RAV MEIR SHAPIRO

A Blaze in the Darkening Gloom

RAV MEIR SHAPIRO

A Blaze in the Darkening Gloom

by his devoted disciple Rav Yehoshua Baumol

who became one of the six million

MAY HEAVEN AVENGE HIS DEATH

rendered into English by *Charles Wengrov zt"l*

from the original, unpublished Yiddish manuscript
written in Poland, 5694 (1934)

under the editorship of *Martin H. Stern*

FELDHEIM PUBLISHERS

JERUSALEM NEW YORK

Picture credits: in the preface *About the Author*, the photographs were supplied by Rav Yosef M. Baumol. Source material for the rest were courteously and generously provided by (in alphabetical order): Agudath Israel of America (Photo Archives); *Béth haSefarim haLeumi* (Schwadron Collection), Jerusalem; and mainly, *Ginzach Kiddush haShem*, B'nei Brak. A word of thanks is also due Yosef Friedenson of Agudath Israel, for supplying accurate historical information in one instance.

design: cw

First published 1994
Second edition 1997
Third edition 2005
Fourth edition 2012

ISBN 10: 0-87306-675-8
ISBN 13: 978-0-87306-675-4

FELDHEIM PUBLISHERS
POB 43163, Jerusalem, Israel 91431
208 Airport Executive Park, Nanuet, NY 10954

Printed in Israel

This ספר
is dedicated to the memory of

Raphael (Rudi) and Celia (Zilli) Stern ע"ה
of Hendon, London, England

רפאל ב"ר משה שטרן ע"ה
נלב"ע כ"ט אדר תשמ"ח

צירל ב"ר מרדכי שטרן (לבית קון) ע"ה
נלב"ע ז' אייר תשס"ה

May their concern for their family
and Am Yisrael, together with their charitable deeds,
serve as a guiding light for many generations.

Martin and Lone Stern
Bayit Vegan, Jerusalem

Motti and Idit Stern
Maya, Shira and Guy Raphael
Ramat Gan, Israel

Arye and Keren Stern
Liron, Noga and Mika
Ness Ziona, Israel

Libbie (née Stern)
and Robbie Goldstein
Shani Hodaya and Ashira Tehilla
Bayit Vegan, Jerusalem

Dina (née Stern)
and Noah Rothschild
Tzilla, Liat and Dvir
Ramat Beit Hakerem, Jerusalem

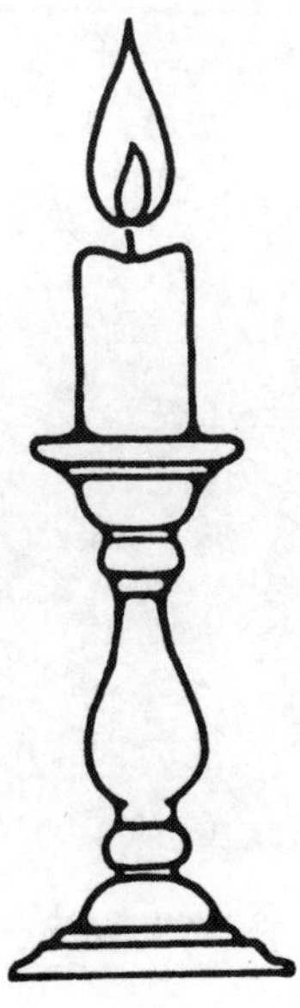

Alan and Lisa Stern
Avraham Yaakov, Rachel
and Sara
Los Angeles, California

Rhona (née Stern)
and Keith Davis
Hendon, London, England

The author as a young rabbi, on his porch

contents

****

An adventure into the past

On a heady summer day in 1967, I walked with my father (of blessed memory) through the Old City of Jerusalem to the *kotel ha-ma'aravi*. It was only several weeks after the Six Day War, and now the Western Wall was in the sovereign hands of our people for the first time in almost two millennia. After nineteen years, Jews could freely reach this last sacred remnant of our ancient Sanctuary. The Western Wall was no longer captive in Jordanian hands.

It was a heightened moment when my father and I walked together through the old historic streets; and in the great emotions that bestirred his heart, a memory returned to him, which he related to me then. His mind went back not to the year 1938, when he arrived in England as a refugee from Hitler's fangs that spread across Europe; not to the beloved parents and brothers who perished in Auschwitz, but still earlier — to a bitter day in the month of Cheshvan, 5694 (November, 1933), when the Jews in his home town of Ungvar learned that Rav Meir Shapiro (*z'tz'l*) had passed away. Then too, as my father recalled, all the Jews around him became caught up in one emotional wave — in a common sense of tragic loss.

Ungvar is a small town near Munkacs, in the Carpathian Mountains that border Czechoslovakia, Rumania, Russia and Hungary. I knew that my father's family had always been *chassidim* of the Rebbe of Munkacs, and indeed were close to him in a warm, abiding friendship. My brother was born on the Rebbe's *yortzaït* (the anniversary of his passing), and he was then given the Rebbe's name: Cha-yim El'azar.

So I found the matter puzzling. The "political orientation" of the Rebbe of Munkacs was clear enough. He would cite the statement of the Talmud (*bavli*, Gittin 55b), that "on account of Kamtza and Bar Kamtza, Jerusalem was destroyed" (and with it the Second Temple, in our distant past). Then the Rebbe would take the four letters of *kamtza* in Hebrew and interpret them: The *kuf* (he would say) denoted the Communists; the *mem*, Mizrachi (the National Zionists); the *tzaddi*, said he, meant the Zionists; and the *alef* stood for the Agudists, the members of Agudas Yisra'el. Thus the Rebbe rejected them all as reliable pathfinders or trailblazers to show a way forward for the Jewish people.

Why, then, did the Jews of Ungvar, including the *chassidim* of this Rebbe, mourn the death of the Rav of faraway Lublin, who had been a key figure in Poland's Agudas Yisra'el? One thing, though, was clear: Rav Meir Shapiro had been a rare type of leader: the kind who could become respected and beloved among all the circles and levels of the Jewish people, from the most pious to the most worldly.

Since that memorable walk with my father, I was determined to learn about that man, to discover why his departure could move the Jewish masses in Europe to mourn for him, whatever their political orientation. In time I obtained a remembrance volume in Hebrew about him that contained a good, full biography; and thereafter, in my leisure hours, I kept reading and learning more about the man.

I learned how he headed Agudas Yisra'el in Eastern Europe, especially in Poland; how he served in the Polish parliament as the deputy of his people; how he founded the imperishable program of the *daf ha-yomi*, so that all over the world, Jews might study the same two pages of Talmud on any given day, on a firm, clear schedule that would take them through the whole Talmud, from beginning to end. I read how he served as the Rav of Piotrkov, and then of Lublin, as he built and headed the legendary *Yeshivas Chachmey Lublin.* And I marveled at the fact that he had done all this in a lifetime that ended before he reached his forty-seventh birthday.

Year after year I would ponder sadly on the need of our generation for a spiritual leader of his ability and stature. With time I could only come to esteem and honor him so much more, thinking of him, as it were, as if he had been my own Rebbe.

As the sixtieth anniversary of his passing began to approach, I felt a strong urge, even a need, to do something that would make our people newly aware of this spiritual giant — especially the young who knew little or nothing about him. I wanted to bring this great personage back into our lives.

The wish was there, strong, imperious. Yet how was I to do it?

Divine providence came to my aid and provided the answer.

I had to attend a meeting on a matter of public concern, together with Rav Avraham Schapira, the highly learned and highly esteemed head of *Yeshivat Mercaz Harav* in Jerusalem, who served in the past as a Chief Rabbi in our Holy Land. Before the meeting began, I mentioned to him, in sadness and yearning, how sorely our generation lacked spiritual leaders of the stature of Rav Meir Shapiro and Rav Kook *z'tz'l*, the Land of Israel's first Chief Rabbi in our century. Giving free rein to my imagination, I wondered aloud what might have happened had those two met and been able to work together in the years after they were gone. What chemistry might have formed and operated between them, with all the great love that they had for the Jewish people and which the people so strongly reciprocated? What might they have been able to do, perhaps, for the poor and threatened masses of Eastern Europe, while the old dream of return to the Jewish homeland began to burgeon into reality?

Indeed, I meditated aloud, what might have happened if only an inscrutable Divine will had not taken these two valiant leaders from this world in the years before the Holocaust?

My musing set off a train of memory in Rav Avraham Schapira, and in his friendly, smiling manner he promised to send me, by fax, two relevant historic documents. Within an hour after the meeting, my fax machine produced a letter that went from Poland to Jerusalem, from Rav Meir Shapiro to Rav Kook (may their memories bring blessing) asking Rav Kook for his blessing on the occasion of the opening of *Yeshivas Chachmey Lublin* in the year 5690 (1930).

The second item that I received by fax was a letter to Rav Kook from a certain Rav Baumol, dated in 5694 (1934). He introduced himself as a ranking *talmid* of Rav Meir Shapiro and gave a full, impressive résumé of his life. Then he importuned Rav Kook to use his good services to obtain for his family and himself a precious "Certificate" (one of the permits to immigrate into the Holy Land which were issued under the British Mandate with such maddening stinginess).

I was left wondering: Did this Rav Baumol ever receive the Certificate he sought? Did he manage to escape the inferno of the Holocaust and reach the Holy Land?

A few weeks later I received the telephone number of a family in Efrat, a town midway between Bethlehem and Hebron — a number that I was to call in connection with a certain communal matter in which I had become involved. In the ensuing conversation, I realized that the woman at the other end was named Mrs. Baumol. I suddenly wondered if this American immigrant, the mother of eight children, might be related to the Rav Baumol in my second fax from Rav Avraham Schapira. She had no idea, she told me; but, she added, her husband's uncle was a retired American Rabbi who lived now in Israel. Perhaps he could help me.

Soon I was speaking with him by telephone, and discovered that he was the older brother of the Rav Baumol in the second letter that Rav Avraham Schapira had sent me by fax. Over the phone I read the letter, almost sixty years old, to this surviving brother, and he confessed that he had never known anything about it.

That evening I sat facing him in his home — a tall scholarly Rabbi, who had left Poland and reached New York in the year 1935. Sadly Rav Yosef Baumol informed me that his younger brother had never received the precious document he sought. Rav Yehoshua went on to become the dynamic head of a community in Poland, a prominent figure in the younger generation of spiritual leaders — until his flame of life was extinguished by the German murderers, among the six million who perished in the Holocaust.

Yet in the sorrow we shared that evening, a glowing ray of light shone for me unexpectedly. Rabbi Yosef Baumol produced a small bundle of narrow yellowing pages, filled with Yiddish words from edge to edge and from top to bottom. This, he explained, was a biography of Rav Meir Shapiro that his martyred brother had written within weeks after this unforgettable spiritual giant had passed away.

As I sat in the evening in that living room in Jerusalem, I felt the reality of Divine providence as perhaps never before. How and why the Yiddish biography was written, how it reached Rabbi Yosef Baumol in America for him to keep and treasure, why it had never been properly published — all this is related by Rabbi Baumol in the pages that follow, in his poignant memoir about his martyred brother.

All I felt then was that Heaven had answered me. A strong yearning had welled up in me to find a way to make Rav Meir Shapiro live again for us, for our generation that came into the world in the decades after the Holocaust. There was a sense of a mission in me. I felt I had a duty to a Jewry that had been born in the half-century after that horrendous,

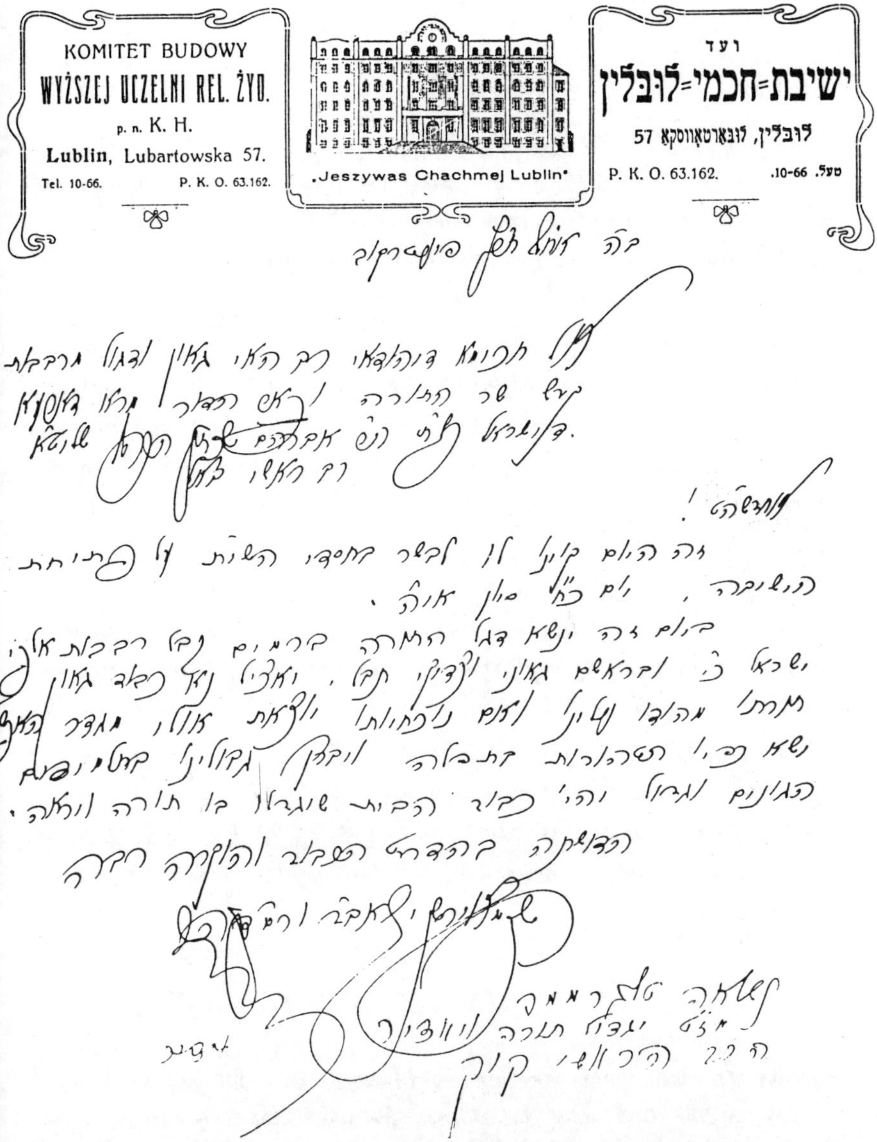
KOMITET BUDOWY
WYŻSZEJ UCZELNI REL. ŻYD.
p. n. K. H.
Lublin, Lubartowska 57.
Tel. 10-66. P. K. O. 63.162.

"Jeszywas Chachmej Lublin"

ועד
ישיבת=חכמי=לובלין
לובלין, לובארטאווסקא 57
P. K. O. 63.162. טעל. 10-66.

The letter from Rav Meir Shapiro to Rav Kook, informing him of the forthcoming opening of *Yeshivas Chachmey Lublin*, and asking that if Rav Kook could not be present, would he give the Yeshiva his prayers and his blessing as a ***kohen*** (***birkat kohanim***), that it might produce worthy ***talmidim***. At the bottom is a notation of the reply: "A telegram was sent: *Mazal tov. May the Torah grow greater and mightier.*"

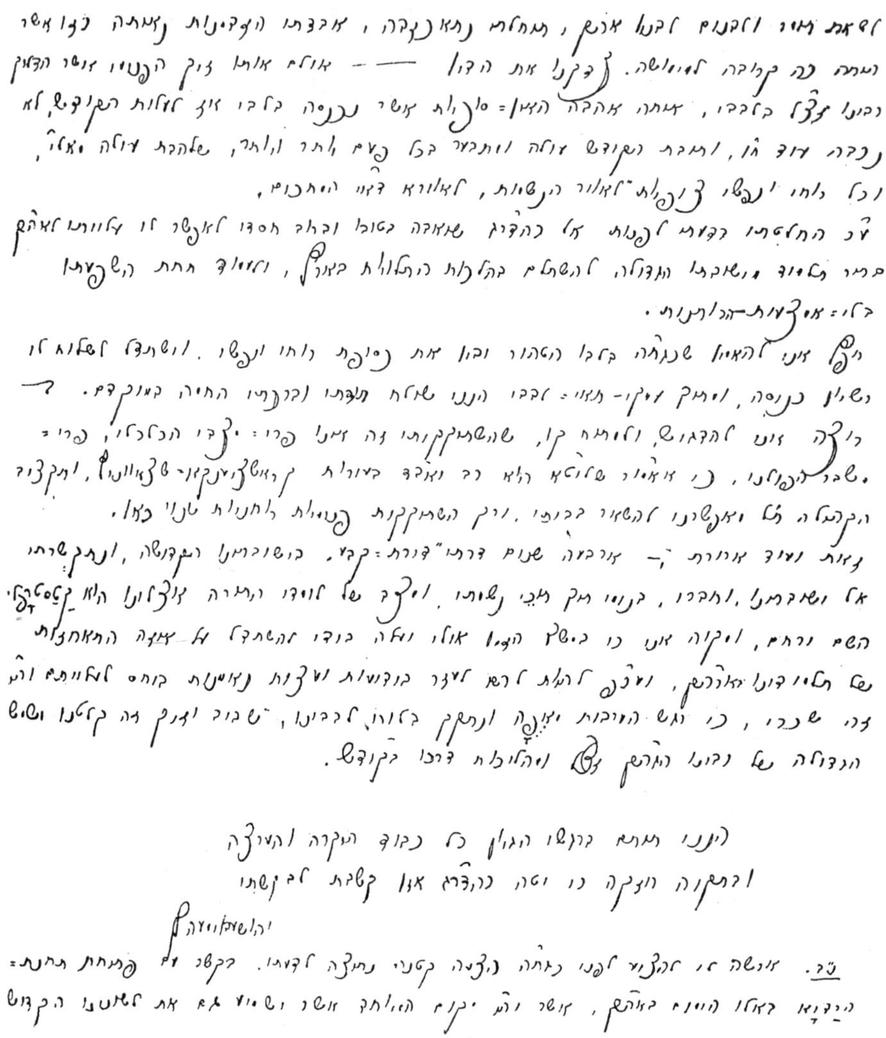

The 2-page letter that Rav Yehoshua Baumol sent to Rav Kook when he turned 21, asking for a Certificate to enable him to migrate to Eretz Yisra'el. He tells of his years of study at *Yeshivas Chachmey Lublin* and of his "graduation with honors";

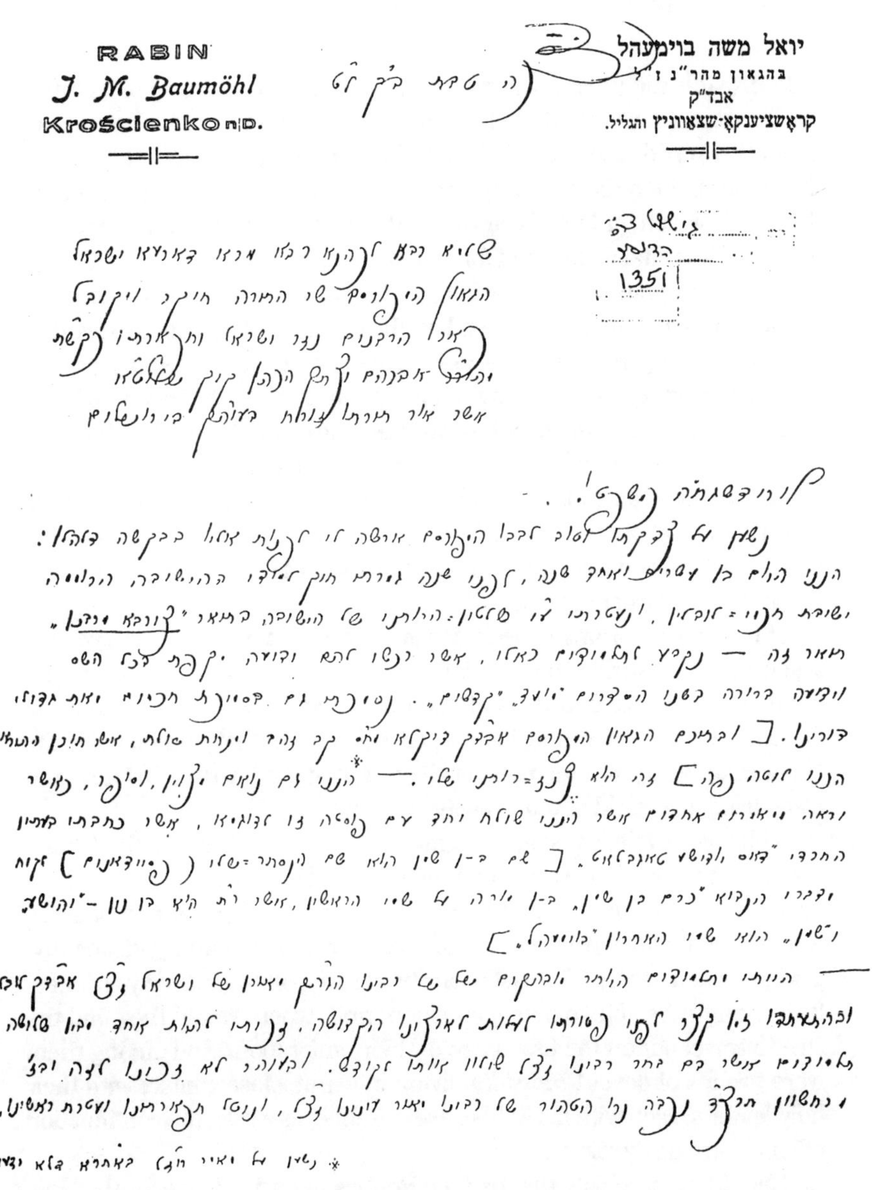

RABIN
J. M. Baumöhl
Krościenko n/D.

יואל משה בוימעהל
בהגאון מהר"נ ז"ל
אבד"ק
קראָשציענקאָ-שצאָווניץ והגליל.

שלום רב להגאון רבא מרא דארעא ישראל
הגאון המפורסם שר התורה חו"ב וכו'
[illegible]
[illegible]
אשר אור תורתו נוהרת בעיה"ק בירושלים

[illegible]

and he writes further that when Rav Meir Shapiro planned to visit Eretz Yisra'el, he was to have been one of the 3 disciples accompanying the great leader; but alas, with Rav Meir's untimely death, the whole project came to nothing.

indescribable nightmare which erased an entire Jewish world of its time.

Do we not owe it to ourselves and our children to learn what we can about that world? Eleven million Jews lived in Europe then. In their midst there was an incredible courage and dedication to the G-d of Israel and to the Torah which, in Jewry's eternal faith, He gave us. How little we know about it. How vital is the need for us to try to learn more.

Time moves us only forward. Outside the world of science fiction we cannot turn back the clock, much less the calendar. Yet good, trustworthy literature can open the way for our minds and our hearts. And there, on the desk before me in that living room in Jerusalem, lay the means to bring us a living, dynamic image of Rav Meir Shapiro *z'tz'l.* Through that manuscript, written in the rich, pulsing, vibrant Yiddish that Rav Meir heard and spoke, we could all go back to the early decades of our century and learn so very much about the fateful years that brought Hitler to power, and the time that followed, when terror loomed over that poor, helpless Jewry through ever darkening clouds.

It is so easy to romanticize the past, to create a past of pure nostalgia and wallow in a world of pure delight that never was. It is so easy to remain blind to the abject poverty that scourged and bedeviled our people in Central and Eastern Europe in those fateful decades that culminated in the Holocaust. We must remember, at all costs, that the Jewry of that time and place lived in a world of utter reality.

Millions traveled west and migrated across the Atlantic to the United States of America. The variegated Jewish population in *Eretz Yisra'el* kept growing at a steady pace, and occasionally by small leaps and bounds. Among the millions who remained, there was a tiny minority of wealthy, landed Jewish gentry. The vast majority were appallingly poverty-stricken. If they might be able to obtain an exit permit, where would they find the fare to travel out on the first stage of their emigration? And among them were groups of devout *chassidim* living in warm, close contact with their holy leaders, each with his Rebbe, every Rebbe, as a rule, the continuation of an illustrious dynasty.

Should we speculate that had the Rebbes moved to leave for the Holy Land, a good number of their followers would have moved with them, and large numbers would have escaped the Holocaust? A trenchant teaching in *Pirkey Avot* (2:5) warns us sternly, "Do not judge your fellow-human until you arrive at his situation!" If this was told us about an ordinary fellow-human, how much more cautious should we be in regard to spiritual leaders of distinguished lineage.

Yet to our mortal eyes, Rav Meir Shapiro appears to have towered over them. At the end of his life he made plans to move to our Holy Land: he intended to come on a visit, and then remain. Had he lived to do so (and Rav Meir was always a man of action who never sat idle), he might have served perhaps as a Rebbe setting a path for his flock, and Polish Jews might have striven to follow. In the historic letter that his *talmid* Rav Yehoshua Baumol wrote to Rav Kook *z'tz'l*, he conveyed clearly that this had been his great teacher's hope and plan, before Rav Meir's untimely death killed this dream too.

Be that as it may, that evening in Jerusalem I saw clearly the task that lay before me. I spared no effort to make sure that the biography would appear in English, and I had the sense of a mission accomplished.

The natural publisher for the book was Feldheim in Jerusalem, due to a long relationship between Yaakov Feldheim and myself, and my great personal esteem for him. And then the natural choice for the translation became Charles Wengrov, whose association with the firm in our eternal Holy City goes back for many years. Not only does Wengrov have a command of the Yiddish he has spoken fluently since his childhood years, but he is also scholar and historian enough to know when he had to go and read elsewhere for background knowledge. Time and again a single word in the Yiddish manuscript, every letter deciphered, sent him searching for information that would make it understandable to us all, so many long decades after it was written.

In these pages we can return to Poland across the years and find valuable information and inspiration. We can learn of a vanished world that set all its hope and trust in the Torah that it studied and carried in its daily life, and from which it drew courage against the growing tide of doom that would come to destroy it.

Here is a story of one man's life among his people, that ended early on a Friday morning in Lublin. A few hours later, the Jews of Poland might have heard the following on their radio:

"This is the 9 o'clock news from Radio Warsaw. The German *fuehrer* Hitler has opened two new armament factories in Bavaria, thus creating 18,500 new jobs. The British Government of Ramsay Macdonald . . . "

In this book we can learn of a tremendous leader of an incredible people with a faith and a courage that can teach us the meaning of one phrase in the Book of *Iyyov* (Job 13:15), "Though He slay me, yet will I trust in Him."

Let us go back into the past and learn from it what we can, so that we can move toward our future.

I remain grateful to the Almighty Who brought me to the manuscript and let me arrange for its publication in English.

Martin H. Stern
Jerusalem, Erev Shavuos 5754 (May 1994)

Editor's Foreword to the Second Edition

Three years have passed since *A Blaze in the Darkening Gloom* first appeared, and the reception that the book received worldwide has been truly gratifying. In Jerusalem, London, and New York — even in far-off Hong Kong — wherever I traveled, I found that the flame of Rav Meir Shapiro's life has been rekindled in readers' hearts. Comments and reactions kept pouring in.

I have good reason to believe that one day history may show how this book acted as a catalyst now, before the last survivors of the Holocaust leave this world, to help bring compensation for Jewish property that was taken ruthlessly when our people seemed doomed to extinction. As I write, I have before me the insurance policies of my own grandparents, on which no payment has been made to this day. When my grandfather insured his life, it was his wish that his family should inherit him. On moral grounds, so it should be. When Rav Meir Shapiro died, the institution to which he had given his life, Yeshivas Chachmey Lublin, was on the verge of bankruptcy. Some uncanny sixth sense (that believing Jews prefer to call a flash of *ruach ha-kodesh*) had made him take out a life insurance policy, with the Yeshiva as the sole beneficiary. And thus his tragic, untimely death brought the institution a sorely needed rescue.

Following the fall of the Iron Curtain in 1990, links between the East European countries and the Jewish people slowly formed anew. From

Budapest to Prague, Lublin to Warsaw, cities, towns and villages returned to the Jewish traveler's itinerary. And last summer an honored group was invited to spend a Shabbos in the original Yeshivas Chachmey Lublin — not the vibrant Torah academy in B'nei Brak, Israel, but the historic building in Lublin that was arrogated to become a Polish nursing school. That Shabbos, the voice of Torah came alive again in the holy edifice which Rav Meir had struggled to erect. It resounded again in the magnificent corridors and halls which have remained almost untouched since they were built. I pray that I may yet merit to experience such a Shabbos there, with my family.

Meanwhile, the time is approaching to recall another creation of Rav Meir: the *daf yomi*. It is planned next month to celebrate worldwide the forthcoming *siyyum ha-shass*, the next completion of the study of the Babylonian Talmud, on the schedule that Rav Meir Shapiro created — to go through the entire *shass* every few years by covering one *daf*, one leaf, 2 sides of a page, every day. As he looks down from his eminence on high, I pray that on that day he may be a *meilitz yosher*, an eloquent defense advocate, for all our people in these times of tension and uncertainty.

Martin Stern
Jerusalem, Tu be-Av 5757 (August 1997)

Editor's Foreword to the Third Edition

Over seven years have passed since the above lines were written. The necessity for a new edition has arisen since we find ourselves, *baruch Hashem*, on the eve of another *siyyum ha-shass* and not a single copy of the previous two editions, to the best of my knowledge, is available on the shelves of any Jewish bookseller worldwide.

The success of this book is proof of the growing awareness of the life of Rav Meir Shapiro and his ongoing contribution to the Jewish people. May his memory and all Am Yisrael go from strength to strength.

Martin Stern
Jerusalem, Tu bi-Shevat 5765 (January 2005)

Editor's Foreword to the Fourth Edition

When I penned the Preface to the First Edition of *A Blaze in the Darkening Gloom* in 1994, it was just five years after the fall of the Iron Curtain. For the first time since the Second World War and the revelations of the terror of the Shoah, Eastern Europe was moving toward democracy, and Jews were coming back to see the world that once was. Unfortunately, there is very little left to see.

It has been eighteen years since we published the first edition, and with this fourth printing, the intervening years have seen the rebirth and revival of Yiddishkeit in places that were once the center of global Jewish life, where millions of our ancestors lived and learned for 1,000 years, until the Holocaust destroyed almost everything.

But all is not well when we forget what came before the Shoah. I recently met a very young grandmother-to-be here in Jerusalem who breathlessly told me that she had just returned from Lublin, Poland, where she had visited Yeshivas Chachmey Lublin. She toured the country, davening in shuls in Krakow and Warsaw. I asked her what she thought of her visit to Rabbi Meir Shapiro's yeshiva in Lublin, which was the European center of Jewish learning before the war.

She looked at me in amazement. "What do you mean?" she asked. "I saw Jews in Warsaw, Krakow and Lublin. I davened in shuls. Yiddishkeit is alive and well."

I asked her what she knew about the 3,000,000 Jews who had lived in Poland before the war and if she had learned anything about them before she left on her trip or while she was there. She said she lived in 2012 and couldn't relate to the past.

This is the tragedy facing our younger Jewish generations. This young woman and others have no idea about the rich, diverse, religious and cultural life that existed in Eastern Europe before the Shoah. Barely seventy years after the destruction, when our grandparents were murdered in Hitler's blood bath, we are forgetting the world that was. The fourth edition of *A Blaze in the Darkening Gloom* is our way of preventing such dangerous amnesia. Our future as Jews is inextricably linked to all that came before us. We must never forget where we came from, how that has an impact on who we are today, and on the Jewish generations that will hopefully follow us.

Martin H. Stern
Jerusalem, Tu bi-Shevat 5772 (February 2012)

About the Author

This book was written by my brother shortly after the passing of our eminent Rebbe, teacher, mentor, Hagaon Harav Rabbi Meir Shapira. At the time, my brother, Rabbi Yehoshua Baumol, was still a relatively young man — barely twenty-one years old. He was born on Purim in 1913, in Buczacz, to our parents Rav Joel Moshe and Rabbanit Slova, *z"l*.

Two years my junior, my brother and I grew up and were educated together. Regardless of our overlapping childhoods, however, I have always felt that my brother considerably surpassed me in knowledge of Torah, in erudition, piety and personal attributes. The uncommonly high caliber of his traits and talents were such that his mentors singled him out as a rising star in the firmament of the Polish rabbinate.

Few fragments of his widely-read articles in *halachah* and *aggadah* were published in *Ha-Talmid Ha-Gadol* ("The Great Disciple"), a memorial volume dedicated to the memory of his unblemished soul. His myriad brilliant *chiddushim*, were completely destroyed. My brother was burned together with his Torah. Only one scholarly work remained intact: this biography of our educator, Rabbi Meir of Lublin.

Constrained by lack of time and burdened by looming pressures both personal and public, my brother wrote this book intending for me to publish it under my own name. He invested his precious resources in this project so that I, a young rabbi taking my first tentative steps in American Jewish communal life at the time, might bear the laurels. My brother made this herculean effort on my behalf in the hope that it would enhance my stature in America as a rabbi and an author and help me land a respectable job in the rabbinate.

That he labored days and nights to craft this scholarly work, without my asking that he do so — while maintaining a formidable schedule of Torah study and Divine service — is an indication to me that he was blessed by God: his keen mind and buoyant personality were complemented by a loving, magnanimous nature.

The unlikely turn of events was such that I had been chosen to be rabbi and dean of the Crown Heights Yeshiva in Brooklyn, at the time a prominent American Jewish community, even before my brother's manuscript reached me. Needless to say, I did not publish the book in my name, because I did not wish to exploit my brother's benevolent gesture. But neither did I publish it in his name. I had vainly hoped to be able to publish his works in ***halachah*** and ***aggadah*** first.

For many years, I kept the manuscript concealed in a drawer, where I cherished it as my most precious possession. After I had learned of the appallingly tragic destruction wrought during the Holocaust, I got into the habit of taking the manuscript out and perusing through its numerous pages. I felt, during those moments, as though my brother was with me, his iconic image hovering before my eyes.

On those occasions I felt so deeply bonded to him, I felt as though I too was "experiencing" the frightful shocks and suffering which he and his family had doubtlessly undergone. That awareness made me feel as though my heart would literally rupture in pain. In my imagination, I saw the atrocious misery, the freezing cold, the cruel blows and humiliations and the death-train cars in which they were taken to Treblinka — and I nearly became mad. I grieved for him. Thus, my brother was constantly in my thoughts over a period of many years. To me, he bequeathed a memorial flame, one that can never be extinguished.

Now, in the twilight of my life, I have decided it fitting to publish his work, lest those who have perished be forgotten. I thank God that I have been privileged to publish this book —first translated from the original Yiddish into Hebrew — under its rightful author's name in the Land of Israel, for which the author, my brother, undeviatingly longed.

In order to unravel the past, to glimpse into my brother's virtue-steeped inner world, it might be fitting that I begin by describing his physical appearance, as it was portrayed by a relative recording youthful impressions:

"His face was like that of a holy being, as if hardly of this world. His deep-set eyes captivated your attention. They were compassionate and kindly, but radiated an inner fervor and perspicacity. The black ***payot*** framing his face lent an air of softness and mystery to his expression.

While his easy smile reflected a zest for life, those same intense, coal-colored eyes bespoke a passion for what was intellectually obscure.

"He listened to the troubles of an eleven-year-old boy and to the tale of woe of an old beggar with the same degree of patience and commiseration. His innate concern and empathy encouraged people to pour their heart out to him. Moreover, he enchanted us with his marvelous sense of humor, which never left him.

"A stroll with him in the verdant countryside was an unforgettable experience. He was keenly aware of the wonders of nature and would often express feelings of amazement and delight in what he perceived as a reflection of the Creator's majesty.

"If one of us became ill, he would instinctively sit alongside the sickbed and entertain with distracting stories. There were days in which he thus spent hours changing bandages and attending to us. He was always gentle, full of hope; cheerful and patient. There was never any need to solicit him to help because he was somehow always 'there' when needed. All at once, his imposing, handsome physique would appear and the mere sight of him eased the burden off one's shoulders. He would delight in response to any feeble comment and he would proceed to joshingly tease and enlist the attention of the patient, until the sickroom became filled with a convivial air. His presence was inspiring. He would leave behind an agreeable and refreshed ambiance — one which lingered."

My brother was gentlemanly and decent to anyone and everyone he encountered. Regardless of his being a natural *matmid* and his diligent, all-encompassing commitment to Torah study, he always had the time to lend a sympathetic ear to the problems and difficulties of others, to aid them in practical matters, to convey words of encouragement. My brother, who was so utterly considerate to all human beings, was also as forgiving as an angel.

One of his admirers, the noted author Dr. Hillel Seideman wrote (*Eleh Ezkerah*, III, pp. 291-92): "He always evinced a willingness to help his fellow man in times of trouble. He was as sensitive as a seismograph and he responded to emotional jolts others experienced, however slight and however remote. He had a discerning ear when it came to being attentive to the heartache of another person. His whole being responded to every call, both those spoken *sotto voce* and those spoken without words."

Above, the author as a young student, in his dormitory room at Yeshivat Chachmey Lublin. *Below,* from left to right: the author, our father, and our uncle, the *av bet din* of Shczawnitz.

Above, from right to left: our uncle, Rav Naftali Hertz, the ***av bet din*** of Shczawnitz; Rav Meir Shapira; our father, Rav Yoel Moshe, Rabbi of Kroscienko-Shczawnitz; myself; and the author (my brother) in his adolescence. ***Below,*** in a picture taken in Lublin, 1933, Rav Meir Shapira appears second from right, and my brother second from left; the others remain unidentified.

The effect of this was that for a solitary few moments, the listener might have the feeling that, in the eyes of my brother at least, he alone existed in the world.

His intellectual prowess was established at an early age. It was at the Lublin Yeshiva, however, that Yehoshua began to develop as a scholar.

The Lublin Yeshiva was already well known as the magnet that attracted the élite of *bnei Torah* of Europe. It was here that his star began to rise. When he was only 18, the Rav of the Yeshiva told my father-in-law, Rav Yehoshua Baumol, author of *Emek Halacha*, that "Yehoshua's *chiddushim* resemble those of the *Gedolim*."

The Dukler Gaon, Rav Tevel Sehman, who conferred Yehoshua's initial *semichah*, once remarked that he could read the word *illui* (prodigy) on his forehead.

His intellectual gift grew simultaneously with his personality development. He was not an intimidating "genius," but in fact was much beloved by his peers, who sought and cherished his friendship.

At this time he began to mature also as an orator and writer. His *chiddushim* were published in Torah journals, while his essays and articles on topical issues were published in the *Das Yiddishe Tageblatt*.

An intimate relationship developed and continued between the Rav and my brother.

It was felt by many that Yehoshua reflected the image of the Rav — albeit in miniature. He had the same rav-like approach, the same sweep of vision, the same enveloping charm which distinguished the Rav's personality.

When the Rav perceived the potential of Yehoshua, he did not relax, but continued to prod and encourage him to reach ever higher goals. Occasionally, he would take him for a walk and talk to him about the most sublime matters in Jewish life. It was as if the Rav sensed that a weighty and responsible role was awaiting his gifted *talmid*. It was necessary to prepare him for what the future would have in store for him.

In the autumn of 5694 (1933) all this was cut short by the sudden passing of the Rav at the age of 47. This tragic event shook Orthodox Jewry throughout the world. It is hard to even imagine what this disaster meant for his beloved students who were suddenly orphaned of their great Master.

While grieving for their loss, they were quick to realize that there was a serious danger that the Yeshiva would collapse and fall under its burden of debt. The senior students mobilized a rescue campaign. Among the stalwarts mustered was Yehoshua, who had already gained the reputation of an orator. His fiery rhetoric, striking appearance, and eloquent language struck the mark. The community was alerted and responded to the call. The campaign was a success: not only was the Yeshiva saved, but the people were lifted and elevated to a higher understanding of their duties in *Yiddishkeit*.

Yehoshua returned to the Yeshiva. But a few years later, our father, *z"l*, became seriously ill and was rushed to Vienna for treatment. Yehoshua did not leave his bedside, tending him to his last breath.

Our father, *z"l*, was only 51 years of age when he was *niftar*. His passing was felt in the Jewish world, as was recorded in the press. He was well-known as the Rav of Kroscienko-Shczawnitz, a famous spa. When the *shiva* was over, the community turned to Yehoshua and asked him to take on the position of *Rav Ha'ir*. He accepted the call as a way of honoring our father, *z"l*.

Around this time, Yehoshua married Chana Shapiro, an outstanding and talented Bais Yaakov Seminary student from Cracow. She was the daughter of the late Rabbi of Opoczno.

In due course, he was asked to come to Opoczno as a candidate for Rav. His first appearance there was during Chanukah, and he addressed the congregation for eight days, after the lighting of the candles. His topic was Chanukah and each evening he treated the subject differently: Chanukah in *Halacha*, *Aggadah*, *Chassidut*, philosophy, etc. The people were amazed and deeply impressed with his all-encompassing knowledge.

But days of quiet did not continue for long. After the invasion of Poland, Jewish communities were subject to suffering and devastation. We do not know much of my brother's activities during the frightful war years. From the survivors, we learned that those years had the effect of impelling him to an even more vigorous pursuit of Torah prayer. His service to Hashem manifested itself also in his tireless devotion to his decimated and suffering congregation. His end was like that of the majority of Jews in his town, of Poland — tragic.

In 1942 my brother was killed in Treblinka along with his wife and two children and our mother, *z"l*. He was 29 years old. May Hashem avenge their blood.

(RABBI) YOSEF M. BAUMOL

לזכרון בהיכל ה׳

אבי זקני הגאון האדיר חסידא ופרישא מ״ה **נחום** אב״ד קרושצ׳ינקו־שצ׳בניץ זצ״ל
נתבקש לישיבה של מעלה **כ״ו תשרי תרפ״ז**

אמי זקנתי הרבנית הצדקת מרת **שרה** נרצחה בידי הגרמנים
ביום **כ״ד אב תש״ב** ב־ניו יורק

דודי הרב **מאיר רפאל** אב״ד לאנצק, ורעיתו הרבנית ובניו ובנותיו

דודתי **רייזל** ובעלה המופלג בתורה ויראה מו״ה **יוסף בוימל,**
ובניהם ובנותיהם, נרצחו בבלזיץ **ערב ראש השנה תש״ב**

דודתי **רחל** ובעלה הרה״ח **לייב** הגאון הרב **ניסן שנירר,** ראב״ד דקראקא,
ובניהם

דודתי **גיטל** ובעלה הרה״ח **אלטר,** נכד הגה״ק בעל ״אמרי נועם״.
ובתם היחידה

דודתי **שיינדל** ובעלה הרח״ח **מאיר גרינשפאן,** נרצחו ביום הרג רב
בעיר טורנא

דודתי **פסיל** ובעלה הרה״ח **דוד אייכנשטיין,** נכד הגה״ק מזידיטשטב
ובתם היחידה

אבי זקני אמי הי״ד הרה״ח **עזריאל אורבך** ז״ל מזקני חסידי
הוסיאטין, נפטר **ט״ז טבת** ורעיתו, אמי זקנתי, **רייזל,** נפטרה **י״ג אב**

יזכור אלוקים נשמות דודי ודודתי, אח ואחות אמי מורתי זצ״ל,
שנספו בימי הזעם בלבוב ובוצ׳ץ
דודי הרה״ח **מיכל** ורעיתו **מחלה** ובניו

דודי הרה״ח **זאב** ורעיתו ובנו המצוין עדין לתפארת

דודתי מרת **חיה** ובעלה הרה״ח **אשר צייגר** ובנותיהם
יום היא״צ הוקבע **לי״א שבט**

דודי רחימי **יוסף,** נפטר **י״ז טבת תשל״ב,** ורעיתו **אסתר,**
כ״ט טבת תשל״ב

ראה ה׳ והביטה ונקום נקמת דם עבדיך השפוך

ונתתי להם בביתי
ובחומותי יד ושם

(ישעיהו נ"ו)

הורי היקרים עט"ר זצ"ל

אבי מורי הגאון החסיד
הרב **יואל משה בוימל** זצ"ל
אבד"ק קרושצ׳נקו
נפטר ב׳ ניסן תרצ"ז
ומנוחתו כבוד בוינה

אמי מורתי העדינה
הרבנית הצ׳ מרת **סלאווא** הי"ד
נספתה בטרבלינקה כ"ג מרחשוון תש"ב

תודה והוקרה
למרת **רחל גבירץ** ע"ה
ולמשפחתה הנכבדה

לקרן
אהרן מ. שרייבר
ומשפחתו נ"י

לזכרון בהיכל ה׳

*

הרה״ח מו״ה **יוסף זיסקינד** ז״ל

רעייתו מרת **מלכה** ע״ה

ובתם **רייצל** ע״ה

הי״ד

הונצחו ע״י בניהם ואחיה האחים היקרים

משה אהרן ושלמה

*

הרה״ח הנכבד מו״ה

אלכסנדר דוד זיסקינד

ורעיתו, מנשים באוהל תבורך, וצאצאיהם

הרה״ח הנכבד מו״ה

משה אהרן אנגלדר

ורעיתו, מנשים באוהל תבורך, וצאציהם

הרה״ח הנכבד מו״ה

אברהם יהושע שעהן ובניו

שנהרגו על קדוש השם בשואה הי״ד

ת.נ.צ.ב.ה.

הונצחו ע״י נכדיהם ואחייניו

האחים הדגולים

משה אהרן ושלמה זיסקינד

A blaze in the darkening gloom

Chronology

7 Adar, 5647 / March 3, 1887: born in Shatz, northern Rumania.

5656 / 1896: at the age of 9, he became known as "the *iluy* (prodigy) of Shatz; tested, he showed full knowledge, by heart, of the entire *Shulchan Aruch Yoreh Dé'ah.*

5661 / 1901: aged 14, he gave his first public oration from the pulpit of the main *shul.*

5666 / 1906: at 19 he married the daughter of the wealthy Ya'akov Breitman; unfortunately, no children were born to them.

5670 / 1910: with the consent of Rav Yisra'el of Tchortkov, he became the Rav of Glina at 23.

5674 / 1914: appointed head of the Education Department of *Agudas Yisra'el* in East Galicia (but in the First World War that followed, no major activity was possible).

5680 / 1920: became Rav of Sanuk (Sonik), Galicia.

5681 / 1921: aged 34, he participated in meetings of the *Mo'etzess G^e^doley haTorah* (Supreme Torah Council) of *Agudas Yisra'el,* and attended in Warsaw the first convention of the *Agudas haRabbonim* of Poland, as the principal representative of the Rabbis of East Galicia. In the same year he was made Honorary President of the community of *Machzikey haDass* in Jerusalem.

5782 / 1922: with the advice and support of the Rebbe of Ger, he became President of *Agudas Yisra'el* in Poland; then he was elected to the Sejm, the Polish parliament, as a delegate of the organization.

5783 / 1923: at the first *K^e^néssiya G^e^dola* ("Great Assembly") of *Agudas Yisra'el,* he launched the program of *daf ha-yomi,* the daily Talmud study plan.

Lag ba'Omer 5784 / May 22, 1924: the cornerstone ceremony for *Yeshivas Chachmey Lublin.* In the same year, he was appointed Rav of Piotrkov.

5785 / 1925: his acclaimed volume of responsa, *Or haMeir,* was published.

5786-87 / 1925-27: he traveled through Europe, then spent 13 months in the United States and Canada, gathering funds to build *Yeshivas Chachmey Lublin.*

28 Sivan 5690 / June 24, 1930: the formal opening of *Yeshivas Chachmey Lublin*; directly afterward, he was appointed Chief Rabbi of Lublin.

Shavu'os 5693 / May 30, 1933: he began a daily study session with students on the Torah's laws for Eretz Yisra'el, in preparation for travel to the Holy Land.

Eve of Shemini Atzeress 5694 / October 12, 1933: in a break with his annual custom, he attended the *hakafos* at the *shul* of the *Chozeh* (Seer) of Lublin, since he planned to be in Eretz Yisra'el for Pesach. Directly after Succot, he accepted a temporary or tentative appointment as Rav of Lodz, to alleviate the Yeshiva's burden of debt.

7 Cheshvan 5694 / October 27, 1933: his earthly life ended.

In the entire Jewish cemetery of Lublin, his was the only *ohel* (mausoleum) that remained intact, inexplicably, after the Holocaust. In 5718/1958, at the initiative of the *Mo'etzess G^e doley haTorah* of Agudas Yisra'el, his remains were removed and reburied in Jerusalem.

compiled by Martin H. Stern

NOTE: Throughout the book, certain passages and paragraphs appear enclosed in brackets [which the British call square brackets]. In many cases a paragraph begins with an opening bracket, but has no closing bracket at its end; sometimes there is a whole series of such paragraphs, until one finally ends with a closing bracket. A full explanation is given on pp. 395-96.

Key to the transliteration

a: as in *quality*.

ai: as in *Sinai*.

ch: as in *challah* (the loaf for Shabbos) or in the Scottish (and Yiddish) *loch*.

^{e} or ^{e} (smaller letter *e* set high on the line, like a "superior number" that indicates a note): as the first *e* in *conference*. This is to denote a *sh^{e}va na*.

é: as in *obey*.

i: the vowel sound midway between *bit* and *beet*.

o: generally as in *from*; sometimes as in *hot*.

u: as in *put*.

By way of introduction

A most difficult task have I taken upon myself; perhaps an impossible one: to present in a series of chapters a life portrait and biography of a legendary Torah giant, a world-renowned Talmud scholar, my great, holy instructor and educator, Rav Meir Shapiro of blessed memory, the Rabbi of Lublin who conceived and constructed *Yeshivas Chachmey Lublin* as a world center of Torah study.

For how can any one person evaluate and comprehend his amazing brilliance, his broad, encompassing grasp of his world, his greatness of spirit, and the universal renown that he gained? And bear in mind that this was also a man of extraordinary geniality, gracious affability and modesty, who lived with a crystal-clear Torah knowledge that suffused and cleansed his heart. Then add to it all an extraordinary paranormal intelligence and and a singular goodness of soul.

Can any one individual portray his multi-faceted character, all the aspects and components of his being that ranged across an entire spectrum with all the colors of a rainbow? Can words describe a Divine light filtered through a prism of crystal clarity? Is it possible at all to blend into one portrait a full description that will convey the unforgettable radiance and splendor of the Rav of Lublin? In truth, only someone like himself would be equal to the task.

Nevertheless, I have mustered my courage and set myself to the task, in the face of the difficulties to be confronted, be they surmountable or not. For I believe that our Jewish people, present and future, have earned it.

The time came when this great Rebbe of mine traveled to other countries, principally America, to gather funds for his young, fledgling yeshiva, so that it could become a full physical reality. And the response abroad was most generous — enough to get the yeshiva building completed and to let it continue without difficulties for a good long while. Young people like myself were able to continue our intensive education in our Torah, under his unforgettable influence.

One of the main, great principles in our Judaism is the obligation of *hakaras ha-tov*: to recognize and acknowledge a true favor when it has been done. If Jewry in other parts of the world, especially America, rallied to Rav Meir's support when he asked for it, I believe I owe it to our people, now and for all time, to write this account of his life: to convey to others some of the events and episodes that I experienced and shared with him, along with certain facts and happenings in his life that I came to know and could verify as accurate and authentic.

In honesty, I cannot give any assurance that I will succeed in presenting a comprehensive, full, rounded description of his flourishing, creative years that produced such monumental, lasting results. For such was the effect of this man on the people around him that with every step he took, another legend seemed to arise.

I do hope, however, to be able to reveal certain radiant aspects and blazing sparks of his life that will portray something, at least, of this spiritual giant and stalwart champion of our people who illuminated our life like a radiant sun. And perhaps even this small something will be of benefit not only to those of our time who knew him or learned about him, but to a great many others in the years to come, when time will have left of him little more than a few dry facts in history.

1

A lineage of distinction

The family name of Shapiro (or Shapira) is among the oldest historic appellations in the annals of our people — a name that recalls a full chapter of Jewish martyrdom in the Middle Ages. For the origin of the surname is Speyer (called *ashpira* in the Hebrew of the period), one of three small cities in Franco-Germany whose distinguished Jewish communities came under savage attack in the Crusade of 4856 (1096; the other two cities were Worms and Mayence, later called Mainz). In the pages of Christian history, the barbaric Crusaders might have won great delusions of undying glory. In these three small cities, on the way, as they marched to wage their holy war in the Holy Land, they brought a readiness to murder and pillage, out of a "holy religious" brutality toward Jews. In Speyer they gave the distinguished Jewish families a simple choice: convert to their "true" faith or be murdered.

The small community saw this as a test by Heaven of its loyalty to the Torah — and it passed the test. One human being survived to bear witness: In his *kuntress tatnu* ("a brief compendium on the year 1096") Rabbi Eliezer ben Nosson (Ra'avan, one of the *ba'aley tos^{e}fos*) recorded the quiet heroism and determination of the people as they rejected all the offers and exhortations to convert — even if only in public, for show, without any inner commitment — and accepted the alternative, with the immortal words of *sh^{e}ma yisra'el* on their lips: the alternative of savage massacre by the "holy Crusaders" that followed.

In later times, this act of heroism, indelibly recorded in our people's consciousness, inspired many Jewish communities in Germany with a hallowed fiery determination to emulate such resolve, to show the same loyalty to the Jewish faith. And in commemoration and commitment to such bravery by its Jewish inhabitants, the descendants of the scholar who survived derived their surname from this city *(ashpira)* where the martyrs' blood had been shed. For those descendants, the surname became *Shapiro.*

Into this family were born a long line of great Torah scholars and men of holiness, in whose hearts burned the same fire of passionate fervor and loyalty to the Jewish faith that inspired their forebears in Speyer with a readiness for self-sacrifice. Among the most renowned of them was Rav Pinchas of Koretz, a main *talmid* of Reb Yisra'el Ba'al Shem Tov, who became one of the builders of the chassidic world in Eastern Europe. On his gravestone the family name of Shapiro was inscribed. Chassidic tradition relates that this was done by his instructions, because for him the name symbolized a readiness for self-sacrifice, a readiness to give one's life for the sake of his Jewish faith, so as to hallow in this mortal world the Divine name of Heaven. Moreover, the Ba'al Shem Tov himself, the creator of the chassidic way of life, would always tell of his love for the members of the Shapiro family line: because in their veins flowed a holy, purified blood.

In the same genealogical line we find Rav Nosson Nota Shapiro [Spira], the Rabbi of Cracow well over 300 years ago [around the turn of the sixteenth century] whose published volume, *M^egalleh Amukos*, shows a rare homiletic mastery of Talmud, Midrash and *kabbala*.

In the years that followed the First Crusade, later Crusaders and their cousins and kindred spirits continued to vent their irrational hatred of the Jews in recurrent outbursts of destruction and pillage, to which local rulers added, in one community after another, their orders of expulsion. At last, unable to live any longer under the constant double threat of massacre and expulsion, as the incidents seemed only to grow more frequent in the area that would eventually become Germany, branches of the spreading family line fled eastward from that land of Jewish misery.

At least one branch eventually found its way to the province of Bukovina, in the region that became known as *Siebenbergen* ("the Seven Hills"), which in time became part of northern Rumania. There they settled in the small town of Shatz, that was spread at the foot of the lush, fertile hills, amid a lanscape of scenic loveliness. [For the Jews the name was Shatz, pronounced *shutz*, to rhyme with *huts*; but the town's proper name was Sutchova, officially spelled Suczawa, which was changed to Suceava when it became part of Rumania; it received its name from the river which flowed through it.] It might be noted that it was to this branch of the Shapiro family, which settled in Shatz, that the renowned Reb Pinchas of Koretz (mentioned above) was born.

The Jews in the town formed over a third of the population. The non-Jews who settled and lived there were a mixture of Germans, Hungarians, Rumanians, and Ukrainians; and since all were of immigrant origins, the Jews, whose origins in the little town went back to its very beginnings, lived among them quite amicably. The local Jewish people were plain, simple folk who made their living by their handicrafts and trade, as they carried on their own lives, with their own Yiddish language and their own customs and ways. A good number of them made sure to keep up their ongoing Torah studies, including the inspiring teachings of the chassidic world.

2

Birth and childhood

On the seventh of Adar, 5647 (Thursday, March 3, 1887), a child (their eldest son) was born to Reb Ya'akov Shimshon Shapiro and his wife Margulya (Margalit); and they named him Yehuda Meir. With the passage of time, the parents might have been reminded, perhaps, of the Torah's words about *Moshe rabbénu* (Moses our Master): According to the Talmud (*bavli*, M^e^gillah 13b), Moshe was born on the seventh of Adar — and so too their Yehuda Meir. In the Book of *Sh^e^mos* (Exodus 2:2), the Torah tells us that Moshe's mother saw at once how good the child was; and the Midrash explains that the home was filled with light. From his earliest years, Yehuda Meir evidently filled the heart of his parents with a light of happy anticipations; they saw in him a wondrous potential and set great hopes on him.

Reb Ya'akov Shimshon was a great-grandson of the renowned Reb Pinchas of Koretz, and was himself considerably learned in Torah and *chassidus*; for a short while, in fact, he served as Rabbi of the local community in Shatz. And the little boy's maternal grandfather was Reb Sh'mu'el Shor (known as the Manestritcher Rav), who was descended from the authors of the two standard commentaries in *halacha*: *bach (ba-yis chadash* on the *Arba'a Turim*) and *taz (turey zahav* on the *Shulchan Aruch)*. In her own right, though, the woman who became Yehuda Meir's mother was regarded as a great *tzadékess*, with a character of notable goodness and piety — so much so that her own father would often praise her with the well-known sentence in *Mishley*: "Many daughters have done valiantly, but you surpass them all" (Proverbs 31:29).

It was only natural, then, that about the child both parents were in complete agreement: They would strive to have him devote himself entirely to Torah study. They would strive to elevate him to a spiritual level that befit a descendant of such great men of learning and holiness.

His mother especially had a great share of influence in the relatively ideal upbringing that he received. She used to speak directly to his heart, in a variety of ways that his heart would absorb and remember. Thus she would say, "Meir'l my child, see to it that you study well and learn Torah:

because every day that goes by with no Torah learned is something precious lost that can never be gotten back; and who knows what the next day may bring?"

Such were the words he heard, that seemed to croon in his ears like a lullaby; and as he learned, in early childhood, to read and grasp the words of what his people called the Torah, he applied himself with zeal. Yet his mother only drove him on to greater effort: "For such a great and mighty Torah," she would say about all his efforts in studying it, "this is too small a sacrifice."

The years went by, and in his mature years he still remembered well those two maxims of his mother's. Twice in *Mishley* our sacred Scripture cautions us, "do not forsake the Torah of your mother" (Proverbs 1:8, 6:20); and this is how Rav Meir Shapiro obeyed. He made full use of those two messages from a devout, pious woman to her tender child, when the time came for him to rally support for his two great creations, the *daf yomi* and *Yeshivas Chachmey Lublin*:

"We have to spend time with Torah every day," he would say, "by studying the *daf yomi*, because every day that goes by without Torah study is something precious lost that can never be gotten back; and who knows what the next day may bring?"

And when a man of means gave an all-too-modest donation in support of the yeshiva, explaining in excuse that times were so bad, business conditions so dreadful, that every penny (kopeck) he gave was a true sacrifice for him, Rav Meir Shapiro would reply sharply by citing his mother's other maxim: "But, my dear sir, for such a great and mighty Torah, this is too small a sacrifice."

The warm, devoted, attentive upbringing that he received from his parents meshed and merged with the inborn prodigious abilities and talents of his mind and the fiery chassidic temperament of his heart, that evidently came to him by heredity. The sum total effect on the little youngster was that he made such progress in his study and in the development of good sense from one day to the next, that everyone was amazed.

At the age of four it was time for the bright, precocious boy to begin learning *chumash* (the Written Torah, the Five Books of Moses). In keeping with a beloved age-old tradition, the parents made a great "*chumash* feast," to which all the worthies of the town were invited. And the highlight (again by tradition) was the sermonic discourse by the boy, in which his *rebbe* had fully prepared him, on some of the words of *Va-yikra* (the Book of Leviticus) — a "Torah talk" in which the boy held forth for over half an hour.

He spoke clearly and resonantly, with such fervor, conviction and confidence, so fully in command of himself, that the response was a great sense of wonder among all who were there. The unanimous conclusion was that here stood before them a future great orator, a true master of rhetoric.

One of the invited guests who heard him was the learned Reb Cha-yim Brody, whose brother Reb Leyb was due to become the Rabbi of the major city of Lemberg. Having listened attentively to the fascinating discourse of this amazing child, he exclaimed, "If not for the enormous difference in age between this young fellow and my brother, I'm afraid the boy could have competed successfully against my brother for the position in Lemberg."

3

Young genius (iluy) and young masmid

In the world of the yeshiva, the norm has always been to differentiate between the *ga'on*, the brilliant mind that grasps and retains, with a penetrating understanding, and the *masmid*, the industrious pupil who will spend hours on end studying away, conscientiously. The *ga'on* receives his "title" soon enough in the yeshiva world, though he does not devote the whole day to his study. For him a few hours in the day are quite enough to supply his keen mind and quick understanding with all that he needs.

On the other hand, the title of *masmid* often connotes a pupil endowed by fate with a slow, dullish mind and a somewhat dense understanding. All day must he sit before his folio page of Talmud and toil away at it; and no matter how much he studies, it is never enough, apparently, to let him climb onto some proper level of esteem as a young scholar.

In fact, we have become so inured to this distinction, this "normal" dichotomy, that we can hardly imagine a synthesis of the two: one human being who is both a *ga'on* and a *masmid*. That would seem to us a plain contradiction in terms. To us they seem two mutually exclusive modes of being which could not exist together, harmoniously, in one person.

And yet this is exactly what young Meir was: a singular exception to the rule. He had a rare mind of unmistakable genius, a lightning grasp and comprehension; and with that he was an extraordinary *masmid*. Not a minute seemed to get lost as he spent the day. Every moment was precious as gold to him.

He would be called to the lunchtime meal; but another few minutes would have to elapse before the food actually appeared on the table. At once he would take up a volume of Talmud and do a lightning review of a page, or perhaps it would be a paragraph of *halacha* in a volume of *Shulchan Aruch*. Then, the midday meal over and *birkas ha-mazon* (the Grace after meals) ended, there he would be, back in the *beyss medrash*, seated at his regular place, immersed entirely in his study, completely immune to what might be going on in the rest of the world. To absorb

Torah learning: this was his sole purpose and goal; and this goal he pursued with all his being, with a maximum of energy and application.

As it were, he showed the way of a ga'on in being a masmid!

****

To what lengths could the young scholar go as a masmid? Let these few facts from his chilhood serve as an illustration:

Not far from his home there was a delicatessen store which stayed open into the late hours of the night. Once, having decided to close up, the couple who owned the shop began making their preparations, when they noticed a light still on in young Meir's home; and there was the boy, studying his Talmud as zealously as ever.

"Well," thought the owners of the store, "if it pays for that thin, weak little scholar to stay up so late, it should certainly pay for us to stay on. Another customer of some sort may still drop in." And they decided to remain for another hour. Then, certain that the boy must finally be asleep, they decided to shut down at last. How amazed they were when the melody of young Meir's chanting reached their ears. The small scholar was still at his Talmud study!

Now, across from Meir's home lived a locksmith who generally rose very early. Once Meir's Talmud chanting reached *his* ears as he woke to start a new day. Curious to know how early this lad began *his* day, the locksmith decided to get out of bed the next morning an hour or two before his usual time — but it was of no use: There was the boy, working away at his Talmud study since some unearthly hour that only Heaven knew.

Evidently he went to bed later than anyone, and rose again earlier than anyone. No one could weary him out; no one could surpass him — this ga'on of a masmid.

Soon enough, however, the abnormal, impossible schedule that he kept was brought to the attention of his parents, and they were warned that this would harm his health and impair his physical growth and development. Quite naturally, they decided to watch over him more and reduce his hours of study. So they made it a policy to put out all the candles and lamps in the home, at a fairly early hour of the night. In the darkness, they thought, he could certainly not go on being a masmid.

It was of no use, however. Just as soon as he received a bit of pocket money from his parents, so that he could buy himself something to eat occasionally as a treat, off he went to the little nearby store to get himself a small candle — and he continued with the Talmud through the hours of the night.

When he was left without any money for candles, he found another way. There were always little tests and examinations for the neighborhood youngsters on the Talmud, and since Meir invariably excelled in them, he kept receiving various items as prizes; or presents were awarded him at other occasions for his outstanding knowledge of his studies. These he sold among his friends, to keep himself "in funds"; and so the supply of candles continued for many more hours of study in the night.

In time, however, his zealous application to the Talmud reached its acme. He himself felt his energy beginning to wane from day to day. Under the tremendous strain his eyes became bloodshot, and he could feel his heart growing weaker. At last he was taken to a medical doctor for an examination.

The medical man diagnosed a condition of general debility — an overall weakness — which, the doctor warned, could fatally affect the boy's health. What he prescribed was a strict "study diet": the youngster was to spend no more than a few hours a day at learning his Torah.

Desolated, the small scholar had no choice but to accept the "cruel decree"; as much as possible, he would have to try to abide by the doctor's order.

Yet what was he to do? To go idle the entire day was out of the question; it was more than he could bear. So he found his own solution: what he could not learn inside — by sitting in a study room and working away at a Talmudic text — he would learn outside, strolling through the town. He took his *chavrusa*, his learning companion, and the two went off to the park, the public gardens, as they reviewed by heart the Talmud tractate *Shabbas*, together with the commentary of *tos^{e}fos*. This was material which young Meir had known by heart since the age of eight.

So they walked together, getting more and more involved in their study, till a heated argument developed between them: At the particular point in the Talmud that they had reached, who was the Sage who made his statement there? One young Talmudist said it was Rava; the other declared it was Raba; and each insisted that he was right.

As one might expect from scholars of such tender years, the argument kept growing more vehement and heated — till they decided on the only possible solution: They must have a look in the Talmud!

Fine; but where? Meir's home was too far off; they could not possibly contain themselves till they reached it. Near the park, however, lived the town *shochet* (the ritual slaughterer). Without another thought they headed for his dwelling — only to be met by a frustration: When they reached the door of the *shochet*'s house, they found it locked, and no one was home. Unable to stanch their burning curiosity, they found the solution together: "Through the window," came from both mouths. Before they knew how it happened, they found a pane had been pushed out of its frame, and they were inside, standing at the bookcase.

The upshot was that both young scholars were right: In the printed Talmud text the name was Rava; but in the margin, it was found corrected to Raba in *hagahos ha-bach* (glosses by the author of *ba-yis chadash*, Rabbi Yoel Sirkes).

Their happiness was indescribable. Imagine: both won the argument!

Only one problem remained: When neighbors heard a window pane pushed out of its frame, they were certain that thieves were at work, and began raising the alarm. To their astonishment, amid the hubbub and confusion, as they entered the *shochet*'s home they found that the "thieves" were two youngsters standing at the bookcase, with a volume of Talmud in their hands.

4

The iluy of Shatz

Slowly, slowly, like ripples widening out in a calm lake from a stone dropped in its center, the reports spread about the "wonder child" of Shatz. In ever widening circles, in a world where such matters were of the highest importance and the greatest interest, the news traveled about young Meir's mastery of Talmudic study: his phenomenal memory, and his depth of understanding. Everywhere people sang his praises to the sky, beyond any limit.

There were those, however, who remained skeptical, dismissing the reports as overblown legends. They refused to believe that in such a small, insignificant provincial town as Shatz, where not one reputable Talmudic scholar lived, such a great *iluy* could develop — a veritable genius.

The result was that people began to notice various visitors at Meir's home. From time to time, rabbinic personages and men of learning appeared, wanting to see the little genius with their own eyes and to learn for themselves how much truth there was in all the rumors about his Talmudic prowess. . . .

One day two chassidic notables, renowned for their learning, arrived in Shatz: the Rebbe of Antunya and the Rebbe of Vizhnitz. While traveling together in the region, fairly nearby, they had heard the rumors and reports about the youngster, and decided to make a detour into Shatz and examine him for themselves.

To their utter amazement, they found that in reality the boy surpassed all the rumors and tales about him. All of nine years old, he knew by heart the entire first part of *Shulchan Aruch Yoreh Dé'ah* — precisely what a young adult had to know before he could be ordained as a rabbi, fit to serve as religious head of a community and answer the questions that would arise on whether something was kosher or not. The boy was able to discuss the material like any old, seasoned rabbi who had been answering such questions for years.

There were other rumors, though, which the two eminent scholars had heard about the boy: that in addition, his mind was exceptionally sharp, and in his studies he could find sudden points of interest and solutions to difficulties with lightning speed.

Seated as guests at the Shabbos table, after the kiddush that came before the daytime meal, Reb Cha-yim of Antunya and Reb Yisra'el of Vizhnitz joined in the *z^emiros* and sang the verses of *chai haShem uvaruch tzuri*. Without warning, the guests drew young Meir's attention to the last line of the sixth verse: *el he-harim essa eynaï, k^ehillel v^elo ch^eshammaï* ("to the hills will I lift up my eyes, like Hillel and not like Shammai"). "Tell us," they asked, "what does that mean?"

The young Meir thought for a moment, then launched into a small but masterly bit of *pilpul* — incisive Talmudic reasoning. "The hills," said he, "are a symbol for the thirty-nine kinds of labor forbidden on this day of rest"; and he told where the symbolism is found in the Talmud (*bavli*, Chagiga 10a-b). There, though, the Talmud makes an important point about this forbiddance: The thirty-nine kinds of labor are exactly those that were needed in building the *mishkan*, the temporary, portable Sanctuary in the wilderness; but there these labors were always done consciously, deliberately and for a purpose. Hence, the Talmud conveys (Chagiga 10b — see Rashi), the Sabbath is violated only when one of these labors is done likewise: consciously, deliberately, for a purpose. Otherwise, no sin has been done.

Here a word of explanation must be added: What links together the labors in the construction of the *mishkan* with the laws of Shabbos? The answer is in the Midrash. In the Book of *Sh^emos* (Exodus 35:1-2) Moshe instructs the people that since Shabbos must be observed as a holy day of rest, no work may be done then — on pain of death. Immediately afterward (Exodus 35:4ff.) we find him instructing the people to gather all the materials they would need for the *mishkan*, and to go ahead and build it.

Hence, says the Midrash (Mechilta, cited in Rashi), we interpret that Moshe clearly meant to convey: "I am giving you a commandment (a positive mitzvah) to build the *mishkan* (which will require thirty-nine kinds of labor). Yet just before, I gave you a commandment (a negative mitzvah) to do no work on Shabbos: The thirty-nine kinds of labor that you must do to get the *mishkan* built, you must not do on Shabbos. On the holy day of rest, precisely these kinds of work are forbidden."

At any rate, at the Shabbos table in Shatz, the nine-year-old explained to the two distinguished guests that according to the Talmud, the "hills" in the *z^emiros* can be taken as a symbol for the thirty-nine kinds of labor forbidden on Shabbos — and with their background, they followed him perfectly.

"But," continued the sprightly young Talmudist: it could be argued that the whole source for this basic law, that precisely these kinds of labor are forbidden on Shabbos, is a matter of *s^emuchin*, proximity. It is derived in the Midrash from the fact that two themes occur in the Torah in proximity, close together. And he cited another bit of Talmud (*bavli*, M^enachos 40a, top, with Rashi), to show that the rule of *s^emuchin* is a valid way of interpretation only according to the School of Hillel, but not for the School of Shammai: This rule, that a binding, normative law can be derived from the fact that two themes occur in the Torah close together — is held only by the School of Hillel.

The boy had shown his mettle. . . .

****

Around the same time, his mother's father, the Manestritcher Rav, came for a visit. When he went to pay his respects to the local rabbi, the eminent visitor took his small grandson along. In the course of the visit, the two men of learning became involved in an interesting discussion on some rather complicated matters in the Talmud. The little fellow stayed there quietly the whole time, seemingly lost in thought; and it never occurred to the adults that he might be listening attentively, understanding every word.

Soon enough, however, the discussion became a debate, then an argument, on a point of *halacha.* In a few minutes, the Manestritcher Rav found himself in a small dilemma. The local rabbi demolished the halachic view that his eminent visitor had formulated, and the Manestritcher Rav could find no way to refute him.

It was then that the nine-year-old Meir spoke up. "It seems to me," he said, "that the true explanation of the matter is this — which would mean that my grandfather is right." And he sailed blithely into his sharp Talmudic explanation. . . .

The grandfather could hardly believe his ears. How beautiful the explanation was — how apt! And he, an eminent Talmudist with years of learning, had never thought of it! Beaming with happiness, he showered the small scholar with kisses. "Well," said he, "I hope that soon you will become my *talmid* and study regularly with me — the kind of pupil that our Talmudic Sages called a *talmid* who makes his teachers wise!" (*bavli,* Chagiga 14a).

In due time this hope became fulfilled. As soon as he turned thirteen, and passed the age of bar mitzvah, the boy rode off to Manestritch, where his renowned grandfather reigned in eminence as the Rav. And there he found the right soil for his spiritual development. Despite his powerful inclination for *pilpul,* to find his own incisive, insightful explanations in Talmudic matters by creative, dynamic reasoning, he restrained and restricted himself, so as to increase and enrich his store of Talmudic knowledge. With an iron determination he studied night and day, undaunted by any difficulties that faced him. Thanks to this rigorous program, he mastered there most of the Talmud and the four parts of the *Shulchan Aruch,* along with a wealth of approaches and opinions, decisions and views, in the literature of *halacha.*

Simultaneously, in the time he spent there, the growing youngster received an invaluable, inestimable education in the proper functioning of a Rav, a rabbinic head of a Jewish community. With receptive, eager eyes he watched all the great, important cases that came before his grandfather — every *din torah* over which this venerable rabbinic authority sat in judgment. The Manestritcher Rav was famed throughout Galicia for his great Talmudic acumen and extraordinary wisdom, that he combined with a sound knowledge of business matters and the practical world. In consequence, as a rule, when he gave his decision, both sides in a *din torah,* both parties in the dispute, were satisfied.

The time that the young Meir spent with his grandfather brought him, as well, a wide general knowledge of the Jewish milieu in Galicia. He became acquainted with various communal enterprises that his grandfather conducted; and this gave him an invaluable background and conception of possible activities in the communal life of Eastern Europe. It was a basic education for him, that matured in his mind in later years, leading him on to acclaimed community activities of his own, which were to revolutionize the rabbinic world that he knew.

For only a short period was the growing youngster able to stay with his grandfather, but it was enough to give him a rounded supplementary education and potential training in skills of community-wide rabbinic leadership, in all areas of devout, religious life. It was a unique education that lodged in his memory, to stand him in good stead for the rest of his years.

****

Thus a year and a half went by since his arrival; and then, one day in 5663 (1903), his grandfather suddenly fell ill. The malady turned very serious, till it became alarming; and the venerable Rav felt he had only a few weeks left to live.

Having no wish to distress the family needlessly, he kept his thoughts to himself, but only called young Meir secretly to his bedside and told this gifted grandson: "You see for yourself that my severe illness won't let me study with you any more. Ride home, then, to your parents. The truth is that I believe you really don't need me any more; I hope and trust that you will be able to learn and absorb more Torah than I ever could."

Meir obeyed and traveled home.

The forebodings of the venerable Rav proved true. That very winter, on the seventh of Adar (February 6, 1903), the great scholar known as the Manestritcher Rav passed on to his eternal reward.

5

The young kabbalist

His return from Manestritch was to lead to the beginning of a new period in the life of the brilliant budding scholar. As he entered his sixteenth year, he was possessed of an immense spiritual treasure, a Torah education that many could only envy. By now he was versed in just about the entire *Talmud Bavli*, the four parts of the *Shulchan Aruch*, and a good number of tractates of the *Talmud Yerushalmi*. And so he began to analyze in depth all that he knew, to set in order the full range of the Torah he had learned and absorbed.

This he did despite the fact that the entire little town of Shatz could not provide him with all the volumes of learning that he needed. Thus, when he had to study something in the tractate *P'sachim* of the *Talmud Yerushalmi*, he sent off a letter to an uncle — the son of the departed Manestritcher Rav — in which he wrote: "I would herewith like to ask you, if you will forgive me for imposing on you, to kindly take the trouble to copy out for me . . . part of the second chapter, from the first *mishna* to the second; and if that is too much, at least do this much for me: Copy out the view of Hizkiya and Rabbi Eliezer precisely, letter by letter." Even such difficulties could not daunt him or prevent him from making progress.

With a passionate zeal he devoted himself to creative study, to produce masterly original thought, wondrous *chiddushim*, impressive insights. At the same time, however, he found that a new psychical urge had come imperiously alive in him: His spirit yearned to know the hidden, mystic side of the Torah — the rich, fascinating body of thought that lived in the world of *kabbala*. For better or worse, there was a powerful longing in him to know also this part of our Divine, immortal heritage.

He realized full well how much endless labor this new study would require, how much precious time it would consume, till he could gain some proper mastery of a body of sacred learning that was all veiled and concealed in vision and metaphor, locked away in its strange, imaging, esoteric terminology.

There were no illusions about it for him. He foresaw how much sheer toil it would cost him till he could succeed in gaining some proper grasp of the sublime mystic teachings that went by the name of *kabbala.* He was aware of it all, in full; and yet the yearning was strong enough to break through all the barriers and thrust every difficulty aside.

In his heart he made a full accounting, a complete reckoning of what it would mean to learn *kabbala.* He calculated quite accurately how weighty a burden a human soul would have to carry once such study was undertaken. Not for nothing did the great sages refuse to permit just anyone to pore over the strange, visionary material, but only exceptional individuals. He sensed how slippery and dangerous was the road before him. It could well mean walking a knife edge poised over an abyss, where more than one mind had lost its balance, and a human soul had gone to perdition.

He took stock of his own mind and its treasury of knowledge; he purified his heart and spirit of all extraneous influences; with the greatest caution and care he considered the matter from all aspects. And try as he would, he could not rid himself of the longing. Struggle as he would, he could not give it up. It was a hunger not to be denied, a hunger that overpowered him till he had to yield. He had to learn this esoteric body of holy knowledge — and it would brook no delay.

With his usual fiery energy and enthusiasm he set to work.

In the fairly small community of Shatz, however, there was no way to keep such a thing secret. The townspeople began to know that their *iluy*, their young genius, had embarked on the study of kabbala; and soon enough a great hubbub and commotion arose in the community: Who had ever heard of a fifteen-year-old studying kabbala? True — it was known what a masterful knowledge he had of so much of the plain, open, unhidden Torah; but how could that justify the study of Jewish mysticism at such a tender age — and moreover, all on his own, without a sound, mature teacher to instruct him and guide him? Such a thing had never been heard of. It was simply *chutzpa* by the boy: an act of arrogance and hauteur!

From mouth to mouth the bit of news traveled, till it became "the talk of the day"; and finally, inevitably, it reached the ears of the town rabbi, Rav Shalom Moskowitz, who, as it happened, was not only a great Torah scholar but a redoubtable master of kabbala as well. (In later years he was to migrate to London, where he would become known as the chassidic Rebbe — *admor* — of Shatz). Unfortunately, there was one bit of knowledge he lacked: he was barely acquainted with young Meir and had no idea of what the growing adolescent was really like. And so he saw the whole matter as a youthful whim — an adolescent caprice, nothing more.

In his role of local Torah authority, the rabbi saw it as his duty to dissuade the lad from such perilous study. He was resolved to make it clear to the young scholar that such study was highly improper and unsuitable for him; or, alternatively, the youngster should at least postpone the study for a good many years, till he would be more matured and replete with a sound knowledge of the open, unconcealed Torah.

So he decided to send for young Meir, and when the young lad came, he began lecturing him sharply, berating him for daring to embark on such a perilous course on his own, at such an early age.

Between the two, however, somehow a serious conversation sprang up, that went on for several hours. Thus the rabbi had a chance to learn what an exceptional young adolescent this was. He had to realize that despite his youthful years, there was an enormous treasury of Torah knowledge which Meir possessed — a strong enough anchor in "normal" Torah learning to ensure that the young scholar would never become imbalanced in the study of kabbala.

The rabbi abandoned his sharp, critical tone and went on talking with the youngster in a softer voice. He was ready to accept that in this particular case, when the boy was already master of such a vast amount of Torah, and when he had so evidently the mind of a genius, an exception to the rule about kabbala could be made.

The conversation went on for another short while — long enough to convince the rabbi that he would find no way to persuade this young fellow to change course and relinquish his new study. Whatever might be, this boy would go further into Jewish mysticism with the greatest persistence and perseverance, with all the burning energy his young spirit could muster, till he would reach the goal he had set himself.

Finally the Rabbi of Shatz conceded: "Well, I have to admit: I don't see any way to stop you from studying kabbala. You do have a very satisfactory foundation in our open, unconcealed Torah. But I think it a great pity that you are going to waste a great deal of precious time, which you could put to very good use. You should go on studying Talmud and Rambam [Maimonides' code of law] and so on; devote hours to that every day, and you are certain to produce valuable chiddushim, new, insightful ways of understanding their teachings. But now, if you go on studying kabbala by yourself, you will lose an enormous amount of time till you get your bearings and begin finding your way. So, then, I am prepared to devote a set time every day for you, and we will study together. I can thus give you the fundamentals of kabbala, the basic terminology and conceptions, till I bring you up to a proper level, where you can continue quite easily on your own."

Needless to say, the young scholar left the rabbi's home in a mood of elation that knew no bounds. He was almost dancing on air. Far from having his path blocked, he was to have a teacher to guide him firmly in his all-important first steps in the strange, unknown world of Jewish mysticism — the very man who might have opposed him implacably.

He became a regular visitor to the local rabbi's home; and in a short while he found himself making rapid strides into the mysteries of this esoteric field of study. Here especially, however, his gift for intuitive insight found a rich field to work; and his teacher could not cease to wonder in amazement at the revelations that this stripling kept discovering in the texts that they studied. It became clear to him, beyond the shadow of a doubt, that this young scholar's intense yearning to learn kabbala had been the furthest thing from a passing whim, but rather a sublime, Divine directive, welling up from the depths of his being.

For here was a powerful longing to attain a complete mastery of the veiled and hidden aspects of the Torah, whereupon he would discover new horizons, new realms of awareness in the open, unconcealed parts of our Divine heritage. It was thanks to this intense longing that he was able to make such incredible strides.

In those daily visits, then, the rabbi and his pupil did a thorough study of the entire *Zohar*, the "Book of Splendor" that constitutes the basic text of Jewish mysticism, and went on to the later great, classic works of kabbala, such as the writings of Rav Moshe Cordovero and Rav Cha-yim Vital, respectively the teacher and the talmid of the renowned Rav Yitzchak Luria (the *Ari*) of Safed. From there they continued with the basic volumes of chassidic thought which developed from kabbala, such as the works of Rav Ya'akov Yosef of Polonoye and Rav Shné'or Zalman of Liady — till the young Meir had a thorough grounding in all the branches and ramifications of kabbala and *chassidus*.

With this, however, the chapter is still not ended. In his firm desire that the growing lad should not neglect or abandon his brilliant, progressing studies in Talmud and *halacha,* Rav Shalom Moskowitz set aside a room for him where he could pursue his learning program undisturbed. And when time allowed, Rav Shalom would join him and the two would discourse and study together; and thus he made further strides in his Talmudic prowess — so much so that as he grew older, yet before the time came for him to marry, he found himself teaching others of his age in what became, in effect, the local yeshiva.

6

Into astronomy

At the same time, while he was plowing ahead in the sublime realms of Jewish mysticism, this young scholar decided that he had to learn as well the fundamentals of astronomy. He was troubled by certain complex, difficult topics in the Talmud that he knew he would not understand unless he could learn and apply the proper astronomical principles.

Without further ado, he studied several volumes on the subject that Jewish scholars produced in the course of our history, such as the two classics, *Y'sod Olam* and *T'chunos haShama-yim.* Having gained a broad basic knowledge of the subject, he went on to "practical field work" and began studying various changes in the sky at night over a period of time, paying particular attention to certain constellations of stars and astral bodies. Out of all that he had read, he tried to understand what he saw — the phenomena that his eyes beheld in the panorama of the nighttime sky.

As no one paid any particular attention to this young adolescent going about his daily routines, his new interest in astronomy remained entirely unknown in the community. It was assumed that he was pursuing his normal Torah studies as usual, with no interest whatever in anything worldly. And this suited him perfectly. He, for his part, did all he could to keep this new field of interest secret, disclosing nothing to anyone. He had no wish to be disturbed or troubled by peering, probing eyes. He wanted no one's obtrusive interest or unwelcome opinions.

When the time came, however, it was fated to become known that this young genius had also become quite expert in astronomy — and it could only evoke a widespread amazement in the small town.

This is how it happened:

One night he was strolling in the town park, his mind busy with his thoughts on what he had been studying during the day, when he happened to glance up at the starry sky — and he stopped short in his tracks. There, before his eyes, was some extraordinary, astounding astral phenomenon that was in absolute contradiction to all he had learned till now.

Completely baffled, he stood there a good while lost in thought, trying to puzzle it out, to get to the cause of it. He cogitated and reckoned, and kept looking up at the stars. Soon enough his rather strange behavior drew the attention of one of the people passing by.

As fate would have it, the man was a full-fledged *maskil*, a member of the Jewish people who had decided to leave the sacred Torah tradition in favor of a non-Jewish secular education. And the hand of fate (or Providence) went even further: he had a doctorate in philosophy, a university degree, having majored in astronomy! It was a subject he loved, having devoted years of study to it.

Unfortunately, though, a love of astronomy was not all he carried in his heart. As a true *maskil*, he also bore within him a fine, cordial abhorrence and hatred for the "old fashioned, reactionary element" among the Jewish people who refused to give up their "antiquated culture" to move with the times. And in fact, he especially detested the *yeshiva bochurim*, with their side curls and old-fashioned garb.

Now the sight of a *yeshiva bochur* staring at the sky left *him* puzzled: Why was a young good-for-nothing like that studying the stars? What in the world could he know about the firmament at night? Quite unable to restrain himself, he went over and asked with a derisive sneer, "What is it that you see up there in the sky? — something so fascinating that you can't stop feasting your eyes on it?"

So wrapped was the young Meir in his thoughts that he did not notice the biting sarcasm in the man's voice. In plain humility he replied, "Of course, for someone who knows astronomy well, I'm sure there is nothing strange to be seen there; but I'm only a beginner, and that formation of stars has just stopped me in my tracks. I've been standing here a rather long while trying to puzzle it out."

The simple, honest words, spoken without any guile, made a deep enough impression on the *maskil* to stop him in *his* tracks. He could not help being impressed; and his only response before such eagerness to learn was to begin an answer to Meir's problem.

To his amazement, he found this young *yeshiva bochur* following his thoughts with lightning speed, with a grasp that many a mature astronomer would envy. Almost inevitably they went on into a discussion of the most profound and complicated questions, as the doctor of philosophy realized that he was dealing here with a young genius.

Every trace of dislike or derision vanished in the man, to be replaced by a feeling of warm affection. The man was overjoyed to have found in this little town, so unexpectedly, someone of his own mettle, with whom he could talk as an equal about his beloved subject. The result was that he took to cultivating Meir's friendship, and readily gave this "young astronomer" full help, out of his own considerable, advanced knowledge, in solving various difficult problems.

At the same time, however, he saw no reason to hide young Meir's light under a bushel; and he began spreading the word through the small town that it had a young genius in astronomy in its midst. All the hopes that the young adolescent had had to keep this side interest secret, all his efforts to keep it unknown, went with the wind. . . .

How advanced he became in this field, how deep and far his knowledge reached, could be gauged from writings of his that he included in his published works, *Imrey Da'as* (on *sidra va-yéra*) and *Or haMé'ir* (section 13). In these two places, with his own genius and compelling talent, he sheds a clarifying, illuminating light on the difficult passages in Talmud tractate *Rosh haShana* 11, 12 and *Shabbas* 129, making them accessible to any initiated learner. For systematically he analyzes and explains, in clear, precise detail, *sod ha'ibbur* ("the principle of intercalation" — literally, on adding a thirteenth month to the Jewish year at the proper times, but more inclusively, the entire system of calculating the Jewish calendar in advance, year by year). With a matchless brilliance and all-encompassing knowledge he sets out the necessary fundamentals and axioms, and with a sound, consistent logic builds his entire structure from them, making the whole thing seem self-evident — simplicity itself. At the same time, with his singular gift of penetrating insight, he manages to use his conclusions to bring a new clarity to various obscure points in the Talmud.

How apt are certain expressions he used: in *Imrey Da'as*, "What we have been instructed from the heavens [a plain allusion to the sky of the astronomer], and after God has made us know all this [a paraphrase of *B^eréshis*/Genesis 41:39]"; and in *Or haMé'ir*, at the end of the responsum in section 13, "Blessed be the One who favors a human being with sensible knowledge; may He lead us in the way of truth." For so much brilliance and profundity, so much inner consistency and indisputable truth, could only have come from sources beyond ordinary human intelligence. One senses there a pure Divine illumination that only certain rare human beings merit to attain.

Beyond dispute, he was among them.

7

The spreading renown

Meanwhile his reputation began to reach further and further in earnest. It went beyond local, nearby regional borders and traveled on into the entire territory of Galicia. Wherever people traveled or journeyed, wherever they moved and met, the general subject of conversation seemed to become "the *iluy* of Shatz": Everywhere, apparently, people had amazing things to tell about him, and everyone had a different wonder to relate. One told about his immense creativity, his tremendous *chiddushim* in bringing a new light of understanding to many a Talmudic problem. Another told of his profound knowledge of kabbala; and so on.

Yet while the sources and causes of his growing fame were various, there was finally one incident which made everyone everywhere believe that all the fabulous things told about him were true:

In a neighboring small town, quite near Shatz, a severe conflict broke out about the rabbinic position, which became alarming in its intensity. To settle the matter and quench the fire of controversy, the local community decided to bring in the two most distinguished and respected rabbinic personages of Galicia: the revered Rav Shalom Mordechai Schwadron of Berzhan, and the no less learned Rav Shalom Lulenfeld, known as the Rabbi of Podhaïetz. Whatever verdict these two reached, it was certain to carry enough weight for all to accept as decisive.

As the two scholars rode together to the small town in response to the invitation, they found that between trains, they would have to remain for a long waiting period at the railroad station in Shatz, and decided to go immediately to a local hotel and spend the time there.

The news spread swiftly through the little town that the two greatest Torah authorities of that time were now right there; and anyone and everyone seized the opportunity to go and meet the two, to chat with them a bit and get to know them.

Particularly elated to hear the news was young Meir. Launched well into adolescence, he was eager to know what two such illustrious minds would make of some of his *chiddushim*, his writings on the Talmud. Now, he decided, he might have a chance to find out.

For the rest of his years he would remember this first meeting of his with these supremely eminent scholars, as one of the most blissfully wonderful episodes of his life.

His heart beat rapidly with a mixture of reverent, fearful awe and unbearable eagerness, as he stood at the door of their room at the hotel, mustered his courage, and knocked; and in a moment he stood before the two gray-haired patriarchal figures of renown. Having presented himself, he went on to tell them the purpose of his visit.

The two could hardly believe their ears. What in the world was this? Here, in this remote, faraway corner of the earth, so distant from any proper center of Torah learning, a mere stripling like this wanted to talk with *them* — seriously — on Talmudic matters? And if that were not enough, he wished to convey to them some of his chiddushim, his own creative thoughts on the Talmud! Really . . .

Whatever their first impulses might have been, they could not bring themselves to dismiss him with disdain; and so they bade him go on and present one of his expositions of insightful thought. Without further ado, Meir launched himself into one of his *chiddushim*, as the two listened gravely.

Within a moment their attention was riveted. In his flow of words they heard an incredible mastery of the Talmud, with its *rishonim* and *acharonim* (the earlier and later commentaries), as Meir marshaled his introductory material for the thesis he wanted to present.

By now, their interest fully aroused, the two great scholars waited eagerly, even impatiently, for Meir to present his arguments and reach his conclusions. On he went with a razor-sharp agility and keenness, through points and thoughts of such profundity that the two scholars of eminence had to concentrate their minds and give him their full attention, to follow the flashes of brilliance that he seemed able to produce with lightning speed.

All at once the Rav of Podhaïetz interrupted him: For all his erudition, said the venerable Torah scholar, the young fellow had overlooked a clear, explicit passage in the Talmud which flatly contradicted the conclusion in *halacha* that he wanted to reach. "On the contrary," young Meir shot back: That Talmudic passage could provide strong support for his conclusion. And he went on to explain the piece of Talmud his way.

All this while, the Rav of Berzhan had sat by impassively, listening in silence even now, as the argument between his learned companion and their young visitor became impassioned. At last, however, as he saw his eminent companion about to be vanquished, he rose to his feet and spoke: "The truth of the matter is as the Rav of Podhaïetz holds!" Yet the Rav of Berzhan said not another word to support his contention, and the perceptive adolescent sensed that this venerable scholar was not really, wholly convinced that he was right. He had spoken only to try to rescue his colleague from a dilemma.

For a moment young Meir was still. Then, weighing every word with care, he faced the Rav of Berzhan and replied courageously, "I'm afraid that your support of the Rav of Podhaïetz comes as no surprise to me. Apparently you have been guided by a phrase in the Talmud (Chullin 59a): *kahana m^{e}sa-ya kahani* — a *kohén* helps other *kohanim*. In keeping with that, I see here how one Rav supports another."

Evidently, with these rather daring words, the meeting ended. What remained, however, was the overwhelming impression that Meir had made on the venerable Rav of Berzhan. He and his colleague rode on to the neighboring small town to carry out their mission, then returned to their respective homes. Once back in Berzhan, this great Torah scholar proceeded to tell the local worthies about this amazing young genius in the little, wholly unremarkable town of Shatz.

Soon after, the time came for the Rav of Berzhan to write to the heads of the community near Shatz of the formal decision which his eminent colleague and he had reached about the controversy regarding the rabbinic post in that small town. When he finished this *p^{e}sak din*, the official verdict that would settle the matter, he added a postscript about his travel through Shatz with his distinguished colleague: for evidently, the meeting with the young Talmud scholar there was still sharply alive in his mind.

Without hesitation, he took a statement in the Talmud about the *tanna* Rabbi Meir (*bavli*, Sanhedrin 24a), made a small change in it to suit his purpose, and then wrote, "Then I saw Rabbi [*sic*] Meir sitting in his house of study uprooting the mightiest mountains [of Talmudic teaching and thought] and grinding them against one another [*thus far the modified citation from the Talmud*] by pure reasoning; and I recited over him the benediction, *baruch yotzér ha-m^{e}oros* (Blessed be the One who formed the heavenly luminaries)." In his unquenchable, enthusiastic admiration, he decided that nothing less than a blessing would do, and deciding on a play on words, he chose a bit of the benediction in the morning prayers about *ha-m^e^oros*, "the luminaries," meaning literally the sun and the moon — because in it was a clear allusion to *Meir* (whose meaning in Hebrew is one who illumines or sheds light).

These words, stamped with the authority of none other than the Rav of Berzhan, a man regarded as probably the greatest Torah scholar of his time, did much to enhance and spread still further the growing renown of the young genius; and it helped persuade a great many to believe all the stories that kept traveling about him by word of mouth.

****

Stranger than fiction, however, are the ways of Divine providence. Eventually the time came when a family relationship formed between the two. As recorded above, Meir's maternal grandfather, the Manestritcher Rav, had passed away, leaving his maternal grandmother, the mother of Meir's mother, an old widow; and the Rav of Berzhan lost his wife. Needing someone to maintain a normal, well regulated home for him, so that he could go on with his important rabbinic duties, in due time he made a second marriage — with none other than Meir's widowed grandmother.

For the young adolescent it was providential. It gave him the opportunity to spend a few weeks in the great Rav's proximity: an unforeseen precious chance to watch him in action, in the practical aspects of his rabbinic life. Most significant was the orderliness he observed — the overriding importance of a methodical approach which dealt with everything systematically, bringing every detail into order and control.

This, he realized, was one of the main characteristics of this eminent authority; and this alone enabled the Rav of Berzhan to send his *t^e^shuvos*, responsa, in reply to the many thousands of *sh^e^élos*, vital questions in Jewish law, which he received from all over the world.

In his later years, Meir was to realize how valuable were these two weeks that he spent with his new family relative. They were a priceless education in rabbinic leadership and action — an education that stood him in good stead when he himself had to assume the mantle of rabbinic leadership and chart his own pathways to action. In his memory the matchless model he saw remained indelibly imprinted.

As time flowed on, leading him ever further toward adulthood, along with his ongoing creative Talmud study, he mastered faultlessly the basic literature needed in the practical side of a rabbinic authority's life: the four parts of the *Shulchan Aruch*, and important volumes of responsa *(sh^e^élos ut^e^shuvos)*. Then, at the "ripe, mature" age of sixteen, he felt ready to seek *s^e^micha*, formal ordination as a rabbi, with the right to serve his people as a religious leader. His next steps would have to take him to the eminent personages regarded as the *g^e^doley ha-dor*, the great Torah authorities of the age. It would be for them to decide if he was worthy of *s^e^micha* now.

His first journey in his quest brought him to his newly acquired relative, the justly renowned Rav of Berzhan. After all, this eminent Torah authority already knew him well. . . . Nevertheless, the Rav turned him down flatly: True, he explained, he was fully aware of Meir's consummate mastery of both the Talmud and the *Shulchan Aruch*; but just because there was now a family link between them, for proper procedural, formal reasons the Rav wanted Meir to acquire a document of *s^e^micha* from another eminent authority first. Then he, the Rav of Berzhan, would be able to act in turn.

Meir set off immediately for his next destination: the major city of Lemberg (Lvov); and he found his way to the distinguished rabbinic head of the community, the notable Rav Yitzchak Schmelkisch, whose printed volumes of Talmudic erudition had helped him attain his eminence as one of generation's foremost scholars.

To him, however, Meir was a completely unknown quantity. He had never seen this young scholar before nor heard of him. And so, as he always did with young candidates for *s^e^micha*, he opened an ordinary, routine discussion on some topic in *halacha*. As the discussion continued, it grew more involved and complex — until this rabbinic personage realized that no ordinary Talmud scholar sat there facing him. He was evidently dealing here with a level of intelligence amounting to genius, a source of Torah knowledge that seemed to spring and pour as from a fountain.

At that, the Rav of Lemberg switched the discussion to a matter of *pilpul*, where a keenly analytic approach was needed to resolve a very difficult ruling by Rambam (Maimonides) in his code of law. Without any preparation, entirely extemporaneously, Meir set off on a train of thinking that left his listener in helpless admiration: This young scholar was a Talmudist of absolutely first rank!

The normal, regular work schedule of this rabbinic authority was a heavy one. In the city of Lemberg lived the largest Jewish community in all of Galicia, and Rav Yitzchak's duties as its spiritual leader were extensive. In addition, being a Torah scholar of the first eminence, he too (like the Rav of Berzhan) received questions of law from all over the world, which had to be answered properly. The fact was, then, that every moment of Rav Yitzchak's working day was precious — planned and allotted for a specific purpose.

With all that, the Rav of Lemberg detained his young visitor for a full ten days, so that in the course of each day he could find some small segment of time for delightful conversation and discourse with him in the fascinating fields of Talmudic learning.

At the end of the ten days, although the two had met only this once in their lives, the Rav of Lemberg felt he knew this candidate for *s^emicha* quite well. In the formal document that he wrote, to confer on Meir full rabbinic ordination, the Rav emphasized the phenomenal mental powers and exceptional abilities that he had come to recognize in the young scholar; and he went on to prophesy a radiant and luminous rabbinic future for him. But the most unexpected feature of this document is that in it the eminent Torah authority wrote of his young visitor as an equal, without a trace of superiority or condescension.

On his return journey, the young scholar stopped again in Berzhan, and there he received his second official attestation of *s^emicha*, from his renowned step-grandfather, who wrote of him in much the same tone as the Rav of Lemberg had done.

From both men of eminence he now had full rabbinic ordination; and both documents foresaw a resplendent future for him as a spiritual leader and educator of his people when the time would come.

Early in the year 5666 (autumn of 1905), he received yet another missive, filled with admiration, that formally bestowed *s^emicha* on him. It was from the renowned chassidic leader Rabbi Yisra'el of Vizhnitz, who had known Meir as a young genius yet in his early years. This illustrious Rebbe likewise foresaw a luminous future for him, as a great mentor and educator of his people.

In the course of time he managed to become acquainted with the foremost rabbinic authorities and Talmud scholars of that period; then, when he returned home, he felt a strong wish to develop and deepen the bond of friendship that he had formed with them. Since he had no way of maintaining personal contact over the distances that separated them, he began a broad, wide-ranging correspondence with them. The subject matter of his letters became, quite naturally, various questions and thoughts that came to him in the course of his ongoing Talmud study.

From this program of correspondence with eminent personages whom he had come to know personally, it was an easy step to write as well to others whom he had never met, giving as his reason for daring to intrude on them in this way, the great renown that they enjoyed in the world of Talmud learning. Thus he came to exchange letters with the noted rabbinic authorities in Stanislav, Butchatch, Brod, and others. Some of their replies were to appear later in their printed volumes of responsa *(sh^e'élos ut^eshuvos)*.

[An interesting "by-product" of this correspondence was yet another formal missive of *s^emicha* — this one from the Rav of Butchatch, a personage of considerable renown in Galicia, who included felicitously a phrase from the Midrash (B^eréshis Rabba 20:12) about "the Torah of Rabbi Meir."]

All this intensive learned correspondence that he initiated and maintained gave Meir the opportunity to probe further in the realm of Talmudic thought; and at last he began writing the first pages of the material that was to appear in a later year as Imrey Da'as, his first published work. Now, when his first few essays were done, he sent them off to the rabbinic authority of Stanislav, who enjoyed considerable renown at the time, and asked for a *haskama*, a formal letter of approval.

When that Talmudic luminary read the pages he received, he had not the slightest hesitation in sending his *haskama* at once: He could only describe the contents as simply wondrous, products of pure genius from the mind of a young *iluy* on his way to maturity. And he expressed his hope and wish that the writings would appear in print, assuring his young correspondent that he would gain world-wide acclaim and recognition.

8

The period in Tarnopol

As his fame and reputation continued to spread through the entire region of Galicia, in time the young Meir came to the attention of a well-known man of means, a wealthy landowner named Reb Ya'akov Breitman, of the city of Tarnopol; and from what he heard, the man felt a great desire to have the young scholar for a son-in-law, as the bridegroom of the youngest of his four daughters. Not in the least miserly, he was prepared to promise a sizable part of his wealth as dowry for so renowned and acclaimed a young scholar.

The matter was duly pursued and negotiated successfully; and in the year 5666 (1906), having turned nineteen and having duly married, Meir became a resident in the home of his wealthy father-in-law. Here, with all his needs provided, new, wider gates opened to him for his further development, both in character and in prodigious mental prowess. In the local world of observant Jewry, the palatial home of Ya'akov Breitman was known as "the domain of Jewish royalty"; as such, it had a great effect on Meir's entire being, casting a decisive influence on the direction of his future life.

His father-in-law was no ordinary person. In addition to his wealth, the man possessed a great store of Torah learning as well, and a profound love of Jews in general to boot — being an impassioned, devoted *chassid* of the noted Rebbe of Tchortkov. In his home it had long been the practice for a group of Talmud scholars and men of rabbinic learning to gather regularly for study; and with them Reb Ya'akov loved to spend his time in spirited Talmudic discourse and debate.

The palatial dwelling was thus literally a *beyss va'ad la-chachamim*, a "meeting place for learned men of wisdom"; and Ya'akov's young son-in-law quickly came to feel entirely at home within the group, as the regular members completely accepted him, from the start, with great affection.

Somehow, automatically, he became at once the focal, central figure in the group; all the learned, scholarly visitors to the regular sessions patently settled themselves around him. And more: he seemed to have some magnetic attraction that drew them: for all the people of the town with a

Talmudic background came now, even from the furthest reaches, enlarging the group in the spacious, hospitable dwelling.

In this comfortable, carefree setting, the young scholar had a priceless opportunity to develop his preparation for life in one important respect: He was able to study a fair variety of human natures, to learn the differences between various types — everyone's superior qualities and everyone's defects. In short, he began studying and learning human beings — how much truth, how much untruth he might find in a given individual.

At the same time he cultivated an important social skill: He peppered his conversations with brilliant aphorisms and flashes of wit that kept the visitors delighted and entertained; and the lasting effect was that they formed ties of firm friendship with him and with the entire household.

With that, he also developed the skill of turning every conversation toward some point or thought of the Torah, so that the time should not have been wasted in idle chatter. For him every bit of social talk became an opportunity and an occasion for a bit of unobtrusive, unexpected Torah learning — to insert some fragment of Torah wisdom.

As for his own regular Torah study, that continued as regularly and intensively as ever. During the day he took to learning with young pupils, engaging them in the spirited discussions and volatile debates of *pilpul*, to make them experience the joys of such lively, explosive Talmud study. The night became the set time for him to study alone, in the privacy of his reflections and thoughts. Then he was able to continue work on his beloved volume of Talmudic studies which he planned to publish: *Imrey Da'as.* Quietly and steadily he made the chapters ready for publication.

Many a time he simply did not go to bed at all. In the night he might become involved in some difficult points in a Talmudic passage, and would just work away at it; and before he knew it, the first rays of sunshine were already on the horizon. Then he would shut down the tempestuous ferment of his searching mind and lie down on a couch to nap for half an hour. When he woke, he felt alert and fresh enough to face a new day of further study with his young *talmidim.*

****

In 5670 (1910), fully adult now at the age of twenty-three, he received two further documents of ordination, that invested him with added authority to serve as a rabbi in Jewry, with the full power of *yoreh yoreh, yadin yadin* ("he shall instruct, instruct; let him judge, let him judge"), the technical legal phrase which gave him the right to answer doubts and render decisions in questions of Jewish law.

One of these documents was from his step-grandfather, the great Rav of Berzhan; the other, from the venerable Rav Meir Arik of Tyrna. Both these giants of Talmudic learning praised him without stint for his level of knowledge in the present, and predicted for him a glorious future.

It was about this time that he began receiving queries on matters of law from the entire region: questions arising from actual life, requiring decisions and guidance to proper action. These he duly answered, in the best traditions of the responsa literature; some of this material was to appear eventually in his volume of *sh^e^élos ut^e^shuvos, Or haMeir*, when it appeared in print some two decades later, in 5686 (1926), when he was the rabbinic head of Piotrkov.

The need and the scope for action

From his earliest formative years, he had felt an inner drive toward social, communal activity — especially in connection with the education and upbringing of the young. Somehow he had always felt a bond, an attachment to this field of interest, and a driving duty to get involved.

Soon, he knew, he would emerge as a religious leader, to serve as the rabbi of a community. Yet neither the esteem nor the practical duties of a rabbinic position appealed to him. All that seemed to him of no real value or significance, compared to what he considered really important: the education and rearing of the young.

Certainly it was a rabbi's duty to watch over all the religious needs of his community. Certainly he must never lose sight of the provision of kosher food, the proper observance of Shabbos and of family purity (the laws of *mikveh*), and so on. Yet in his view, the "square one" of a rabbinic position, the fundamental area where a rabbi should focus his attention, had to be the faultless, undamaged education of the young.

And so he dreamed of recreating the Jewish life of the past, the time of earlier generations when every reputable rabbi of a community maintained a yeshiva. This was a fact, with historical evidence to support it: In letters and documents from earlier eras, many a notable rabbinic signature would be followed by the title, *rav v^e^résh m^e^sivta*, "rabbi and head of an advanced yeshiva"; and the position of *rosh yeshiva* (head of the yeshiva) carried far more prestige than the seat of a rabbi.

The highest rank that a Torah scholar could attain was indeed the title of *rosh yeshiva*; and so the situation remained, well into the current century, in such lands as Bohemia and Moravia (that were combined afterward into Czechoslovakia), Hungary, and particularly Lithuania: the greatest dream, the greatest hope for happiness of any man of Torah learning, was to become a *rosh yeshiva*. For it had been understood that in this position, a person would merit to teach young members of a further generation, on advanced levels, the Torah that had always been the ongoing sustenance, faith and hope of this believing people.

What misfortune he saw in the changes wrought by the ravages of time. In his day, the very concept of *rosh yeshiva* had long become distorted and crippled out of all recognition, till it had almost vanished from sight. What remained in its place for a person who taught Torah to the young was a title of derision: the *m^e^lamed* — at just about the lowest place in a community's ratings of prestige.

It was this deeply wrong point of view that Rav Meir wanted to demolish in the Jewish world of Eastern Europe, and to restore the prestige levels of old in the sphere of Torah education. He was still far from the bold public position he would take many years later, to introduce wide-ranging reforms in the rabbinate, with proposals and ideas that he would implant in his *talmidim* at the prestigious *Yeshivas Chachmey Lublin*. Now all he dreamed and hoped for was, ultimately, a rabbinic position in which he would be able to add after his name, as others had done in days of old, *rav v^e^résh m^e^sivta*.

Yet Heaven saw to it that while still in Tarnopol, he should be provided with a wide field for action on a broad scale.

In the Galicia of his time, one major trend became too blatantly obvious to be ignored: There was a steady stream of Jewish youth flowing into the junior colleges and universities of the non-Jewish world, to study the various branches and fields of secular knowledge; and from day to day the stream grew larger and stronger.

The great luminaries and authorities in observant Jewry, the foremost men of Torah learning and piety, could only be gravely concerned. They saw the dire danger that this boded for the Jewish people: such a steady trend could well undermine Jewry's entire religion and faith, till it could disappear without a trace, Heaven forbid.

For the simple fact was that once the young folk entered the world of secular learning, all became intoxicated with its dubious "aromas and flavors"; and then just about everyone found it beneath his dignity to regard ancient Jewish tradition and law with any respect. The "proper, stylish" attitude for this youth seemed to become a posture of derision and contempt.

However, when perceptive, discerning minds examined the miserably doleful situation in search of root causes, it became apparent that the young folk chose this path in life not from any great thirst for worldly knowledge and absolute truth, but from plain, mundane practical motives: Trade and commerce offered the Jews an ever diminishing prospect of earning a good living; competition became ever more fierce. And so they saw better prospects in the world of secular learning: On that road they could hope to attain a proper profession or perhaps a government position. In those years, such prospects were brighter and better than they became afterward, when conditions grew bitterly darker in Eastern Europe.

The main problem, then, was a practical one of economics and survival; and its effect was devastating. For actually, its invidious effects infiltrated the consciousness of Jews long before they could head toward a secular education with its disastrous effects on Jewish identity. They felt its effects keenly when they were still only small boys. As they began to learn about the world of reality in which they lived, by and large the young lost all interest in the traditional *limmudey kodesh*, the holy Torah study that had always been the very essence of Jewish education. For as a rule, they were members of poor families, sharing the dismal poverty that afflicted so great a part of the Jewish people in Eastern Europe. A specter of deep insecurity and fear hung over them: If they received their education only in the traditional *chéder* and the yeshiva, they might grow up with no way of earning a living.

The literal meaning of *chéder* is "a room"; but the rooms in which Jewish children were expected to sit and learn their Torah became ever more empty, till the survival and continuity of this kind of education — the only guarantee of an authentic Jewish identity — became a matter of grave doubt.

Already the ravaging effects of the problem could be seen in Jewry's ranks: Whole families severed their ties with the Jewish religion, and more often than not, they became part of the secular movements coming to life among the people. Heaven only knew how matters might end if nothing was done to deal with the problem.

The vision of a school

It was the well-known chassidic Rebbe of Tchortkov, one of the greatest *tzaddikim* in Galicia, who conceived a way out of the dilemma: As he saw it, there was a vital necessity for a basic change in the entire *chéder* system; it was necessary, said he, to add a new kind of *chéder*, under the label of "Torah and labor"! In such places, along with a traditional Torah education, a craft or trade would also be taught, simultaneously, that would enable a young person to support himself when the time came for him to leave the chéder.

It should be borne in mind that in this part of the world, in this period of time, a youngster generally ended his schooling at about the age of bar mitzvah, or even a few years earlier, and then he went to do what he could to support himself and to help in the family situation. So when a boy studied in a chéder, once he left to enter the workaday world, as a rule his Torah education ended there. Only if he could earn a living in a way that left him free time in the day — only then he might be able to continue his education through adolescence.

For his new kind of chéder, therefore, the Rebbe of Tchortkov wanted a fundamental change in the curriculum. Through the long decades of its existence, in the chéder only *chumash* and *g'mara* were studied — the Hebrew Bible (more specifically the Pentateuch, the Five Books of Moses) and the Talmud — which could not be seen as immediately relevant to ordinary, everyday life. If a youngster could continue on to a yeshiva, there he would learn *halacha*, the great mass of normative law and religious practice — which an observant Jew would need to guide him through life.

In the new program of the Rebbe of Tchortkov, he called resolutely for the inclusion of simple, practical *halacha* in the study program of the chéder. If a youngster was to have only a few years of Jewish schooling, it was crucial to give him *then* this minimal preparation for an observant life.

As the program was conceived, this new kind of school would be called *cheder k^{e}lali* (the General Chéder); and children grown to school age would be divided into two categories: If there were good prospects or intentions for a youngster to continue his education in a yeshiva, he belonged in the first category, and should attend only a traditional, "old style" chéder. Into the second category went children for whom the knowledge of a craft or trade was essential once they left the school; and for them the envisioned *cheder k^{e}lali* was an absolute necessity.

There was one further proviso in the plan, which followed naturally. As the Rebbe of Tchortkov conceived it, wherever a *cheder k^{e}lali* was established, it should have an attached "workshop" or vocational room; and there, in his juvenile years on the way to adolescence, every boy could learn whatever practical skills he wished, under the supervision of the chéder staff, concomitantly with his *limmudey kodesh* —which would include and emphasize selected parts of the *Shulchan Aruch* and other texts, as guides to religious practice for a Jew's entire life.

The Rebbe of Tchortkov was under no illusions. Simple and obvious as his plan might seem, for that period in that region of the world it was utterly revolutionary. Once he tried to put his plan into effect, he knew he would meet powerful resistance from circles in observant Jewry that would regard any attempted modification or change in the old, traditional chéder system as a move toward Reform! He knew it well.

Yet how could he sit by passively and watch the steady deterioration in the chéder system, the erosion day by day in the ranks of traditional education? If those circles could remain impassive, telling themselves that all was well and would be well — he could not; if they could carry on as usual, never giving a thought to the signs of imminent danger and how it might be averted — he could not. He had to act.

Yet he knew that if his plan was to have any chance of success, he would need the full consent and cooperation of every circle and element in observant Jewry. He had to win their trust and support for the new kind of chéder that he envisioned. Otherwise he was bound to fail, and his efforts might lead, instead, to conflict and controversy rather than any constructive results.

The move he took was to call a major conference, in the city of Tchernowitz, of all the chassidic religious leaders, the Rebbes, whose lineage linked them to the renowned original Rebbe of Ryzhin. He was certain that if he could get their consent and cooperation, all the other chassidic notables would join his ranks.

On the day before Nissan, 5672 (March 18, 1912), the conference opened. Quite a large number of chassidic personages came to attend, as well as the esteemed Rabbi of Tchernowitz, Rav Binyamin Weiss. The result was that the Rebbe of Tchortkov's proposal was endorsed with great enthusiasm, and plans were set in motion for intensive work to put the idea into effect.

As the Rebbe himself had foreseen, however, the storm of reaction was not long in coming from a considerable part of observant Jewry. With full, one hundred percent hidebound conservatism, rejecting as unthinkable any modification whatever in the age-old system of schooling, this camp determined to fight the whole campaign tooth and nail.

By his nature, the Rebbe of Tchortkov always cherished peace and strove for it in every possible way. His dearest hope and wish ever remained for harmony and unity among all the religious elements and factions in the Jewish community. Once he understood what a stormy hullabaloo his planned campaign aroused, how violent the depth of antagonism and hostility that the project could yet bring, he decided to postpone the whole matter for the time being. In time, he believed, even these factions and elements in religious Jewry would realize how harmless and innocuous his plan was, and on the other hand, what great benefits the proposed new chéder could bring, and how much damage it could repair among this people of faith.

In short, then, the plan was "put on the shelf" and nothing was done with it in the reality of Jewish life.

Yet the conference in Tchernowitz also produced good, positive echoes and reactions through the entire regions of Bukovina and Galicia. Everywhere lively discussions went on about the envisioned "General Chéder"; and a great many insisted that this was the only realistic, feasible plan to save the entire system of the chéder from moving steadily and inexorably into oblivion. They were eager for someone with courage to seize the initiative and take action on the plan.

Thanks, however, to the widespread opposition and hostility, no one came forward to take up the challenge and champion its cause. Everywhere people paid great lip service to the great idea of the Rebbe of

Tchortkov, in very heated discussions; and they left it at that.

The young scholar takes action

In Tarnopol, however, the soil for this idea happened to be exactly right. Rav Meir Shapiro became completely entranced by it, fully applauding and supporting the resolution taken at the conference in Tchernowitz: to implement the plan without delay.

As he gauged the community in Tarnopol, he saw a broad area of action before him, where the proposed new kind of chéder could do a world of good. And he set to work.

Thanks to the relatively prosperous situation of many in the community, he had no great difficulty in raising enough money to buy a large building, where he hoped to establish a sizable model school — to serve as a model and example for the whole of Galicia. Beyond the financial aspect, he was fortunate also in another respect: As he went into action, what he was doing and planning aroused no great opposition. For most of the observant Jews in Tarnopol were lively, devoted followers of the Rebbes who had attended the conference in Tchernowitz and had warmly accepted the new plan.

Thus the young, dynamic Rav Meir Shapiro was able to proceed step by step. In a series of meetings and consultative sessions, the practical details of the planned new chéder were worked out carefully, as attention was paid to the curriculum, the learning program, and the goals. This done, he went ahead and bought a sizable, imposing structure which had been a government-owned school building until then.

One important feature (not to be underestimated) was its first-rate bathroom facilities, meeting the best sanitary standards. And needless to say, the rooms where classes would be held were large and airy.

Since he wanted the proposed new school to be recognized and approved by the government, he founded a "religious cultural-educational society" under the name of *Tif'eress ha-Dass*, under whose aegis this *cheder k^{e}lali* would function.

The difficult pioneering stages were over. It would not take much more to make the new school alive and operating. But then, as fate would have it, a change of circumstances occurred which made it necessary for the young, brilliant scholar to leave Tarnopol. And with him, alas, the entire dynamic energy of the project left too. The wind went out of the sails.

Gone was the spirited initiative, the animated drive and verve to move it forward the next few steps toward fulfillment. Everything remained at a standstill — until the First World War broke out; and that brought rack and ruin entirely to Jewish life in Poland. The people were left depleted and bereft of any life energy, of any will to create and build. Of course, the community in Tarnopol suffered with the rest.

So it was that even there, where the idea of the *cheder k^e^lali* had the best chances of becoming a reality — even there it was never able to materialize. In Jewish history it remained no more than a beautiful dream, a vision of hope in a melancholy, sorrowful world.

9

The first published volume

If all the labor he invested in the "General Chéder" that he tried to open in Tarnopol bore no practical results whatever, there was another project into which Rav Meir Shapiro poured the energy and brilliance of his heart and mind while in Tarnopol, which did bring blessed tangible results.

In the few years that he stayed in the city, he was able to finish *Imrey Da'as*, his volume on the Shabbos portions *(sidros)* of the Written Torah, and to make it ready for printing. This he did, actually, in response to the importunate pressure and appeals of *talmidim* and friends. They kept urging him to finish the contents and bring it to press, so that they could get to know well, at close hand, some of the fascinating creative insights of his dazzling intelligence.

The work finally went to press in his last year in Tarnopol, after he had already accepted his first rabbinic position.

The volume can be described as one of the most interesting of its kind, which human ability has produced in recent times. A radiant wealth of grace suffuses its contents. From its very first lines, any reader with the Talmudic background and ability to appreciate it becomes fascinated and held, perhaps even spellbound, unable to break off and turn away, till he has read through to the end of a chapter or section.

Rav Meir's approach is to take various statements and teachings of one particular *tanna* (Sage of the Mishna) or *amora* (Sage of the G^emara) which apparently have no connections or links with one another. Then, with sinewy threads of luminous perception, with methods of thinking that Eastern European Jewry labeled *pilpul*, he proceeds to weave and draw his links of ideas and thoughts between the diverse, disparate teachings and statements — with such an incredible keenness and brilliance that the reader in this world of Talmudic thinking finds himself simply dazzled.

One goes on reading, and the "magic" approach goes on unabated: Plumbing ever greater depths of insight, his mind goes on linking statement with statement, teaching with teaching, building so perfect and consistent an edifice of thought, till the receptive reader finds the whole so naturally, integrally right that his only possible reaction must be: Yes, of course it is so; how could it be otherwise?

The greatest power that lies in the volume's pages is their singular ability to draw the appreciative reader on. As he looks a bit ahead, his interest is ever renewed and refreshed, and he finds himself continuing, without getting tired or bored. On the contrary, curiosity carries the reader ever forward in an eagerness to learn more. Again and again he willingly concentrates his faculties and marshals his alertness to follow fully the great profundity and razor-sharpness of this author's mind.

This utterly amazing ability to find and develop brilliant connections of thought between disparate teachings in our Oral Torah was not something that came late or suddenly to Rav Meir Shapiro. Well before he married the daughter of Reb Ya'akov Breitman, that worthy man of wealth sent one of Tarnopol's foremost Talmudists to Shatz — Rav Mannes Gold, a noted *dayyan* (judge) in the city's *beyss din* (Jewish court) — to get to know the young scholar and gauge the true depth of his Talmudic erudition and intelligence. Reb Ya'akov wanted a reliable report that would either verify or refute all the rumors and stories he had heard about the young scholar's astounding prowess.

Rav Mannes Gold stayed a few days in Shatz, then rode back with his conclusions: He could never have imagined, he told Reb Ya'akov Breitman, that in this orphaned age in which they lived (such a bereft, directionless era without the great Torah luminaries of earlier times), a Talmudic genius of such power could yet be found. All the time that he (Rav Mannes) spent listening to this brilliant young learner expound his creative, innovative thoughts on Talmudic matters, it seemed to him that he was in the presence of the legendary Rav Ya'akov Pollack, the singular scholar who founded the entire approach and method of *pilpul* in Talmud study, in the Poland of an earlier century.

Flashes of lightning, said Rav Mannes, seemed to spurt from this young genius's mind, as sparks of utter brilliance kept blazing through his words, that left a profound impression on this listener's heart.

And then Rav Mannes recalled a curious occurrence. At one point an argument developed between him and young Meir over a detail in the Talmud. Without further ado, he stepped over to the bookcase to get the volume he wanted and check the matter; but to his surprise, he found the tractates in no sort of order. Why, asked Rav Mannes, were they not arranged in the proper order, as a set of Talmud should be?

To this the young genius replied that even thus, as the various volumes stood, for him they were in order. And he threw down a challenge: Let Rav Mannes take a few volumes out in the order (or rather, disorder) that they stood, and open each at random to some page whatever. Then he, Meir, would choose a passage on each of these pages, and with an extemporaneous *pilpul* he would show how they could all be linked together in one interconnected structure of ideas.

Rav Mannes Gold took up the challenge. When the various volumes lay open before him, the young Meir studied them a while, gave the matter a long period of reflection, and within a couple of hours or so, he showed how all the passages he had chosen could be linked up together into one skein of unified Talmudic thought.

****

As this fascinating encounter between Meir and Reb Ya'akov Breitman's learned emissary happened when Reb Ya'akov was interested in the young man as a potential son-in-law, Meir must have been then about eighteen or nineteen. Going back in time, when he was only sixteen he displayed the same astounding mental agility-ability. For *Lag ba'Omer* of that year (May 14, 1903) the growing young scholar went to the Rebbe of Vizhnitz. He wanted to spend in the aura of that noted chassidic leader the minor holiday which marks the day when the immortal Rabbi Shim'on ben Yochai left this world for his eternal reward.

By then the young scholar was already well known as something of a genius; and so the Rebbe turned to him at the semi-festive table and asked, more in jest than in earnest, "Do you think you could give us a good, rousing discourse of *pilpul* — some fine, sharp reasoning — that would tie together all the passages in the Talmud by, or about, Rabbi Shim'on ben Yochai?"

The question could only bring a small smile to everyone's lips, as a bit of the Rebbe's teasing humor. No one really expected anything to come of it. The only exception was Meir himself. To everyone's amazement, he took up the challenge and began talking. Out came the words in an uninterrupted flow of Talmudic citation and reasoning. For a good few hours he continued, doing exactly what the Rebbe had jestingly requested: out of his memory he quoted every passage in the Talmud where

Rabbi Shim'on ben Yochai's name occurred, and by sinewy logic and flashing insight he proceeded to make of them all one interconnected structure of thought. . . . In the middle, however, night fell, and he was forced to break off before the end.

Let us move ahead in time now, to the year 5675 (1915), when the First World War was in full blaze and Russian forces occupied Poland. Rav Meir was then the Rabbi of Glina, but under the dreadful conditions that the occupation brought, he was forced to flee; and he headed back to Tarnopol. Just about the time he arrived there, a few thousand Jews from various towns and small cities in Galicia were taken prisoner, and the danger hovered over them that they might be sent off to labor camps or godforsaken villages deep in faraway Siberia. By Heaven's grace, however, the political situation changed afterward, and they were released; yet conditions were still so hazardous and uncertain that they could not return to their homes, but had to remain quartered in Tarnopol for a long while.

Places were found for all the refugees in the private homes of Tarnopol's Jews. In the dwelling where Rav Meir lived now, about two dozen Torah scholars and learned Talmudists found accommodation. And thus the days passed there in relative calm, as the refugees paid the fullest possible attention to all the news they could get about the military and the political situation.

In a while it seemed to them that matters were getting better, and very soon now they would be able to travel home, back to the forlorn wives and children they had been forced to leave. To their dismay, however, the fierce clashes and battles only grew more violent — so bad, in fact, that it seemed to them they might be confined to Tarnopol for years to come. With no certainty to hold to, they grew confused and doubt-ridden, till they were gripped by a dismal despair. They became resigned, feeling only defeated and hopeless. There was no spirit left in them, no patience to go on with the daily sessions of Torah study which always gave them consolation for a while and helped them forget their dire plight.

One day Rav Meir (then twenty-eight years old) entered the large study room where they were gathered, and he saw them seated well enough before their volumes of Talmud, but quite unable to concentrate their minds for any serious learning. What they needed, he saw, was encouragement; and he began to talk to them:

"Consider yourselves fortunate that in such a frightful time of war you can sit in a warm, well-lit room and study Torah. I know your wretched situation; I realize how dreadful you must be feeling; but you know it is written (in *séfer t^ehillim*), 'The Torah of the Eternal Lord is *t^emima*, simply whole, *m^eshivas nafesh*, restoring the spirit' (Psalms 19:8): Torah study can always bring us back to hope and make us cheerful. It can make a human being turn optimistic, no matter what."

He looked at their faces and saw that their deep depression had not lifted one whit.

"Do you know?" he exclaimed, "when I was younger I really knew how true those words in *séfer t^ehillim* could be. One of my greatest pleasures was to lock together into one interlinking body of thoughts, one ingenious *pilpul*, various bits and pieces in the Talmud — to make of them all one unified mental journey in Talmudic perception. Then I felt I truly understood how the Torah is *t^emima* — simply, really whole — one whole, undivided entity, in which various teachings in the Talmud, apparently unrelated, can be parts of a single, integral thought structure. And this was for me a genuine *m^eshivas nafesh*, a way of profoundly restoring my spirit."

Their curiosity aroused, their interest awakened, the learned scholars asked him if he could perhaps produce such a *pilpul* then and there, on the spot.

"Well," he replied, "it has been a long time since I tried my skill at it; but I hope I won't have to go to any great trouble or strain to do it again. We can find out right now. I see you have various *g^emaras* opened before you (different tractates). Let each one read out a passage from the double page open before him."

When all had done as he asked, he put his mind to work and began talking — and his uncanny ability worked as well as ever. The Talmudists in the room could not help being fascinated as they listened — even spellbound. And before he was done, their deep melancholy mood of depression was entirely gone. They had become too absorbed in the lightning thoughts of his mind; and soon they found themselves involved in impassioned debate and discussion on the various ideas and insights he produced.

As it happened, one of the learned people quartered there was absent at the time. When he appeared later and heard of the scintillating discourse he had missed, he implored Rav Meir to repeat it for him; but Rav Meir refused: "I did not go through that whole mental exercise," he explained, "for its own sake, because it would have lasting value in itself. It was only a means for me to get you all out of your sunken despair. Now that the goal has been achieved, there is no purpose in repeating the means that I used."

****

Years later, when he was the Rabbi of Lublin, he entered once a well-known learning center known as the *beyss medrash* of the *aïzerner kop* (the House of Study of the "Iron Mind"); and there, as he might have expected, he found young learners seated before various Talmud tractates, busy at their individual *g^emaras*: Chullin, B^echoros, Bava Kamma, Kiddushin, and so on. Moved by a sudden mood of elation-inspiration, he went among them selecting a passage from each of the opened volumes, and without further ado, he began addressing the astonished *talmidim* — to show this uncanny, incredible power of his once again. With one profound, far-reaching idea he linked all the passages together.

****

This amazing gift, then, stayed with him well into his mature years; but by then (as we saw two paragraphs above) he had no wish to give such displays of his power in *pilpul* any permanence. He used the gift when the spirit moved him or when he saw a need for it; and then he was quite willing and happy to let the *pilpul* he produced go and be forgotten.

Radically different, however, was his attitude during his first stay in Tarnopol, as a young married Talmud scholar, who would yet have to make his way in the world. Then there was a great desire in his heart to publish the volume that he called *Imrey Da'as*, to set before the entire world of Talmud study a wealth of such dazzling displays of his intellectual power — one masterly exercise in *pilpul* to tie together wholly unrelated bits of Talmud, for every *sidra*, every weekly portion of the Written Torah. It was a project truly dear to his heart.

With loving care he had the volume set in type, printed and bound to the finest esthetic standards of book production that he could attain. And the product that came at last from the bindery was truly handsome. But needless to say, it cost him a pretty penny — an investment not only of time and labor but of solid money as well.

His friends advised him to set a high price on it, for two reasons: one, so that there could be a greater income from the sales, to repay him part of what he spent on it; and two, if people paid a higher price for it, it would have a greater value in their eyes. They would hold both the work and its author in higher regard.

"My opinion is different," replied Rav Meir with a small smile. "What printed work is more precious to our Jewish people than the *S'fer Téhillim*? Into that little Book of Psalms, as he says its words in prayer, a believing Jew pours out all his thoughts and feelings, all his gratitude, all his needs, all his longings. And yet it is the lowest in cost among all our printed works. . . .

"This shows that the greater and loftier the contents — the more noble and sublime — the smaller we must reckon its material, commercial worth. Spirituality and materialism are two contrary concepts, diametrically opposed. So I think I ought to set the lowest price I can on this volume of mine." . . .

There was not the slightest doubt that this published work was very dear to his heart. He set great hopes on it, that it would enrich the world of Torah learning that he knew. Yet an inscrutable fate decreed otherwise: it was doomed never to be sold and never to circulate among the Jewish people.

In the unpredictable, uncontrollable vagaries and nightmares of the First World War, the Russians occupied Tarnopol; and one small, incidental effect was that his entire library went up in flames — including virtually all the copies of *Imrey Da'as.* Only two copies remained, which he cherished for the rest of his tragically short life. [When that life ended, the two copies were placed reverently on his bier (the *aron*) and brought with his body to their final resting place.]

10

Into the first rabbinic post

To the lot of the Jewish community in Glina, a little town near Lemberg, fell the privilege of providing the young Rav Meir with his first position as an active, practicing rabbi.

The townlet's official name was Glinyany, but if you called it that, the Jews might not know what place you were talking about. Out of a total population of some 4500, the Jews numbered about 2000. And when the small, little community invited Rav Meir to become its spiritual leader, no one could have any idea that this acclaimed prodigious Talmudist would gain an unmatched international renown one day in the world of Torah study.

One result of this rabbinic appointment was that in the Polish Jewish world he would come to be known as *der glinner rov*; and the title stayed with him through the later years, as he moved on, respectively, to his later rabbinic positions in Sonik, Piotrkov and Lublin.

It was no small thing that this community did by taking him as its rabbi. For it became an open secret, hidden from no one, that if not for the Jews of Glina, the prodigious talents of this prime Talmudist might well have been developed and used not at all for his brilliant leadership amid the Jewry of Poland. Instead, all his formidable abilities might well have been swallowed up in the far-flung business affairs of his wealthy father-in-law. He might have been forced, by pressures too strong to withstand, to seek outlets for his boundless energy and singular talents in that alternative direction — if not for the Jews of Glina. And they, in turn, gained an imperishable place in Jewish history, by thus becoming linked with his name.

****

Having spent a good few years in Tarnopol after his marriage, living comfortably in his father-in-law's palatial home, the grown man believed he now had a complete, fully rounded preparation for the rabbinate. He felt ready at last to undertake and carry the full responsibility that a rabbinic position would bring. With his entire being, he yearned now to start actualizing and achieving in reality the dream that had gone with him through all his years to manhood, the goal that had always been at the center of his heart: education — an approach to teaching and rearing the young that could remold an entire generation.

Into this field of activity he wanted to pour his dynamic energy, his sparkling, effervescent creative thought. And the one, single way he could see to accomplish any part of his dream was through a rabbinic position. As a spiritual leader with authority, a *rav* could exert pressure on his congregation and community, to make the people do what he demanded, what he saw as a vital necessity.

His name was certainly known in Galicia; and various rabbinic positions in the region, with larger and smaller communities, stood vacant, while suitable candidates were sought. He only needed to put his name forward, to let it be known that he was available, and without the slightest doubt, many a community would have taken him as the best choice in sight; then he in turn would have accepted readily.

One mighty, powerful force, however, stood in his way: his father-in-law. Many were the heated, impassioned arguments that took place between them about it. "Why in the world do you need to become a practicing rabbi," asked his father-in-law, "when you really want to devote your whole day to Torah study? Right here you have the ideal conditions for it. Why in the world do you want to take on the heavy burdens of a rabbinic position? Whatever for? You will have to spend your whole day on community affairs. For Heaven's sake, keep away from that kind of life!"

Galicia at that time formed part of the domain of Austria-Hungary; and this father-in-law of his, Reb Ya'akov Breitman, was one of the richest and best-known men of wealth not only in Tarnopol, not only in Galicia, but in all Austria-Hungary. The man shuddered at the thought that his refined, delicate daughter, raised as a veritable princess (as one might expect in such a palatial home), should ever be reduced to the status of a rabbi's wife — to depend for her support on the meager stipend that some straitened community could afford. It gave him the willies even to think that strangers should have to give her the means to live, that she should need to look forward to such "extras" as Purim gifts *(mishlo-ach manos)* and *chanuka gelt* that communities generally gave their rabbi in addition to his paltry salary.

(In truth, though, had Reb Ya'akov possessed the gift of prophecy, this would never have troubled him. He would have foreseen that this son-in-law of his would never accept any such "gifts" or "extras" in any of the rabbinic positions he was destined to hold. In fact, he never even took any payment or fee from people in dispute when he sat in judgment to try their case.)

[Actually, some four decades later, one resident of Glina recalled that for many years after he became its spiritual head, Rav Meir refused to take any salary either. Finally the community council insisted that this was highly unsuitable, and he must accept a salary. So he did, and divided part among poor students of his yeshiva, while the rest went into the funds for running the yeshiva. All this was years later, though. Now he still needed a way to leave the home of his wife's wealthy parents.]

Apart from these considerations, however, there was a deeper reason for Reb Ya'akov's strong refusal to let Rav Meir leave Tarnopol. In his heart an extraordinary bond of affection had formed for this young man to whom he had given his daughter. He was astute and learned enough to appreciate, better than anyone else, what a precious jewel he had acquired as a son-in-law. He saw how, as a result, his home had been transformed into a living, dynamic setting of animated Torah study. The young man had made it a focal center for the foremost Talmud scholars in the city to gather, so that they could listen to his effervescent outpour of brilliant lively thought, which he produced so abundantly and effortlessly, like an irrepressible wellspring.

Thus there was now another thought that Reb Ya'akov could not bear to consider: that the vibrant life and vitality which the young man brought regularly into his home could suddenly disappear without a trace. How could this man of wealth allow his home to grow completely quiet all at once, as still as a tomb — a plain, ordinary dwelling like any other home? He could not even think of it. He had become too accustomed to the happy, convivial evenings of Talmudic discussion and debate to give them up without a powerful struggle. He was determined that such evenings must never be taken from him: he would not permit it!

And yet he also wanted to keep his son-in-law happy. The older man was too decent and sensible to quash Rav Meir's aspirations and hopes with blunt brutality. Instead, he had an inspiration:

"Very well," he told Rav Meir. "You want to become a practicing rabbi, the spiritual head of a community, so that you can accomplish something for our religious life. I won't stand in your way. But you must understand: For you to announce yourself as a candidate in search of a position — for you to go and look for a rabbinic post like any young man in need of employment — to ask, to search and beg for a place — that would be absolutely beneath my dignity. That, I cannot allow a son-in-law of mine to do. . . . If, however, a community turns to you with an offer of its own accord, asking you to become its rabbi — then I will consent immediately."

Unable to take any firm stand against his father-in-law's forceful argument, having nothing in his nature to let him mount any strong opposition, the young Rav Meir had no choice but to consent.

Now the magnate felt much better about the situation. If his gifted son-in-law took no initiative in the matter, if his longing for a rabbinic post did not become widely known, it was not very likely that an offer would come to him out of the blue.

There was, however, another thought in the back of his mind which made him quite certain that the gates to a rabbinic position would remain shut forever to the young man. In the Jewish world of Galicia, it was the accepted custom that any announced candidate for a rabbinic post had to declare, from the start, a sizable sum of money which he was prepared to give the community if it chose him. It had never yet happened that when a candidate was appointed the rabbi of a community, he then failed to give the amount he had promised.

Well, then, thought the complacent Reb Ya'akov Breitman, should any community learn that Rav Meir was eager to find a position, as long as the community heads knew who his father-in-law was, they were certain to demand a nice fat sum as the price for accepting him. After all, this famed man of wealth would have no trouble paying whatever they asked. Why not try to "skin him alive" and ask for something really ample? — even exorbitant? And he, Reb Ya'akov, had no intention of paying anything.

So then, thought the contented father-in-law, now the young man could sit and wait till the cows came home before an offer came along that he would be able to accept.

Rav Meir understood his father-in-law quite well; he knew that this was probably what the older man had in mind. He was also well aware that he himself did not have the means to pay a community an acceptable sum of money if it appointed him its rabbi, even if he received an offer without doing anything to get it.

And yet, if Reb Ya'akov Breitman thought his son-in-law had capitulated and resigned himself to staying put — he sadly underestimated the young man. Rav Meir remained in full hopes — in fact he remained certain — that in the course of time he would receive a good offer from a community that would be willing to forego the usual condition and accept him as its *rav* without demanding a kopeck in return.

However human beings may conjecture and contrive, Heaven has its own ways of working. Evidently, though he took not the slightest step to seek a position, the word must have spread that he was open to offers, if a certain special condition was met: for not long afterward a delegation of Jews arrived from the small town of Glina, formally and respectfully inviting him to become their spiritual leader — and they added not a word about any payment on his part.

The news struck like a thunderbolt in Reb Ya'akov's regal home. In consternation the wealthy man realized that his whole ingenious attempt and clever scheme to keep the young man at home had failed. It was all of no avail. The impossible happened. Here was an ideal, idealistic community demanding no money whatever — nothing that Reb Ya'akov could absolutely refuse to pay!

Dismayed, the man saw that he would have to accept failure. There was nothing he could do now to bar Rav Meir's way. He had given his word, and he would have to keep it. . . .

And yet, even with this, the matter was still not finished. If Reb Ya'akov was ready to admit defeat, his wife was not. Having seen how her husband had failed in all his stalwart, vigorous efforts to persuade Rav Meir to give up his ambitions in the rabbinic field and remain with them, she still had one idea left. She well knew that her husband would never be willing to implement her idea, but she was prepared to go ahead on her own. In her life of wealth she may have learned that with money one could do practically anything; and as it seems, she decided to try to solve this problem in the same way.

Without a word she went over to her husband's safe and opened it. Taking out an enormous amount of money, she brought it to Rav Meir. "Here," she said. "Here you have as much as you can earn in your whole life as the Rabbi of Glina. It is yours, absolutely and completely. All you have to do is give up this whole idea and let us hear no more about it!"

Whatever close friends and intimates were there in the room with them, could only stare in spellbound amazement at the amount of money she was offering him. They felt certain that at last the young man would have to capitulate and yield to the powerful wishes of his wife's parents. Why insist on facing all the trials and tribulations, all the toil and trouble, that a life in the rabbinate was certain to bring him, when here was a small fortune instead, his for the taking?

The young man, though, remained undazzled, unimpressed, unstirred. In moving words laden with emotion he completely spurned the offer, in a blazing rejection: "Heaven is my witness that I don't want to become a practicing rabbi so that I can make a career for myself; nor do I want it for the honor and prestige I can gain. My only craving is to study Torah and share it with others; and I am completely convinced that the only way I can really attain my goal is with a rabbinic position. What value does a world of money have for me, compared with the longing of my whole spirit? Believe me: if I didn't feel a revulsion for money, if I didn't detest unearned income, I would never put on a rabbi's garb."

These words, that could only have come from the very core of his being, could not fail to leave their mark, profoundly, on everyone in the room — including his mother-in-law.

Knowing this was the full, openhearted, absolute truth for Rav Meir, she could only plead with him and beg him to make one last compromise: Let him not hasten to answer the community of Glina immediately that he was ready to accept the position. Let him wait with his reply till the Rebbe of Tchortkov would come to Tarnopol. All in the family, including Rav Meir, were his fervent, devoted *chassidim.* They would put the whole question before him, and his authoritative decision would finally settle the matter.

The time came when the Rebbe appeared on a visit, and when the whole affair was put before him, he listened gravely to both sides. He saw how desperately the father-in-law wanted to keep the brilliant young man in his home, to what lengths he was willing to go to prevail on Rav Meir to stay. Nevertheless, he sided with the gifted young scholar and told him to go ahead and accept the offer from Glina. To this decision of his he added on words of encouragement, good wishes and blessings that the young rabbi should be able to realize all the noble plans that he wanted to implement in the life of the community.

Nothing more remained to be said. The decision of the Rebbe carried enough weight and authority to preclude any further attempts to detain or dissuade Rav Meir from the rabbinic post in Glina. When a delegation arrived a second time from the little town, this time to invite him for a Shabbos, he accepted at once. His road was clear now, without obstructions.

****

On that Shabbos he made his debut as a rabbinic speaker: He gave his first *d'rasha* in the *shul* of Glina, to a congregation that filled the House of Worship — a congregation curious and eager to hear what kind of sermon the newcomer would give.

The effect on his listeners could only be described as electrifying; and the decision about him was unanimous. All the members of the community, of every political type or party, of every stratum, agreed to have him as their spiritual leader.

And thus, in the early months of 5671 (late 1910), at the age of twenty-three or twenty-four, he came to be known everywhere as *der glinner rov*: the Rabbi of Glina.

****

Something most interesting happened a good bit earlier, at the last time that the young man went to Tchortkov before the Rebbe visited Tarnopol and decided the family dispute in his favor. The occasion was the arrival of a *yom tov*, a holy Festival, that Rav Meir wanted to spend in the Rebbe's domain.

Thousands of *chassidim*, however, also had the same wish, and the throng around the Rebbe's table was formidable. Yet as a devoted follower of the Rebbe, the young scholar bent every effort to push his way through and get close to his great spiritual mentor, so that he could hear clearly the inspired Torah thoughts which the Rebbe was about to voice. At last he reached a fairly good position, and leaned on the the rim of a bench.

As the Rebbe began speaking, however, the press of the attentive listeners became ever stronger. People bickered and shoved, till there was an actual danger to human life. Suddenly, situated at the midpoint where the pressure was greatest, the young man felt ill, and he lost consciousness and fainted.

A small clamor of alarm arose, and the Rebbe had to interrupt his Torah thoughts. When the young man was brought back to consciousness, the Rebbe said to him, "It's nothing dreadful — just *chassidim* pushing and shoving — showing their eagerness to hear me. I promise you, though, that it is a sign from Heaven: This year you will become a practicing *rav*!"

The Rebbe evidently had in mind the peculiar proclivity of Jews in Galicia, with all the respect they had for their spiritual leaders, to cause them pain many a time. . . . At any rate, his words were prophetic. That very year Rav Meir Shapiro began his career as the Rabbi of Glina.

11

The Rav in action

Having arrived and settled in the little town, the young rabbi looked about and saw a spiritual wasteland everywhere. In every aspect and area of religious life, chaos and disorder reigned. All was an abandoned wilderness. At every step, wherever he turned, he found neglect, with no one to care a whit. In short, if Heaven wanted a "training ground" for this young man that would test his every ability as a spiritual leader and forge his spirit into a dynamic, effective instrument, Heaven's choice fell on Glina with good reason.

Carefully, methodically, with his perceptive eyes he took stock of the entire situation, and he saw an immensity of work before him — an abandoned, woebegone field that would need hard labor to start from the very beginning and cultivate it properly.

Ideally, he ought to work in order, fixing and repairing matters bit by bit. Yet everything was in such a mess, in such tragic ruin, that he knew he could not afford the luxury of a slow and steady approach. Let him delay the least bit, and he might find everything beyond repair. It was imperative to replace confusion and chaos with absolute clarity, with unwavering certainty.

It was time to muster all his young, dynamic energy, to gird on firmly his mantle of rabbinic authority, and to set to work with his unfolding, developing initiative and determination. For his motto he took the charge that *Moshe rabbênu* (Moses our Master) gave the men he appointed as judges: "Be not afraid before any man!" (*Dvarim*/Deuteronomy 1:17).

He went into action on a wide-ranging program of reconstruction and rehabilitation, to rebuild the town's Jewish spiritual life from the ruins.

Every penetrating glance he threw, every forceful gesture he made, created a response, as people reacted to this charismatic dynamo. With every word of his, clarity and order came to replace dereliction and disorder. Every act of his hit its target, with its own impact, in a clear, consistent program to enact a whole series of guide lines and rules regarding family purity and the supply of kosher food. Without hesitation he did what was necessary to strengthen the proper observance of Shabbos as a holy day of rest — a matter in which he found all the barriers and restraints completely broken down.

Late on a Friday he found a barber plying his trade well after the time for lighting the candles that would welcome in the holy day of rest. Resolutely he walked into the barber shop and broke the man's instruments. After Shabbos he went back to the man and paid him the damage.

There was a butcher dealing in kosher meat whose personal conduct fell short of the moral, ethical and religious standards that the new Rav had set for trustworthy suppliers of meat. Rav Meir decreed a ban on his wares for three months, forbidding the Jews of the town to buy from him. Yet the man had small children at home, orphaned by the loss of their mother; and he needed some way to sustain them. As the son-in-law of Reb Ya'akov Breitman, Rav Meir did not lack for money; and for those three months he saw to it that the children were provided with food.

In the seven days following a wedding, friends and family blithely decided to hold *shacharis* (the morning prayer service) in the bridegroom's home. Since there would have to be *k^eri'as ha-torah*, a brief reading from the Torah, on Monday and Thursday mornings, they decided just as blithely to "borrow" a Torah scroll from the *shul*. This was a violation of Jewish law, however, being considered utterly disrespectful to the Torah; and when the Rav learned of the planned "transfer," he forbade it implacably, with the full weight of his authority behind his action. It was his job to impose the authority of Jewish law as he knew it, down to the last details, not as others might think they knew it.

At another time he learned that young men and women planned to dance together at a forthcoming wedding. He sent word that unless this plan was promptly forgotten, he would not perform the wedding. Then another bit of "charming" news reached him: A theater group planned to put on a play which poured scorn on the "old-fashioned" pious Jews whose lives were centered in the *beyss medrash*, the hallowed House of Prayer and Study. He banned the theater group, and the play vanished from sight.

So he worked to repair and rebuild, reconstruct and remodel one area of Jewish life after another, one aspect of religious observance after another. Eventually the neglected, spiritually desolate *beyss medrash* would become again a proper House of Learning, as he became able to establish regular *shi'urim*, lectures and lessons, for the adults. Soon there would be committees to help people in distress with interest-free loans and to give attention to the sick: societies of *g'millas chessed* and *bikkur cholim.*

In later times, he once recalled his early days in the town: "I went to war," said he, "on eight fronts simultaneously, at one and the same time: I battled against the desolation that reigned in the *beyss medrash.* I waged war against *am haratzus,* abysmal ignorance in the Judaism of the Torah. I battled the strong, ruthless members of the community and the lawlessness in Glina's Jewish life — since they thought they could do as they pleased. I fought against despair and the feeling of helplessness, which overcame every good idea by good, decent people. I declared war against the breaches in the walls of proper religious life and conduct. I fought ruthlessly against the contempt and derision shown toward Torah study and its earnest, dedicated teachers. Then there was the battle against the secular, non-religious Jews; and finally, the battle with the lukewarm Jews who regarded everything with indifference and equanimity, ready to compromise and live at peace with everyone and everything."

The time came when he could write to his uncle (the son of the deceased Manestritcher Rav), on Friday the twenty-sixth of Elul, 5670 (September 30, 1910): "My thanks go to the Eternal Lord for His lovingkindness, that His goodness is with me and my household constantly. My prestige is great in this town and all its environs; if all were told, it would not be believed. All the esteemed worthies of the community attend upon me and seek my company and approval. Without me, no one lifts up his hand . . . for they heed and obey my word, whatever I bid them; and [thus] many remedying, repairing regulations have been enacted here on my account, since I came here. . . . "

****

One thing that clearly helped him rise in esteem and prestige, to establish his authority in Glina beyond question, was the brilliance of his mind, that could find ingenious solutions to problems which could only make people admire and respect him.

In his very first year in Glina, a fierce controversy broke out between two of the most eminent members of the community, over a road that belonged to both of them, which had deteriorated to a condition of ruin. It simply could not be used unless major repairs were made — and each of the two wanted the other to pay the heavy costs. The true focus of their heated dispute, however, was not the money involved, heavy as the expense would be: for both were wealthy enough to meet the costs without a second thought. It was rather a pure clash of wills (or egos), in which each of them was determined to emerge the victor and enjoy a sense of triumph over the other.

The arguing and wrangling grew ever worse, ever more fierce and complex, till, eventually, it involved most of the Jewish townspeople, as some sided with one of the two, and some with the other.

On the Fast of Esther (the day before Purim — Thursday, March 24, 1910) one person in the town had a splendid idea: "Look," said he: "Just a little while ago we took that fine new *rav* to be our spiritual leader. Why not put this whole big dispute before him, and leave it to him to decide? Should that not be *his* job?"

Both parties to the controversy readily agreed, and away they went to set the case before Rav Meir, whereupon each presented his arguments. As he listened, it did not take him long to realize that it was not the money at stake which bothered these two antagonists, but a simple matter of pride and prestige: Each wanted the other to lose the case, so that he could emerge as the winner — nothing more.

The pronouncement he made was as clearcut as it was surprising: He ordered each of them to produce the full amount of money that it would cost to repair the road properly. Thus he soon had in his hand twice the amount that was needed. Without another word, he gave the money to one of his trusted attendants, with orders to deliver it to the *gabbo'im* ("managers") of the *talmud torah*, the local Torah school for the community's children. The money, he explained, was his fee for trying the case, and it was to be used for the school's upkeep.

"Now," said he to the two astounded worthies in dispute, "I will decide your case. Did you ever study the Mishna?"

"Certainly, certainly," the two replied almost at once.

"When you have a chance, take a good look at the beginning of tractate *Sh^{e}kalim*. There you will find a plain ruling that on the fifteenth of Adar, the roads and byways have to be repaired. Why particularly on that day? By then spring has certainly come. The winter is over, with all the rain and the snow that must have melted, which has quite certainly left the roads an impossible and impassable mess of misshapen mud dried hard. So the fifteenth of Adar is a fine time to get all the pathways and byways properly fixed and made usable. . . .

"On whom, though, does the duty fall to get the job done? Like the other rulings in the Mishna there, it is obviously the obligation of the *beyss din*, the court of judges that must deal with all matters of Jewish law. . . . This means that the matter is no business of yours" (said he to the man at the right) "nor is it any business of yours" (thus to the man at the left), "but entirely my affair." And with that he took the needed amount of money out of his own purse, to give it to a trusted attendant. "Of course," continued Rav Meir, "since today is the Fast of Esther, that means today is the thirteenth; and since today is Thursday, the fifteenth falls on Shabbos; and consequently, the work cannot be started till Sunday — but that is a mere detail. On Sunday," he ordered his attendant, "you will bring all the laborers you need and set to work."

The impression that this stunning decision made on the community was beyond words. Everyone realized that by this masterstroke of his, the new Rav of Glina had hit the target perfectly. Resolved and gone was the long-standing conflict which had begun to turn acrimonious, drawing in ever more members of the community to take sides and make matters worse. Now peace and quiet could return to the Jewry of Glina.

Just as important was the fact that Rav Meir emerged completely clean and unharmed, untouched and uninvolved. Had his decision favored one of the two, the other would likely have remained resentful and perhaps would even turned into something of an enemy of the Rav. Now both the antagonists, and the Rav, could all live in peace. Neither had won, neither had lost.

And for Rav Meir there was one further reward. True, the case had cost him money out of his own pocket; but he had gained twice as much for the cause that was dearest of all to his heart: education in Torah for the young.

****

During his stay in Glina, something else happened which gave him a chance to use the unusual resources of his mind.

On a Shabbos morning, while the Torah portion was being chanted as sacred tradition required, one person in the congregation went and insulted another. Deeply offended, after Shabbos the insulted man went to the Polish court of justice and brought suit against the other for "creating a disturbance in a House of Worship during a prayer service" — a serious crime under Polish law in that predominantly Catholic country, for which the prescribed punishment was quite severe.

When the case was heard in the Polish court, Rav Meir was summoned to give evidence, so that he might verify that the accused man had indeed caused a disturbance. The Rav, though, had a mind of his own. However dreadfully the man on trial might have insulted the other, that man had no business running with his grievance to the Polish court. Such an action was in complete violation of sacred Jewish law. The matter could (and should) have been brought before *him* to decide. However hurt and distressed the insulted man felt at what the other one had said to him, however furious he was, the punishment that now faced the other man if the case went against him would be out of all proportion to his crime.

On the witness stand the Rav spoke clearly. In the Torah, said he, there are three kinds of laws: *mitzvos* ("commandments") are for every Jew; all, old and young of any age, must know them and keep them, because even children must realize and acknowledge that one Creator made this world and rules over it. Then there are *chukim*, decreed laws, such as *t'fillin*, which the Torah requires a Jew to keep only when he reaches the age of thirteen. And finally there are *mishpatim* ("civil laws"), given only for rabbis to know and to enforce, since they include our rules of punishment for violation of our religious laws.

"Now, then," continued Rav Meir, "when this alleged disturbance was supposed to have occurred, the part of the Torah being read aloud dealt only with *mishpatim*, which, as I have explained, apply only to someone like me. Yet I heard no serious disturbance whatever. I could hear every word of the Torah reading clearly, without missing a syllable." . . .

The case was dismissed.

****

To return to the beginning, however, the truth was that whatever triumphs he achieved in his early months in the small town, he remained unhappy. No matter how much he accomplished, no matter how firmly he established his authority and put matters right in the woeful conditions that he found in the religious life of the people, till the community life was no longer a shambles that resembled a wasteland, Rav Meir remained dissatisfied, far from any feeling of solid, crowning achievement. And he knew why.

He had to set to work at the same time toward his main goal, that really was dearest to his heart: education — another area of frightful neglect in Glina, which would not let him rest.

The local Torah school, known as the *talmud torah*, was located in a dark ramshackle structure, dilapidated enough to repel every sensitive, decent youngster. Every *beyss medrash*, every House of Study where young and old might gather in search of Torah learning, stood in a miserable state of disrepair. Among the older youth and the adults who should have filled those Houses of Study in some sort of learning program, absolute ignorance ruled, along with a lack of any meaningful Jewish content in their lives.

[There was far more to the problem, however, than the dilapidated or woebegone condition of the buildings. While the *talmud torah* had a long history in Glina, in the year 5655 (1895) a new school had been opened bearing the name of the Jewish man of wealth, Baron Hirsch, to provide the same education as the Polish schools maintained by the government; and all the teachers were Jewish. Thus the students could get as good an education as any Polish youngster in Glina, without suffering from the strong hatred toward Jews that the teachers shared with the non-Jewish pupils in the government schools.

[When their studies ended at the Baron Hirsch school, those youngsters who could not continue into a secondary school were apprenticed to artisans and craftsmen, so that they could learn a practical skill; and they were given the money to buy their own tools and equipment, so that they could work independently to support themselves.

[If the classrooms of the *talmud torah* were poorly attended and rather empty, it was because the classrooms of the Baron Hirsch school were rather full.]

It was never in Rav Meir's nature, however, to throw up his hands in despair and admit defeat.

He looked at the wretched situation, and of itself the dream formed in his heart to bring an end to this whole misery by establishing a General Chéder, a *cheder k*ᵉ*lali*, following the "Tchernowitz plan" of the Rebbe of

Tchortkov that was described in an earlier chapter: in short, a *talmud torah* that would offer a youngster practical, useful vocational training along with the standard Torah studies.

[Here he could see with his eyes how sound and right the Rebbe's plan had been. With the *talmud torah* that he envisioned, he could meet the Baron Hirsch school's competition on its own ground, and prevail against it with one simple argument: If in later life a youngster would in any case make hardly any use of a "theoretical" schooling from "book learning," because at a painfully young age necessity would drive him to go to work, evidently his main need was to learn a trade, a practical skill; and this he could do at either school. Why prefer the Baron Hirsch, then? — because there he could get a fine Polish secular education in order to live as an educated Pole among Polacks who would hate him as a Jew? Why not a Jewish schooling in the Torah instead, to enrich his life with a meaningful, deeply rooted identity?]

Rav Meir was a man of vision and dream, but a most practical dreamer; and without further ado, he set to work on the project that was vital for him.

Yet even as it began to take concrete form, an inscrutable fate intervened and his wife suddenly fell ill. It became necessary, on medical advice, to take her to a sanitarium. After due consultation and consideration, he decided to take her to the healing institution of Dr. Jacob Lange in Frankfort, Germany. This medical doctor was known to be a scrupulously observant religious Jew, and under his firm supervision, Rav Meir could feel entirely confident that the food would be absolutely kosher.

A visitor in Frankfort

So it was that in the year 5672 (1912) he could be seen in the streets of this thriving German city, where he spent the entire summer.

It did not take long for the intelligentsia in the Orthodox community to recognize the greatness and brilliance of this young Torah scholar. Despite the deep, inbred dislike and contempt that a German Jew generally felt for an *Ostjude* or *ein polnischen Jude* (an East European or Polish Jew), he soon found himself the center of a small circle of prominent figures concentrated around him — notables such as Dr. Gershon Lange (professor at a junior college), Dr. Posen, Herr Raphaelsohn, and so on.

With them he engaged in illustrative talks and discussions on the way of *pilpul* in Talmud study, and on matters of *halacha*. So interesting and engrossing did they find him that all of them used every stretch of free time that they had to visit him and listen enrapt to the brilliant Torah thoughts that came from him like sparkling jewels. Thus the small, select group of Orthodox Jews came to gather regularly and listen to his *shi'urim*, his full-length discourses on the Talmud.

To a certain small extent, this calmed in him some of his passionate desire to share with others some of the Torah thoughts that always stormed and raged within him.

At the same time he made the acquaintance of the local rabbi, the noted, esteemed Rav Salomon Breuer [the son-in-law of the legendary Samson Raphael Hirsch, who founded and headed the Orthodox community in Frankfort through the years when the heady winds of Reform Judaism blew through Germany like a hurricane, felling so many Orthodox communities and leaving most of German Jewry altered beyond recognition]. Regrettably, though, no real friendship formed between them — on account of a small witticism that the somewhat impetuous Rav Meir allowed himself to make, which left the Rabbi of Frankfort quite offended:

Rav Breuer was confident that in the religious condition of his community there was nothing to be ashamed of. Here one could find professors, attorneys-at-law, research scholars — intellectuals in every walk of life — who observed the *mitzvos* scrupulously and devoted their free hours to Talmud study. As he saw the community, he believed he could be justly proud of it; and he felt certain that it could only make a truly favorable impression on this unusually gifted visitor from Galicia, quite possibly leaving the young man at a loss for proper words of praise that would do justice to the high, exalted level of the city's Jewry.

At what he thought an opportune moment, the Rabbi of Frankfort turned to Rav Meir and asked confidently, "Well, how do you like my city? I really mean my Orthodox Jews." . . .

"If you will permit me," said the rather ebullient, irrepressible Rabbi of Glina, "let me answer metaphorically: Today I passed by a confectioner's shop, and my eye caught a notice in the window: *Kosher ice cream, under the strict supervision of Rabbiner Breuer.* That seems to me the clearest description of Frankfort's Orthodoxy," he added with a smile. "They are 'kosher' Jews of course, but they exude such a freezing coldness. They don't have the warm, fiery heart of a Jew in Galicia."

After the warm, complimentary reply that the Rabbi of Frankfort half expected, half hoped for, the answer he received left him mortally offended; and no warm, friendly relationship could develop between them after that.

Only in the year 5684 (1924) did Rav Breuer's cold, negative attitude undergo a change. Then, as Rabbi of Sonik, Rav Meir came again to Frankfort, this time to raise money for his *Yeshivas Chachmey Lublin.* And he explained to Rav Breuer that as he saw it, over the intervening years a closer relationship had formed between the Jewries of Germany and Poland. By now, he continued with a smile, the "temperatures" were rather "evened out": The German type had lost some of his coldness, and the Polish type some of his fiery warmth. . . .

Moreover, in the course of the years, Rav Breuer himself had come increasingly into contact with Polish Jews, and he realized that there had been some truth in this brilliant scholar's unexpected reply on his first visit to Frankfort. Thus a bond of genuine friendship finally did form between the two notable Jewish leaders.

12

Beney Torah

As soon as he was back from Frankfort, Rav Meir set to work to make his planned General Chéder a reality — which would mean, at the same time, a reconstruction of the entire *chéder* system.

Unfortunately, he did not have the means to launch the new school in a proper building of its own. For the time being he would have to make do with temporary, rented quarters that were suitable for classrooms. This did not prevent him, however, from taking certain departures from the accepted norms, which worked to good effect on the formation of the school: Thus the teachers were taken on as employees of the *chéder*, to be paid a monthly salary on which they could live decently.

[In other lands and in other times, this might seem an ordinary, obvious policy to adopt in running a school. It was quite certainly the norm in Glina's well-funded Baron Hirsch school, that was described in an earlier chapter. In a *chéder* in Poland, it was revolutionary:] The new policy would firmly erase the sorrowful, miserable results that came from the individual dependency that a teacher (a *melamed*) had on the parents of each and every pupil:

For every month, each set of parents would always have to pay the *melamed* his fee per pupil *individually*. And this standard, accepted system had a twofold deplorable effect: First, the *melamed* would devote most of his efforts, and attach most importance, to the progress of the wealthier parents' children. For the education of the young sent by the poorer parents, he would have precious little concern, since as a rule, Heaven alone knew when or if he be would paid his due for trying to educate *them*.

Understandably, a large number of poor but capable, gifted children were consequently deprived of any chance or hope of developing properly. They never found an opportunity to reach any decent level of psychological growth and spiritual fulfillment.

The second wretched consequence of the system was the effect it had on the teacher himself. In his situation of economic inadequacy and insecurity, the thought always festered and gnawed in him that he must bear the lot of a *melamed*, at the mercy of the parents of every boy in his classroom in regard to his livelihood, and he must therefore bow to their every notion and whim.

With Rav Meir Shapiro's new, "modern" approach, the whole picture changed. Now a teacher would feel far more free, released from the yoke and chains that had dragged him down, able to lift his head and enjoy a new sense of self-esteem. It need hardly be added that the effect on the youngsters' education was highly beneficial.

Remembering well the policy that the Rebbe of Tchortkov had formulated at the conference in Tchernowitz, Rav Meir divided the school's program into different courses of study, for two categories of pupils: those with hopes and prospects of continuing their Torah education beyond the *chéder*, and those who would have to go to work once the years of elementary or primary school were over (forced by bitter economic conditions of the time). In general, he did what he could to tailor the learning programs to the inclinations and proclivities of the pupils.

[According to the rules set by the man who built and owned the school building, it was to be used only as a normal *chéder*; but Rav Meir prevailed on him to let him have his way. In addition to working out the two courses of study and hiring the teachers, he did the most important thing of all: from the pulpit and by personal visits, he worked energetically on parents to send their children there.]

Going further, in the same building he established as well a *yeshiva g^e^voha*, a full-fledged secondary Torah school for older boys, which was headed in entirety by none other than himself. Only a small number of students came. Not many in that age group could avoid the dire necessity of going to work. But those who could be there, with Rav Meir as their excellent teacher, really thrived.

With the greatest energy and zeal he devoted himself now to both the educational enterprises that he had created, so that they should turn out human beings of the highest caliber. Slowly but surely he became father, leader and teacher to the youngsters; and they began to feel his paternal love — something to which they were utterly unaccustomed in the prevailing atmosphere of their world.

Of themselves the pupils responded: a fire of enthusiasm kindled in their young hearts, and they took to their studies with a passion, to satisfy both themselves and this unusual educator that they had found. He, however, did not stop there. He held interesting, engrossing talks with them about the material they were studying, suited to their level. More important, they could gain knowledge and inspiration from his fiery, worshipful behavior when he joined them at the regular prayer services. They could listen and learn when he burst into snatches of chassidic melodies, or when he threw out some problem in their Talmud study that had suddenly occurred to him. And as often as not he threw out jokes, inspired pieces of wit, from which there was also much to learn.

And there was more: He arranged various kinds of special meals for them on school holidays; yet more special were the "little banquets" of *m^elavveh malka* that he made for them on Saturday nights, and the "small feasts" on days of *rosh chodesh*, when a new Jewish month began.

The psychological effect on the youngsters was all he wanted and hoped for. The conscientious, selfless, heartfelt education and upbringing that he gave them produced results that he welcomed: latent talents and abilities emerged and grew keen. The number of students with a zest for learning increased, and out of them came eventually many a *talmid chacham*, a considerable number of fine Talmud scholars in every sense. Grown to manhood, some of them took worthy rabbinic positions in various towns and townlets of Poland and other countries.

****

[All this energetic, successful education, however, could never have taken place in Glina's single building for Torah study. Under Rav Meir's dynamic leadership, it had become inadequate quite soon for all the youngsters who came eagerly.]

The dynamic young spiritual leader saw only one solution. With his unflagging initiative he drove ahead with the construction of a new, specially planned school building. It meant working relentlessly to raise money in the community; yet as long back as memory extended, the Jews of Glina could never be counted among the affluent. They barely earned enough to live on. (It was far worse after the First World War, when most of Glina went up in flames: Then the town became simply impoverished and learned to live in a state of distress.) And still, there was the Rav of Glina exhorting, bestirring, demanding of his flock that his building plans must be acted on: the Torah structure that he wanted, for which the foundation stone had been set, must be built!

He refused to be subdued by economic realities. As though he was a rich member of the community, he took a sizable sum of his own money to get the building program launched and under way. . . . Yet where would he ever find the money to continue?

There were a number of rich people with whom he was on friendly terms, and he went to them now without hesitation, to ask for their help. They gave him their contributions readily enough; but the sum total was far short of what he needed for the handsome building he planned. And so he sat at his desk one day, wondering what to do next: Should he stop — accept that this was as far as he could go, and no further? Yet he knew, past any doubt, that with the building he wanted he could save the entire youth of this town of Glina from losing a precious spiritual identity: he could inculcate in them the commitment to the Torah that had sustained this identity through centuries of exile and dispersion. . . .

He sat there musing, till he knew what he had to do: He was well aware of his power of oratory. He knew how he could stir people to their depths when he spoke. This gift of his kept the *shul* filled to capacity by residents eager to hear his sermons. With that power he would exert a moral force over the members of his community; he would bring a moral pressure to bear, till they found the means, beyond their ability, to put together the support that he needed.

It was on an ordinary Shabbos that he rose from his place in the *shul* and went up to the pulpit, to face his congregation. Yet something in his manner told the people that this was to be no ordinary sermon. Some important matter was on his mind. . . . An earnest silence developed in the House of Worship . . . and this is the story they heard:

****

The town of Sassov in Galicia (began Rav Meir) became renowned on account of the famed Reb Moshe Leyb, the great tzaddik who lived there — who excelled so powerfully in *ahavas yisra'el*, in his love of Jewry and Jews. In his boundless love for this people, he would always query and question travelers who came passing through Sassov, about the situation of the Jews in this little town or in that.

One day he was told about a man who was noted for the *tz^edaka* he gave, the help that he always provided for the poor, although he himself could have used help like any penniless beggar, since he was himself as poor as could be. Sometimes as many as twenty, thirty or more indigent souls slept the night in his plain, simple home. He had no fine, sumptuous, regal beds to offer them. He did not sleep on one himself. But he did set out pallets of straw for them, with small straw-filled pillows for their heads. And with each sleeping-place that he prepared, he said a prayer: "Almighty Master of the world, You know the thoughts in the minds of Your human beings; and so You know that I can't give them anything better. Let this be as worthy in Your sight as if I prepared here the softest mattress and covered it with the finest bedclothes."

Quite a large number of poor folk used to come to eat at his table, and he certainly couldn't give them the kind of meal that *sh^e^lomo ha-melech* (King Solomon) could provide when he ruled in ancient Jerusalem. He served them just bread and coffee, no more; but with every serving he added a prayer: "Almighty Master of the world, You know I have nothing more to give. May this be as acceptable to You as if I served them the finest and best of foods."

Reb Moshe Leyb listened earnestly, and he decided to take a trip and see this *ba'al tz^e^daka*, this wondrous "master of charity," for himself. It was a long journey, but at last he reached the *shtétl* he wanted; and then Reb Moshe Leyb went to spend the night at the home of this most unusual poor man, along with all the indigent souls who were there.

Now he watched and saw for himself how this man gave freely what he was able to give, and how he added his little prayer with every place for sleeping that he prepared, with every bit of food that he served. . . . Well, when the time for him to leave, the great Rebbe of Sassov turned his heart heavenward and said, "Almighty Master of the world, what harm would it do, then, if this poor man were really able to provide good, comfortable beds for the poor, indigent folk? And why should he really not have the means to serve the best foods for the hungry souls who come to him? You see how much he tries to help those poor folk, how devoted and selfless he is!"

Sensing that his words had been heard clearly in Heaven, Reb Moshe Leyb assured his host that he could expect to become wealthy; and with that he left to travel home.

A few years sped by, as the Rebbe kept asking visiting travelers about the conditions and the situation of the Jews in every possible location of their life in exile. And at last someone turned up from the small *shtétl* that the Rebbe had visited to see that remarkable man of charity. "Tell me," said the Rebbe: "How is Reb Velvl the *ba'al tz^e^daka*?" The Rebbe remembered that this was how the man was known in the *shtétl*; but the present visitor only looked at the Rebbe in bewilderment: "Who?"

Reb Moshe Leyb put his memory to work and described where the man lived and how he looked; and finally a light dawned in his visitor's eyes: "Oh! That could only be Wilhelm the Rotten Informer! About him the Rebbe is asking?" And he launched into a full account about this man: By some strange, unknown means he suddenly became fabulously rich, almost overnight; and since then he had turned into the worst skunk in town. To his fellow-Jews he was now like a sore plague. Not a single poor person, no matter who, was allowed to go through his doorway and enter his home. He was an overweening tyrant, nothing more.

As soon as his visitor left, the Rebbe burst into a flood of tears, and he lifted his heart to Heaven: "Almighty Master of the world, what did I go and do? What did I perpetrate? In Your world I found a sweet, precious soul; and through me, because of me, he took off his entire *tzelem elokim*, the last vestige of his Divine image, till he is little more than a rich animal. . . ." Then, without another thought, he set off again on the journey that would bring him to the little town. Whatever happened, he was determined to see that unusual, amazing *ba'al tz^e^daka* who had turned into such a vile and wicked human being. Perhaps, thought the Rebbe, it was not too late: perhaps he could still do something with that deformed, disfigured soul.

When he came at last to the exact spot he sought, he stood still a moment, hardly able to believe his eyes. In place of the simple home, almost a hovel, where the man had done his heartfelt daily acts of charity, stood a regal mansion, literally fit for a king. Uniformed guards stood at the door, and lackeys and flunkeys in resplendent livery went about in haste on Heaven knew what important errands.

Having taken note of the whole scene, Reb Moshe Leyb of Sassov went up as close as he could, till a little gate stopped him. "You there!" he called out to one of the guards. "Go and tell your master that a Jew from the town of Sassov wishes to speak with him." The guard, however, only sneered: "You are wasting your time. The master left strict orders to let no Jew inside: absolutely none." At that the Rebbe only shrugged. "Go tell your master," he continued, "that I want to ask him a scientific question, something to do with the laws of physics. I believe only a scientist on his advanced level will be able to give the answer."

About a request like this the guard had no orders, and he took the message inside. Highly flattered to be thought (apparently) an advanced scientist in matters of physics, the lord and master told the guard to let the Jew in. "I'm in a little hurry," he said, "but I'll talk to him." This once, he thought with a shrug, he would break the iron rule he had kept for the last few years. He would grant the visitor a few minutes, to satisfy his curiosity and hear what intriguing question the man wanted to ask.

Reb Moshe Leyb entered the sumptuously furnished salon, and he found the "lord and master" somewhat embedded in the soft, luxuriant cushions of an easy chair, with a large mirror close by. Into that the man kept looking, as he adjusted his clothes, especially a very fine cravat around his neck. As soon as he saw this unexpected visitor, he snapped out, "All right, Jew, come and ask your question — quickly. I don't want to be late to the party of Polish noblemen that I've been invited to attend!"

Said the Rebbe, "Why is it that when we stand before a mirror and look, we see only ourselves; but when we stand before a window and look, we can see others?"

Loftily the "lord and master" replied, "The glass in the window is left clear, plain; but to make a mirror, the glass is coated on the back with silver. That is why we see only ourselves in a mirror."

The Rebbe raised his voice: "Ah . . . so . . . now I understand: As long as we still turn our eyes to plain, unadorned glass, we can still see another human being. Once a heavy coating of *silver* comes along, we cannot see anyone else any more. We can see only ourselves!"

Now the Rebbe's voice became a shout: "You vile, rotten, wicked animal! Can your befouled brain still remember a few years back, when you were a penniless pauper? Then they called you Velvl the *ba'al tz^e^daka*. I came and saw how wonderfully you did your acts of charity, and I prayed to Heaven for you. I sensed that my small prayer was accepted, and I assured you that you would know wealth instead of poverty. The wealth came to you — and this is why, now, you will not let a Jew enter your home any longer! Now they call you Wilhelm the Informer. You go to the parties of the Polish 'nobility' and you sneer with those haughty *p^e^ritzim* at your fellow Jews. You tell tales about poor, struggling Jews, so that one more *poritz* might decide to be harsh and cruel to Jews under his power. . . .

"Do you know why I have come here now, to see you again? I have come to scrape away the coating of silver from you!"

The man looked at the Rebbe, and his face turned pale and ghastly as the words sank in. All his sneering hauteur and arrogant lordship vanished. He began weeping and wailing till he was near to fainting. He fell to the Rebbe's feet and implored him not to bring him back to the abject, bitter poverty that he had known most of his life. He gave his solemn word, made every kind of promise he could, that from this day forward his home would become a place of warm hospitality for the Jewish poor — just as his plain, simple home had been years ago.

Remembering all the good that the man had done in the past, knowing how much merit the man had amassed in his Heavenly account, Reb Moshe Leyb of Sassov took pity and prayed for him with compassion; and the repentant Velvl remained well-to-do.

****

So ended the story that Rav Meir Shapiro told in the shul in Glina. There was little more that he had to end to his sermon. His listeners understood his message. Whoever lived anywhere above the level of absolute penury, however much or little above, gave what he could, if not more. . . .

"With that story," Rav Meir used to recall, "I was able to scrape together the money I needed — and there was even a small surplus left over."

After long, wearying work and intensive effort, in the year 5671 (1911) the building he wanted stood complete at last in the loveliest part of the town. It was a handsome edifice, with cheerful, comfortable rooms; and it became the permanent location of the *chéder* and *talmud torah* (the primary school), as well as the *yeshiva* (the secondary school).

****

Yet even then, with the handsome building standing and the classrooms filled, his "educational ambitions" were by no means satisfied. In his heart lived a further dream: to set up somewhere, somehow, a proper pedagogic center for training sound educators and capable teachers.

At a gathering somewhere outside Glina, he once had occasion to speak, and he tried to drive home the overriding need for a good teacher-training institute. "Just think," he said: "How many qualifications do we demand from a *shochét* before he will be accepted to do the ritual slaughtering in even the smallest *shtétl*, to provide the little community with kosher meat? He must know well all the relevant laws, down to the last detail. He must have those laws well in mind when he does his work, and his hands must move efficiently, so that he doesn't make any blunders. In addition, he must be a devoutly observant Jew, or else we won't trust him. . . . Then, after all that, what do we put into his hands? What do we entrust him with? — an ox!

"Consider, then, what qualifications a *m^elamed* should have — a teacher in a classroom — when we entrust to him our children, the young souls who will build and form the future of our people. The children are the foundation of Jewry's next generation; and that makes them the most precious possession we have. . . . "

****

Rav Meir, however, was as much a realist as a dreamer, and he knew that for now there was not a hope in sight of starting any kind of institute for training teachers. Action on such a dream would probably have to wait years.

For the time being there was work enough for him in the imposing new building he had in Glina. For the present, he could devote himself completely to the pupils in his school, to his work as an educator. And he gave of himself without stint, always trying to do more.

[With its growing reputation, *B^eney Torah* attracted quite a few pupils from beyond the borders of Glina. Without a second thought, he had them stay at his home, to receive full room and board without any payment.]

From time to time he would examine the pupils in the classrooms and give them little tests; and he would give the boys marks, to rate their degrees of proficiency. To those who proved to be good, capable learners he gave more personal attention, taking them more under his wing; and at times he would even study with them privately.

Once he gave a quiz to a classroom of youngsters, a short oral examination to see how well they were faring with the Talmudic material that they were studying at the time. To his surprise, one boy showed, quite unexpectedly, a grasp and an acumen whose like Rav Meir had never met in this new school of his. The boy's father was an ordinary shoemaker, and he himself a plain, ordinary pupil with nothing remarkable about him. And suddenly he seemed to bask in the radiance of a new sunlight, as he astounded Rav Meir with his keen understanding and brilliant perception.

The Rav put a few difficult questions to him (the kind that could be called "stumpers"), and the lad answered them with so much sagacity and sharpness that the Rav could only look at him in wonder. So moved was he that he gave the boy a kiss on the forehead; and turning to the *rebbe*, the teacher of the class, he quoted the prophet Yirm^eyahu, "A precious son, truly, is Ephraim to me" (Jeremiah 31:19) — for the boy's name was Ephraim. Then he asked the youngster, "Do you remember the words in the *chumash* (the Written Torah) that *Ya'akov avinu* (our Father Jacob) said — what kind of blessing our people would give to children? *May God make you like Ephraim . . . (B^eréshis/*Genesis 48:20). Well, starting tomorrow, your place will be two grades higher. You have just been promoted."

This small, precious encounter with the Rav put so much new life and vigor into the boy that from then onward he devoted himself entirely to his study, with every fiber of his being, with all the fire in his spirit; and he advanced prodigiously from day to day. The Rav could only watch with deep satisfaction and joy, setting great hopes on him.

Once again, however, the inscrutable hand of fate struck. The boy suddenly fell ill, and the medical knowledge of the time found no way to save him. When the Rav had to stand before the open grave of his beloved Ephraim and give the *hesped*, to eulogize his dead pupil with tears in his eyes, his anguish was indescribable.

Once again he quoted the prophet Yirm^eyahu: "*A precious son, truly, is Ephraim to me, indeed a child of playful delights.* How precious, how wondrous was this boy, Ephraim; how delightful the play of his mind when he studied his Talmud. *For whenever I speak of him, how I remember, remember him* 'od, *still.* When I think and talk about this boy that has been taken from us, I remember him so clearly, and I think of *'od*, how much still, how much yet, how very much more he could have given us of his brilliance, to enrich our enjoyment and delight in our Oral Torah. *This is why my innermost being is moved with yearning for him* (Jeremiah 31:19):

This is the deepest, strongest sorrow we must bear in the calamity that has stricken us!"

So spoke the heart of this father of his community over the child with so much promise, who was taken from him at so young an age. He wept and wept in his grief; and those who listened wept with him.

****

Yet life had to go on for the living, in its normal ways; and the young Rav Meir was soon completely back at work as educator in his school and spiritual leader in the community.

For all that Glina was only a small town near Lemberg, with his dynamism, his scintillating wit and superb oratory, his reputation among the Jewish people of Eastern Europe continued to grow, and invitations came to visit other communities as a guest speaker.

On one such occasion, as he entered the Jewish auditorium escorted by the heads of the community (including the local rabbi), he noticed portraits on the walls of certain well-known secular Jews who presumed to act as leaders and spokesmen for their people though they had neither any knowledge nor any concern for the Torah or its age-old sacred values. One prominent feature of these portraits was that their subjects were very obviously and proudly bare-headed, to emphasize that they were "modern and enlightened," with virtually no connection to the Torah.

"It is not fitting," said Rav Meir to the men escorting him, "that in this self-respecting community of believing Jews, such portraits should appear." The local rabbi (who evidently liked to function with at least half a foot in the "modern, enlightened" camp) felt rather offended by the remark, and he retorted, "I don't understand why rabbis of other communities should come and meddle in our affairs!"

"I am reminded," shot back Rav Meir on the instant, "of a butcher who found that with an animal which had just been ritually slaughtered, there was a question of a possible defect in an organ that made it uncertain if the meat could be considered kosher. So the butcher went along with the *shochet* to the *rav* to find out.

"Having listened carefully to the problem, the *rav* replied (in the Yiddish idiom of Poland's Jewry), 'According to the *T'vu'os Shor*, that animal is not kosher; its meat may not be eaten.' The *shochet* understood well what he meant: In the volume named *T^evu'os Shor*, its learned author had dealt with exactly this problem perhaps a century and a half ago, and his decision was to declare the animal's meat forbidden. That decision had to be followed here.

"All the butcher understood, however, was that this meant a most serious loss of money for him, and he banged the table in anger. 'What connection,' he raged, 'does the *T^evu'os Shor* have with my animal? What is his business with me? What right does he have to come meddling suddenly in my affairs?' "

****

Among the many striking, thought-provoking dicta in the Talmud is the statement (*bavli*, Y^evamos 97a) that when the teaching of a departed sage in *halacha* is cited here on earth by living students, however long ago that sage was taken to his eternal reward, *sifsosav dov^evos ba-kever*: literally, "his lips are moved to speak in the grave." It would seem to denote that when the living engage in dynamic, animated Torah study, by paranormal channels the discarnate souls whose teachings and thoughts are being studied become participants in the ongoing process of discussion and learning.

Since Rav Meir was generally known as a foremost Talmudist, wherever he appeared on a visit yeshiva students always came flocking around him to bring up points of interest or difficulty that they found in their study; or they set forth new ways of explaining certain matters in the Talmud, which had occurred to their creative minds, to see if he would accept or reject their ideas.

Once, as one young fellow began talking to him, Rav Meir sensed soon enough that this particular youth was not genuinely interested in getting at the truth of the Talmudic passage he quoted. All this young fellow wanted was to be able to boast afterward that he had engaged the great Rav Meir in a Talmudic discussion, and the two had talked as equals!

Since the youth's mind was quite shallow, more than once he presented some supposed interpretation by a *rishon* (Early Authority) or an *acharon* (Later Authority) which simply did not exist. His "creative mind" dreamed it up.

Thus, he suddenly cited something impossible to understand from the commentary of *maharsha* (Rav Sh'mu'el Edels, found in the back pages of every volume of Talmud in the standard editions). Rav Meir thought for a moment, then replied, "There is no such interpretation in the *maharsha.*" Yet the young fellow insisted that there was. "Very well," said the Rav. "Let us take the volume in question and see."

As might be expected, Rav Meir was right. The youth could find no trace of what he claimed to have cited from the commentary.

Rather resentful at such a shallow approach to Talmud study, the Rav remarked sharply, "Do you know what you have just done? With this claim of yours you made the *maharsha* remain reclining with his mouth open, while *mashi-ach* kept standing on one foot!"

"What? What do you mean?" asked the young fellow, a bit frightened by these puzzling words that the Rav uttered rather sharply.

"It's quite simple: You know that the Talmud states that when someone conveys a matter of *halacha* in the name of a scholar who lived in the past, that scholar's lips move in the grave. Then we learn further that when a person quotes something in the name of the person who said it originally, he brings *g'ula*, redemption, to the world (Pirkey Avos 6:6).

"Well, then, what happened here? As soon as you announced, 'The *maharsha* says,' that great scholar, may his merit protect us, opened his mouth to whisper the next words with you. On the other hand, when *mashi-ach* heard you about to quote something in the name of the one who said it originally, in this way he expected you to bring the messianic redemption to the world. Being the Messiah, he therefore lifted up one foot, poised in readiness to go racing off and make the world experience the ultimate redemption.

"Then they learned that what you quoted was something the *maharsha* had never said. So of course the *maharsha* was left with his mouth open, and the Messiah with one foot poised in mid-air!"

****

On one visit to another community, he was accosted by a "modern" Jewish gentleman who fancied himself rather learned in the Torah, but quite "emancipated" from *emuna*, from any sacred Jewish belief. Knowing Rav Meir's reputation as a master of the Torah, this gentleman began quoting bits of Scripture that he could deride with a bit of irony and contempt — to bear down lightly, perhaps, on Rav Meir's nerves.

One choice text that he quoted with relish was the phenomenon that when the Ten Commandments were given at Sinai, "all the people were seeing the sounds" (*Sh^e^mos*/Exodus 20:15). Striking a pose as a plain, naïve soul trying to understand, he asked, "This would mean that the people not only heard the Almighty's voice; they also saw it. I understand that this could happen somehow because it was a miracle; so we have to believe it. But was it necessary? Why did the people have to see as well as hear? It wasn't enough just to hear the Almighty?"

"Let me explain it for you," replied the Rav. "In Hebrew we have two different words that are pronounced *lo*. One, spelled with an *alef*, can denote only a negative: 'No, do not.' Spelled with a *vav*, however, it doesn't mean anything negative at all. It means 'to him' or 'for him.' So if the people only heard His voice as He commanded us about such interesting things as murder, adultery, theft, and so on — a modern, enlightened type like you could have understood Him to mean we *should* do these interesting things, under certain conditions. That is why it was so important, especially for people like you, to see the words that they heard — so that they shouldn't give the Almighty the benefit of any fancy interpretations."

13

For the Beilis trial

True, Glina was only a small town near Lemberg; however, with all he had been able to achieve there by his dynamism and brilliance, and by the strong impression he made wherever he visited, the young Rav Meir's reputation was anything but small now among the Jewish population of Poland and Russia.

Soon a black, ominous development of events filled the newspapers of the world, as it struck fear in the hearts of East European Jewry. And the result was that Rav Meir was brought face to face with the renowned Rav Mazeh, the distinguished Rabbi of Moscow.

[However accustomed the Jews were in Eastern Europe to the danger and insecurity that had filled, for centuries, the very air they breathed, from the middle of 5671 (1911) their underlying, pervasive sense of anxiety grew stronger. It would take over two years till the cause of this extra anxiety and fear disappeared.

[On the twentieth of Adar, 5671 (March 20, 1911) a Russian boy's mutilated body was found in a cave on the outskirts of Kiev. The press decided at once that he had been killed by Jews, because they needed his blood for their ritual purposes. The investigations of the police led them eventually to a gang of thieves, but with strong pressure and support by reactionary, antisemitic groups, the chief district attorney of Kiev refused to be bothered by facts. Instead, he looked for a Jew to arrest. Once he found some kind of a victim, the entire Jewish people could be blamed, condemned and damned by the Russian populace.

[On the twenty-fifth of Tammuz (July 21), on the flimsy, inconclusive evidence of a Russian lamplighter and his wife, a Jew named Mendl Beilis was arrested and sent to prison, where he was to remain for over two years, till his trial could finally begin.

[One thing was clear: It was not one individual alone who stood accused here of the age-old "blood libel" — that Jews need the human blood of a non-Jew in their ritual preparations for Pesach and in their celebration of Pesach. The entire Jewish people stood in the dock, waiting to be tried. And should the dark, mindless forces focused on this case find some way to make the "blood libel" stick, not one Jew might be able to go on living anywhere in the Russian empire of the tsar.

[And even more than the Jewish people faced trial here. The case could decide the fate of the Talmud too. In the black minds of the Jew-haters there was not the slightest doubt that the Talmud taught and guided the Jew in his nefarious, hostile, even murderous attitude toward non-Jews and in his relationship with them. To prove their case, it was believed that they had a list of citations from the Oral Torah, mainly the Talmud, which, as they understood those passages with their interpretation and commentaries, could only show how right they were.

[In the Jewish world of Poland and Russia, there were concerned and responsible people who knew that a good, strong defense had to be prepared not only for Mendl Beilis but for the Talmud as well. Otherwise, every printed volume in Russia might be ordered burned, and if any volume ever appeared again, it would be a criminal matter.]

That summer, Rav Mazeh of Moscow was in the health resort of Marienbad, Bohemia (later Western Czechoslovakia), where he stayed at the Luxemberg Hotel. It was known by then that when the Beilis case came to trial, he would probably have to take the stand to answer whatever charges might be brought against the Written and the Oral Torah, primarily the Talmud.

When some of the concerned, responsible people learned that certain individuals were also in Marienbad, they saw to it that these should take rooms at the same hotel — so that they could work together to formulate answers on the citations from the Talmud that would be hurled at the trial against the Jewish people. The answers they could prepare would give Rav Mazeh the effective basis for his defense.

The individuals in question were the Rebbe of Tchortkov; Aaron Marcus, the noted genius who had come from the "modern, cultured" world of Germany to learn the world of Poland's *chassidim* and to join it; and finally, the young Rav of Glina.

As the four studied the citations and accusations which had been flaunted abroad by the bigoted, fixated minds of the antisemitic forces, the most serious problems, which clearly presented the greatest difficulties and therefore the most serious dangers, were given to Rav Meir. He accepted the challenge to formulate satisfying answers.

The first statement under scrutiny came from the Midrash: *tov she-*

bagoyim harog: "the best among the non-Jews, kill!" (Mechilta on *She-mos*/Exodus 14:7). Did this indeed typify Jewish morality? Were Jews actually directed by the Talmud to put to death even the best of their fellow-beings of other faiths?

In reply, Rav Meir pointed to an old debate between a bishop and Rav Shelomo ibn Verga, the author of *Shévet Yehuda* who lived at the time of the catastrophic expulsion of the Jews from Spain in 5252 (1492). The debate is mentioned in the commentary of *Meiras Ena-yim* (popularly known as the *sema*) on *Shulchan Aruch Choshen Mishpat*, sec. 425, par. 18. In that debate, Rav Sh'lomo ibn Verga explained the statement in this way:

There is reason to believe that in the ancient Land of Israel, the *sanhedrin*, the highest court of the Jews, hardly ever had anyone put to death. Rabbi El'azar ben Azarya makes this clear in the Mishna (Makkos 1:10; *bavli*, 7a): "If a *sanhedrin* had anyone executed even once in seventy years (said he), it was labeled a brutal court!" For this reason, however, murders must have occurred fairly frequently — since the attitude and practice of the *sanhedrin* presented no serious deterrent to people given to robbery and violence. In fact, this is hinted at by what we read further in the Mishna: "Rabbi Akiva and Rabbi Tarfon said: Had we been in the *sanhedrin*, no one would ever have been put to death." They could always have found some technical grounds for setting anyone free from a murder charge. Evidently they had an abhorrence at the very thought of causing anyone's death. Yet the Mishna itself continues with a strong objection: "Said Rabban Shim'on ben Gamliel: So would they indeed increase the number of murderers in Jewry." No one would hesitate to kill out of fear of the death penalty.

Therefore (Rav Shelomo ibn Verga explained) we understand the words of the Midrash as applying to that very question. The advice of the Midrash is: *tov shebagoyim*: the best way, the best policy, is the one that generally prevails among the non-Jews: *harog*, kill! All murderous outlaws and robbers should be executed, so that others will be frightened off from pursuing such a way of life.

****

The second problem was a teaching in the Talmud (*bavli*, Yevamos 61a, original version, unaltered on account of censorship): "You are called *adam*, a person, a human being; and the nations of the world are not called *adam*." Was that a fair, just, humane and ethical attitude — to consider only Jews as decent human beings and no one else?

This was Rav Meir's answer: Among all the nations, when a single person is arrested on criminal charges and is brought to trial, only he stands accused, not his entire people. They are not considered involved and responsible for what he is believed to have done. One person is on trial, no more. As the Jewish people existed in its long, historic European exile, when one Jew was brought to trial, Jewry was always there with him, awaiting the outcome in fearful trepidation — as all could see now, all too clearly, in the ordeal of Mendl Beilis.

That, said Rav Meir, was just what the Talmud meant: "*attem*, you, are called *adam*"; but the word *attem* is a plural form. It means not a single "you" but a great many taken together: The entire people are considered as *adam*, one individual — facing Heaven knew what punishment whenever one Jew was brought to trial; "but the nations of the world are not called *adam*." Where Jews were not involved, it would never occur to anyone to hold an entire people guilty and responsible for one person's crime.

****

The third problem was the Talmud's teaching (*bavli*, Sanhedrin 59a, original version, unaltered on account of censorship): "A non-Jew who engages in Torah study is punishable by death." What normal, intelligent reason could there be for such an idea? Did the Jews consider their Torah so holy, so inviolate and untouchable, that if anyone else dared study it, they were ready to sentence him to death? Did any other nation or people have something so barbaric?

For this, too, the Rav of Glina had an explanation: Suppose, said he, that a non-Jew failed to fulfill some solemn order or holy command in his religion that was meant for him, and as a result, he was held to be guilty enough to receive a death sentence. He could defend himself with the simple argument that he was not aware of the matter: No one had given him any stern instructions or any warning. If he studies, however, and learns all about the solemn order or the holy command, then it is certainly a different matter.

In this statement, then, the Talmud is merely giving the rest of mankind a word of caution, for its own good: If a non-Jew studies the Torah, he may learn enough of what we know to be Heaven's absolute truth to become liable to a death sentence through Heaven's agency, if he ignores the Torah's warning afterward and disobeys what he has learned.

****

The fourth topic was not something in the Oral Torah at all, but a sentence (a verse) from the Book of *T'hillim* in the Hebrew Bible: "Let the faithful people of piety exult in glory . . . exaltations of God in their throat and a two-edged sword in their hand, to carry out revenge upon the nations, chastisements upon the peoples" (Psalms 149:5-7).

Was this a fine, proper, humane moral attitude for a Divinely chosen people to have toward other people and nations on this earth — to be so openly vengeful and bloodthirsty in their prayers? And what of the Almighty's injunction in their Torah, "You are not to take revenge, nor to bear a grudge" (*Va-yikra*/Leviticus 19:18)?

For this too the resourceful Rav Meir had an answer:

As we understand it (said he), it refers to the ultimate, messianic future, when the Almighty will judge the people and nations of the world for having failed to keep the ethical and moral commandments that He gave them. To defend themselves they will argue, "We were much too busy and involved in world politics, dealing with our problems of government in all the hostility and distrust that went on among the nations. We simply had no time left to give even a thought to the moral imperatives or ethical, humane commandments that we were given."

In the time of *mashi-ach*, however, when the ultimate Redemption comes for the Jewish people, it will live once again as a sovereign nation in its homeland, in the greatest good fortune that this long-suffering people has ever known. Then it will show how it is possible for a nation to deal with severe political problems, to maintain a viable government amid lethal hostility and mortal dangers — and yet to keep the Almighty's commandments scrupulously in a life of faith. There will be "exaltations of God in their throat" as they worship and pray, even while they hold "a two-edged sword in their hand" to defend themselves against all the mortal enemies that surround them.

Then, with this example for all to see, the Almighty will deal with the nations as they deserve, for all the enormous crimes and sins that they committed: for their arguments in self-defense will have become unacceptable.

****

These, then, were the replies that the young Rav Meir prepared for the four most difficult and thorny questions that Rav Mazeh might have to face when the Beilis case came to trial. When he heard them, at the Luxemberg Hotel in Marienbad, Rav Mazeh looked at Rav Meir Shapiro in open admiration. Beyond any doubt, he was impressed.

"The answers are good — very good," said he. "It is not at all certain if the questions will be asked; but if they are, I will most surely use these answers. And even if not, I will most likely use them at some other occasion. For apt, felicitous thoughts like those there is always a need and a use: if not today, then tomorrow."

****

[On the twenty-third of Elul, 5673 (September 25, 1913) the "blood libel" murder charge against Mendl Beilis finally came to trial. Among the mass of testimony that went in all directions, the important point was that the prosecuting attorney's main evidence, on which his case depended, was what the Russian lamplighter and his wife had seen or not seen. When the presiding judge questioned the couple directly, their reply was, "We really know nothing at all." They declared that the secret police had confused them and made them answer questions they did not understand.

[The jury had been carefully chosen from the most boorish and simple Russian peasants that could be found; but when the case finally ended on the twenty-seventh of Tishri, 5674 (October 28, 1913), even they had no trouble reaching a verdict: Mendl Beilis was not guilty.

[As to the Talmud, in the course of the trial, a priest with a criminal record testified that the dead boy's body bore all the marks of a "ritual murder as the Jewish religion required"; and with a spurious air of learning, he purported to cite the Talmud to prove his charge.

[It was not difficult for Rav Mazeh to take the stand and show up the priest for the abysmal ignoramus he was. But to drive the point home, the defense attorneys then asked the priest what the names of two Talmud tractates meant: *Eruvin* and *Chullin*. He admitted he did not know.

[Then came the *pièce de résistance*: Prompted by another learned *rav* who was present, one of the defense attorneys decided to ask the "erudite" priest a fascinating question about the tractate *Bava Basra*: "Tell me: Where did the Buba Basra live, and what did she do?" As *buba* denotes a grandmother in Yiddish, so it denotes an old woman in Russian. And thus the dear clergyman, suspecting nothing, sadly admitted that he really knew nothing about the Buba Basra. . . .]

****

[It would seem, then, quite clearly, that the four thorny questions on which Rav Meir worked never came up at the trial, and Rav Mazeh found no need there for the answers that Rav Meir supplied. But they were told and retold among the Jews of Poland and Russia, till they became, one might say, part of the people's *torah sheb^e al peh*, Jewry's Torah lore that was passed on and shared by word of mouth.]

14

In the Russian occupation

[As the Beilis trial receded into the past, life in Glina resumed its normal course for Rav Meir — but not for long. On the ninth of Av, 5674 (August 1, 1914), in the Jewish season of mourning over the destruction of the *beyss ha-mikdash* and Heaven's decree of exile, the First World War broke out, to bring new destruction to all of Europe; and in time its disastrous effects reached Glina too.

[As it had been for decades, Poland was divided then into three parts, each ruled by a different power. The largest part, some sixty percent of what the Poles considered Poland, was included in the Russian empire ruled by the tsar. This was generally known as Congress Poland. To the west, a northern chunk belonged to the German kaiser within his empire. And the southern part, Galicia, which included Lemberg and Glina, formed part of the Austrian empire.

[With the outbreak of the war, Germany and Austria joined forces, to become the Central Powers, while the Western countries united to become the Allied Powers (or, for short, the Allies); and they were joined by Russia under the tsar. And thus Austria and Russia became fighting enemies.

[As the war got under way in earnest, the whole of Poland became a natural battleground for them. Russian forces marched through Congress Poland and into Austria's part of the land. A series of stunning successes in Galicia enabled them to occupy Lemberg on the twenty-fourth of Elul, 5674 (September 15, 1914); and within the next three months most of Galicia was overrun. It came under the control of a warring, conquering force that did not hesitate to wreak havoc, as the Russian soldiery pillaged and looted to their hearts' content.]

Thus Glina became a victim of the early months of the war, as the Russian troops trampled and tramped, bringing their "normal share" of damage, devastation and ruin.

Rav Meir Shapiro had no choice but to take his young wife and flee back to Tarnopol, where they could hope to find greater safety in her parents' home. Some time later, the Russians burned down his house in

Glina, and in the conflagration, his large private library, probably worth a small fortune, was lost for good. Into the flames went also (as mentioned in an earlier chapter) virtually the entire edition of his cherished first volume of writings, *Imrey Da'as*, only a very short while after it had come from the bindery. And for good measure, a few manuscripts of his further writings also went up in the devouring blaze.

Yet Rav Meir was never one to sit and bemoan what was past. In the relative safety and calm of Tarnopol he gathered around him a new group of young learners, and with these students he concentrated on the Talmud day and night.

[Even such a fairly tranquil, orderly life, however, was not to last for long. A new time of bitter trouble and dire hostility was on the way.

[As the World War progressed, by the spring of 5675 (1915) the tides of battle turned, and the ruthless, mighty Russian army began suffering defeat. In Iyar (the beginning of May) the combined forces of Germany and Austria launched a mighty offensive in southwest Galicia, and within a few weeks the Russians were driven out of almost all of Austrian Poland. In the month of June (Sivan-Tammuz), the Austrian forces took back eastern Galicia and Lemberg; on the nineteenth of Tammuz (July 1, 1915) they began a campaign of attack which was to drive the Russians out of Congress Poland too.]

Thus a time came in the spring when the Russians, still very much in firm control of the region, realized that a major offensive was on the way, to force them out. They sensed the danger, and in their angry frustration, the Russians vented their rage on the handy traditional scapegoat, the Jews. They issued decrees right and left against this fairly helpless element of the local population; but the worst decree of all, that the Jews found the hardest to bear, was an order that compelled them to dig defensive trenches which would hamper and delay the advance of the Austrian forces.

How did the Russians try to enforce the decree? They simply set about snatching whichever Jews they found: old and young, the sick and the feeble; and these they dragged off, to subject them to forced labor that would turn the life of the victims into a bitter, woeful nightmare.

Without hesitation, Rav Meir took the initiative now; and the suffering captive victims saw him literally as their stalwart savior. Unable to bear their distress, he went directly to the commandant of the local garrison and guaranteed him enough money to pay for a much better labor force than the one that his soldiers had managed to scrape together from the Jewish population. Let the commandant hire a crew of strong, able-bodied Polacks, said Rav Meir — as many as he needed — and he, Rav Meir, would see to it that enough money was provided to pay them for digging the defensive trenches.

The plan was effective. As the commandant welcomed the idea eagerly and set to work on it, Rav Meir moved to organize a committee, with himself at its head, that would have to raise the needed money.

Thanks to his dynamic energy, the plan worked. The seizure of Jews right and left was stopped in its tracks, and those who had been taken were sent home. Once again Jews could move freely and safely through the streets and roads of the city, as the "rescue committee" worked intensively not only to raise the sum that the commandant needed but to help any and every Jew in distress with both material support and sound advice. And to this entire action Rav Meir contributed not only his leadership but a sizable sum of money out of his own pocket.

****

Long ago our Sages of the Talmud taught, however, that *s'char mitzvah mitzvah*: the reward for doing a mitzvah is the ability to do another one. As the frightening threat of forced labor in Tarnopol was made null and void, a new problem came flooding in: Elsewhere in Galicia, several thousand Jews had gone into flight from the approaching Austro-Hungarian enemy, only to be taken captive by the Russians; and now they were brought into Tarnopol to be kept under the most miserable conditions as prisoners of war.

Rav Meir took stock of the situation. He reckoned that quite easily, he could get the prisoners released into the care of the Jewish community: The Russians would be happy enough to have these captives off their hands. But then heavy funds would be needed to provide the refugees with the care they needed.

One thing was clear to Rav Meir: The amount of money that this severe problem required could never be raised in Tarnopol. With its own limited resources, the local community simply could not take care of such a mass of refugees and provide for them. Without further ado he traveled across the Dnieper River to certain wealthy Jews who lived in that part of the Russian empire. Once they heard why he had come, they responded very generously. And once more the wise author of the Book of *Koheless* was shown to be right: ***and money answers everything*** (Ecclesiastes 10:19). With funds enough to cover their basic, minimal needs, the Tarnopol community was able to cope somehow with the refugees.

****

Such were the conditions, however, that human personal help was needed too, while the money was stretched as far as it could go. With his natural propensity for appraising a situation and taking charge, Rav Meir knew that except for Shabbos, not a single day while he was back in wartime Tarnopol would he be able to take vacation. And now he issued a series of orders and decrees for the Jewish residents — among them, that no one was to use more than one pillow for sleeping; all remaining pillows were to be given to the refugees.

A good number of people understood, accepted and obeyed; but a larger number muttered something resentful or derisive, and did their best to forget about it. Soon the situation was reviewed . . . and a new cry of alarm went up: Too many refugees still had nothing but a section of bare earth to sleep on, with nothing to ease their discomfort and distress. A clamor went out: *Fellow Jews, where is your pity? Brothers, where is your compassion?*

A mass meeting was called, and one great Talmud scholar rose to speak. His dedication to his study was well known. This was a man who devoted his nights and days to nothing but Torah and Divine worship. "Everyone," he declaimed now, "must accept this ruling and adjust to it. You can take me as an example. I give you my word that I have given away every bit of extra bedding, and when I go to sleep, I rest my head on one small pillow — no more!"

"How can you compare anyone else with you?" a plain, unlearned man interrupted him. "How much sleep do you give yourself at night? — an hour at the most? So of course a small, little pillow is enough for you. I need a full twelve hours' sleep at night to get my proper rest. So you want to tell me to make do with one little pillow?" . . .

That "charming" interchange between the Talmud scholar and one listener in the audience stayed in Rav Meir's memory, and he often repeated it in later years. Then he would add, "Here you have a fine example of *da'as ba'aley batim*, the view of ordinary, unlearned members of the community; and as noted many a time in our Torah lore, such a thought is invariably the opposite of the Torah's view!" . . .

****

Such were the vicissitudes of those bitter times that hardly had one serious problem been brought under control, than another came up to hang over their heads and darken their horizon.

One fine day this decree was proclaimed: New work projects had come up for which a labor force had to be organized. A force of one thousand workers had to be provided without delay by the Jews of Tarnopol; and if this demand was not fulfilled, Cossacks would be let into the city to do the needed work instead.

What this would mean — letting in a mass of Cossacks — the Jews of Tarnopol understood only too well: There would be an invasion by a horde of barbarians, bringing pogrom and slaughter, havoc and ruin. Any caprice or whim that occurred to these human animals, they would carry out to excess.

Yet what was the community to do? With the best will in the world, with the utmost effort they could make, it was impossible for the Jews of Tarnopol to supply a labor force of a thousand Jews:

First of all, just a while back, the Jewish laborers had been subjected to unexpected torment and duress. Ordinarily they were day workers. Having done a day's work, they had always been free to go home for a normal night of rest and recuperation. Recently, however, they had been kept at work for days at a time, sometimes a whole week, with no regard for the clock. They had been forced to keep toiling.

Deprived of any regular periods of sleep, they tended to become extremely nervous and irritable, and this threw them into panic. They became more and more distraught, till they felt unable to function properly, in any organized fashion; and now, in reaction, none were willing to go to work any more — any kind of work.

Nor was this all: Even if the Jewish community organized a work force of a thousand, the men would have to be paid by the community for every day's labor; and there was simply no way to find and gather enough money for the purpose.

The community was in a dilemma, with no solution in sight; and tension and anxiety grew worse as the day grew nearer and nearer when, by the decree of the Russian commandant, the work crew of a thousand had to be produced — or else the Cossacks (Satan's special forces out of hell) would come.

The night before the "deadline" became a grim time of vigil. Virtually no one slept. People everywhere wracked their brains in search of some solution, some plan or idea that might help — and all to no avail. All they knew for certain was that so far nothing practical or useful had been done — which meant they would have to be prepared for the worst when morning came: a nightmare of the calamity and catastrophe in which the Cossacks specialized.

The night's end would mean that all was lost, all hope gone: The city would become a disaster area . . . and no one could foretell who would survive and who would not, who would remain uninjured and who would not.

The very air was thick and oppressive with the pervading sense of anxiety and dread. The people longed only that the night should never end, that morning should never come. . . .

And then a rescuing answer came with the morning, from a totally unexpected source. Swift as lightning, the news spread through the fairly small city: With the morning the Rabbi of Glina appeared with his *talmidim*, his Talmud students of late adolescence or older, ready to volunteer as part of the needed work crew.

The news evoked a response from every part of the town. Without hesitation worthy, esteemed members of the community came forth to join the volunteers. As they went marching through all the streets, others of all ranks and kinds joined them. Within the hour a volunteer force of over a thousand had been collected.

The harrowing sense of oppressive despair was gone. All kept talking only of the great thing that the Rabbi of Glina had done, of his readiness to sacrifice himself for the sake of the community. And there was a sense of exhilaration in the knowledge that the doom they had awaited would not come.

The simple fact that a rabbi had taken the lead to head the work force

— a recognized religious leader (a "clergyman") who was exempt from any decree of forced labor — shook the Russian authorities considerably and left a strong impression that stayed with them. The result was that they "diluted" the sternness of their decree and made it much milder.

Yet the impression of the Rav's action on the Russian authorities was as nothing compared to the effect it had on the Jewish population. That was just indescribable. All and everyone regarded him now as a winged angel, a sublime savior who had rescued them in their darkest hour. For a long time to come, the incident was to remain a topic of conversation among Tarnopol's Jews, as his heroic action was held up as a model of one Jew's readiness to act and to make sacrifices out of a true love for his people.

****

[As winter had given way to spring, so spring left to make way for summer; and with the summer came the powerful Austrian army, driving the forces of the Russian tsar before them, first out of Galicia, and then out of Congress Poland too. In leaving, however, the Russian forces followed a policy generally known as "scorched earth": Whatever territory they were forced to yield, before going they made sure to ruin and destroy everything possible, so that when the Austrian forces entered, they would find as little as possible for their benefit and comfort.]

In this poor, helpless land, needless to say, the poorest and most helpless people were the Jews. For them the new development could only bring more chaos and ruin, pathos and poverty, than ever before.

It did not take Rav Meir long to realize how impossible it would be to stay on in Tarnopol. In the new circumstances, there was no longer anything he could do to help the stricken, suffering community. If his wife and he stayed, they would only share in the general misery, to no useful purpose.

With regret, the two moved on to the city of Lemberg. Since it could be described as the metropolis of Galicia, life there could be expected to remain relatively even and peaceful.

Soon the Jewish community became aware of his presence as a major force in its religious life. Refusing to sit idle, he established a large yeshiva for a sizable number of older students, and this he headed as administrator and educator for all the three months that he had to remain in the large, bustling city of Lemberg.

However, having become a public figure of considerable renown, he soon found himself involved in a community problem.

One day, a delegation of eminent members of the community came to him, seeking his help. In the sizable ritualarium (*mikveh*), built to serve the Jewish population of this major city, part of the water heating was still being done by an old, antiquated method called "the samovar system," which had long been used in the small cities and towns. Could there be any doubt, asked the members of the delegation, that the system was altogether unsuitable in the city of Lemberg? What they wanted, then, was that Rav Meir should take the initiative to have a new, efficient system of water heating installed, in accord with Jewish religious law.

Rav Meir's reply was sharp and clear: There was a Rabbi of Lemberg, named Rav Aryeh Brody. The problem was in his province, in his domain of authority. Let Rav Aryeh deal with it. He, Rav Meir, was no more than a visitor, a sojourner, living in Lemberg for only a while.

Obediently, the delegation went off to see Rav Brody, and put the problem to him. He, however, would give them no clear, decisive answer that would satisfy them.

What were they to do? Back they went to Rav Meir and told him exactly how Rav Aryeh Brody had replied. And Rav Meir realized that with all due respect, the Rabbi of Lemberg had indeed been evasive. He had hesitated to meet the problem head on. In his own forthright way, Rav Meir promised the delegation that on Shabbos he would take the pulpit in the main *shul* of Lemberg and speak to the congregation about it.

Now he gave an example of his remarkable homiletic ability to use the words of the Sages for his purposes, most aptly and felicitously. He began by citing a passage in the Talmud (*bavli*, M^{e}nachos 109b): "Said Rabbi Y^{e}hoshu'a ben P^{e}rachya: Originally, had anyone said to me, *Go up there*, I would have tied him up and set him down before an *ari*, before a predatory lion." Then Rav Meir interpreted: "Originally, when a delegation came to me and said, 'Go up to the pulpit and speak about our thorny problem with the *mikveh*,' I readily bound them and compelled them to go to your *ari* — your Rav Aryeh, the Rabbi of Lemberg."

He continued with the Talmudic citation: "Now, should anyone tell me to go down, I will pour over him a kettle of heated water." And he interpreted: "If anyone will tell me now to go down from this pulpit — for what business have I, an outsider, to come and speak about your affairs? — I will pour over him the samovar of your ***mikveh***: the boiling-hot problem of the antiquated, inadequate 'samovar system' for heating the water in your ritualarium. This is a burning issue that affects the entire community of Lemberg, and it must be dealt with!"

Thus he launched a campaign to acquire and install a new, modern, fully adequate system, in keeping with Jewish law.

****

[Sooner or later all human creations come to an end — even the hells that "great rulers" unleash. On the seventh of Kislev, 5679 (November 11, 1918), the First World War came to an end. Needless to say, Poland was in utter ruins. But as soon as the situation was settled enough to make it possible to travel safely, Rav Meir Shapiro returned to Glina.

[As he could only expect, the economic situation of the Jews was a total disaster; and their spiritual condition matched it exactly.

[His response was a simple assurance to them: "I will not leave you until I see the community back on its feet — rebuilt." Then he went to work in his typical dynamic, indefatigable way. Slowly but steadily a normal orderly life was restored. For Rav Meir himself, the most important thing he did was to take a good house which had survived the war and to have it repaired, refurbished and enlarged, till it could become the handsome new *B^eney Torah* school, the Yeshiva of Glina returned to life.

[For years after he left, as long as the community existed the yeshiva lived on with it — until Nazi Germany's "wave of the future" erased everything in its "heroic" march of destruction.]

15

The challenge of Sonik

The official name was Sanok, but to the Jews of Poland it was Sonik. One of the largest towns in central Galicia, in southeastern Poland, it had a Jewish community with two notable features: The first was the community's size: it was indeed among the biggest in all Galicia: some forty-five percent of the town's total population of ten thousand. The second feature was its peppery propensity for quarrels, especially about the rabbinic position.

The blistering quarrels had a way of flaring up and blazing all the time: for the community was hopelessly splintered into factions, with robust antagonisms and cordial dislikes raging among them fairly constantly. Deceit and distrust, suspicion and disparagement, were the regular order of the day.

The reason for this sorry state of affairs lay in the "merry mix" of *chassidim* that, by and large, made up the community. In this largest of the towns in Galicia, set right in the center of the province, you could find a *kloyz* or *shtibl*, a warm and vibrant House of Worship and study, for just about every group and type: sober, dignified *chassidim* of dynasties of spiritual leadership that derived from Ryzhin: devoted adherents of the Rebbes of Tchortkov, Sadygora and Boyan; ebullient, effervescent, lively *chassidim* of Belz and Bobov; and the sharp, keen mentalities that characterized the adherents of Ger.

For anyone familiar with such different types of devout, believing Jews, no explanations would need to be given why full peace and complete harmony could never reign; why, from time to time, some outburst of blazing controversy had to erupt like a small tornado, leaving no cordial good feelings in its wake. As often as not, the after-effects of some small sharp quarrel could even be disastrous.

Such was the community of Sonik, numbering some forty-five hundred souls, and such was its reputation.

And then, one day, an announcement appeared in the newspapers: "The town of Sonik is seeking a Rabbi."

On the surface it was an attractive position. In a bustling town of this size, the income for the rabbi would certainly be handsome. . . . And yet, very few candidates applied for the post. Whoever considered it realized only too well what the rabbinate there entailed: becoming involved and remaining embroiled in endless rancor and dispute, wrangling and arguing, for the rest of his life. A fine income there would be — enough and more to support himself and his family. Yet with it would come enough and more of insolence and disrespect, insult and disparagement. . . .

However attractive the position might seem to a fine learned young man eager and ready to serve a community, as he pondered on this offer it lost its attractiveness completely. Soberly and objectively considered, to find a suitable candidate, the community would have to look for a man of courage and stature with a sterling character and a brilliant mind, who would feel able to rise above the entangling web of interlocking and interacting quarrels, and to evoke admiration and esteem among each and every segment and group in the community — every element, every level and class in the Jewish quarter, without exception.

It was easy enough to give the qualifications needed for the job; but to find such a person was another matter. If any existed, they were certainly very rare: "I have seen scions of excellence," said Rabbi Shim'on ben Yochai, "but as I see, they are few" (*bavli*, Sukkah 45b).

Yet the teeming, energetic community would not give up. The toilsome, wearying search went on, till at last the heads of Sonik's Jewry found their man. To their ears came highly favorable reports of the dynamic young Rabbi of Glina. Not only was he a genius in Talmud, said the reports, but he was brilliant in all facets of the rabbinate.

Eager to seize the opportunity, all the various community heads agreed to inform him that he had been unanimously chosen to serve the Jews of Sonik as their spiritual leader, and he was earnestly implored and cordially invited to honor them by taking the position.

Under no illusions, early in the year 5681 (late 1920) Rav Meir accepted the post, knowing that he had done enough in the fairly small community of Glina, in the time he had been there, so that other religious leaders could well take his place and continue with what he had been able to accomplish.

****

If he needed the right introduction to the Jews of Sonik, to give him a fast education in what he would be facing as their Rabbi, he received it directly on his arrival. No sooner had he settled into his new home than he learned of a sizable commotion going on in town, agitated by weighty arguments and discussions on all sides: Since a famous Rebbe lived in Sonik, who should pay the first visit to whom, to show deference and courtesy?

By and large, the town's *chassidim* argued passionately that it would be no more than right for the new Rabbi, a young man in his early thirties, to pay a respectful social call to the eminent older chassidic leader, known for his great piety and deep devotion to the Almighty. And the plain, ordinary members of the community insisted just as vehemently that the eminent Rebbe should pay a welcoming visit to the new Rabbi, since the younger man was now invested with the authority of the Torah and the rabbinate over the whole of Sonik. Even if the new Rabbi were willing to forego personal honor and forget personal pride, the glory of the Torah was involved here, together with the prestige of the rabbinate. Any slur to them, any slight to their honor, would be unforgivable.

After endless wrangling and bickering, a satisfying compromise was reached: First the Rebbe sent his adult sons to visit Rav Meir in deference and courtesy, and afterwards he went to pay his respects to the renowned Rebbe.

As the conversation opened between them, Rav Meir told his host, "Now I have been able to understand something interesting in the Talmud: As the Sages tell it (*bavli*, B^e^rachos 10a), a silent, unspoken dispute developed in ancient times between Yeshayahu the Prophet and Chizkiyahu the King: Yeshayahu held that Chizkiyahu ought to come to him, since he was the Prophet of the people; and Chizkiyahu insisted that by right Yeshayahu should come to *him*, since he represented the honor of the kingship. There was no way to resolve the conflict, says the Talmud, till the Almighty made the king become mortally ill (Isaiah 38:1), and Yeshayahu had to perform the duty of *bikkur cholim*: he had to go and visit the ailing monarch.

"Well, we read further in the Talmud that on this visit, the first thing that Yeshayahu did was to berate the king for never having married. Imagine: Here is the king of *Y^e^huda* (Judea) lying mortally ill; he is likely to lose his life; and rather than say something cheerful and heartening, to lift the stricken monarch's spirits, Yeshayahu decides to upbraid him because he has never married. Does this make sense? Is this what the Prophet should have done?

"After the events of today, however," continued Rav Meir, smiling, "we can understand it very well: Yeshayahu meant to intimate that the only reason for Chizkiyahu's illness was the fact that he had never married. Had he taken a wife, she would likely have borne him sons; and when the Prophet and the King came to differ on who ought to visit whom, Chizkiyahu could have sent his sons to visit Yeshayahu first, and then the Prophet would have visited the King. There would have been no need for the Almighty to make Chizkiyahu mortally sick, so that Yeshayahu would be forced to come to him for *bikkur cholim*!"

****

Thus the mind of Rav Meir found a felicitous "Talmudic" way to end the whole matter on a pleasant note. But if here he touched on the mitzvah of *bikkur cholim*, his attitude of great reverence and courtesy toward this Rebbe of eminence was destined to have a sequel involving the mitzvah of *halva-yas ha-meyss* — escorting the dead to pay a final honor on the way to the burial ground:

To move ahead in time, several years later Rav Meir was no longer in Sonik but in Warsaw, having been elected by then to serve as a Jewish deputy in the Sejm (pronounced as *same*), the parliament which governed Poland.

One day the sorrowful news reached him that this esteemed Rebbe in Sonik had passed away. [Knowing the strong, warm bond of friendship that had flourished between the two as long as Rav Meir lived in Sonik, the community heads decided to inform him at once by telegram; and they added that they would hold back with the funeral until he came.]

At all costs, he was determined to attend — only to discover that the last railroad train he could have taken from Warsaw to reach Sonik in time, was already gone.

This, however, was simply not enough to stop him. Exercising his rights as a member of the Sejm, he insisted that the Ministry of Transportation must put on a special train that would get him there in time.

[It was a bitter winter's day; all the roads were covered with ice and snow, making travel virtually impossible; and the railroad trains were no exception: the tracks were frozen with a covering of ice. Yet all this Rav Meir ignored. He stood on his rights, till he was granted an engine and a railroad car to get him there. He was warned, however, that the government could take no responsibility for his safety, and could not even guarantee that he would ever reach his destination. Then the Ministry notified the entire railroad system of this special trip, and gave stern orders that the little train must be given full clearance.

[At various stations, as Jews learned who was traveling and why, many joined him as space in the single railroad car allowed. The weather, however, slowed the train considerably; and when Rav Meir arrived, the funeral had already started. It had not been possible to delay any longer.

[Through the massive throng he forced his way, till he stood before the bier (the *aron*); and then, since the revered Rebbe's name had been David, he took a well-known phrase from the Talmud (*bavli*, Rosh Hashana 25a) and declaimed it for all to hear, *Dovid melech yisro'el chaï v^eka-yom* — "David, King of Israel, lives and exists!"]

Then he went on with his hesped, his heartrending eulogy to make every listener aware of the great loss that the Rebbe's death would mean to Jewry.

But Rav Meir did not stop there. While all were gathered around the freshly dug grave, in a mood of utter reverence for the departed soul, this well-known visitor from Warsaw boldly proclaimed the Rebbe's son as his successor: the next leader of his *chassidim* in a continuing dynasty of spiritual guidance. To drive his point home, there and then Rav Meir wrote on a sheet of paper what *chassidim* have always called a *kvitl*: his very personal Hebrew name and his needs and requests from Heaven; and before everyone's watching eyes, he handed it to the man he had just proclaimed as the new Rebbe. There he stood waiting, like any supplicant *chassid*, while the new Rebbe read it and gave him his blessing.

Originally, when Rav Meir had decided to accept the rabbinate in Sonik, he had been under no illusions about the community. He had acquired no illusions about it since then. He knew well that only in this way would he prevent any arguments or conflicts about the proper successor to the departed Rebbe. He had publicly given the title now to the son, and had performed toward him the act of a worshipful *chassid*. Now, Rav Meir knew, no one would stir up any opposition or controversy.

****

Having digressed and moved ahead in time, we must return now to Rav Meir's first arrival in Sonik.

He was aware that in general, he was well known and highly regarded by the Jewish population of all Galicia; but if he thought that the entire community of Sonik was ready to welcome him, he learned soon enough that he was mistaken. Most of the devout Jews did accept him wholeheartedly, but there were elements which took a negative attitude toward him and felt that he should not have been given the rabbinic position.

Since there was nothing he could do about it, he went ahead and gave his "acceptance address" in the main House of Prayer: a full, solid sermon that gave the people a chance to get to know him by listening. So successful was he, so beguiled by his sermonic talent were they, that all opposition to him vanished, and he found himself entirely welcomed as the new Rav in Sonik.

In reacting to the favorable change, he noted that this sort of change was foreshadowed or prefigured in the last sentence of the Book of *Esther*: "For Mordechai the Jew was . . . great among the Jews and well liked by the majority of his brethren" (Esther 9:3):

"You see," said Rav Meir cheerfully, "Mordechai was a great person among his people as a whole; but among his brethren — those close at home — he was well liked only by the majority, not by everybody. So what do we read next in that sentence? ***dorésh tov l'ʻamo***: he sermonized well to his people; he gave a fine ***d'rasha***; and then ***he bespoke peace for all his progeny***: Once he gave a fine sermon, peace and harmony reigned, because then he became as an affectionate father to all those around him: all became his progeny spiritually, and ***everybody*** liked him. . . . "

****

The first formalities over, he settled down and took a long, hard look at the public, formal aspects of religious life in the town: the areas and domains of such matters as kosher food supplies, education, the ***mikveh*** structures (ritualariums); and so on. A few words were enough to describe everything: completely, utterly dreadful; in fact, catastrophic. Anarchy ruled wherever he looked. People were doing whatever they pleased. The formal power of a ***dayyan***, a judge with rabbinic authority, was far too little established and recognized; by any usual approach as a usual ***dayyan***, he could never hope to achieve anything much. Alone, behaving as a normal, ordinary rabbi, he would never stem, even somewhat, all the disastrous, chaotic lack of order and discipline.

And so a weighty burden fell upon him now, as the brand-new Rabbi, to devise new rules and regulations, establish new approaches and methods, that could repair the damage and wreckage which the past had left for him.

As in other arduous situations, in the past, he took no refuge or comfort in illusions. He accepted the fact that he had come upon a difficult, thorny path, and there was no choice for him but to walk it. In response, he simply mustered all his strength and forceful energy, and set out to wage his battles with the miserable situation.

In his very first sermon as the new Rabbi, at the first chance that the people had to hear him speak, he delineated the areas where he intended to go to work. He left no one in doubt of his ability for sharp, clear, wide-range observation, as he began with words of the Prophet Yeshayahu: "Go, my people, enter your chambers, and lock your doors behind you. Hide for a brief moment, until *za'am* (wrathful fury) passes" (Isaiah 26:20). Then he interpreted: "In the word *za'am* we have the letters *za-yin, a-yin, mem.* For me they stand for *z^evachim, éruvin, mikva'os* — or, if you prefer, matzos; in other words, the problems of kosher, ritually slaughtered animals to provide meat; the problems of a proper *éruv* for this town [a technical arrangement by posts and wires that would make it permissible to carry things in public on Shabbos]; the problems of maintaining every *mikveh* in Sonik in satisfactory condition; and the assurance of a good supply of kosher matzah for Pesach for the entire community."

He paused a moment, and continued: "The situation in every one of these areas of my concern is a matter of utter pathos and miserable neglect — more than enough to arouse Heaven's wrathful fury. If others till now have ignored everything, seeking safety in their own chambers, in the privacy of their personal lives, I cannot. I intend to work. I intend to fight."

****

He began with the *shoch^etim,* determined to put every last one of the ritual slaughterers under his unflinching supervision. By his stern orders, no *shochet* was permitted any longer to practice his craft without the presence of another *shochet.* He knew that two together would have the courage, presence of mind, and sense of responsibility to deal properly with any problems that might arise about an animal's physical condition that might be found after it was ritually slaughtered. Above all, he broke the bonds of dependency between the *shoch^{e}tim* and the butchers who employed them and paid them. He made it clear that the ritual slaughterers would be under his direct jurisdiction and protection, and they could therefore deal freely and honestly with questions about the kosher status of a slaughtered animal, with no fear of a butcher's wrath and retaliation if the man lost money because a slaughtered animal was declared not kosher.

With this single act, Rav Meir achieved a major breakthrough in the problem of providing kosher meat in Sonik.

He went further. He found some butchers selling both kosher and non-kosher meat in the same store (simply telling the customers which was which and asking everybody to depend on their word). His next decree was that in any and every butcher-shop with such wares, a wall had to be erected to divide the store into two completely separate parts: kosher and non-kosher; and each part had to have its own entrance. In effect, the one store would have to become two.

The reaction among the butchers was a most stormy and turbulent one. They implored and pleaded, then sent him anonymous, unidentifiable threats, in search of a way to prevail on him to rescind his edict — and all to no avail. Ruthlessly, with all the power at his command, the decree was put through and enforced.

Some butchers, ready to stop at nothing, even tried to arouse the dangerous hostility of non-Jews against him. They did their best to convince the non-Jews that the real reason behind the Rabbi's decree was his strong wish not to come into contact with them when he entered a kosher butcher store — because he considered them lesser, untouchable, filthy breeds, or something like that.

Yet all this availed the rebellious, resistant butchers nothing. Rav Meir's absolute devotion to the truth of his purpose could be seen and felt by all.

One butcher presented him with the most difficult problem of all. He did not merely sell both kosher and non-kosher meat. He had a non-Jew for a partner in his store — a black-hearted scoundrel who treated Jews brutally and never hesitated to make trouble for them. Many suffered a great deal from him. When Rav Meir issued his implacable order, this execrable character sent someone to him with a clear personal message: Let the Rabbi not dare cross the threshold of the store. If he did, this villainous character would show the Rabbi just what he could do to him!

The naked physical threat made no impression on the new religious head of Sonik's Jewry. He would not even call the police and report it. From the youngsters who studied Talmud with him regularly he chose one and took him by the hand; and the two set off together.

On the way, Rav Meir cited a passage from the Talmud (*bavli*, Sanhedrin 7b), so that the two might have it in mind together: "When Rav [a well-known Sage whose real name was Abba] would walk to the *beyss din* (the Jewish courthouse, to act as judge), he used to say: Of his own good will should one go out to death by violence." And Rav Meir continued, "This is how a rabbi in Jewry should conduct himself — not to be frightened off by any human threats — not even a death sentence that someone may imagine he will carry out!"

With quiet, measured steps, without any emotion of fear, he walked on to the butcher-shop. His simple arrival in full command of his dignity, his appearance in the doorway as an imposing figure that could only arouse respect, unnerved the two partners and left them speechless. So frightened were they of this image as he stood before them that, with tears in their eyes, they gave him their solemn word that they would do everything he demanded.

The incident gave its own evidence for all in Sonik to know: his fearless devotion to his task was absolute. Whatever quarrels and arguments might go on thereafter in the community, about his character and authority there would be none. From then on, in religious matters his word was law.

Knowing that he could work with a free hand now, without a soul to oppose him, his next project was the *éruv.* By the time he was done directing his laborers, the carefully built arrangement of pillars and posts, with strong wire, cable or sinewy cord drawn tightly on high from one to another, turned Sonik into one private domain under Jewish law, so that Jews might carry what they wished on Shabbos. He made sure to include even the furthermost corner where a Jew might venture or reside.

He turned his attention next to every structure in Sonik that housed a *mikveh.* To these ritualariums he brought the latest developments in sanitary construction and the provision of hygienic convenience and comfort. By the time he was done, even the most "modern, enlightened, progressive" elements were willing to adhere faithfully to the laws of family purity.

In time, the Pesach season came, and Rav Meir put aside all thought of resting on his laurels. Every aspect of matzah production was placed under his authority alone, and wherever proper, reliable supervision was needed, he appointed one of his own trusted people.

Every evening at six, he rode through the town and snapped a lock on the door of every matzah bakery. At six the next morning he unlocked them. No unauthorized, unsupervised baking of matzah for Pesach would be done in Sonik while he was the Rabbi. Down to the last detail, everything was done with precision as he directed.

The plain result was that the bakers benefited. The reports spread through all of Galicia that the matzos of Sonik were absolutely kosher, beyond any possible doubt — and ever larger orders kept coming in from near and far.

****

In the course of his rabbinic career, occasionally small piquant interchanges or incidents happened, which he recalled in later years.

Two members of the community appeared before him one day, to ask him to sit in judgment over a dispute that had arisen between them. Rav Meir listened gravely while one man presented his side of the case, with his arguments, and then the other told his side, with his counter-arguments. With his keen, analytic mind, Rav Meir realized that justice lay with the first man: his arguments were sound and true; whereas the second man suffered from a slightly distorted view of the matter and from a bit of faulty logic.

Patiently, steadily and clearly, Rav Meir explained his line of reasoning to the second man, to make him understand why he was going to decide in favor of his opponent. The second man listened, and kept nodding his head — apparently to indicate that he was grasping Rav Meir's line of thought. Satisfied, the Rav finished his explanation and formally gave his verdict.

Now, however, the penny fell in the slot: this second man realized that he had indeed lost the case. So he launched into his side of the matter all over again: the facts as he saw them, the arguments that justified him. He made it very clear that not a word of Rav Meir's explanatory talk had penetrated his mind enough to convince him of anything.

"Right now," said Rav Meir to him, "you look to me like a Lavan [Laban] — the same type as the father-in-law of *Ya'akov avinu.* And I'll tell you why: When Lavan chased after Ya'akov and caught up with him, we read in the Torah that he came at Ya'akov with a big argument: Why did you sneak off without telling me that you were planning to leave me? (*B'réshis*/Genesis 31:27). Ya'akov explains the whole thing clearly: how he worked for this father-in-law of his with such devotion for so many years, suffering from the unbearable heat by day and from the bitter cold at night, bearing responsibility for every single sheep in the flock; and Lavan always tried to flim-flam him and avoid paying him . . . and so on (verses 38-41). Hence he had every right to take the family he raised at such heavy cost, and the flock that was rightfully his, and to go off with them; and he had good reason for not saying a word to this father-in-law of his.

"Lavan listens, and he knows Ya'akov is right. Yet what does he say to Ya'akov a minute later? 'The daughters are my daughters, and the children are my children, and the flocks are my flocks, and everything you see is mine!' (verse 43). He holds to his argument; he doesn't change a word of it. All that Ya'akov just told him so vehemently meant absolutely nothing to him. . . .

"And you, dear sir, are just the same: Justice is one thing for you, and your arguments are something else altogether: you won't budge from them."

****

One day he was asked for a decision on an interesting question. In a certain town, it was proposed or expected that the Jewish community council should allocate a total sum of money that would finance a worthy purpose of the devout, religious community; but as a result, an institution of the irreligious and anti-religious Jews would also benefit. Under the law of the *Shulchan Aruch*, was the council permitted to make the allocation?

The Rav pointed to a commentary on the Torah called *Da'as Z^e^kénim* (that was written by some of the scholars who created the commentaries of *tos^e^fos* on the Talmud). At the beginning of the Torah portion (*sidra*) titled *lech l^e^cha* there is a little allegory: In his orchard, someone had two trees. One grew fruit that produced an elixir of life, which would give new vigor and strength to anyone who drank it. The other grew poisonous fruit, that would kill anyone who ate it. The man refused to water the tree with the life-giving fruit, because then, as a result, the tree with the poisonous fruit would also be watered.

That parable, said Rav Meir, answered the question about the community council exactly. . . .

****

While he was in Sonik, it became almost painfully obvious that he had an innate hatred of money not justly earned, an abhorrence of ill-gotten gains. Most of all, he loathed any person who was obviously greedy for money, making no secret of his avarice, and who would hoard what he had like a miser, becoming increasingly unable to part with any of it.

Rav Meir simply could not understand such a creature. He would wonder: how could someone love money inordinately? Everyone has to be master of his money, so that he can have control of it — not the other way around. . . . And he would do his best to drive this lesson home to his pupils and to members of the community.

In support of this lesson, he would note a striking statement in the *talmud yerushalmi* (Yoma 1:1, 38c) that the second holy Temple in Jerusalem (the *beyss ha-mikdash*) was destroyed only because "they [the population at that time] loved money and possessions."

He also focused on the words in the Book of *D^e^varim* about the management of *ma'asér shéni* (the Second Tithe), which had to be taken to Jerusalem and eaten there. However, says the Torah, if Jerusalem is too far off and taking the food and drink there will be too much trouble, they may be sold, *v^e^tzarta ha-kessef b^e^yadecha*: "and you shall take the money compactly in your hand" (Deuteronomy 14:25), to convey it easily to Jerusalem and buy food and drink with it, and then that will be eaten there.

In those three Hebrew words, emphasized Rav Meir, the Torah gives a clear indication that a person's money should be in his grasp, so that he can do with it as he pleases, in accord with the Torah's wishes.

Thus he became known in Sonik for his scathing attitude toward niggardly types who would examine a coin three times before deciding to spend it.

Once, however, a Talmud learning group came to the end of its study of the tractate Bava Kamma, and as usual, the event was to be celebrated by a *si-yum* ("Completion"), marked by homiletic talk and suitable refreshments. And Rav Meir was invited to attend.

One person there decided to tease the Rav by citing the very end of the tractate. The Talmud deals there with items on one person's field that another comes and takes: is it considered robbery or not?

We read there: Said Rabbi Yehuda: With *k^e^sus* [cuscuta, a parasitic weed] and *chaziz* [young green blades that grow with grains, which can become hay — fodder], there is no robbery; in a place where they [the farmers] mind, it *is* a matter of robbery. Said Ravina: and Massa M^e^chassya is a place where they mind.

What the man implied by citing this was clear enough: Here the Talmud tells of people who minded strongly about little, insignificant things that grew of themselves — minded so strongly that if anyone came and took such items, they were guilty of robbery. The smallest thing was precious to them. And yet the Talmud does not look down on them in scorn!

With a smile Rav Meir replied, "Rashi comments on that spot on the map that it was a place of *b^e^heymos* — a bunch of animals."

****

Once he paid a visit to a neighboring little town, where he made the acquaintance of the local rabbi. The man was very learned and devout, but with all that, he found himself pulled and dragged into controversies with the townspeople, to remain helplessly embroiled.

At a small feast held by worthy, eminent members of the community, Rav Meir spoke: "Here," he said, "I've been able to understand at last a difficult teaching of the Midrash (P^e^sikta Zutrassa, B^e^midbar 19:2). The Midrash asks: What made Korach decide to quarrel with Moshe? (*B^e^midbar*/Numbers 16). And the reply is given: He saw the *para aduma* (the Red Heifer: there, 19).

"Our master teacher Moshe was the most humble of human beings (there, 12:3); he was King and Prophet to the people. And yet Korach went ahead to mount a quarrel and a mutiny against him. Why?

"Well, other Midrashim declare that we have no reason, no explanation, for the precept of the *para aduma*: For all the mitzvos of the Torah we can find an understandable reason or purpose — all except the Red Heifer (Midrash T^{e}hillim 9; B^{e}midbar Rabba 19:3, 8). What I believe the Midrash means, then, is that when Korach saw that the Torah ordained a mitzvah with no apparent reason that anyone could find, he decided that so could he go ahead and quarrel with Moshe, even organize a mutiny, for no reason that anyone could find.

"And this seems to hold true in every age and period: Just as we are baffled by the *para aduma*, so we remain baffled if we try to understand why any and every Korach in every generation simply must quarrel with a person who reaches, in some way, an aspect of *Moshe rabbénu* — why the Korach types just have to mount attacks against such a person.

"This seems to apply to community leaders in every generation; and this is evidently the reason behind the major quarrels in this *shtétl* of yours. . . ."

****

Sonik was "blessed" with a large number and variety of chassidic groups, with allegiance to different Rebbes of their past and their present. As he watched the ongoing life in the Jewish community, Rav Meir came to notice that one particular group tended to badger and harass a certain other group, and then, later on, it assumed the posture of an injured party, claiming that it was being made to suffer.

One day he found the opportunity to talk about this in public, and he began, "The Talmud tells us (*bavli*, Bava Kamma 30a): 'Whoever wants to be a *chassid*, let him observe the [legal] matters of *n^{e}zikin* (damages).' Well, now, why does the the Mishna of tractate Bava Kamma begin, 'There are four "fathers" (major categories or modes) of *n^{e}zikin* (damages)'? Surely it should have said *mazzikin* (damagers), since the Mishna deals there with entities that cause injury or damage to others?

"The answer is that many a damager, who causes others trouble, irritation or pain, can turn around later and wail and cry that he is really the injured party, that he has really suffered injury or pain. Hence the Talmud cautions us that if a person wants to be a *chassid* truly, let him observe matters of *n^{e}zikin*, damages, injuries, properly and honestly: which means that if he becomes a *mazzik* and causes others injury and pain, let him not go and camouflage himself with the cloak of a *nizzak*, an injured, suffering person. Let him admit and confess his guilt. Then he may have the right to call himself a *chassid.*"

16

On with education

With the public aspects of Jewish religious life in Sonik well under his control now, Rav Meir Shapiro could give his attention to the area that would always be his greatest concern: proper schooling for the young.

In his order of activities in Sonik, to set matters right in the community's public religious life, it had to come last. In his heart, an aching care for the education of the young would always hold the center.

Back in Glina, when he received their message that the heads of the Sonik community had decided unanimously to offer him its rabbinic office, his response had been clear: He was willing to accept the post, but only on one condition: the community must give him the right and the means to conduct a yeshiva. He explained that as he saw it, only a fully functioning, living yeshiva could give a community its *raison d'être* and justify its existence. And he made it clear then to the eminent Jews of Sonik that if this condition was not granted him, he would be quite happy to stay in modest, little Glina and continue conducting the yeshiva that he had erected there.

However larger and greater the Sonik community might be, however more prestige its Rabbi might enjoy, for him the prime consideration was to be able to function among his people as *av beyss din v^erosh mesivta*, "head of the religious court and head of the yeshiva" — like every important religious leader in the Poland of earlier times.

Needless to say, the condition was accepted; and now the time came for him to get to work.

If he had been able to establish his exemplary learning center in the small, fairly poor community of Glina (less than half the size of this community), no one who knew him could doubt for a moment that soon enough he would have an even finer and better school in Sonik. . . . And so it was.

It did not take long till he had a first-rate primary school going as a dynamic center for sound Jewish upbringing: both a *chéder* and a *talmud torah*. [With his drive for quality, Rav Meir did not hesitate to look for first-rate teachers for his classrooms and to hire them when he found them. The result was that wealthy and well-to-do parents also took to sending their children there; and since they could pay tuition fees, the funds available for running the school increased considerably. With the growth of the school's reputation, the time even came when a fair number of women from non-religious homes came to the Rav to plead and beg him, with tears in their eyes, to take in their children, even though they themselves kept nothing of the Torah. . . .]

Of even greater importance to him, however, was the *yeshiva g^evoha* that he established — a secondary school for older students — which, as in Glina, he named *B^eney Torah.*

As news of the yeshiva's existence spread, several dozen new young faces appeared in the town: older boys from beyond the boundaries of Sonik, drawn as by a magnet by the prospect of studying under the illustrious Rav Meir Shapiro. [Without proclamation or publicity, by pure word of mouth, they learned of the new project — and they arrived. They were indeed students of caliber, budding young scholars of first rank, the kind that Rav Meir eagerly wanted and sought.

[In a short time the number of "out-of-towners" was to grow from a handful to several hundred, from every level and kind of Jewry that could be found in Poland. Physically, the yeshiva would be typical, the same as most secondary schools for Torah study in Poland. There would be no single suitable structure to house everything and everyone. The youngsters would do their studying in various buildings, not all of them well suited for the purpose. They would sleep wherever lodgings could be found for them in the town. For lunch (the single good meal of the day) there was the system of "eating days" — in Yiddish, *ess'n teg*. A youngster would go to a family which had agreed to give one *yeshiva bochur* a meal on this day of the week.

[And yet they came, a handful that would grow to hundreds, drawn solely by the reputation of Rav Meir Shapiro as an unparalleled teacher, an amazing source of Jewish education with every fiber of his being. A rabbi of another town in Galicia sent his only son (a brilliant but slightly spoiled youngster), and in the accompanying letter the rabbi cited a single sentence from the Book of *T^ehillim,* daring to address words to Rav Meir that were originally meant for the Almighty: "Let your work be visible to your servants, and your glory to their sons" (Psalms 90:15).

[His reputation, that was to grow with the years, would rest not only on his consummate mastery of Talmud and his ability to teach it, not only on his deep fatherly interest in the intellectual and spiritual growth of his students, but another aspect as well: his unflagging concern for their material welfare — to do all he could about the food they ate, the clothes they wore, the places where they slept. He knew how important all this was: the better their physical state, the better they would study.]

****

On *Lag ba'Omer* in 5682 (May 16, 1922), the yeshiva formally began to function; and Rav Meir duly rose to address his incoming body of students, all who had gathered from near and far.

He began with a phrase in the Written Torah: "and Yisra'el camped there, facing the mountain" (*Sh^{e}mos*/Exodus 19:2). Then he cited the Midrash on it, which notes that both the noun and the verb are in the singular, not the plural: "This teaches us that they [the Israelites] camped there with one heart, as one man" (Mechilta on the verse).

"Thus the Torah tells us," said he, "that when the time came for the Torah to be given, all personal interests vanished; all individual, self-centered concerns disappeared. Every trace of hatred and animosity between one Israelite and another was wiped away. One purpose and goal united them in complete harmony, till they thought and felt as if with one heart: They were there in readiness to receive the Torah.

"In you, sitting here today and facing me, I discern that goal of Mount Sinai: the yearning aspiration to study and know our sacred Torah. And therefore we must engender in this yeshiva that same utter harmony, that same unity and singleness of heart among companions that should envelop you all and encompass you into one entity. In this way alone lies your only hope that you will receive the Torah as our people received it at Sinai, and that it will remain with you — so strongly, so thoroughly, that you will not be torn away and swept into any of the alien currents that are flowing so torrentially through our Jewish world today."

With sustained passion in his voice he continued: "The Talmud tells us (*bavli*, Gittin 36a) that when Rav had to sign a document, instead of writing his name he drew a fish.... Why? What did it mean?... From our sources in the Talmud, it appears that he lived a long life — over ninety years. The last of the *tanna'im* [the Sages of the Mishna] and the first of the *amora'im* [the Sages of the *g^emara*], he must have witnessed many periods of trouble, many kinds of turbulence, in the existence of our people, till his head turned grizzled and hoary with age.

"And yet he was never overcome. His Jewish soul was never conquered. To the end of his days he would not bend or yield. He remained the same Rav, with the same breathtaking, fascinating hues of the Torah in the persona and aura of his being. And when the world around him wanted to know the secret of his being, wanted to know from where he drew the iron strength in his character that endured with a consistency steeled against every adversity — he showed the world a fish.

"Do you remember Rabbi Akiva's fable about the fishes and the fox (*bavli*, B^erachos 61b)? As they were swimming close to the shore, frantically trying to escape the fisherman's net, they saw a fox standing at the river, and they asked him for help. That sly, cunning creature tried to trick them. Let them come up on the shore, he told them, and they would be safe. But the fish were too clever for the fox: 'If we face such great danger as the net pursues us, trying to capture us, how much worse will our fate be if we come up on dry land!'

"Those fish of Rabbi Akiva were meant to teach us of the great power of survival that our Torah Judaism gives us. When times in this land were relatively good, when the worm of heresy and apostasy was not yet festering and gnawing away everywhere at our sacred faith, when the atmosphere in which our Jewish people lived had not yet become so completely poisoned, the best forces and elements of our youth were uprooted from us. Whole sections of our people were torn alive from the living, pulsing heart of the Jewish body that lived in Torah study.

"How much greater is the danger that our people face today, when the fishermen's nets of heresy are spread wide to ensnare us at every step we take, offering us visions of glorious utopia if only we leave the Torah and follow the worldly paths to perdition that seem so tempting.

"Our task now, in our day, is to keep well in mind the fish of Rabbi Akiva's fable and the fish that Rav drew as his signature: to make sure that no matter what, we never leave the atmosphere of Torah learning as long as we can draw breath. . . .

"In the *talmud yerushalmi* (K^esubos 8:11, 32c) we learn that one of the early Sages, Shim'on ben Shettach, enacted a ruling that Jewish children should go to Jewish schools. In the *talmud bavli* (Shabbas 16b) we find another ruling by Shim'on ben Shettach: He decreed that the metal vessels of heathens, of non-Jews, should remain *ta-mey* (ritually unclean — 'polluted,' defiled), even if they were melted down and remade.

"What is the connection between the two? What single thought in his heart made this Sage of ancient times pronounce both rulings, that are so different and disparate?

"When a ritually unclean vessel becomes broken, and it undergoes some process to make it whole again — even if it is melted down and recast to make it as good as new — even then, said Shim'on ben Shettach, it is still *ta-mey*, polluted, unclean. So pernicious is the corruption in the basic material, in the very metal, that no process of renewal or repair can make a clean, usable vessel out of it. . . . And the same thing, as Shim'on ben Shettach saw it, held true in the molding and formation of a Jewish human being. The earliest layers, from the start of a child's education, must be molded and formed in purity.

"Evidently, until his time, children were brought up any which way, at home or in the street; and Shim'on ben Shettach saw that this was not good enough. Proper Jewish schools had to be built, and the children had to go there. . . .

"You are among the fortunate few who began your schooling in a proper *chéder*, avoiding the tragic flow of so many children out of life by the Torah and into other schools. We watch in despair how they become contaminated and defiled by the so-called culture of Western civilization, till they are beyond any hope of recovery and return into the sublime, Divine atmosphere of the Torah.

"By coming here to continue studying the Torah, you continue in the tradition of Shim'on ben Shettach, to which our people have held through the centuries: to become so thorougly imbued with the Torah, to have it so well baked deep into your very being that it can never evaporate out and disappear. In this way," he continued into his blazing conclusion, "you will become the fundamental stratum, the basic material of the future that will leave its mark forever in the ongoing formation and continuity of the Jewish people.

"My dear, cherished *talmidim*, our world looks at you with pride: for only with you, living completely and thoroughly with the Torah, does our people's sacred historic identity have a hope of survival and continuity.

"Be aware, then, of the great responsibility that lies upon you. Lift high the Torah's banner through your entire future. And this alone will take you through a life of good fortune forever."

Those were the words of a devoted father deeply concerned and involved in the education of his children; and they left an ineradicable impression in the young listeners' hearts. Under Rav Meir's dynamic direction, the studies flourished with vibrant life — till, eventually, the Yeshiva of Sonik gave the Jewish people, worldwide, a cadre of learned Talmud scholars and major Torah authorities.

****

One day, as he was in the midst of giving the young learners a *shi'ur*, a keen discourse on Talmudic matters, in walked the *rosh ha-kahal*, the official head of the Jewish community in Sonik — obviously a man of considerable wealth and importance. Wasting no time, he informed Rav Meir that there was a certain matter which he had to discuss with him. The Rav, however, had absolutely no wish to interrupt his *shi'ur* and let his whole flow of thought peter out and evaporate into nothing; and he indicated as much to his unexpected visitor. That gentleman was very resolute, though; he insisted that the matter was too important to be delayed: they had to talk it over at once.

"Very well," said Rav Meir. "Then come and have a meal with me."

"What?" asked the bewildered man. "Where should I go with you to have something to eat? And why right now?"

"The Talmud states: If anyone breaks off from words of Torah and gets himself involved in words of conversation, he is fed the burning embers of a broom fire (*bavli*, Chagiga 12b). So why should I eat alone? Come: we'll go and have that tasty dish together!"

****

Out of the blue, a youth of about seventeen once turned up at the yeshiva. He had come all the way from the depths of Lithuania, far away to the north, with a wish to enter the school and learn: for the school's fine reputation had come to his ears.

"Do you have any Talmudic learning?" Rav Meir asked him. "Have you studied any Talmud?"

"No, no; nothing at all. That is why I have come here: I want to learn it."

It transpired that the young fellow knew only how to read Hebrew and how to say the prayers. With this pitifully minimal background he had come to the esteemed Yeshiva of Sonik!

For obvious reasons the administrative staff wanted to send him off at once, without another thought. Not so Rav Meir. To him such a strong, simple desire to learn Talmud, however naïve it might be, was to be admired. He took pity on the boy and decided to accept him.

Well and good; but what of this young fellow's crying need for a background education? To this problem Rav Meir had his own unique solution: At his own expense he hired a private tutor for the youth, in addition to which he himself gave the eager pupil lessons. A born, gifted teacher, Rav Meir soon found this unusual pupil responding well, as his comprehension and understanding ripened and grew.

In a fairly short time the newcomer from Lithuania was able to change into a regular, normal student of the yeshiva. And then he shot ahead, to gain an enviable reputation as a prime Talmudist. So remarkable was his advance, in fact, that a time came eventually when the Rav had to go out traveling and be away from the yeshiva — and it was this young Lithuanian scholar whom he chose to give the *shi'urim* (the regular lectures in Talmud) to the students in his stead.

****

This would seem to have been indeed a basic characteristic of the Rav: to take young folk under his wing most unexpectedly, in a way that could lead to quite unexpected results. It was evidently something inborn and innate in his makeup, with which he simply lived and breathed.

If we might leap ahead once more, let us record here something that happened a few years later, after he left Sonik to become the Rabbi of the major city of Piotrkov. It was a small, insignificant event, which was eventually reported in Piotrkov's weekly Yiddish newspaper, *Unzer Lebn* ("Our Life"):

Since he was appointed the city's new spiritual leader, the time came when Rav Meir had to travel and ride into Piotrkov in state — in regal style. When he entered the city, he was accompanied by a few young adolescents clad in the traditional garb of religious folk in Galicia. Once they were well past the city gates, they took their leave of him.

The unusual clothes they were wearing — black plush velvet hats and long black coats (caftans, *kapotas*) — drew the attention of several people passing by. Curious, they asked the young folk just who they were.

What they received in reply was a brief biography of the youngsters, which these visitors told as they kept wiping the tears now and then from their eyes:

"We are from the Ukraine. Our parents were people of means: they were able to live a life of dignity and esteem — until one day a pogrom struck our town like a hurricane and destroyed every trace of its quiet, comfortable Jewish life. The attackers pillaged and robbed everywhere, mercilessly, with nothing and no one to stop them. Yet had that been all they did, we might have borne it and returned to some kind of normal life. Only, they wielded their bloody swords too, ferociously. With the savagery of wild animals they slaughtered whole families. A stream of blood was running through the town by the time they were done. . . .

"In that pogrom, that indescribable nightmare, our families were murdered: parents, brothers and sisters; and we remained young helpless orphans. So we became distributed among the farmers in the villages, to work for them. You see, on account of the war there was a big shortage of farm hands everywhere. For long months on end we slaved away then, homeless, scattered about among the Ukrainian farmers. Our situation was just horrible! Who knows how we might have ended up, if that wonderful Rabbi of Sonik hadn't worked with all his might to help us.

"He didn't rest till he was able to get us out of the hands of those wretched Ukrainian farmers. And then he set up an orphan home, where we could live like human beings. We were provided with everything we needed: food, drink, clothing — and a proper education. For those of us who had good heads there were first-rate Torah studies. The others were given training in a practical vocation, so that they could go out in time to earn a living.

"He was a true father to us. If not for him we would probably have died from hunger in absolute misery.

"So now, when the time came for him to leave our region and come to Piotrkov, in the heart of Poland, we decided to escort him as a mark of honor. . . ."

17

Into Agudas Yisra'el

[Thus far we have followed the career of Rav Meir Shapiro in the southern part of Poland called Galicia. For over a hundred years it had been a land of its own for the Jews who lived there — as good citizens of the Austrian empire. In the year 5575 (1815) at a historic conference known as the Congress of Vienna, the powers that ruled in Europe decided to divide Poland into three chunks, each to become the prized possession of a different monarch:

One small part to the northwest became an extension of Germany; Galicia (as noted) became a part of the Austrian empire; while the main portion of Poland went to enlarge the Russian hegemony. In consequence, the large Russian part would always be known as Congress Poland. Through the years this territory remained under the autocratic, tyrannical control of the tsars, who ruled over their empire like something between an eagle and a buzzard.

[In this main part of Poland (some three-fifths of the entire country) the Jews were fated to suffer an endless variety of bitter troubles and tribulations, as the Russian government under the tsars issued one harsh law after another, one vile decree after another, to "homogenize" this stubborn minority into good Russian subjects. Added to all that were the sporadic, intermittent pogroms, which occurred whenever local rulers and their good Polish subjects decided it was time to vent their frustrations and hatreds on the inevitable scapegoats.

[On the other hand, under the benign, fairly liberal rule of the Austrian monarchs, the Jews of Galicia were left relatively free and untroubled, to live their own peaceful lives, rather much as they pleased. And thus matters went, until the horrors of the First World War, that no one could have ever imagined, brought chaos and destruction, misery and ruin, to just about every community in every part of Poland.

[As noted in an earlier chapter, Austria and Russia fought on opposite sides in the war; and in consequence, the Russian army overrode and occupied Galicia, till the Austrian army was able to regain the territory. To the Jews in the land, whatever happened, the result was always the same:

more impoverishment and suffering, more lethal damage and danger to their lives.

[After the war, the Poles in all three parts of the divided country demanded to become again a sovereign independent nation in the land that should be theirs rightfully. To the Treaty of Versailles that followed the end of the war, Woodrow Wilson, the President of the United States, brought his famous Fourteen Points that were supposed to bring healing solutions to the bleeding problems of a ravaged Europe; and the thirteenth Point was a call to give the citizens of Poland what they wanted. The Treaty of Versailles proclaimed it and guaranteed it: That country must become a single national sovereign state.

[As the Polish people tried to form a national government, however, after over a century of division and subjugation, problems emerged. From the populace of Austrian Poland came a Leftist party with socialist ideals and policies; from Congress Poland came the Rightists, mainly the bourgeois men of means of the middle classes who had always lived in contentment under the Russian tsars and wanted to ensure their well-being.

[The core part of the Rightists was known as the Endecja (pronounced *endetzya*), and the heart of their policy was pure nationalism: Poland for the true, indigenous Poles (mainly themselves), and to hell with all the minorities — especially the Jews. They made no secret of their endemic, black-hearted antisemitism; they thought it one of their more attractive features. Their main interest, though, was to fight the Leftists and to make sure no other group gained too much power.

[As for any kind of economic policy and direction that might make sense and might work, in their blackened hearts and clouded brains they never found anything like that. Their only predictable response to the country's economic troubles was to follow the Russian policy of over a century: wherever, however possible, blame the Jews, oppress them, and squeeze out of them as much revenue as could be extracted.

[As the new, independent, laughably democratic Poland came into being, the secular, non-religious Jews felt very ready for it. During the war years they had sensed that some sort of new country could arise when the world conflict was over; and they were quick to organize their own political parties — mainly three:

[One of the three was the *Bund*, the Jewish labor party. Like all good Marxists, socialist or communist, they believed they could achieve all their goals, all the happiness they wanted, by being good, organized workers in Poland, true to the wondrous, magical, utopian ideals of Karl Marx, Lenin, *et al.* Of course they wanted nothing to do with the Torah: according to the gospels of Marx, religion was the opium of the masses, that could only impede and deaden their true progress to the *goldeneh glikn* of their true Utopia. Consequently, except for the label of *Jew*, there was absolutely nothing Jewish about them.

[Then there were the General Zionists. Their way to Utopia led to the barren grounds and pest-ridden marshes of the Holy Land, and they actually sent immigrants as they were able to. Those who came in the early waves of immigration did valuable work, though in their way, by their own lights (or darknesses), to help prepare the Homeland for their people. Unfortunately, their attitude to the Torah and those who believed in it varied between indifferent, negative, and downright hostile. (The Revisionists, a much smaller group, were merely a very militant, drum-thumping variation of this stronger party.)

[Finally, there were the Labor Zionists, which combined the blind but unquestionably glorious ideals of the first two: Of course the main idolatry should be the glorious labor of the working class; but since, unfortunately, they were Jews in an irrational world of *goyim*, their goal was to take the idolatry to the Holy Land.

[As socialists, they believed in the holy value of solid work. Large numbers migrated, and with fearless courage they put in the gruelling, backbreaking labor to prepare the Homeland physically for their people. As at least one veteran remembered long afterward, they would read certain chapters of *tanach* to draw the inspiration and energy they needed to keep going. It is doubtful if any other sector of Jewry would have done that fearful, tremendous task in that place, at that time. Regretfully, though, their attitude to the Torah and its devout adherents had to be hostile — on their entrenched ideological grounds.

[In Congress Poland, these heady winds and movements had begun among the Jews yet well before the First World War, when the territory was still under Russian rule. Thus, in the election of candidates to the Fourth Duma (the Russian legislative assembly), left-wing Jews rallied to the support of a socialist candidate who promised to fight for Jewish rights against the vile Polish nationalists. In response, the black-hearted, right-wing Polacks called for a boycott of all the Jews in the country, and the general hatred of this poor, downtrodden people increased.

[When the new, independent Poland arose after the war, the secular, non-religious Jewish parties continued to play politics and meddle in national affairs, out of a sense of their numerical and political power. Sooner or later, the only tangible result was a sharp increase in the bitter hatred of the Polacks toward all the Jews in the country, while deep conflicts and acrid controversies flared among the Jews themselves. In short, with no rudder of Torah to guide them, by and large the secular Jewish parties tended to make life ever more miserable for their plagued and buffeted people in Poland.]

****

[Thus the second and third decades of the twentieth century brought their bouts and storms of confusion, upheaval and misery to Poland; and for the devout, believing Jewry of Poland, which tried to contain its entire life within the Torah, there seemed only one way to try to protect themselves and their interests in their hostile, irrational world: to organize into a united party of its own — under a name that had originated among the Orthodox of Germany: *Agudas Yisra'el.*

[The idea of an international body of world Jewry loyal to the Torah arose rather naturally in Germany, with its tendency toward organization, order and united action. It was promulgated at a series of conferences in Hamburg in 5669 (1909), when the new, young movement was headed by Dr. Salomon Breuer, the Rabbi of Frankfort, and Isaac Halevy, the author of *Doros haRishonim*; and the first conclaves were attended by such important visitors as Rav Cha-yim Soloveitchik of Brisk (Brest-Litovsk) and the chassidic Rebbe of Ger.

[On the eleventh and twelfth of Sivan, 5672 (May 27-28, 1912), a historic conference was held in Kattowitz, Upper Silesia, in the part of Poland which belonged then to Germany. With some 300 delegates from four countries in attendance, the formation and the program of the World Organization of Agudas Yisra'el were proclaimed. In the years that followed, inasmuch as Rav Cha-yim of Brisk had participated fully in the formative stages, and now the movement had the solid backing of the Rebbe of Ger, a great part of Poland's Torah Jewry united under the banner and became one of the world organization's important branches.

After the war, if it was to survive and function to any effect, Agudas Yisra'el in Poland would have to become one of the Jewish political parties.]

From its inception, Rav Meir Shapiro took a keen interest in the rise and development of the movement in Poland, and in his heart he knew that he was for it. Soon enough he became a registered, "card-carrying member of the party." Knowing his people, however, he was not surprised to learn that not all devout, believing Jews welcomed the new organization. A good many opposed it strongly, holding that the Torah they studied and the mitzvos they kept were enough to take care of everything for them, and Jews should do nothing more in response to the world around them.

Well, a day came in the years before the war, at the time that his sole field of activity was the modest community of Glina, when a delegation from Warsaw arrived to see him. Evidently reports of his redoubtable achievements in the small town in Galicia had reached even the capital of Congress Poland: for the delegation came to offer him the rabbinate of Warsaw's Jewish community — a chance to rise meteorically in the Torah world! A small condition was attached to the offer, however: He would have to give up his membership in Agudas Yisra'el and have nothing further to do with it. . . .

[Strange were the vagaries in Jewish life. At a later time the heart and center of the national organization in Poland would be located in Warsaw; but now, by and large, the city's Jewish community opposed it — quite certainly, one must suppose, under the influence of *Mizrachi*, a smaller political movement of observant Jews in Poland, which held that the world of Torah should work with and within the Zionist camp.]

Rav Meir's answer was clear and decisive: He wished his visitors well, and he wished them farewell. They could go. The condition was fully, utterly, totally unacceptable.

Here he showed again a character trait that he had displayed in the past: Once he had an ideal in his mind, a goal worth struggling to attain, no consideration of personal gain, in either prestige or money, would have the slightest effect on him. And for him the welfare of Agudas Yisra'el had become important.

[What was it, however, that made him link his heart and mind so firmly to Agudas Yisra'el when it struggled to survive and grow in Poland, groping to find a clear way forward among a stricken, starving people ravaged by a world war? This is what he recalled in later years:

["When I traveled to Kattowitz in the year 5672 (1912), to take part in the conference for the sake of Heaven that Agudas Yisra'el convened, a hard question held my mind in its powerful grip, and I could find no peace: How in the world could a Talmudic genius like Rav Cha-yim of Brisk of Lithuania find common ground for discussion and debate with Reb Ya'akov Rosenheim of Frankfort, a major city of culture in Western Europe? The whole yearning and desire of Rav Cha-yim of Brisk is certainly to see our entire authentic Judaism contained within the confines of *halacha*, normative religious law; and just as certainly, Reb Ya'akov Rosenheim's outlook is altogether different! Again, what likelihood is there that a religious Jew from the materialistic land of America will acquiesce and agree to the views and ideas of a devout Jew from the mystic city of Safed? And who can understand how a modern, enlightened Jew from Holland can possibly join forces and go hand in hand with Polish Jews who carry so strongly their minutiae of Tradition?

["I am not ashamed to admit that even when my foot crossed the threshold of the convention hall, this strange, fascinating phenomenon was still beyond my comprehension; and the harder I tried to understand it, the more bewildered I became.

["*Nu,* What does a Jew like me do in such a case? I opened my valise and took out a volume of tractate B^{e}rachos, and I began sinking my mind into it, from the beginning. Having finished the Mishna text at the start, I went on to the opening question in the *g^{e}mara*: *tanna mé-heycha ka'i* — From which point of departure does the Sage in the Mishna come to take his stand? From which point in the Written Torah does the Sage begin with his question in the Mishna?

["Somehow, I found myself completely unable to understand the question. So I went searching through the commentaries for some sort of explanation: through Rashi, *tos^{e}fos*, Maharsha, Maharam of Lublin . . . and when I was done with everything they had written on it, I understood rightly what the *g^{e}mara* meant with its question.

["And then, all at once, the answer to my great perplexity flashed into my mind: We all know that the Mishna was created in the Holy Land, and the *g^{e}mara* in Babylonia; Rashi and *tos^{e}fos*, in France and Germany; Maharsha and Maharam, in the regions of Eastern Europe — and yet all focus and consider one single question: *tanna mé-heycha ka'i?* I understood it then: This was the secret of the existence of Agudas Yisra'el: a golden chain of unity that binds together the Jewish homeland, Lithuania, Germany, Holland, America and Poland."]

****

Eventually a direct and forceful attempt was made to persuade Rav Meir to become not merely a "card-carrying member" but an active, dynamic participant in the activities of the party — and he hesitated. Perhaps, he thought, it would be best not to take such a step: As an official "party man" he was certain to be attacked from all sides, while all sorts of people would try to get favors from him. Would it not be better, then, to keep well away from political party affairs?

Then he looked at the other side of the question: the wretched, tragic condition of so many Jews, the pathetic situation of his people in this dour land of misery; and the knowledge that beyond any doubt, only a well organized political party offered any hope of improving their lot.

Not feeling ready for a firm decision either way, he decided to wait for some sort of sign from Heaven that would show him clearly which way to choose. . . .

While the question kept percolating in his mind, the new political organization of Torah Jewry kept gathering momentum, and it soon began publishing its own newspaper, titled *Der Yid* ("The Jew"). It was a small, modest thing, that would not tax the party's meager resources too heavily. The secular, non-religious Jewish world had long been publishing *its* newspapers, more substantial and prestigious affairs: *Haïnt* and *Moment* [which tended to serve as brass trumpets for the political pied pipers who thought mere pipes and flutes not strong enough to lure the Jews of Poland down their secular paths to spiritual perdition].

Then Rav Meir noticed that shortly after *Der Yid* began appearing, the other two newspapers took to attacking Agudas Yisra'el in general and its new journal in particular. Evidently the large, powerful secular parties believed that all Polish Jewry should belong wholly and solely to them in political matters, and only they had a Divine right to produce journalism that could exert a major influence in molding public opinion.

Rav Meir reacted by writing an article in *Der Yid*, in which he reported a piquant little incident: Walking down the street one day, he came upon a man selling newspapers. "Do you have a copy of *Der Yid*?" he asked. "Why a *Yid*?" asked the street vendor. "Take an important paper with substance: *Haïnt* or *Moment*. My copies of *Der Yid* are still wrapped up and lying at the bottom of my pile."

"But I want *Der Yid*," replied Rav Meir; and the vendor had to go to the trouble of extracting one to sell him.

At a later opportunity the curious vendor asked Rav Meir, "Why do you insist on *Der Yid*, in preference to *Haïnt* and *Moment*?"

"I will tell you," the Rabbi of Glina replied: "The name *Haïnt* means 'today'; so it denotes only one day. The name *Moment* denotes likewise only about a minute, here and now. So both will soon disappear into the past. *Der Yid* means 'the Jew'; he may lie at the bottom of the pile, downtrodden and oppressed; but the Jew is eternal."

It was an apt and telling answer, that had come readily to his mind; yet as he thought about it, he reflected that this was also Heaven's answer to him: the Almighty's way of telling him to join Agudas Yisra'el with all his heart and to become fully involved.

This is what Rav Meir related in his article in *Der Yid* — the incident that made him ready at last to enter the front ranks of the fledgling organization.

While the war loomed and flared, however, his renown and authority were mainly in Galicia. There almost every Jew knew to tell something of his abilities and achievements — especially in Eastern Galicia. To go back in time to the years before the world conflict broke out, in the year 5674 (1914) a rabbinic conference was held in Lemberg, to establish a branch of Agudas Yisra'el in Eastern Galicia, as part of a world organization.

As the young Rabbi of Glina, Rav Meir participated, and he delivered an address. Such was the impression he made that he was immediately chosen to head the program of education which the conference wanted to launch. It was obvious that with his extraordinary abilities, he was the ideal man for the task.

About two years earlier, while Galicia remained a peaceful part of the Austrian empire, he was chosen to be a delegate from that part of Poland to the all-important conference at Kattowitz [mentioned above] at which the World Organization of Agudas Yisra'el came into being. And there he was chosen to be part of a delegation to negotiate with the government of Turkey on problems concerning the Holy Land. [Apparently, though, with the outbreak of the full, worldwide war, nothing could come of all the plans and hopes.]

Eventually, as the fires of battle raged and spread, it was noted in an earlier chapter how the Russian forces marched freely through Congress Poland and captured East Galicia. It was then that he set to work organizing a branch of Agudas Yisra'el there, as a means of providing possible help for the suffering Jewish victims of the conflict. Several conferences took place, at which he was the dynamic moving spirit and his word was generally decisive. [In fact, not one serious conference or assembly took place without his active, forceful presence.

[Nevertheless, he could only feel frustrated and hampered at every turn. Once the Austrian forces drove the Russians out of Poland, while the German armies were victorious in the northern parts, Germany and Austria (the united partners known as the Central Powers) decided to make a brand-new partition of Poland — just between the two of them. Thus Warsaw became the capital of the German part, while Galicia, with Lemberg (Lvov) as its main city, remained Austrian property. So once more Galicia remained separated by a frontier from the more northern parts of Poland.

[With the country ravaged and gutted by a war that was not of its making, Rav Meir saw only too clearly how little he could accomplish in an isolated Galicia, while the Jews struggled for sheer survival. He knew he would have to bide his time till, by Heaven's grace, all the cruel fighting would end. Then perhaps the rabbinate of all Poland could unite for meaningful action, most probably under the banner of Agudas Yisra'el.

[Meanwhile, during the war years, Dr. Pinchas Kohn worked energetically in Congress Poland to keep the organization alive and well. Since that was now under Germany's dominion in the new partition, and Dr. Kohn was a German national, he could act with a free hand — until the Allies defeated the Central Parties and the war ended. Then Poland could move at last toward freedom, independence, and unification.

[And religious Jewry moved too. In Adar I, 5679 (February 1919) a conference was held in Zurich, Switzerland, to infuse new life into the resuscitated World Organization of Agudas Yisra'el.

[In Poland, however, the situation was still far from peaceful. It was one thing to proclaim national independence. It was a very different matter to get all foreign armies to leave, define the boundaries, and establish some sort of government. For another two years or so, after peace came in Kislev 5679 (November 1918), a newly formed Polish army would have to fight on a variety of fronts, now against the Czechs, now against the Ukrainians, and finally against the Bolsheviks, once they were able, after the Russian revolution, to produce their armed forces and send them into battle.

[For the Jews of Poland, the nightmare they had known in the years of the World War went on, or perhaps even grew worse. Whoever was battling whom in any given place and time, Jews were always among the victims. They could suffer severe damage and injury inadvertently; they could be exploited ruthlessly for the benefit of the occupying troops; or, in the paranoid atmosphere that prevailed, they could be thought to have sided with the enemy — it never mattered, at any given time, who was the enemy and who had the thought — and there would be mindless and merciless punishment.

[From the start of the First World War, the Jews in Poland went through a period that can only be described as a reign of terror. Not till the civil calendar marked the year 1922 did enough peace and quiet come to the land as a whole to let the Jews give some thought to their situation of misery and to see what might be done about it.

[Necessarily, most attention was paid to the need for purely physical recovery. There were, however, great Torah authorities who gave thought to another overriding concern: What could be done to repair and rebuild a decent, orderly, regulated religious life for the people? It was high time to stop staring in frustration and dismay at the utter wreckage, the abysmal ruin that the years of war had also brought to the proper observance of the Jewish faith. It was time to take action.]

In the year 5682 (1922), then, great scholars and authorities in Polish Jewry convened a national rabbinic conference in Warsaw, from the twenty-third to the twenty-fifth of Tévés (January 23-25), to consider and decide how to set their "rabbinic house" in order. It was vital to "repair the fences" and mark the boundaries anew, so that the people would know clearly, once again, what was right and what was wrong, what was permitted and what forbidden.

Among the several hundred rabbinic personages who attended, Rav Meir Shapiro was most certainly there; and he was asked to deliver an opening address: a greeting in the name of the worthy rabbis of Galicia.

However renowned he was in his "home territory," now, at thirty-five, he was by no means well known in Warsaw: until the war's end, Congress Poland had been virtually foreign territory for him. As Rav Meir began to speak, however, it did not take the gathered delegates long to realize that before them stood a luminary of first rank who could bring a new radiance of hope into the country's Jewish life.

These are some of the words he spoke, which left his listeners in no doubt about the valor and the fervor in his heart; which conveyed his profound awareness of the destruction and ruin in the physical and spiritual life of Poland's Jewry — and of his readiness to give of himself without stint in a battle to help:

"Distinguished conference, honored assembly of our people's most learned Torah scholars:

" . . . You have come together here; and graven into your foreheads I see bloodied signs of a despairing pain, a frightful sense of shame and degradation. You have come with your hearts torn and your heads bowed.

"Yes, the hearts are torn: for which heart among us would not burst when we see how science flourishes, technology abounds with success, surrounded by friends and supporters, while our sacred Torah, the greatest science of all for us, lies isolate and desolate, abandoned and forgotten somewhere in a corner?

"And we have come with our heads bowed low, because an aching doubt also probes in our minds: Perhaps we are to blame?

"In the early years of the World War, the spiritual leaders in Galicia, myself included, founded an *Agudas Rabbonim Galitzo'im*, an Association of Galician Rabbis; but this Association never fulfilled its duties: because we knew that the living pulse of the Jewish people, its heart and soul, was in Congress Poland, and for such a long time we kept hoping and yearning, dreaming and longing for the historic hour when we could meet together, face to face, with all of you, the rabbinic personages of a united Poland. . . .

"As we are assembled here today, rabbinic representatives of Congress Poland, Galicia, Lithuania, Volhynia [Wohlin], pages of our history may mingle and blend together in our thoughts; whole time-slots and periods from past generations can pass before our eyes — periods in our annals when healthy, authentic Jewish life blossomed and flourished — periods when great, distinguished rabbinic conferences were held to establish authority — the times of the *va'ad arba arotzos* (the Council of Four Lands). . . . "

With undisguised bitterness in his voice, Rav Meir exclaimed, "Yet what kind of comparison can we make? How remote is that past from our present! Then all that was needed was to mend a few fences in religious practice, repair a few enactments to ensure compliance with the Torah's law, and then announce and proclaim the va'ad's decisions far and wide.

"And everywhere, in every Jew, the historic *va'ad arba arotzos* would find a listening ear and receptive heart that caught up with a holy tremor every single word, every declaration which came from those historic conventions. Following the example that our people set at Sinai, the Jews of Poland responded, *na'aseh v^enishma* (*Sh^emos*/Exodus 24:7): *We shall do, and we shall heed!*

"And what have we today? The prestige of the rabbinate is torn down and left fallen to the ground. Every coarse and pompous boor allows himself to give advice, as he attacks and scorns whatever we say.

"Today it will not be enough to announce and proclaim the mended fences and repaired enactments for our religion on which this conference has decided. We have to reach the very core of our people; we must get down and get through to the lowest levels; and then we must awaken the old sense of trust that our people once had toward us. We have to capture their interest and create new ears for them: a new receptivity, a new willingness to listen to what we say. . . .

"The spiritual leader of an individual community has neither the means nor the strength to protect and lead a rescued remnant as it struggles to survive almost a decade of wholesale conflict and slaughter; and for this reason we have all suffered frightfully. All we could do was to hide the anguish in our hearts. We let no outsider feel the appalling, abysmal tragedy that we lived through — what we felt in the innermost depths of the soul. Each and every leader of a flock sat in his own hidden corner and wept silently, trying to choke down the tears; but he sensed the hearts of his colleagues as well. He knew that if his spirit was throbbing and tossing about in the dreadful debacle that befell us, the heart of his colleague in the next town was most probably weeping too, privately, in isolation, over the catastrophic destruction in the lives of our people. . . .

"Many years from now, some future historian will probably come to write an account of our period. He will leaf through the printed and written records of all that happened in the social life of our people, in the various times that we lived through; and he will quite certainly pause to look for source material on what the rabbis of our generation did: What had their activities been? What did they accomplish?

"All he will find will be empty pages — pages upon pages filled with letters and words, but devoid of any content. He will find words, sentences, paragraphs that lie so lifeless on the page — unmoving — adding up to absolutely nothing! He will read of rabbis who achieved nothing!

"He will stare in amazement and disbelief — till his blood boils at their utter apathy and indifference; and he will pronounce over them a frightful verdict of condemnation: For how could he know then anything of their inner pain? How will he ever discern or detect the anguish that burned in the hidden chambers of a soul?

"Rage will be the verdict — a rage welling up from the Jewish people that will include, encompass and envelop all the spiritual leaders. All the rabbinic figures and personages will be placed under a fearful accusation of betrayal and desertion.

"How the heart trembles when such thoughts rise unbidden in our minds . . . How well you know it. And therefore your suffering is doubled and redoubled. . . . "

****

Such was the key part of the address that he gave at the convention, in a voice charged with electricity. Then, with his powerful gifts of rhetoric, he drew on the radiant, inspiring thoughts of the Talmudic Sages to rouse his colleagues, to animate in them an energy and will for noble deeds that might infuse new life into their depressed, downtrodden people.

As long as Poland had been partitioned and divided under separate ruling powers, no rabbinic figure in Congress Poland or Lithuania could have had any great knowledge or conception about Rav Meir. He was in Galicia, and that had been virtually a foreign country. Now, as he revealed his heartfelt, impassioned thoughts, his blazing hopes and dreams, he revealed to the eyes and ears of his listeners a singular image: a man of the people, whose knowledge, love and concern for them knew no bounds. As he spoke of Poland's Jewry, it was clear that his heart included everyone, of whatever type, of whatever class or level.

When he was done at last, when he left the rostrum and returned to his seat, not one individual in the assembly hall was left unmoved. To the last participant, he had shaken them. It was the first time they had encountered a *rav* with so much sincerity, with such an open, undisguised depth of concern for the tasks that lay ahead for them.

The result was that this relatively young Talmudic genius, only in his mid-thirties then, became recognized as a foremost spiritual leader of undeniable authority. In the dimension of acclaim and the acquisition of fame, it can be said that by the impact of his address, he "conquered" Congress Poland. From then on, his renown in the Polish Jewish world grew from day to day.

As if to give his "conquest" and spreading reputation extra force, it was at this convention that he was elected President of Agudas Yisra'el in that newly unified land.

18

Into party leadership

Until that historic convention in Warsaw, Agudas Yisra'el in Poland had been little more than a name and a hope. The bare truth was that in the calamitous war years it had been able to do hardly anything solidly meaningful. For the Jews who would readily join it, the mere effort to stay alive was taxing enough.

Thus Agudas Yisra'el was still in its early stages of development now, groping to find its way forward. Its main effect till then had been to draw down on its head the clamorous attacks of secular Jewish camps on all sides, on both the Right and the Left, as they tried to drown out its voice.

And the truth was that the organization had yet to find even a clear, consistent voice of its own, so that it might play a significant role in Poland's political life. In fact, it could be argued that it was in a dire situation then, actually on the verge of disintegration, facing a very real danger of total disappearance. In retrospect it can be seen that a man of Rav Meir's caliber, with his brilliance and multiple abilities, was vitally necessary, like a life-belt, to keep Agudas Yisra'el afloat and alive in the turbulent ocean of Polish Jewry's existence.

He had a position, though: he was the Rabbi of Sonik and the head of a reputable yeshiva; and as at least one student realized years later, everything Rav Meir did in making and heading that yeshiva was an exact "rehearsal" for his eventual establishment of the renowned *Yeshivas Chachmey Lublin* in his later years. The truth was that his ebullient, tempestuous mind and heart were filled already then with ideas and plans, dreams and hopes, for the resplendent Torah center which he envisioned.

And so, when the news was brought him — the "glad tidings" that he had been made President of Agudas Yisra'el — his first reaction was a most ardent wish to refuse the position. He pleaded and implored to be left free to pursue his own work for Torah education.

He reckoned, however, without the revered Rebbe of Ger, who saw the dire need for the organization more clearly, perhaps, than anyone else in Poland. That front-line spiritual leader went to Rav Meir personally and importuned and pleaded with him to accept the presidency. When Rav

Meir explained his fundamental reason for refusing, the Rebbe made him a promise in reply: Let Rav Meir take the helm of Agudas Yisra'el, and with Heaven's help, the Rebbe would give him major, massive support to realize his dream of the great, resplendent study center.

[There was another factor which influenced him. Well before he was asked to accept the position, he sensed which way the wind was blowing, and he wrote his great mentor and guide, the Rebbe of Tchortkov, describing the dilemma into which he would be put. The venerable spiritual leader replied that he himself should do nothing to seek the post or to encourage others to elect him; but if he found himself chosen, he should accept.]

There was nothing Rav Meir could now do but acquiesce; and thus Agudas Yisra'el in Poland had a president.

[As if to remove any last doubts whether he had made the right decision, he received a heartening message from the Chafetz Cha-yim: "May *haShem* (the Lord) strengthen you to do His work in the tents of Yefess (Jafeth) — a metaphor denoting the non-Jewish world — to gladden the hearts of all the despised and groaning Children of Israel. For who will stand by them to champion their cause, if not the great men of Torah in our time?"]

****

Having accepted, Rav Meir Shapiro set to work. Not for him were the gimmicks and trickery, the artifice and claptrap, in which other organizations excelled in their hunger for publicity. He had neither the time nor the stomach for empty phrases. He was a man of action, and he focused instinctively on the solid work that had to be done.

It became his task now to restructure the very essence of Agudas Yisra'el. With his extraordinary mind, trained in Talmudic analysis, he clarified the organization's philosophy and outlook. He delineated the pathways of truth that were open to the Jews of his time and place. With a cartographer's skill he mapped out directions in life for any Jew willing to believe in the Torah.

Once he had done this, a program of wide-ranging fruitful activity followed naturally. Under his direction the Agudah began to breathe and pulse with a new animation. It lived and surged with a content of inspiration that cast its effect into the people, ineluctably and inevitably — into the very streets and marketplaces of Jewish life.

Step by step Agudah's influence rose; it captured bastion after bastion in public life, till it became a powerful factor in Polish Jewry — a factor that could be neither mistaken nor ignored.

It was Rav Meir himself who pointed unerringly to the core reason behind his achievement with the organization. A journalist once asked him whether it was true that he was now in Agudas Yisra'el. "No," he replied: "I am not in the Agudah. The Agudah is in me!" And whoever knew him well could understand what he meant. Rav Meir had never made a secret of the idea that had formed in his earliest years, in the vividness of his imagination. When barely an adult in Tarnopol, he had been impelled by the idea to found a religious organization that he named *Tif'eress haDass*, which embodied quite exactly the tenets and the aspirations of Agudas Yisra'el.

Evidently, then, in one form or another the idea and the vision had always lain buried in his heart, never dying but quiescent; and from there, from within, it had kept speaking to him, driving and urging him on to great, lofty actions with but one goal in mind: to unite his people into a force that would perceive and acknowledge the Creator openly, "to do Your will with the whole heart!"

Everything stemmed for him from the single guiding thought which built the Agudah's foundations: to reach and inspire the faith-filled, believing, observant masses of Polish Jewry; to infuse a sense of ability and strength into them; and then to mold and weld them into one organization, with the confidence that they could stand firm, proof against all the destructive winds of foreign, radical ideology, against all the miasmas of glorious and gorgeous delusion, that tore with tornado force over the Jewish horizon.

So he worked with a sound integrity and a solid effectiveness for the purpose and principle of Agudas Yisra'el, as a major organization in adult Jewish life.

Nevertheless, either deliberately or unwittingly, his labors tended to aim toward a target of educational work, toward the most cherished goal of his life that would always be his greatest aspiration. He had a sense that to him had been entrusted the mission of rearing the next, growing generation of observant Jewry. With a bit of word play, one great Torah scholar once applied to him the name of an early Talmudic Sage, Avtalyon, in the sense of *av talyon*, "the father of the lambs" — the remarkable man remarkably chosen for the father's role in the education of the young.

Inevitably, when the youth-division of the organization came into being — *Tz*e*irey Agudas Yisra'el* — his heart went into that with all his sympathies. To the youngsters willing to unite under a banner of Torah, willing to declare openly and boldly their readiness to live by the Torah, went his very soul. To them he gave steady attention and encouragement, till it might be said, metaphorically, that he raised them "dandled on the Torah's knees."

It was only to be expected that the young would respond to Rav Meir as to a good father. Whatever he did, he seemed to penetrate naturally, easily, to the depths of their being. Whatever he produced for them was so naturally suited to their aptitudes and tastes.

Here is one typical fragment from a message of greeting that he gave to a conference of the youth organization:

". . . Has this not been the whole dream of my life? — to see a devoutly religious youth living and battling will all its energy for our faith! I hope and pray to find this yearning of mine realized in you, *Tz*e*irey Agudas Yisra'el.* If anyone asks you, 'What is this organization of yours, this *Tz*e*irey Agudas Yisra'el*'? — with these words can you answer him: *Tz*e*irey Agudas Yisra'el* is a Jewish religious legion, the equal of any national legion. Our homeland is the Torah. Our shield is our morality! . . ."

He gave time and thought as well to the ranks of religious labor which had united under the organization's banner as *Po'aley Agudas Yisra'el.* He delineated clearly for them their proper tasks in a life under the Torah; in plain words, he set out for them a clear, understandable life program. And this is how he ended his message: "The most beautiful day of my life will come when I see the Jewish laborer with one hand on the plow and a volume of Talmud in the other" — the achievement of a holy ideal in the dreams of age-old authentic Judaism: the fusion of Torah study and productive labor.

****

So he worked at the helm of the organization for years, serving, when the time came, as its delegate to the Polish parliament, the Sejm. Eventually, however, through his work as head of his outstanding yeshiva in Sonik, his dream of a world center of Torah study began to mature and move toward realization. Simultaneously, as the years called the 1920s moved steadily along on the civil calendar, he became aware that the need had grown less and less for him to remain as the President of Agudas Yisra'el. [Another man had come to the fore, to develop as a stalwart, capable leader: Rav Yitzchak (Itche) Meir Levin, the notable son-in-law of the Rebbe of Ger.]

Nor, late in the twenties, would he return to the Polish parliament for a second term as a delegate of his people when the present Sejm ended its time in office and new elections were held. By then the other deputies from Agudas Yisra'el had learned, with him at their head, how to function there as effectively as possible; and his duties in the Parliament had come to absorb too much of his time, with very little to show for it.

A good number of years later, then, he was to distance himself from these duties, to remain intensely involved only with Agudah's educational work; and there he achieved solid results that were truly amazing.

Now, however, having become the President of the organization, he was about to enter politics in a most unusual way that would be long remembered.

19

Into the Polish parliament

"In a time of peril, a *séfer torah* is even to be taken out into the town square!" So went a well-known saying in the "oral Torah" of the people, in the highly insecure, often irrational world of Poland's Jewry. [It was a dictum derived from the Mishna (Ta'anis 2:1) and Rambam's code of law (*hilchos ta'aniyos* 4:1). And wasn't it written in *Targum Shéni* on the Book of Esther (4:1) that this is what Mordechai did when Haman's decree of destruction faced the Jews?]

At any rate, this became the guiding principle of Rav Meir Shapiro in the third decade of the twentieth century when he threw himself into the maelstrom of Polish Jewish politics. It became his motto when suddenly, to the amazement of a great many, he entered the political arena.

For all he knew, perhaps he was the greatest Talmudist in Poland. He might have absorbed enough sacred learning to be considered the very embodiment of the Torah — a living *séfer torah.* But he knew this was no time to stay in the safe, cozy confines of his *beyss medrash*, studying away.

He could never bury his head in the sand before threatening danger. He could never ignore reality or blind himself to it. And he saw what a time of danger it was for the observant, believing Jews of Poland. When it came to organizational activities, the need for any mass action to exert influence or achieve any specific goal, the observant, Orthodox Jew was simply at the mercy of the secular, irreligious organizations. Everything in Jewish public life had to go under their patronage and power.

The reason for this was especially evident in the Sejm, the parliament of Poland which in effect had supreme power in the land. Whatever their numbers might be, whatever part of the Polish population they might comprise, the observant Jews had not a single representative there. [The Jewish deputies who were elected to the first Sejm, which held its first session on the tenth of Adar I, 5679 (February 10, 1919), were either assimilationists, whose main interest was to lose all trace of their Jewish identity, or Zionists of different varieties, all of whom generally detested the Orthodox.]

The consequences were virtually fatal for the entire range of Torah activities that Agudas Yisra'el inaugurated. The attitude of those in power, Jewish or Polish, was catastrophically derisive: Both the Agudah and its activities were regarded as completely puny and insignificant.

If the situation was to be altered, if Agudah's work was to have any useful, productive results, the need was imperative to have its own representation in the Sejm. It had to throw off the shackles that the secular Jews with political power could impose on it. For sheer survival, Agudas Yisra'el had to work free of any need for secular Jewish patronage or favor in order to exist and do its work. It had to liberate itself from the tragic plight of "exile within the Jewish exile," of being at the mercy of the secularists. Just as it had to breathe, so did Agudas Yisra'el have to be able to express its views, to cast its influence over public Jewish life.

[There was opposition enough that he had to face in his own ranks too: from leaders of devout, pious Jewry who stood adamantly against open united action outside the walls of the House of Study. Thus, one day, a chassidic Rebbe who strongly opposed the idea of Agudas Yisra'el asked him, "In our regular prayers three times a day, we have a paragraph in the *sh^e^moneh essrey* that begins with the word *v^e^lamalshinim*; and there we ask the Almighty to deal with all the evil people who act wickedly and brutally against us. Why isn't it enough for us to bear in mind all those rotten political groups when we say that paragraph, and leave the rest to our Father in Heaven?"

[Replied the Rav: "Directly after that paragraph comes the next section, that begins with the words *v^e^al ha-tzaddikim*, to pray the Almighty for great compassion and kindness toward our good, pious people. If our Jewish enemies would be content just to say that paragraph about the tzaddikim, bearing us in mind, it would certainly be enough for us just to say *v^e^lamalshinim* against them. But they go much further than that: they apply to us the kind of adjectives and titles that we ought to apply to them — and so, just saying *v^e^lamalshinim* is not enough."]

Ever a realist, Rav Meir saw what had to be done. In such a situation of dire danger, it was certainly not the time for a spiritual leader to sit enclosed in the confines of Talmudic study and *halacha*. He had to appear before the people and persuade and compel the Torah Jews to see the situation as he saw it.

Now it was time for masses of Jews, as they assembled to listen to him, to learn of his incredible earnestness, his passionate concern for their spiritual welfare, and for the welfare of their children in the future. He worked without stint, never sparing himself. With all his energy he spoke and spoke, to convince his listeners of the mighty need to send as many delegates as possible to the Polish parliament, who would speak *for them.*

Like some veteran campaigner long trained in politics, he "went on the trail" and "covered territory" as he traveled all over Poland. Nor would he sit in glory on a dais, ensconced in dignified silence while others spoke. He himself expounded and exhorted, to bestir his listeners and rouse them out of lethargic indifference. And he convinced his listeners of the critical urgency of the matter: the prime importance of having religious Jewry represented in the Sejm; the immeasurably good results that could come of it.

Aroused and annoyed by this approach of direct, effective actions, the secular camps looked for ways to deter him; and they did not hesitate to stoop to cheap theatrical tricks: At one occasion they sent in scoundrels to come at him, brandishing knives — evidently to frighten off both Rav Meir and his audience from daring to interfere in the secular Jews' sacred exclusive right to play Polish politics.

When Rav Meir saw the vulgar louts coming at him with their knives, he stood his ground and opened his frock coat and shirt, till he bared his chest. "Here!" he exclaimed. "Here is my heart. Plunge in your knives! Go ahead! My heart is clear, unsullied, undefiled. 'Political attacks' with weapons aren't going to frighten me away! We're used to them by now." And the hooligans dragged themselves off and disappeared.

One goal drove him now. He was determined to get observant, believing Jewry out of the clutches of their irreligious brethren, to make sure that Jews of the Torah would not have to live in "exile under fellow-Jews," subject to hostility and torment by the secularists who hated them. He wanted a loud, clear voice in the Sejm so that all their suffering and all their troubles could be heard there directly, not through the distorting throats of deputies from the powerful irreligious parties with not the slightest belief in the Torah and not the least concern for those who lived by this belief.

Whatever the cost in time and effort, he was determined that this sorry state of affairs must end. On the seats of the Sejm, he would do all he could to make sure that an imposing group of eminent representatives of Torah Jewry would be present — indeed in their long black coats, indeed with skull caps on their heads: rabbinic personages, in their own distinctive clothes. Let the very same human beings who functioned in the midst of the Jewish people, those who worked within Jewry to elevate its moral and spiritual life, also represent this people publicly in the national parliament.

The time had come for Torah Jews to lose all sense of self-doubt and self-negation, to throw off all feelings of shame and inferiority, and to send their rabbinic personages to the Sejm, with the simple statement, "These are our leaders! Accept them with the courtesy and dignity they deserve!"

His yeoman efforts brought results. The campaign was successful. On the fourteenth of Cheshvan, 5683 (November 5, 1922), elections to the second Sejm were held; and as a result, some five new delegates took their seats in the Polish parliament: religious Jewish representatives of eminence — including himself. Not one but two electoral districts voted him in. And thus, at last, Poland's masses of Torah Jewry could consider themselves politically independent, self-reliant, free from the baneful power of secular Jews who wished to think and live as non-Jews. To this extent, a new era had begun for them.

Proud and bold was his demeanor when he appeared in the Sejm; and the pride and esteem of Poland's Jewry could rise with him. One Polish official in the government remarked, "The personality of Rabbi Shapiro bestows great honor on the people of his faith."

And yet, if someone really knew Rav Meir and was familiar with the way his mind worked, he could realize soon enough that the role of deputy in the Sejm was not at all to the great Talmud scholar's liking. It hardly suited his basic nature and innate character.

If proof were needed, he provided it a number of years afterward, when, late in the twenties, the present parliament was dissolved and elections were announced for the next Sejm. To the surprise of many, Rav Meir refused to run again. Under no circumstances would he be a deputy in the next Sejm.

One of his colleagues among the rabbinic deputies asked him why: What was his reason? He replied, "Believe me: more than once I had a good cry when there was only the Almighty to see my tears. I wept before Him over the dozens of hours I had to spend there, in the Sejm, without a word of Torah study. Now," he went on to cite words from the Book of *Shir haShirim*, "I have taken off my robe; how shall I put it on? I have washed my feet clean; how shall I besmirch them? (Song of Songs 5:3). If I finally took off my political garb, if I was finally done with this whole parliamentary business, how can I put it on again? If I have finally gone clean out of it, how in the world can I ever go back?"

The plain truth was that when he had run for election the first time, when he plunged then altogether into the political maelstrom, it was not for the political gains *per se* (empty fame and honor), and certainly not for the financial benefits that a seat in the Sejm could bring. It was only for the specific results he wanted to achieve for the religious Jews; and for this, he saw clearly, his presence in the parliament was no longer vital.

"What?" he remarked once in later years, "a seat in the Sejm for personal benefit? I've ever and always been a *soney betza*, a hater of unearned money and filthy lucre. I could never understand people with a craving for money." In those later years, however, it was well known that he always went to ask for money and gather funds; and so he went on to explain: "Afterwards, when I built the *Yeshivas Chachmey Lublin*, every zloty and dollar became precious to me. So you will ask: Why such a radical change in me? Then let me tell you: My attitude to money *per se* is still the same; only, now I have a very different way of reckoning and calculating. When I look at money for a holy, religious purpose, I don't see the money at all. I see the end result of it. A hundred dollars means another *talmid* in the yeshiva, another ten pages of Talmud studied during the day, with the commentary of *tos^{e}fos*, the chanting sound of the study ringing through the air. And this is so dear to me — so very dear."

In the same way can his approach to politics be understood. Not in political gains did he measure the value of religious representatives in the Polish parliament; not in the ordinary political terms of how much shoddy intrigue could be conducted by these men behind the scenes — how many "shady deals" could they make with other deputies. He saw only one lofty purpose behind it: the possibility of benefit for the country's observant Jews. Jewish religious life in Poland might be able to move and advance in a new direction. Seen in this light, his political activity was veritably epoch-making.

****

Nothing that Rav Meir Shapiro did could ever be mediocre, ordinary or average; and this held true for his stay in the Polish parliament. His behavior there made an impact on everyone. For he allotted his time deftly, to an astonishing degree.

When the Sejm was in session and the time came to speak in defense of the Jews, to demand their rights, he spoke with valor as their official, empowered champion, sent to do what they wanted. One minute after the session closed, while other deputies strolled through the corridors to exchange idle gossip and vapid jokes, he reverted to his rabbinic role as a spiritual leader, and his mind became engrossed in a difficult point in Rambam's code of law on *kodashim*, about a holy animal offering in the *beyss ha-mikdash*, which currently he could not understand. When he saw the solution, whole and perfect, he could not contain himself. He called near one of the other rabbinic scholars who were serving in the Sejm and told him of the solution he had found in the Sejm to the difficulty in Rambam's law.

There is one poignant entry worth noting in the diary he kept while he served in the Polish parliament. First he writes with irony about the subjects that a deputy might or might not touch on when he held forth in the Sejm. Then he muses about the "great thoughts" of the Jewish and non-Jewish "gentlemen" in that "magisterial chamber" and their sense of triumph and superiority on account of their rights and privileges as deputies. And he concludes, "but when all is said and done, I wait for another location, another place . . . under other circumstances . . . the nation of Yisra'el, in the [Holy] Land of Yisra'el, before the Divine King of Yisra'el."

Such were the thoughts that animated Rav Meir's mind when he was in the Sejm. Not all the pride and glory, not all the hauteur and superiority in which other deputies reveled and wallowed, would ever intoxicate him. He dreamed, hoped and waited for another time entirely, when all the people who were truly, authentically Jewish would be settled in their own Divinely promised Land, before their own true, immortal King!

****

Like a magnet, Rav Meir drew the attention of a certain deputy named Professor Lutoslawski. [His title indicates that he received a higher Polish special education, in which he probably majored in the higher and lower forms of antisemitism. In addition, he was a clergyman, learned in the theology of the Polish Catholic church, which had specialized since time immemorial in blackhearted Jew-hatred and the incitement of pogroms. In the Sejm he specialized in clever, convoluted legislation to deprive the minorities of political and economic rights, as much as possible. This policy was dear to his heart, since the Jews, over one tenth of the population, were the country's largest minority.]

One day, this fine-feathered professor gained a particular unholy notoriety by proposing something special in one of his better speeches in the Sejm: that the national railroad service should provide special trains for the Jews — so that the holier, cleaner Polacks should not be contaminated by traveling together with them.

Once, feeling rather sprightly, the "clever" Professor accosted Rav Meir in the corridor. "Do you know, dear, honored Rabbi?" he began, "I have a brand-new idea for the Jews — how they can earn a living: They can skin dead dogs. Then they will have something to trade in."

"But won't their deputies protest about it in the Sejm?" asked Rav Meir coolly.

"Whose deputies?" wondered the witty Professor. "Do you mean the Jewish delegates?"

"No," replied the Rav smoothly: "the doggy, canine deputies. . . . "

"But does the honored Rabbi not know," persisted Lutoslawski, still pleased with his witty mind, "that in Schlesien there is an inscription over the city gates: *To Jews and dogs, entry is strictly forbidden*?"

"In that case," countered the Rav blandly, "neither of us would be able to go in. . . . "

The Professor stood still. Not a word came from his mouth. Only a flush spread over his cheeks, as though he had been slapped full across the face. Never had he expected such a sharp, razor-edged retort from a mere Jewish clergyman.

[It was noted that in general, Rav Meir's presence in the Sejm made a strong impression. Whether in formal speeches or amid informal conversation, he never hesitated to lash out at the Jew-haters, making them feel the rasp of his tongue and the flashing snap of his mind. The arrogant, self-assured antisemites in the Sejm began to fear him. They learned that in his presence it was best to curb their tongues and watch what they said about the Jews.]

****

One day, in the corridor, he was asked by a deputy from the Endecja [the major political party which made no secret of its Jew-hatred], "Tell me: why do you Jews eat hard-boiled eggs at your Pesach Séder?" [Evidently it was something he had heard of, and it piqued his curiosity.]

"It is the symbol of Jewish stubbornness," replied Rav Meir, "to tell the world and remind it that we are a stiff-necked people. Eggs are the only food which, the longer you cook them, the harder they get. The same is true of the Jews, that must cook and stew in all the troubles and hells we are given by our humane, civilized neighbors." Since the deputy from the Endecja was a good Polish Catholic, he must have known the "Old Testament" as part of his Holy Bible; and so, for good measure, Rav Meir added a sentence from the Book of *Sh^{e}mos*, about the Hebrews in ancient Egypt, when their troubles had begun: "But the more they [the Egyptians] afflicted them, the more they increased and proliferated" (Exodus 1:12).

****

[Of all that the new, independent Poland managed to produce in its first years of existence, the new Constitution was most important. It was something that the Western world virtually demanded, and the Poles knew it would have to look good. The world would watch and would read it with interest and care. And so, when the decent, morally upright Pilsudski, Poland's foremost leader, formed the first Sejm, its main task was just this: to draft a national Constitution.

[By the twenty-second of Tammuz, 5680 (July 8, 1920) a special commission had a draft ready, which it duly set before the first Sejm. On the thirteenth of Tishri, 5681 (September 25, 1920) serious debate on it began, and went on and on and on. On the seventh of Adar II (March 17, 1921), it was finally passed. Its "general spirit," noted one writer, "was liberal and democratic." It was described, in fact, as "one of the most democratic constitutions in the world." By its Article 110, citizens of national minorities (meaning Polish Jews also) were to have equality of civil and political rights, the freedom to have their own religious and social institutions and to practice their own religion. And religious discrimination of any kind was forbidden.

[What could be better? What could be sweeter? Secular Jews who set hopes of getting anywhere worthwhile in the new Poland could rejoice, believing all this was worth more than the paper it was printed on. Others, Rav Meir Shapiro among them, knew better.]

However, since the Poles thought the new Constitution a thing of beauty and joy, and it was a subject for endless discussion, one day Rav Meir was asked for his opinion. And he replied:

"The Polish constitution is very good. It gives its Jewish citizens all the legal rights and every kind of equality. The only misfortune with it will come with the interpretations. When a law has to be put into practice, when it has to be implemented, it has to be interpreted: Just where and how is the law to be carried out? I'm sure that thought will be given how to apply the laws stemming from the Constitution so that they will injure and harm the Jews."

Then he continued, "Let me give you an example from the Torah, to show you what I mean: At the beginning of the Book of *Sh^emos* we read of the edict that Par'o [Pharaoh] proclaimed: *Every male child that is born, into the River shall you throw it* (Exodus 1:22). He said 'every male child'; literally it should have meant all without exception, Egyptian babies as well as Hebrew. What actually happened? The Aramaic translation, Targum Onkelos, tells us right there what Par'o meant, as the Egyptians well understood. The Targum reads, 'Every male child that is born *to a Jew.*' Only those unfortunate children were to be drowned. The decree spoke of all, every newborn male without exception. Those who heard or read it knew how to understand it and apply it: Only Hebrew infants were meant. That was the purpose of the decree, and that was how it was obeyed."

[Was Rav Meir right in his devastating criticism about the future of the Constitution? Some fifteen years later, this is what one expert wrote: "But these provisions of the Constitution functioned even during the parliamentary regime in theory and not in fact. At no time was there any real desire of the government to put into practice the clauses establishing and securing the rights of the national minorities. Many old Russian laws discriminating against Jews, such as the one forbidding Jews to acquire land, remained in force in the face of the repeated protests of the Jewish deputies. Specific legislation to give effect to these provisions of the Constitution never achieved passage, despite the efforts of the Jews and of certain liberal groups" (Simon Segal, *The New Poland and the Jews*, p. 33).

[Around the same time, another expert (non-Jewish) noted, "Today the Jews — about one tenth of Poland's population — are the only minority in Poland for which the state has made no financial provision as to minority schools. It does not appear, therefore, that Article 10 of the minorities treaty has been respected" (R. L. Buell, *Poland: Key to Europe*, p. 285). The minorities treaty was older than the Constitution: It had been made between the newly arising independent Poland and the victorious Allied powers after the First World War, on the thirtieth of Sivan, 5679 (June 28, 1919), at Versailles.

[By the summer of 5685 (1925) it was obvious even to the obtuse minds that governed Poland that without heavy aid from the American government, their government was doomed — and there was no rational, helpful way in which the country's Jews could be blamed for it and forced to provide funds that they did not have. There was no choice but to go to Washington with their hands out and ask for a handout.

[The fine Polish governmental minds learned, however, that they faced a difficulty: In America there were Jews of influence and power, and they knew a bit too much about Poland's treatment of its Jewish minority. It was urgently necessary to do something, if their mission to America was not to be given the treatment it deserved, exactly equal to Poland's treatment of the Jews. So urgent discussions were held with the Jewish delegates in the Sejm, and as a result, "a few ordinances were issued to relieve the most pressing . . . difficulties of the Jewish population; but nothing really basic was enacted. Skrzynski — the Foreign Minister — went to the United States in July, 1925, and there gave to a group of American Jews positive assurances that the Polish government would faithfully implement the agreement arrived at with the Jewish deputies in the Sejm. . . . But . . . that government did not change its policy toward the Jews and did not fulfill the terms of its agreement" (Segal, p. 39); "no legislation was enacted to implement the agreement or change the political and economic situation of the Jews" (Buell, p. 286).

[We can assume that when the heads of government reached their agreement with the Jewish deputies in the Sejm, giving firm promises and assurances of new, wonderful laws and even taking tentative first steps that ultimately led to nothing, the non-religious delegates felt a wonderful glow of satisfaction and anticipation. We can assume that Rav Meir Shapiro evaluated the whole business much more accurately — just as a few years earlier he evaluated Poland's new, wonderful Constitution with devastating accuracy.]

****

One day, Rav Meir and a few other Jewish deputies were seated in a hotel lobby in Warsaw, immersed in a heated, peppery discussion, when a Jew walked in with pairs of stockings draped over his hand. He came over to them and presented a few pairs, hoping for a sale.

Rav Meir realized that this was a poor itinerant peddler, trying to eke out a living in this way, walking through the streets of the city. Without another thought, he took out a sizable sum of money and gave it to the man. In response, the peddler took the number of pairs for which the money had just paid, and he held them out to Rav Meir; but the Rav refused to take any.

"We don't need them," he explained. "You see, we are deputies in the Sejm, and our business is politics. Well, the business of politics is all lies — dishonesty and falsehood; and there is a clear teaching in the Talmud that *sheker eyn lo ragla-yim*, 'falsehood has no feet' (any lying story, anything deceitful, can never rest on a solid, stable footing that will hold: *Alfabéssa d'Rabbi Akiva*, beginning). So if there are no feet in our business, what use can we have for stockings?"

****

A Zionist delegate once challenged him inside the Sejm, "Tell me: How does a devout, religious man like you come to enter politics? You ought to be sitting in a *beyss medrash*, a House of Study, working away at your Talmudic learning; or you should be conducting a proper yeshiva. Politics is for people like us."

"This," replied the Rav, "is an old argument; there is nothing new about it. The Sages of the Talmud gave Elisha ben Avuya, the Torah instructor of Rabbi Meir, the derogatory, offensive nickname of *Achér* ('Other,' meaning 'something else'), because he left the Jewish faith and turned heretic. Well, in olden Talmudic times, *Achér* asked Rabbi Meir this kind of question. 'Turn back,' he told Rabbi Meir. 'I have measured the *t'chum* (the distance that may be walked on Shabbos), and you have already covered it. You may go no further.' But this can be understood to mean: So far may you go in your occupation and trade, and no further. What business have you to keep on after me and meddle in politics?

"Now, in the Talmudic passage, Rabbi Meir answers *Achér*, 'Let you yourself go back' — because Elisha ben Avuya had been Rabbi Meir's teacher in Talmud, and now he was out of the Jewish faith" (*bavli*, Chagiga 15a). "This, then, is what I tell you, dear Zionist deputy. Had you remained with your secular, worldly philosophy in your domain, enclosed in your own proper boundaries, I would have stayed in my proper modest world of *halacha* and would never have come barging into your political arena. But you Zionists came into my *beyss medrash* to capture Jewish souls. You came with your heresy and idolatry, with your pipe dreams of a golden future to be found in Herzl's vapors of illusion, to turn the heads of my yeshiva students and make them leave the tried and true pathways of our faith.

"So I went out to the marketplace to capture souls in your political arena. . . . As Rabbi Meir answered *Achér* long ago, in the same vein do I, named Rav Meir, answer you, an *Achér* of our generation. . . . "

****

Even in his greatest battles with his opponents, the secular Jewish parties, when he brought to bear all his fiery spirit and brilliant mind, he maintained a fund of forbearance and a capacity for proper, dignified debate in polemics. He attacked his opponents, but with elegance and courtesy. And for this, even his fiercest political enemies respected him. They fought on the battleground of politics, but personally, his anatagonists held him in esteem.

This brings to mind a rather interesting incident: In preparing for the elections to the second Sejm, Agudas Yisra'el and the General Zionists "made a deal" to form one technical bloc for the electoral listings. The two agreed to appear on the ballot as one political entity. [In each electoral district, a party had to gain a given minimum percent of the votes to send any delegates at all to the Sejm. In certain districts Agudah stood no chance of reaching the minimum percent, and without such an arrangement, all the votes for it would simply go down the drain. Between themselves, Agudah and the General Zionists worked out their own rules to decide which of the two would send how many delegates from each district, according to respective party strength. Thus the "deal" worked to Agudah's advantage, without doing it any harm.]

It brought Rav Meir, however, a pointed, almost nasty query from a leader of the *Bund*: "Tell me," he said when he happened to meet Rav Meir: "If you had to go and make a deal with another party for sound political reasons, why didn't you come and make the deal with us? You like the General Zionists better than us? They don't keep the Torah, and we don't keep the Torah; so why did you pick them?"

"The answer to your question," said Rav Meir calmly (with a touch of a smile), "is clearly indicated in the Mishna. Seventy years after the first holy Temple, the *beyss ha-mikdash*, was destroyed and our people went into exile, great masses of Jews went up from Babylonia to the Holy Land, to settle there and to build the second *beyss ha-mikdash*. So the Mishna states (Kiddushin 4:1): 'People with ten grades of lineage went up from Babylonia.' There were ten grades of genealogical records among them.

"Now, the list there in the Mishna starts off just fine: the first three categories are *kohén*, *lévi*, *yisra'él*. Many a person arriving could show from his family records that he was a *kohén*, a direct descendant of Moshe's brother Aharon in the male line; or that he was a member of the Tribe of Lévi; or at least a good ordinary member of the Jewish people, without any blemish or defect in his genealogical record.

"But then we find something astounding: the sixth category of the ten is *mamzérim*, bastards! With a genealogy like that, they are listed in the Mishna? — to indicate that they were worthy of 'honorable mention'?

"The answer is that if their heart moved them to leave behind a foreign land where their family line had become entrenched and secure for several generations, and to go resolutely to the Holy Land, even if they were bastards they deserved this honorable mention. . . . And this, my dear *Bundist*, is why I rate the General Zionists higher than you. They have their aspirations and ideals, and their people go up to the Land of Israel. . . . "

[He left it to his listener to work out for himself just what "Talmudic rating" Rav Meir assigned to the *Bund*, when it sought its utopia only in Poland, and only by the Communist pipe dreams of Lenin and Marx.]

****

In the city of Lemberg, Rav Meir went about campaigning vigorously, urging his listeners to vote for the bloc and not for Agudah, since the name

Agudas Yisra'el would not appear on the ballot. In the middle of an impassioned speech to a mass audience, a voice suddenly interrupted: "How can this be? Only yesterday you were battling the Zionists tooth and nail, and now you come campaigning for them? You want us to go and vote for them? Really?"

Rav Meir waited for the hubbub to subside, and he launched into his answer: "We find in the Torah that between Eyssav [Esau] and Ya'akov [Jacob] there was bitter enmity; at one point Eyssav planned to murder Ya'akov. Similarly, there was dire hatred between Yosef [Joseph] and his brothers; at one point they talked of killing him. In both cases, however, there was a reconciliation. Yet there was a profound difference between the two instances: After Eyssav made peace with Ya'akov and the enmity was lifted, Ya'akov did not become any true friend of Eyssav. Ya'akov became the ancestor of the Jewish people; he remained with the soul of a Jew. Eyssav remained a heathen. And we know the unalterable Talmudic dictum that Eyssav hates Ya'akov. The underlying enmity remains, alive and virulent, to this day.

"On the other hand, once they were reconciled, Yosef and his brothers remained friends for the rest of their lives: for all of them had the souls of Jews."

Thus Rav Meir Shapiro let his audience understand that a truce for cooperation with the General Zionists was necessary and helpful now, but no long-term reconciliation or partnership was intended.

****

At another time he was sitting with a group of General Zionist deputies, when one of them, failing to notice him well, began to give vent to his visceral ("gut") feelings about the members of Agudas Yisra'el, till his "gut feelings" brought him to the level of the gutter. Suddenly the penny dropped in the slot: he realized that right there was the President of this organization which he was describing in such abominable terms.

In his embarrassment, the man tried to mitigate his frightful social blunder by softening and countering the fulminating words of calumny he had let loose. "Well," he murmured finally, "it really can't be all that bad. After all, the Agudah folk are also Jews. . . . "

With an ironic smile Rav Meir shot back, "Our Talmudic Sages teach us that even if a Jew has sinned, he is still a Jew (*bavli*, Sanhedrin 44a). Woe to us if we have reached a level now where we say: Even if a Jew has *not* sinned, he is, nevertheless, still a Jew!"

****

Once he was in the Sejm and began fulfilling his duties as a deputy, it became clear to all how excellent he was in his new role, as if born to the task. A few of the other religious deputies then asked him why he would want to go on devoting his time and energy to Torah education, yeshivos, and so on. As they saw it, he ought to dedicate all his time and energy solely, exclusively, to politics. In that way, they believed, he could do more for the Jewish people in Poland.

Interestingly enough, exactly the opposite was asked of Rav Aharon Levin, the learned, distinguished Rabbi of Reisha (Rzeszow) who likewise served as a deputy in the Sejm, for well over a decade: How did such an oustanding rabbinic personage ever come to devote his time to politics? Surely he ought to busy himself only with Torah study and religious duties? A man like that should be training and bringing up fine young Talmudists, and so forth.

Well, Rav Meir replied: "We can find a hint of such questions and arguments in the Book of *T'hillim.* There we read, 'Then they envied Moshe [Moses] in the camp, [and] Aharon [Aaron] the holy one of *haShem* [the Lord]' (Psalms 106:16). In those ancient times, long ago, people badgered Moshe, demanding to know why he was 'in the camp': why he busied himself with the internal affairs of the Israelites instead of being their representative in the world; while they stormed at Aharon, asking why he was 'the holy one of *haShem*,' always engaged in holy matters, instead of being involved in politics."

****

To leap ahead in time once more, the time came when Rav Meir had to go to America for a long visit; and as it happened, the rather notorious or infamous Yitzchak Gruenebaum was in the States at the same time. [He was a veteran, long-standing deputy in the Sejm, as the anti-religious leader of the radical Labor Zionists in Poland, with a strange talent for meddling and messing about in Polish politics in a way that generally brought trouble for the Jews and bitter controversies in their ranks.]

A journalist who wrote for one of the most prominent Yiddish newspapers in America asked both for an interview, together, since they had something in common: experience in the Polish parliament as Jewish deputies.

The journalist focused on the welfare of the Jews in the "old country": the economic situation, the social and political conditions, the prospects for the future, and so on. Rav Meir showed an astonishing grasp of Poland's political situation in general, and of the Jewish situation in particular. His keen appraisal of the prospects for the future left the journalist in utter admiration: Here was a *rav*, a rabbinic personage known internationally for his Talmudic prowess, fully immersed then in his work for Torah education, laboring for the creation of a great yeshiva, and so on; and what the newspaper man heard in the interview was the mind of an absolutely brilliant political analyst, with a sound, clear awareness of Polish Jewry's situation.

When he wrote up the interview for the newspaper, the man added on a final paragraph: "That Rav Shapiro, the renowned Talmud scholar, is also a first-rate parliamentarian — of this everyone can become convinced; but whether Yitzchak Gruenebaum can equally succeed in finding a solution to a difficulty in some points in Rambam's code of law — that I greatly doubt. . . . "

****

[The second Sejm met for the last time on the twenty-fifth of Tishri, 5688 (October 21, 1927). Some five weeks later its term of office legally ended. About three months after that (March 4, 1928) elections were held for the third Sejm.]

As might be expected, Agudas Yisra'el put up Rav Meir's name among its delegates, whom it proposed to return to the Polish parliament. He, however, no longer had any desire for it — for one simple reason: There was an enormous, acrimonious conflict going on within his Jewish camp itself. Where there should have been cooperation and harmony, he found division and discord. And so he adamantly withdrew his candidacy.

In a letter to one of the leaders of the party's election campaign, he wrote: "Despite the wounds in my heart and the depressive gloom of my thoughts [in connection with the great conflict and discord within the party ranks] I will not go back on my word. . . . As regards myself, the electoral areas with which I am linked, I will not visit any more [to campaign there]. I will not ignore and forget the honor of my colleagues, but I will forgo and ignore my own."

In the same letter he touched on a tendency among his colleagues and associates to prefer non-Jews as candidates to represent them in the Sejm. [Evidently there was a belief that such people could do more in the Sejm for the Jews than Jewish deputies could; and patently Rav Meir disagreed.] This attitude he criticized sharply [and to support his position, he went to a teaching that the Talmud gives (*bavli*, Y^e^vamos 45b) on a sentence in the Written Torah: "You shall then appoint a king over you . . . from among your brethren . . . " (*D^e^varim*/Deuteronomy 17:15); and he wrote: "But I in my whole, simple faith will go in the way of our holy fathers [the Talmudic Sages] who said: *All* appointments [to positions of authority] that you make, let them be for none but [people] *from among your brethren*."

[Moreover, above all else, there was the accumulation of frustration and exasperation that he experienced in the world of Polish politics, in the atmosphere that prevailed particularly in the Sejm. It was painful for him to have to function as an equal among officials with small minds engaged in management of the public welfare. It hurt him to see them endlessly concerned with petty quarrels and narrow interests. And he had to fritter away precious time that he could have devoted to Torah study!

[When he firmly and finally refused to run for the third Sejm, he declaimed loud and clear, with great fervor, some well-known words from *Pirkey Avos* (6:5): "Do not crave after the royal table of kings: for your table is greater than theirs!"

[Thus, in the year 5688 (1928) he ended his formal political career, and in the third Sejm he was, if anything, conspicuous by his absence.]

20

Daf haYomi: the daily leaf

It sounded like something out of a dream when he first promulgated the idea that was to capture the devout, religious world of Jewish study. It was like an imagined thought out of another age, another realm, not at all suited to the "here and now" in which we lived.

Many responded with skepticism and doubt: Could such an inspiring vision become a solid reality? Just think of it: a whole Jewish world studying on the same day the same *daf* of Talmud: the two sides of the same sheet in the same tractate.

Was the idea not just something fanciful . . . quixotic? In New York, London, Paris, and Heaven knew where else, on a plain weekday, would people actually sit down and begin at the beginning: *Massechess* (tractate) *B*e*rachos*, page 2a? And would they really go on day after day, page by page, chapter after chapter, tractate after tractate?

Rav Meir's calculations were faultless. In this way the entire *talmud bavli* (Babylonian Talmud) would be covered in about seven years. And then the participants could share in a celebration worldwide, a *si-yum ha-shass*, a "completion of the Talmud," in which several hundred thousand had taken part.

The vision was luminous. It pointed to a way of noble, angelic attainment in a mundane world that knew suffering and sorrow enough. It offered a hope of Divine grace, as never before, to any generation that could make the idea a part of its ongoing reality.

Yet was it truly possible? Could the plan actually work? Would it not be the greatest pity even to divulge the idea in public, to begin talking about it? Would not every word spoken of it be a crime if it was bound to fail? Why make any effort for it if it might be doomed from the start?

Such were the gloomy doubts of the few associates with whom Rav Meir shared the epoch-making idea at the start. It rang in their ears like something legendary, spun out of pure fantasy. How could you grasp by the lapels a whole world of weak, tired, hard-working, struggling Jews and tell them, *Go, take a volume of Talmud in hand in your free time, and sit down to study*?

So at first he himself was quite uncertain whether the idea of the *daf ha-yomi* could succeed. He had no basis or cause to reckon that it would be transformed into a worldwide study program. He decided, then, to begin modestly with a smaller dream, that he especially cherished: to institute the program among the religious youth in Poland's Jewry. To the young, who could be reached by idealism and vision, he felt ready to bring the plan. With them he felt on more certain ground.

This is how he explained it to them:

"*T'filla b'tzibbur*, to do our praying with a whole group of at least ten, has a value of importance all its own, apart from the mitzvah of saying the prayers. In a group, the prayer attains a sonority and power that an individual can never match. How great and holy, then, will a *daf* of Talmud be when it ascends to Heaven from the study of hundreds of thousands, with Heaven's help? How immensely important will such a widespread learning program be!"

At one point in his writings he characterized it as "a most worthy *avoda* (Divine service and worship) before the ever-present Creator, blessed is He; a great source of spiritual satisfaction for the Almighty."

At another occasion he explained in a chassidic vein the sublime goal that the *daf ha-yomi* could achieve: "The Talmud mentions a number of creatures in the animal world which have each a gestation period (the time that the creature must spend in the womb after being engendered, till it is ready to be born) equal to the time that something in the plant world needs for its process of full growth. Thus, for example, small livestock have a gestation period of five months. Correspondingly, it takes a grapevine five months to produce its fruit.

"There is one notable exception to the rule, says the Talmud: the snake: 'For this wicked creature we have found nothing that corresponds' — nothing in the plant world that takes seven years till it yields its engendered product — the time a snake needs for its prenatal development (*bavli*, B'choros 8a).

"The snake, however, is not just another creature. The snake brings to mind the primal Serpent, which, as we know well, persuaded Chava [Eve] in the Garden of Eden to eat the fruit of the *étz ha-da'as,* the Tree of Knowledge of Good and Evil; she persuaded Adam in turn — the first man; and so the sentence of death came upon humankind.

"Thus the primal Serpent, a snake, brought all kinds of misfortune and disaster into the world. And if there is nothing in the realm of plant life with a growth-formation time of seven years, corresponding to the snake's gestation period, that means we can find nothing there with which we might counteract the fatal achievement of the primal Serpent.

"Now, however, we have something: By the plan of the *daf ha-yomi* we will study through the entire Talmud in [roughly] seven years. Our holy tradition teaches us that the Torah is our *étz ha-da'as*, our Tree of Knowledge that lets us gain eternal life in spite of the fate of death that awaits us all. With the *daf ha-yomi* we can produce a rare, precious fruit from our Tree of Knowledge once in seven years, and that can counteract and overcome the fatal poison which the hateful Serpent brought into the world. This fruit of our daily Talmud program can repair the damage and defect that came into the world when the fruit of the original Tree of Knowledge was eaten in Eden."

[Thus his creative mind worked to persuade the masses of his devout, believing people to enter the garden of Torah learning and study a *daf* of Talmud every day — a leaf, two sides of a sheet — so as to make a fresh, new green leaf grow every day on our Tree of eternal life. He offered the certainty that once in seven years the tree would produce a fruit which would counteract in the Hereafter the mortal experience of death on earth.]

Here are further thoughts that he expressed, as his keen, lively intellect kept finding ways to promote the great plan:

"This program will create a new, special common language among our people. Two Jews from different towns, or even from different countries, will meet. The knowledge they share in the *daf ha-yomi*, in the pages of Talmud currently being studied, will give them a common interest, a common ground on which to become acquainted and form a bond of cordial friendship directly. The days of a person's life, and even more, certain hours every day, will take on a new importance that will be felt. One will know that if he lets a day go by heedlessly, he loses two pages of Talmud — a *daf*, a leaf; and he loses his place in the steady journey to a Divine afterlife that *k'lal yisra'el*, our Jewish community, is making.

"He will know that he has fallen by the wayside, and no longer belongs to the great brotherhood that has prayed, 'Make us know to count our days rightly, and we will bring a heart of wisdom' (*T'hillim*/Psalms 90:12). For with the *daf ha-yomi* a person will learn to value a day of life, knowing what it can bring him and (conversely) how much he loses if he fails to do his measure of studying.

"The sense of obligation, the stable, ordered regularity of the program, will arouse a person and stimulate him to go on to further learning."

So went the lively ferment of ideas in Rav Meir's mind; for he simply could not stop hoping that a way would be found to proclaim the program and launch it properly.

[Evidently Heaven knew what was in his heart, and decided to help. On the third of Elul, 5683 (August 15, 1923), while the normal life of an evening went on in Austria's capital city of Vienna, the first *K^e^néssiya G^e^dola* ("Great Assembly") of Agudas Yisra'el opened at the glittering, elegant Royal Theater building, with some six hundred delegates in attendance. It was to last for ten days, with such luminaries in attendance as the venerable (octogenarian) Chafetz Cha-yim, the Rebbe of Tchortkov, and the Rebbe of Ger.]

Quite certainly the greatest Torah authorities were there — the most renowned Torah scholars and the revered masters of chassidic learning and piety — met to thrash through the various grave and weighty problems which faced the devout, religious Torah Jewry in the European diaspora.

Sitting and moving among them was the lively, effervescent Rav Meir Shapiro, still looking, irrepressibly, for ways to promote and launch his *daf ha-yomi* program. Then the *K^e^néssiya G^e^dola* went and did it for him: [It put him on the program, to present the idea at one of the formal, plenary sessions. And he spoke:

["If the entire observant community everywhere, in every single location where our observant Jews exist on this earth, will study the same *daf* of Talmud on the same day, could we have any better, more palpable expression of the sublime eternal unity between the Holy One, His Torah, and His people?

["How splendid this could be! A man goes sailing acros the sea, and he carries a volume of *Massechess* (tractate) *B^e^rachos*. He is traveling from the Holy Land to America — and every day, with the setting of the sun, he opens the volume and studies the *daf.* Arrived in New York, he enters a *beyss medrash*, and to his amazement, he finds a group at work on the very page of Talmud that he has reached in his own, private learning program. Delighted, he sits down and joins them. He gets into Talmudic debate with them, and is answered back. The net result is that the Glory of Heaven has become greater, mightier, more holy. . . .

["Suppose someone migrates from North America to Brazil, or to far-off Japan. Having arrived and settled, he will head for the *beyss medrash* and find there what? — a group busied with the very part of the Talmud that he has been studying. . . . Could we have a better way of bringing Jewish hearts into one great, harmonious union?

["Nor is this all. Until now, thanks to the traditions of the yeshiva world, where every young learner is initiated into the Talmud, only certain *massechtos* (tractates) are studied, while others are left to a select few learners and scholars to take pity on them and open their pages. The *daf ha-yomi* program will put all that right!

["One further point: Our youth, the future of the Jewish people — it is they above all who must begin this great mitzvah of 'wholesale study'!"

[The immediate response was purely "local" — but it was ardent enough to launch the program as though with rockets, to send it solidly into the entire Jewish world of learning.]

Amid thundering applause, the whole assembly of some 600 delegates rose and stood to attention; and with a fiery holy fervor, with emotions that rose to fever pitch, every single person there accepted the obligation to participate in the program, that was now scheduled to begin with the new Jewish year: on Rosh Hashana, 5684 (September 11, 1923).

At the same time, the convention called on Jewish communities everywhere to adopt the program and proclaim it throughout the world. And thus it was born into the world in a fortunate hour, to be welcomed and absorbed as an unforgettable and unrepealable part of religious Jewry's way in the world: a global daily study portion.

[After Rosh Hashana he received a letter from his only sister, who lived in a far-off village in the region of Bukovina, in northern Rumania, and knew nothing whatever of his activities: "On the night of Rosh Hashana," she wrote, "I had a dream: I saw you in Heaven, dear brother, surrounded by a great mass of angels with striking figures, all radiant as the light of the firmament; and you, my brother, were standing in their midst, your face alight like the sun in its full strength; and they were all smiling to you, as they thanked you and rejoiced with you very, very greatly. . . . Please, dearest brother: let me know what the dream means. . . . "

[The reactions to the program, as the Jewish people learned of it far and wide, made the meaning of the dream quite clear to him.] Echoes and reverberations of response came, clearly and unmistakably, from all over the world. There was no doubt that the idea took hold, and in scores of farflung locations on the planet Earth, people were taking to studying the Talmud almost in unison — the same leaf, the same two pages, in the same tractate. Only differences on the clock separated them in their timing. And quite certainly the numbers of participants kept growing as the new Jewish year progressed.

Interestingly enough, Rav Meir's acclaimed new program brought a new Jewish custom to very many people in the world of Torah. Ever since it became the generally accepted custom to read a portion of the Written Torah (the Pentateuch) every Shabbos at the prayer service, to complete the entire Torah in the course of a year, Jews everywhere dated their letters accordingly. Thus a letter written on a Tuesday would be dated, "the third day in the week of *parashas* thus and so." Now Rav Meir's simple yet radical idea produced a new custom among a sizable part of the Jewish population: People took to adding to the date in a letter the *daf* of Talmud that was to be studied that day.

Rav Meir had brought not only a new study program to the people, but also a new way of identifying the days. Having acquired long ago a way of dating by the Written Torah, Jewry now had a way by its Oral Torah.

****

When he saw how well the idea had been received, how vigorously the novel learning program was thriving, Rav Meir once gave a most interesting reason for it, in his own characteristic way:

We read in the Talmud that when man (Adam) was created, his body came from Babylonia, his head from the Land of Israel, and his limbs from other lands (*bavli*, Sanhedrin 38a-b). This indicates that if there is a wish that an important creation should exist as a permanent, stable entity and be able to spread through the world, everywhere — then the component parts that comprise the material for it should be varied, from a variety of places. Then it will belong everywhere; it will find its place everywhere.

Now let us have a look at a page in the Talmud: The Mishna, the earlier part, was given its redacted form by Rabbi Yehuda haNassi in the Land of

Israel; so we have a parallel to Adam, the first, created man: the head derived from the Land of Israel. Now, the *g*ᵉ*mara*, the later, major part of the Talmud, was put together by the Babylonian Sage Rav Ashi; again we have a parallel: Adam's body came from Babylonia.

Now further: the commentaries of Rashi and *tos*ᵉ*fos*, printed with the text, derive from France. After a tractate has ended in a printed volume of Talmud, we have more commentaries at the back: Rabbénu Ashér, from Germany; Rambam (Maimonides) on the Mishna, from Egypt; and then the last ones: Maharshal, Maharsha, Maharam, and so forth — all produced in Poland. Thus the analogy continues: Adam's limbs came from other lands.

Hence, said Rav Meir, when we read in the Torah's Book of *B*ᵉ*réshis*, "This is the book of the developments of man" (Genesis 5:1), we can apply the words to the Book of the Talmud: It was composed and formed in the same way as Adam. And that is the reason why the *daf ha-yomi* program has found such a warm reception everywhere among our devout people of the Torah: because there is such a close parallel between a page of Talmud and the human being that the Almighty created.

****

The success of the idea brought a series of other learning programs in its wake, either for people who would find two pages of Talmud a day too taxing or too time-consuming, or for those who wanted supplementary programs for daily learning. Soon enough printed schedules appeared for *mishna yomi*, ongoing sections or paragraphs of the Mishna for study day by day; *nach yomi*, a daily study portion in the *n*ᵉ*vi'im* (Prophets) and *k*ᵉ*suvim* (Writings); *mussar yomi*, a daily portion for study in the sacred literature of ethics and morality; and so on.

So the man who yearned and dreamed of achieving major goals in Torah education for his people found himself the founding father and the inspiration for a sound new system of continual daily study by old and young, amid the Jewish people worldwide. As a result, Torah education in general, in all its aspects, tended to become more orderly, more regular, more invigorating.

How did the creator of it all feel about this epoch-making development? How did he react to its astonishing success? This is what Rav Meir

Shapiro wrote in *Unzer Lebn* ("Our Life"), a Yiddish weekly which appeared in Piotrkov:

"The sublime idea of the *daf ha-yomi* hit home into the soul of our Jewry. With lightning speed, young and old joined its ranks of committed participants. . . . The enthusiasm that exists for the *daf ha-yomi* is the best guarantee for its continued, ongoing life. If a mission gains for itself the harmonious labor of the younger generation together with the efforts of the older, then it has an assurance that it will continue to exist. Should the youth keep its distance and stand away, then the mission is doomed: it will perish."

Yes: the creator of the idea knew he had hit his target: the living soul of authentic Judaism. That collective spirit had moved a bit too far from the Oral Torah. The regular study of Talmud had become a matter for certain individuals only. Exceptional minds alone busied themselves with it. The ordinary workaday Jew remained generally remote from it; and the more time that went by, the further away he found himself from whatever he had studied in his school years. And now the *daf ha-yomi* came and infused a new spirit of life into the collective soul of the ordinary folk.

People burdened, harried, busied all day with the need to earn a living became as scrupulous and careful about attending the daily study session as they were about putting on *t'fillin* in the morning and about fulfilling their duties of prayer every day. Their feeling about the *daf ha-yomi* became quite the same as toward the prayer services: No matter how occupied and involved a person was in his work, let him but be reminded that the daily session was about to begin in the *beyss medrash*, and he would drop everything and tear himself away to make sure he joined his group for the day's Talmud portion. A holy obligation it was — a daily ration of nourishing Oral Torah — and under no circumstances would he forego it.

So, with the passing days, the *daf ha-yomi* became absorbed deep into the heart of Torah Jewry; it became a daily duty that had to be fulfilled. Even a person who studied his Talmud regularly alone would join the great body of observant Jewry afterward in the group study, in order to strengthen and renew his existence as part of his people's collective soul, its spiritual wholeness.

****

[Gratified as he was to see this cherished idea of his proclaimed and welcomed in the world of learning, in his heart he retained his unique abiding interest in the youth of Poland's Torah world, and his unabating concern for their education. When the *K^e^néssiya G^e^dola* ended and passed into history, once he had some free time, he issued a letter of his own specifically to the youth, over and above the mighty call to adult Jewry that the *K^e^néssiya G^e^dola* had proclaimed; and this he sent out for mass distribution together with a small pocket calendar listing the specific pages of Talmud for every day in the coming years.

[This is what he wrote to them:

["Dear companions of the mind: The *K^e^néssiya G^e^dola* decided, at my suggestion, on the daily study period of the *daf ha-yomi*, and all have accepted this great decision with immense satisfaction and happiness; but you young folk, the choice element of our people, its future, have accepted it with something more: a holy enthusiasm.

["You should know then, dear children, that you have taken a great vow to the Divine King of the Jewish people, and you have to go ahead now to the holy task, to study yourselves and inspire others to it.

["Please accept from me the calendar of the daily study portions. You will see from it that our learning program began the first day of Rosh Hashana, 5684, and is due to reach completion, if Heaven wills it, on the Rosh Hashana (new year) for trees, the fifteenth of Sh^e^vat, 5691 (1931). . . .

["Beloved children of the Almighty, you have gone forth to the aid of *haShem* like valiant warriors. Go forward in this valor of yours! Carry high the banner of the Torah, because the eyes of the entire body of pious, devout Jewry are upon you. And may the Almighty be with you, O courageous warriors!"

[In later years he recalled at times: "When the idea of the *daf* blossomed in my mind, I wanted to present it to the *K^e^néssiya G^e^dola* as a program only for the young. I never dreamed that the Great Assembly would adopt it as a resolution for the elders of our people as well; but when I began to explain the great value of the program — the enormous effect if every day the same leaf of Talmud would be studied by tens of thousands and their voices rose to Heaven — then came the overwhelming surprise: It was unanimously agreed that the plan was good for all the Jews!" And he concluded with an apt quotation from his favorite source — the Talmud: "Fortunate is the generation in which the adults listen to the young ones" (*bavli*, Rosh Hashana 25b).

[Over seven years later, on the fifteenth of Sh^{e}vat, 5691 (February 2, 1931), the end of the Talmud was reached. It was time for observant Jewry all over the world to celebrate the first *si-yum ha-shass* ("Completion of the Talmud") in the *daf ha-yomi* program. Since his *Yeshivas Chachmey Lublin* was then in existence as one of the great study centers of world Jewry, the occasion was celebrated there with particular splendor. And Rav Meir spoke with great feeling, citing the Talmud again in his own brilliant fashion:

["Said Rabban Gamliel: Once I was traveling in a ship, and I saw a vessel that disintegrated, whereupon I was in grief over the Torah scholar who had been on it. Who was he? — Rabbi Akiva. Yet when I went up on dry land, he came and sat to deal with matters of *halacha* before me! 'My son,' I asked him, 'Who brought you up to safety from the watery deep?' He answered me, 'A *daf* (wooden board) of a ship came to me by chance, and as every wave came over me, I bowed my head to it" (*bavli*, Yevamos 121a).

[Having cited this small account from the Talmud, Rav Meir continued: "That time, in which those holy *tanna'im* (Sages of the Mishna) lived and functioned, is considered one of the most arduous periods in the life of the Jewish people. It was then that Jewry lost both its political independence and its spiritual center. The wicked, barbaric Roman empire decreed on our people cruel, unbearable edicts. And the great scholars of the nation assembled to formulate some plan and devise some way to rescue the nation from spiritual perdition — to save the ship of Jewry that was foundering and going down.

["Rabbi Akiva gathered masses and taught the Torah in public, in defiance of the decrees (*bavli*, B^{e}rachos 61b), till he succeeded in restoring the crown of the Torah to its former state of glory. Out of his steady teaching, 24,000 students came into being (*bavli*, Yevamos 62b).

["When Rabban Gamliel saw that despite everything, Torah Judaism remained on solid ground (completely out of danger from the foundering, disintegrating ship), he wanted to know Rabbi Akiva's great secret: How had he succeeded in raising up the welfare of the Torah from the fate of perdition? 'My son,' he asked him, 'who raised you up' out of the depths? By what secret method did you rise up and raise the spiritual level of the nation with you?

["To this Rabbi Akiva replied, 'A *daf* of a ship came to me by chance.' In the context of the story it means a wooden board; but today, in retrospect, we can understand it metaphorically: 'I found a simple remedy, to counter our dangerous ills: I instituted the mass study of the *daf ha-yomi.* By this means I raised high the welfare of the Torah and the prestige of Judaism and its people in entirety!"

[So spoke Rav Meir Shapiro at the completion of the first cycle of Talmud study by devout Jews around the world. When the time came for the ***kaddish d'rabbanan*** as required at any ***si-yum*** of a Talmud tractate, it was he who chanted it in the great Hall of Study and Prayer of ***Yeshivas Chachmey Lublin***, standing before the opened ***aron kodesh.*** And for some reason that no one could explain, that ***kaddish*** came from him with a great flow of tears, in which sorrow and joy mingled together. In retrospect it could only be surmised that through some prophetic awareness he had a foreboding that this was the only ***si-yum ha-shass*** he would celebrate. At the next one, over seven years later, he would no longer be alive.]

****

[All this, however, happened seven years later. Let us go back in time, then, to the ***K'néssiya G'dola***, which adopted his idea with such unexpected fervor and launched it to great success.]

Perhaps Rav Meir should have sat back, basking in the glory and honor of his achievement, as "the man of the *daf ha-yomi*"; he was never, though, a person who could rest on his laurels and let the grass grow under his feet.

The great conference of Agudas Yisra'el in Vienna lasted all of ten days, and that was more than enough time for him to have his brilliant conception of the *daf ha-yomi* accepted and proclaimed worldwide. However, with some 600 delegates gathered there to focus on the problems and concerns of observant Jewry, it was too good an opportunity to miss for further action.

And so he spared no effort on behalf of the other great conception that lived in his heart and mind with a dynamic energy of its own: the construction of a world yeshiva, an international learning center that would gather the very best minds, the most gifted intellects among the young who were committed to Torah study.

This vision too he communicated and shared with the delegates to the conference, making it clear that for him it was no vague, abstract plan, like a Spanish castle in the air. He assured everyone with whom he spoke that if given the means, he was ready to go to work and manage the project till it materialized into what he envisioned.

The entire assembly listened to these thoughts of his with great satisfaction. The delegates knew that when Rav Meir Shapiro undertook to convert a dream into reality, they could expect facts about matters accomplished.

And indeed he took his first steps toward the goal right there, at the conference: He tied the plan for the great yeshiva with the *daf ha-yomi* by issuing a further demand: He called on every person who studied the "daily leaf" of Talmud to mark the end of the day's learning by setting aside a *groshn*, a Polish penny, for the construction of the yeshiva.

Thus he launched his two great conceptions into the Jewish world linked together, the one to help the other, the both to float and soar through Jewry's spirit, as each gave strength to the other, toward one purpose and one goal: to lift the Jewish world out of its abysmal ignorance of its heritage, to raise high the prestige of the Torah, and to broaden and deepen its sacred study.

After the *K^enéssiya G^edola* became part of current history, the time came to evaluate and summarize it; and Rav Meir emerged as one of its most significant and commanding figures. To a large extent the entire conference came under his influence. In the oral and written impressions that delegates gave afterward, hardly anyone failed to note, with undisguised admiration, the spiritual stature of the man and the many facets of his prowess — especially the powerful gifts of oratory and eloquence that marked him whenever he addressed the convention.

21

Into Piotrkov: the festive welcome

The year 5684 (1924) moved along, till winter made way for spring, and time continued its course. And the community of Piotrkov started preparations for a great festivity all its own.

The Jewish quarter became a beehive of activity, as ideas were proffered, discussed and adopted, with one purpose in mind: how to make the reception of the new Rav of the city truly imposing and impressive. For the new spiritual leader of Piotrkov was to be the renowned Talmudic authority, Rav Meir Shapiro, at present still the rabbinic head of Sonik.

As the preparations got under way, the city became bathed in decorations, with gala ornamentation everywhere. A general holiday mood prevailed everywhere in the community, as day by day the activities of preparation gathered momentum.

Piotrkov was an old city, with a long, well-known history in Poland's annals. Geographically, it was very favorably situated, and it never failed to make a good impression on visitors. Among all the cities in the land, it stood out for its cleanliness and beauty; and it was noted for its handsome houses, of the kind generally found in large modern urban centers, as well as its picturesque alleyways, and so on.

Piotrkov had grown and taken form as the historic main city of a province. [In times of old it had been the setting for Poland's high court or tribunal; and hence the city was always called thereafter *Piotrkov Trybunalski.*] Moreover, as a rule, high-ranking government officials and ruling officers tended to make their homes there. The result was that care was always taken to provide the city with the best and most modern of installations, to enhance its appearance.

Many might have found it hard to believe that in a Polish region long under the rule of tsarist Russia, such a city could exist — built with a cosmopolitan sense of esthetics. And now, against this urban background, the elaborate adornments and decorations in the Jewish community made a most impressive and striking effect.

There was a sense of exultation in the air, a happiness that could not be measured. People were virtually, and sometimes literally, dancing in the streets. Without exaggeration, it could be stated that when two good friends happened to meet, as a rule they took to talking about the new rabbinic head that the community had acquired: what an illustrious scholar he was, renowned worldwide; what a remarkable speaker; and so pious and devout, and withal so modest and humble. Nor would they forget to mention the distinction he held as a deputy in the Sejm. And with all that, he was so warm and friendly, so accessible, so charming and congenial.

As likely as not, the two would agree, "How fortunate we are! How wonderful to have him for our Rav. Come, let us take a minute and do a little chassidic dance!"

So there they would be, dancing in the street; but not for long would they remain a mere duet. Here others come and join, and the circle grows wider. Still more join, and the circle spreads out further — till at last, almost naturally, inevitably, they allow themselves to move and cavort into the city square.

And why not? It was a day when the Jews of Piotrkov felt they were celebrating a *Simchas Torah* of their own, preparing to acquire a living Torah scroll, a singular individual who had absorbed so well, so brilliantly, the Torah that was Jewry's life-spirit.

There was a plain, ordinary Jew in Piotrkov who earned his living as a porter, by carrying heavy loads. He came into the steet laden with a weighty sack on his shoulders, so heavy that he almost collapsed under it. Then he heard the news: the new Rav was coming that very day, to take up his new position. On the instant the man set the sack down and began a sprightly impromptu chassidic dance. He had to give vent to his joyful feelings. . . .

A few other porters saw him, and they asked, "What happened to you? — you made so much money today that you've gone dancing in the street?"

"He is worth it," replied the man. "Our new Rav deserves it. What a good fortune is ours that we've been privileged to get such a precious, wonderful Rav." And with that he seized the other porters to start up a joyous circle for some sprightly dancing!

****

It was the first time in Jewish history that a community in Congress Poland took a person of eminence from Galicia to be its spiritual leader — and with so much regal pomp and tempestuous parading to boot. [Moreover, it was no secret that Rav Meir was incredibly young for a position of such eminence: only thirty-seven. One would have to go back a long way in the community records to find another brilliant master of Torah who had been chosen for the post at such an early age.]

In short, this was an event of glory in the Torah world, that was celebrated to the hilt.

Quite likely, Rav Meir himself had probably become accustomed to such displays of homage and emotion. In many communities he had received stirring welcomes when he came visiting. Most dramatic of all had been people's reactions when he had to leave Glina a few years earlier. Then some had thrown themselves in front of the wheels of his coach before it was due to start, and others had wept spasmodically, begging him not to abandon the little community. He still remembered how heartrending it had been.

That, however, might have been nothing so strange — perhaps only to be expected. After all, in that first rabbinic position he had stayed, except for interruptions on account of the war, for about ten years, displaying a devotion and concern for his flock that they would probably never find in anyone else.

However that may have been, this was his very first entry into Piotrkov, and the demonstrations of homage and esteem were beyond anything that could have been expected. [For longer than anyone could remember, it had been — and remained — a deplorable but accepted norm among the people in Eastern Europe that Jews in Congress Poland tended to look down in disdain at fellow-Jews in Galicia, considering them intellectually inferior, and so forth.] Yet here were fine, worthy Jews giving a spiritual leader from Galicia a spectacular welcome to the city's rabbinic post.

****

It began at the railroad station. Everybody seemed to be there — men, women and children — dressed in their *yom tov* clothing, all gathered to await the incoming train. A great many delegations, representatives of the entire Jewish populace, rode out to meet the train en route and accompany it in. Within the train, Rav Meir came with an escort of eminent political and rabbinic figures. As the turning wheels brought the train at last into the station, there was a shout from the car where Rav Meir sat:

"Precious Jews of Piotrkov, the whole community of Lodz envies you your great Rabbi!"

The city police and military guard offered the services of their musical band, to enliven the occasion in its own way; but the Rav asked leave to decline the offer, because it was the time of *s^efiras ha'omer* (the Counting of the Omer) between the festivals of Pesach and Shavu'os — a rather mournful period on the Jewish calendar, when observant Jews try to avoid hearing joyful music.

With the entire community in escort, with huge lanterns providing illumination, the Rav rode through the majestic city gates directly to the great synagogue of Piotrkov; and there, in the large, imposing *shul*, he gave his inaugural *d^erasha*. These are the words he spoke which left the deepest impression:

"Dear Jews of Piotrkov," he exclaimed in the middle of his spellbinding address, "what I ask of you is recognition. Accept me as your spiritual head and rabbinic authority. And what you can expect from me in return is a readiness to give of myself unsparingly. Where a matter of religious observance and law is involved, I will stand firm as iron. But at the same time I intend to be a faithful companion and father to everyone, in words and in deeds, wherever and however it will be in my power. . . . "

Special editions of the local Yiddish newspapers appeared, to bid him welcome to the city; and each devoted lengthy articles to him. In one article its author wrote, "A golden age is beginning now in our Jewish life." In the words of another journalist, "A radiant sun will now send its rays across the horizon of Piotrkov"; and so on.

****

Among his early acts of ceremony was a formal visit that he made to one of Piotrkov's most eminent Jewish residents, when that gentleman arranged a courtly reception to receive him. It may have been there, or perhaps at another such reception that was arranged in his honor soon after his arrival, that he aired a light-hearted thought, as he began developing his own brand of friendly, easy-going relations with the people he met:

"You must surely be wondering," he said to the little gathering, "how a fairly young man like myself" [he was only thirty-seven] "has come to be the Rav of such a major city as Piotrkov. Well, I am going to explain it to you; but first we need to understand why as a rule a young learned scholar takes the rabbinic post in a small townlet, while an older man of learning is appointed to the position in a large city. Logically, it should be the other way around: A young man generally has his robust youthful energy, and so he has the strength for the tasks he would have to face in a large city. For an older person, as his strength ebbs and wanes, surely a modest little community would be appropriate?

"We have a teaching in our Tradition, however" [derived from *yerushalmi*, Bikkurim 3:3, 68c] "that when a person is appointed a *parnas*, the managing head of a community, all his transgressions are forgiven him. Whatever sins, misdeeds or wrongdoings there may be on his Heavenly record, his slate is wiped clean. Well, an older man probably has more sins on his record than a younger man; so he needs the heavy burden of the rabbinate in a big city to earn him full forgiveness. For a young man, with a small number of sins to account for, a small, unburdensome position should be enough to get him completely forgiven.

"Now I," concluded Rav Meir, "with all the many sins I have to my discredit, I must have a really large city's community to earn me any serious degree of forgiveness. So I had to come to Piotrkov. . . . Still, though," he went on with a disarming smile, "we see that it is the wicked folk, with heavy sins in their life, who really succeed in this world. For this reason I've left over some of my sins on my record, not forgiven, so that I too can do well in this world. . . ."

****

At the early reception in his honor, mentioned above, in the midst of the lively talking that developed, he was unexpectedly asked a flippant question by a rather witty *moreh tzedek* (a local rabbi and spiritual guide): "We know by our tradition that in the ultimate, distant future, when the great Resurrection comes, all the *rabbonim* are certain to return to life, through the merit they gained with the Torah. Then all the spiritual leaders in the history of Piotrkov, all who were here before, will return here with you, honored Rabbi. What will you do then about a rabbinic position here?"

With a light smile Rav Meir replied, "Their communities, their flocks whom they led, will return to life with them. Then each *rav* will have his flock, and I will have mine."

"But dear honored Rabbi, what will you do if our city's early spiritual leaders return because they were men of great learning and deep piety, but their flocks whom they led won't make it? What will happen then?"

"A *rav*," he retorted, "who will not have the power in the Hereafter to bring his community back to life with him was no proper *rav* in the first place!"

In this brief conversation he gave the clue to his forthcoming rabbinic work in Piotrkov, and the yardstick by which he would measure it. This was to be his guiding principle: that a rabbinic leader must be able to elevate his community with him to a proper level of religiosity; and whoever lacked the power to do so should not be reckoned among Jewry's spiritual leaders. So did he conceive a rabbi's task; and it was in this spirit that he set to work.

That same evening, though, he discovered that if he was eager to take on the tasks which awaited him in this large historic community, the people were just as eager to see him and get to know something about him. As the formal reception was going on at the home of his worthy, eminent host, a huge throng gathered outside, demanding to have a look at him. According to the Midrash (Mechilta on *Sh^emos*/Exodus 19:9), the Israelites at Sinai exclaimed, "It is our wish to see our Monarch!" The same kind of outcry came from the mass gathering.

He went out to the balcony and saw thousands of faces looking up at him. With no other choice, he gave another heartfelt, heartwarming sermonic talk; and at last, they went home satisfied.

22

Back to rabbinic duties

The days of festivity and exultation ended; and then it was time for work. Piotrkov was a major city, and the rabbinic tasks were certainly larger in scope and size; but essentially they were quite like what he had encountered in the past, first in Glina and then in Sonik: serious neglect in the communal areas of religious observance, serious breaches in the fences of public compliance with religious law.

What struck him most forcibly, however, was the frightful absence of young folk immersed in Torah study: not even a tiny nucleus of decent, dedicated students! A baleful ignorance of proper Jewish observance prevailed. And to match this, the Leftist elements in the Jewish population were flourishing and growing in strength. Taking full advantage of the tragic ignorance of the Torah in the city, the radical organizations came preaching and flaunting their doctrines of Jewish salvation, to be achieved by physical labor alone, with a total rejection of the Torah, either in Poland (so the *Bund*) or in the Holy Land (so the radical Leftist Zionists). And they made tragic destructive inroads in the life of the Jewish community.

Rav Meir studied the elements in Piotrkov that remained loyal to the Torah; what he saw was a lifeless body left without skin or flesh — a skeleton without any signs of healthy life.

In his own typical way, he began at the beginning: to set up and develop elementary, primary schools that could take in children not only from the more prosperous families but from the poor, indigent people as well. Let the schools begin rearing religious, observant children, and soon there would be a devout youth movement in the community, learned and loyal to the Torah. Let *his schools* absorb and educate the youngsters, instead of the non-religious, irreligious, and anti-religious schools that were flourishing now, thanks to the *Bund*, the Zionists, and the *maskilim* (the "enlightened intellectuals" who were too enlightened to need the Torah) — and in a few years he would have prime student material for a secondary school — a yeshiva worthy of the name.

Then he could even look ahead to the establishment of *shtiblach* in due time: small-scale, intimate Houses of Prayer and Study for young *chassidim*, devoted followers of certain great Rebbes.

As he set to work in earnest, it was the *Bund* that declared full, open war against him. The leaders of that deluded organization, entirely and permanently intoxicated with the communist gospels of Karl Marx, blasted out at the very idea of founding "outmoded" schools of the *chéder* type, that had been in vogue centuries ago. Of what good could such schools be, they screamed, in the "modern world" of the twentieth century? How could people teach something so foolish and irrelevant as this ancient thing they called Torah?

Not content with propaganda, the *Bund* leaders headed straight for the "jugular vein" of this "dire enemy" of theirs: They demanded of the community council, in charge of sharing out funds for all Jewish activities in the city, secular and religious, to make drastic cuts in the money it allocated for the schools for boys called *Talmud Torah*, and those for girls named *Beyss Ya'akov*.

To their surprise, the deluded, foggy *Bund* leaders met more than their match in Rav Meir Shapiro. In person he led the battle to defeat any attempt to cut the funds for religious schools. [By any standard, he was no ordinary, run-of-the-mill community leader. This was the President of Agudas Yisra'el in Poland, and a delegate of religious Jewry in the Polish parliament. Few could equal him in fighting spirit or in moving eloquence. So he made short work of all the *Bund*'s shrill bellowing and hysterical yiping.]

Now he set to work to do once more what he had done years before in his other communities: He built up a model yeshiva and stood at its head. He served as its administrator, he gave the most notable, outstanding *shi'urim* (Talmud lessons and lectures) during the week, and he became the main, general educator of the students, concerned with all their needs, so that they could study properly.

[Actually, in Piotrkov he had no need to start entirely from nothing — far from it. When the First World War was over and the dust settled from the Bolshevik Revolution over the border, in Russia, the greater part of Russia's Torah Jewry migrated into Poland; and as the Bolsheviks acted with satanic energy and purpose to destroy the Jewish religion and Torah education in the newly created Soviet Union, the young, burgeoning organization of Agudas Yisra'el in Poland reacted by establishing a network of primary (elementary) schools under the name of *Y'sodey Torah*.

One of the first of these schools came to life in Piotrkov, at 81 Pilsudski Street, near the railroad station where people took the train to Lodz. In time the building became too small for all the pupils who were able and willing to attend it, and the school moved to larger quarters in Trybunalski Square.

[A good many years earlier, the legendary Sarah Schenirer of Cracow had paid a visit to Piotrkov and found a receptive community ready to listen and respond when she called for the establishment of a *Beyss Ya'akov* school for girls. Members of Agudas Yisra'el and *Po'aley Agudas Yisra'el* readily formed a committee, and in a short while they bought an apartment in the heart of the Jewish quarter. There the school began with two classes (grades), taught by a graduate of Sarah Schenirer's own, original seminary in Cracow. In time the number of grades grew to eight, as the staff was enlarged and the pupils who attended numbered about a hundred and fifty.

[There was not the slightest doubt that the school filled a major, aching void in the city's Jewish life. Without it, young impressionable girls could only have been carried away headlong into the heady windstreams of the secular Jewish world, to lose all contact with the pathways of authentic Torah Judaism that wove and continued the strong bonds of ongoing Jewish family life.

[Once Rav Meir assumed the mantle of rabbinic authority, he infused a new dynamism in the community to promote his kind of education for both young boys and girls. He worked indefatigably for more schools, more classrooms, more pupils. . . . Yet his main interest focused, inevitably, on the boys in the community of high school (secondary school) age — the graduates of *Y'sodey Torah*, and so on.

[Traditionally, any would-be scholar among these youngsters who wanted to continue his education would find himself a place to sit with a like-minded youngster for a companion (*chavrusa*: partner in Talmud study), in some *shtibl* or *beyss medrash* (a small House of Study). There the two would plow away together at page after page of Talmud text, without guidance or direction, and without a trace of proper encouragement, recognition or reward from anyone. Add to this an economic situation, featuring dire poverty as a rule, that pressured and drove such youngsters to go to work and earn a living, and it becomes only too easy to understand why the number of such students dwindled away, till they virtually disappeared. As they continued to vanish, with them went all hope of finding older individuals, in late adolescence or early adulthood, busy with the Talmud in any of the Houses of Study.

[In Iyar of 5682 (May 1922), under the impetus of Agudas Yisra'el, a proper Torah high school was founded, under the name of *Yeshivas B^eney Torah.* It opened with twenty pupils, who had graduated either from a traditional *chéder* or from the community's *Y^esodey Torah* school. A first-rate Talmud scholar was appointed to serve as the *rosh yeshiva,* to guide and teach them as they sat and studied in the large *beyss medrash* adjacent to the city's great synagogue. . . .

[Such, in sum, was the condition of Torah study and religious education in Piotrkov when Rav Meir Shapiro came to occupy the rabbinic post.

[As indicated, he worked to establish, improve and enhance one *chéder* after another. For him, one school named *Y^esodey Torah,* however excellent and large it might be, could not possibly be enough for a community of about twelve thousand souls. . . . With his enthusiastic support and encouragement, the *Beyss Ya'akov* school also flourished and grew.

[But like a homing pigeon finding its dovecote, he let his heart's main interest focus on *Yeshivas B^eney Torah.* Inevitably, he became fully involved with it; and inevitably the number of pupils grew rapidly, as he gave his own scintillating, stimulating *shi'urim* and added a fair number of outstanding scholars to the staff. It became a model institution of its kind, that acquired a solid reputation.

[Yet he could not neglect the adults either. Under his relentless drive and pull, younger and older men who had learned in their youth how to study Talmud were encouraged to come to *shi'urim* that he either arranged or gave for them, and then to continue on their own regularly, in the evening hours.]

In time he saw gratifying results. Every *beyss medrash* in Piotrkov, all the Houses of Study that had stood abandoned and desolate for years, became filled with the sound of young folk learning their Talmud. With *Yeshivas B^eney Torah* as a nucleus and a matrix, several dozen young scholars gradually matured into prime, devoutly religious Talmudists.

****

Concomitantly, however, Rav Meir had to give his attention to other problems of first importance — the same areas of concern that he had found in Sonik, which he had designated by the word *za'am* ("fury") as an acrostic: *z*ᵉ*vachim* (ensuring a supply of reliably kosher meat), *éruvin* (making certain there was a proper *éruv* for the community, to permit carrying things in public on Shabbos), and *mikveh* (providing the community with a modern, hygienic ritualarium to make it pleasant and attractive to observe the laws of family purity).

With his clear vision, he realized almost at once that there were serious irregularities in all the three areas of religious life. And so he set to work once more on the path he had taken in his previous positions: He formulated new regulations and established new, firm restrictions, making certain that they were understood and obeyed. Laborers were soon at work constructing a new *mikveh*, glistening clean, with the most modern sanitary installations. He formulated his programs of action, and all went ahead with exemplary precision.

In a short while, the firm controlling hand of Piotrkov's new spiritual head was evident everywhere in the community's religious life. And the net result was unmistakable: Jewish Piotrkov became a model community in Poland.

[One further signal contribution by Rav Meir to life in the city's religious community must be noted. When he became the rabbinic head, two Yiddish weekly newspapers appeared, one published by the *Bund* (to peddle its radical Marxist socialism), and the other by the General (irreligious) Zionists. There was only one thing the two shared: an attitude of utter derision and contempt for authentic Jewish faith and for those who clung to it with the Torah. This attitude was freely and fully aired in both newspapers. And the young, budding, struggling local branch of Agudas Yisra'el could hardly even dream of starting a weekly paper of its own. Even if enough money for it might be furnished, where would capable journalists and writers be found in the community?

[Invariably more aware of the world around him than people realized, when Rav Meir came to Piotrkov to take the rabbinic post, he brought with him a young talented writer named Isaac Baer Ackerman, from the staff of *Der Yid*, the weekly paper of Agudas Yisra'el in Warsaw. The young man set to work, and starting in Shᵉvat 5685 (February 1925), *Di Yiddishe Shtimme* (The Jewish Voice) appeared every Thursday in Piotrkov, to the delight of the religious community.]

In general, there was little doubt that under Rav Meir's spiritual reign, Jewry in Piotrkov enjoyed one of the finest periods in its religious history. Rarely was there ever such a rapport between a rabbi and his flock; rarely did such a warm, harmonious relationship ever develop in a community. The people sensed a father in him; they felt palpably how much he was involved with them, how much he wanted them to find good fortune in their present, and how concerned he was for their future.

For anyone who wanted to visit him, his door of his home was never locked. Whatever a person might seek — wise counsel, a bit of material help, some apt, ingenious way to deal with a complex, difficult problem, or perhaps some vital intercession on someone's behalf in high governmental circles — he was always there to listen. In response, he gave words of consolation and comfort, or just encouraged a perplexed or embittered visitor to pour out his heart and give full freedom to his feelings, till a sense of relief came of itself. As often as not it needed only a sympathetic ear or only a few warm, felicitous words from him, or at times some pointed sagacious thought, to lift thc melancholy, dolorous mood that had been pressing down on a visitor's heart like a mountain, and make it disappear.

In the community there was a noted historian named Moshe Feinkind. Writing once about his illustrious Rabbi, Feinkind made a list of the many things that Rav Meir did for the city's Jewry: With an outlay of a thousand guilden out of his own pocket toward the costs, Rav Meir repaired or reconstructed the *éruv* in the city — the needed technical fixtures to permit carrying objects in public on Shabbos. He helped dozens upon dozens of people who came upon hard times and suffered distress, either by giving them money outright or by granting them loans for which he never asked any repayment, as he continued taking an interest in their welfare.

In his essay on Rav Meir, Feinkind recorded a series of incidents — a few things that happened:

On a day before Pesach, the Rav was getting ready to bake his own special matzos *(matza shᵉmura)* to use at his Séder that evening, when a respectable member of the community came to see him, and spoke with him discreetly, in absolute privacy:

The man had been thrown lately into severe business difficulties, till he became unable to meet his obligations. The result was that he faced being put out of business completely, to be left a ruined man; and now he even had no way of preparing for Pesach. He had bought nothing yet of all the provisions that his family needed for the Séder and the *yom tov.* In the city, he added with bitter sorrow, no one knew yet of his dire plight; he was still regarded as a fine, upstanding member of the community.

Without a word the Rav left, and was gone for about an hour. Then he was back, with a few hundred zlotys in his hand — a handsome bit of capital, which he gave his waiting visitor, adding only a minimum of words. It was enough not only to see the man through Pesach but to help him back on his feet afterward, so that he could continue in business.

There was a standing regulation in the community that all kosher butcher-shops had to be concentrated in one part of the city — so that the rabbinic supervision over them would not present any great difficulties. One fine day a particular butcher took a notion to open a store in another location. Needless to say, the Rav placed a ban on the shop, forbidding anyone in the city to buy meat there. Along came the butcher in question to the Rav to plead for mercy. He admitted his error, but, said he plaintively, the venture had cost him an investment of several hundred guilden. Now the loss would hurt him badly. . . .

Here too Rav Meir acted at once, without a wasted word: He went to his money chest, withdrew the amount in question, and gave it to the man.

Now a third incident: In came a man from a neighboring small town with *his* tale of woe: The factory that supplied him with merchandise to sell refused to continue dealing with him. He owed the factory too much money for what he had bought till now. He could have no more goods on credit till he paid up what he owed. . . .

What was he to do? asked the man, weeping. Under the circumstances, he would just have to shut down his little store and become a beggar, wandering around to ask for charity!

Here too Rav Meir took action. He took the man with him, and the two rode directly to the factory. There he spoke forcefully to the owner and persuaded him to let the hard-pressed Jew pay back what he owed in a series of modest payments, while the factory would continue giving him merchandise. Then Rav Meir made the first payment on the spot, out of his pocket.

One year, as the time of Pesach approached on the calendar, Rav Meir was in the United States on a lengthy visit. [He was determined by then to move at full speed with his plan for a world yeshiva, an international study center, and he knew that only in America could he gather the vast sum of money that the project required. But he remained aware that at this time of year he should have been in Piotrkov, running the local campaign of *kimcha d'pis-cha* ("flour of Pesach"), to gather and distribute money for the poor, for their Pesach needs. From information he received, he knew that a large part of the community faced actual hunger.]

Thanks to the system of social organization among the Jews in America, he could deal with the problem. The masses of immigrants from Poland were organized in *landsmanshaftn*, according to their places of origin in "the old country." Now he met with the association of Piotrkov *landslaït* and raised a handsome amount of money from them. To this he added a few hundred dollars out of his own pocket [a most solid figure in buying power at that time]; and the sum total was sent to the proper people in Piortrkov, to reach them in good time.

Such was the bond that linked Rav Meir with the Jews of Piotrkov. They regarded him with a reverence and love that was probably never equaled. His concern for them remained undiminished by a separation of continents. And while he lived with them, when they had reason to rejoice, he shared their happiness; alternatively, when suffering fell to their lot, he shared that too.

[One result of this relationship, coupled with his matchless eloquence and oratory, was the fact that whenever he spoke to a listening audience, whether in a *shul* or in an assembly hall, not a single empty seat could be found. . . . Nor was this all.]

Unforgettable for the Jewish populace were the large-scale *s'udos* (meals, feasts) that he provided periodically on Saturday nights, to which the whole religious community was invited. Such meals bore the name of *m'lavveh malka* ("escorting the queen"), which devout people have traditionally to mark the departure of Shabbos.

At these meals he was a veritable fountain of multifaceted inspiration as he held forth, his voice ringing out for all to hear. He would give keen, spirited *pilpul* for the Talmudists; sermonic gems of interpretation on homiletic teachings of the Sages; an occasional flash of brilliant wit that could come only from a great mind; and for variety, a heartwarming chassidic tale.

The listeners absorbed his every word with the deepest pleasure, learning eagerly from his inexhaustible store of Torah knowledge; and their affection for him grew ever stronger. The rapport that prevailed between the shepherd and his flock could actually be felt, like a living physical presence. And awareness of the phenomenon spread beyond the confines of the city.

It did not take long for residents of the neighboring townlets and hamlets to come as delegations, to beg him to stop being the Rav of the city alone and become instead, quite simply, the "district rabbi," presiding over the entire region: Let him "spread his protective wings" over their small communities too. Let him come to each location for an occasional Shabbos, perhaps, or pay a long visit during the week. . . .

He listened to the delegations, and felt no choice but to give his consent. The ability to turn them away and shut the door on them was simply not in his nature.

Thus we find him in the middle years of the century's third decade with enough, perhaps, to keep three ordinary individuals busy: He was the "district rabbi" of Piotrkov and its environs; President of Agudas Yisra'el in Poland; and a deputy in the Sejm.

For him, however, all this was yet not enough to consume all his time and energy. His heart and mind were restlessly engaged in thoughts, ideas, plans to make a reality of his further dream: a great yeshiva of world renown and world importance.

****

A few miscellaneous, piquant incidents happened during his years in Piotrkov, which might be worth recording:

One day a young man came to ask him for *s'micha*, a formal document of rabbinic ordination. When Rav Meir began conversing with his visitor on matters of Talmud and *halacha*, he saw quite soon that this young man was definitely not a suitable candidate for rabbinic ordination. It irritated him that the visitor came so blithely to ask for something as serious and important as *s'micha* when he was so blatantly unready for it.

"Let me tell you a story," said Rav Meir, and the young man prepared to listen: "The renowned scholar Rav Yosef Sha'ul Natanson, who spent his years as the Rabbi of Lemberg, was once making a journey in his coach, when he noticed a young man walking along with a pack on his shoulders. Rav Yosef Sha'ul ordered his driver to stop the vehicle, and he invited the foot traveler to come up and ride with him — which the young man gladly did.

"As the two got to talking, Rav Yosef Sha'ul learned that the young man was a candidate for the rabbinic position in a nearby townlet; and as they spoke, he took out a letter of approbation and recommendation for him, that a well-known chassidic spiritual leader, a Rebbe, had written to his devoted followers in that little town.

"Rav Yosef Sha'ul was curious. 'Tell me,' said he: 'Have you studied the part of the *Shulchan Aruch* called *Orach Cha-yim*?'

"The young man shook his head: 'No. You see, people generally don't ask a *rav* about the matters that it deals with. Everyone has the handy compendium, the *Kitzur Shulchan Aruch* [by Rav Shlomo Ganzfried], and whatever they might want to ask, they look the matter up there and find an answer for themselves. . . .'

"Rav Yosef Sha'ul went on: 'Very well; but then, did you study the section of the original *Shulchan Aruch* titled *Choshen Mishpat*? That deals with business matters, disputes, damages, and so on. These are certainly matters that come under the jurisdiction of a local Rav. He has the sole authority to act as judge and give decisions. . . .'

"The young man shrugged: 'In that little town, such is the deplorable, sinful state of affairs that when a dispute or a quarrel of any kind breaks out, the parties go straight to the Polish courts. So for that townlet, you see, there is really no need to study *Choshen Mishpat*.'

"Rav Yosef Sha'ul persisted: '*Nu*, so be it, then. What about the section called *Evven ha'Ezer*? That deals with divorce and other matters of marriage and marital relations. You must have studied that; not so?'

"The young man shook his head calmly: 'There are no rivers in that little town, you see; so the technicalities of the law don't allow a *get* (a document of divorce) to be written there. As a result, when anything comes up relating to marriage and divorce, the people take the matter to a Rav somewhere else.'

"*Nu*, Rav Yosef Sha'ul still had one question left: 'But you must have mastered the section of *Yoreh Dé'ah*. You must surely be able to answer with authority if a question comes up about meat that comes in contact with milk, for example? Problems like that come up every day in a devout

Jewish community.'

"For a moment the young man was disconcerted, at a loss for an answer. Then he recovered his wits and shot back, 'If I knew *Yoreh Dé'ah* well, I wouldn't have needed the fine letter of recommendation from that Rebbe to his *chassidim* in the little town!'

"That is the little story I wanted to tell you," said Rav Meir to his young visitor. "Now you can leave and go on your way. With the great amount of knowledge in the *Shulchan Aruch* that you have shown, if you come seeking *s^emicha*, a document of rabbinic ordination, at least you should bring with you a fine letter of recommendation."

****

Once he was called out to a neighboring town where several rabbinic men of learning lived. Among these scholars, though, quarrelsome differences of opinion seemed to go on forever, and as a result, certain important areas in the religious life of the community were left in outrageous neglect. So badly did the state of affairs deteriorate that the community's religious life could be described as a total wreck.

Rav Meir took stock of the sorry situation, and not a doubt could remain in his mind that the rabbinic personages of the town were fully responsible for it. When the leading members of the community were ready to hear his conclusions and advice, he began:

"The state of affairs here has helped me understand something in our Written Torah in a completely new light: You will remember that when the Almighty informed *Avraham avinu* [our Patriarch Abraham] of His intention to destroy the city of Sᵉdom, Avraham tried to save it: he pleaded with the Almighty, 'Perhaps there are fifty tzaddikim within the city?' (*Bᵉréshis*/Genesis 18:24). Now, this can seem puzzling. What need did Avraham have to ask a question like this? Could he truly reckon for a moment that if there were fifty religious, righteous people in Sᵉdom, the Almighty would go ahead and destroy the place?

"Now that I have examined the situation here, I think I understand what he really meant. He told the Almighty, 'Perhaps there are fifty tzaddikim within the city.' In that case, he intimated, there was no need for *Him* to destroy the city. He could just leave it to them, and *they* would transform the place into a total wreck. . . ."

****

With his all-absorbing concern for the education of the young children in Piotrkov, on one occasion when he spoke in the great, central *shul*, he decided to emphasize the role that a young mother could play in the matter, to make the young ladies in the synagogue aware of their own importance and of their consequent obligation.

To drive his point home, he stated simply that the fundamental responsibility for a child's education rests on the mother. The entire behavior of a child depends on the young woman who brings him into the world. "In the Midrash the Sages indicate this," said he, "by telling us (*B'réshis Rabba* 63:6) that when Rivka [Rebecca] passed by a *beyss medrash*, a Jewish House of Learning, then her unborn son Ya'akov [Jacob] thrashed about in the womb, eager to go there. If a mother walks by a *beyss medrash* when she has the opportunity, because the study of Torah and the mitzvos are dear to her — then she will become the mother of a precious Ya'akov in Jewry.

"But, the Midrash teaches further, when Rivka passed by a place of idol-worship, then Eyssav [Esau] thrashed about within her, eager to go there. If a young mother will be drawn to the idolatries of the world today, in pursuit of meaningless pleasure and empty goals, and she will give never a thought to the Torah, then she may well find herself the mother of an Eyssav. . . .

****

At one time, delegates of a worthy institution of charity and mercy came to Piotrkov, to raise funds for it in the community. On Shabbos they joined Rav Meir in the great central *shul*, and during the morning service they made a stirring appeal for financial help. When the Torah was read, many more than seven people (the usual number) were called up, and for each one only a few sentences of the weekly Torah portion were chanted. Thus, in the blessing of *mi she-bérach* that followed every *aliya*, each person in turn could pledge a handsome donation for the institution in question; and after Shabbos the visiting delegates could receive a substantial total.

Near Rav Meir sat one of the very eminent members of the community, and this whole "business" displeased him: To his mind, it demeaned the prestige of the Torah, and it made the reading drag on too long; and so he made his feelings sharply clear to Rav Meir.

Sweetly, the Rav replied: "Actually, there is an explicit sentence in our Scripture that applies to this exactly: '*haShem* (the Lord) has a desire for the sake of *tzidko* (His righteousness); He enlarges the Torah and makes it majestic' (*Y'shayahu*/Isaiah 42:21). The Almighty has a strong desire for the well-being and the purpose of *tzidko*, His *tz'daka*; He wants Jews to give *tz'daka*, charity, for His good causes; and for that, 'He enlarges the Torah': He lets us call up more people to the Torah reading to make it a larger part than usual of our *shacharis* service."

The eminent, worthy man liked the apt interpretation of those words from Scripture, and he accepted it with the same good humor that Rav Meir showed in thinking of it. So all was well.

****

Since he was himself something of a dynamo in the pursuit of his rabbinic duties and educational goals, this energetic Rav of Piotrkov did not look kindly on people in rabbinic posts who were content to live rather passively and do little more than answer questions on matters of religious law when, as and if they were asked. To his mind, they fell far short of fulfilling their rabbinic duties. Once he spoke out about it: "The Talmud foretells (*bavli*, Sotah 49b) that in time to come, in the era before the advent of *mashi-ach* [the Messianic era], 'the face of the generation will be like the face of a dog'; and again, in tractate Yoma (21b), we are told about the fire from Heaven which descended onto the *mizbé-ach* (the Temple altar, where animal offerings or certain parts from them were burned), that in the time of the Second Temple *(ba-yis shéni)* in Jerusalem, this fire was 'like a dog.'

"As the Talmud tells us there, fire from Heaven was always present on the altar; nevertheless, humans were required to provide burning logs as well. Well, says the Talmud, in the First Temple, Heaven's fire was crouched on the altar like a lion: it had power and substance. In the Second Temple too there was fire from on high, but it crouched on the altar like a beaten, wilted dog. It was of such poor quality, says the Talmud, that it 'did not help at all.'

"So we have the simile of a dog for both that fire and 'the face of the generation': the rabbinic gentry who are supposed to guide, lead and direct the people of their time. Thus we can deduce from the Talmud that they will be equally of no value.

"Some of our rabbis try to defend themselves by insisting that there is really nothing they can do, because in any case no one will listen to them. Yet here too lies a curse on the era before the advent of *mashi-ach* [the Messianic era]. For as the Talmud predicts about that distant future (*bavli*, Sotah 49b), in that baleful time, when 'the face of the generation will be as the face of a dog' — 'on what will there be for us to depend? — on our Father in Heaven.'

"Apparently, on the surface, this would seem to be a good quality to cultivate and adopt: faith and trust in the Almighty. Yet we see in this dolorous time before the Messianic advent how it has become the very cause of the attitude that prevails so disastrously in our rabbinic world: When there is such a crying need for so much to be done, our spiritual leaders remain indifferent and aloof, arguing that they themselves can do nothing with our people and for our people; they must leave everything to our Father in Heaven. He alone, they argue, can set matters right in the dreadful, tragic situation of our people. So they need do nothing. . . . "

He saw the need for action; he saw the ways to action, to organize and inspire people into unity under a life by the Torah. And it depressed him to see learned rabbis merely sit in their positions and wait for people to come with questions in matters of religious law, so that they could provide answers. The worst of it all was that he saw how this continually lowered the prestige of the rabbinate. From day to day, respect for such "do-nothing" scholars grew less and less, and the level of religious life in the country suffered.

Once he said somberly, "It is about just such a situation that our Sages said: Skin a carcass in the marketplace and earn something, and don't say . . . *I am a great man!* (*bavli*, P^{e}sachim 113a). If those Talmudists won't realize that they have work to do, and they had better forget about sitting on their dignity and waiting for miracles, the day may come when they won't even have a carcass to skin, so that they might earn something to live on!"

****

If he could be scathingly critical about certain elements in the rabbinate, in Poland, it was only in the privacy of his own domain, in speaking with his *talmidim*, to inspire and guide them onto other pathways when the time would come for them to follow the road of *Moshe rabbénu*, as we read: "Moshe grew up, and he went out to his brethren, and he watched their arduous labor" (*Sh^emos*/Exodus 2:11).

Outside the privacy of his own domain, to the world at large, he remained the stalwart champion of every devout, observant Jew.

One day he happened to encounter a leader of one of the secular, irreligious Jewish parties, whereupon that fine-feathered gentleman proceeded to explain to Rav Meir that for him too, the Torah was something precious and holy. His difficulty, he continued sweetly, was that he found himself unable to tolerate the people who studied it — primarily the learned scholars and rabbinic leaders.

Rav Meir did not remain owing him an answer. His stinging reply came at once:

"I'm sure you recall the Written Torah's account of the quarrel that Korach and his adherents mounted against Moshe in the wilderness (*B^emidbar*/Numbers 16). The result was, as you know, that they all disappeared into the ground. The earth swallowed them up (verses 32-33). Well, the Talmud relates that a certain Arab desert traveler once showed Rabba bar bar Chana just where *b^elu'ey Korach*, 'the swallowed folk of Korach' — he and his cohorts — had sunk in and disappeared. This Talmudic Sage listened, and he heard those vanished souls declaiming, 'Moshe is true, and his Torah is true, and they were liars' (*bavli*, Bava Basra 74a).

"Now, isn't this puzzling? If those souls in the ground really repented and realized how wrong they had been, surely they should have said, 'and *we* were liars,' not 'they'?

"The answer is that those unholy, unlovely souls realized that direct, open warfare against the Torah would only bring disaster on them, to let them sink further into the earth and disappear even more. So they changed their tune: Now they insisted that they really loved the Torah and accepted it faithfully; only, *they* were liars — those who studied it and lived by it loyally were unbearably false and deceitful.

"You see," Rav Meir concluded, "in every age and time there are 'the swallowed folk of Korach': They try to work insidiously, never coming out into the open. From underground they try to gnaw away at the roots of our faith. So they come and declaim aloud, 'Moshe is true and his Torah is true; we are convinced of that; but *they* are liars — the people who live by it faithfully.' Of course, then, those folk just have to be in political opposition. . . . Once a Korach type, always a Korach type."

His father.

The *iluy* of Shatz, growing to manhood.

The new quarters for his *B^eney Torah* school in Glina.

Group portrait in Glina:
Rav Meir with students and staff of the *B^e ney Torah* school.

The dapper young delegate of *Agudas Yisra'el*, on his way to the *Sejm*, the Polish parliament.

Top left: talkinç
with other Jewi
delegates to th
Sejm, religious
otherwise. *Abo*
as the dynamic
of Piotrkov. *Fa*
left: the city's
great shul. *Left*
Shmu'el Eicher
who bought the
for *Yeshivas*
Chachmey Lub

At the historic *K^e néssiya G^e dola* where the *daf ha-yomi* program was proclaimed.

For the cornerstone ceremony of *Yeshivas Chachmey Lublin*, escorted by *talmidim*, he took a horse-driven carriage to welcome the Rebbe of Tchortkov on his arrival at the railroad station.

At the
emony,
on a
pecially
built
atform,
Rebbe
ke with
motion
to the
athered
nasses.

ding under a canopy, Rav Meir declaimed his historic words; and the first bricks were duly set.

As the
buildin
began
go up,
called
report
(religic
and ot
wise) t
come
see, a
to writ
about

On his fund-raising tour across America, he took the time to visit a Jewish orphan home and give the children his blessing.

Left: The day the great Yeshiva was to open at last, Rav Meir was given a "royal welcome" at Lublin's railroad station, when he arrived from Piotrkov. *Above:* The Rebbe of Tchortkov came likewise by train, and was escorted by his sons to the Yeshiva.

orning, holding his small *séfer torah*,
ed on the steps with students and staff.

And he went to the historic cemetery

to pray for the Yeshiva at certain old graves.

: After affixing it to the doorpost, the Rebbe of Tchortkov reverently kissed the *mezuza* ne Yeshiva's entrance. *Right:* At a heightened moment of the opening ceremonies, the bbe spoke from the crowded balcony to the vast throngs that gathered to attend.

ft page, clockwise from top left: students waiting for Rav Meir's first *i'ur* (lecture); in front: his father./Preparing to teach about the *beyss -mikdash*, our ancient and future Temple, he sat by the model in the st basement./2 portraits as the Rav of Lublin./In the Yeshiva's fine ɔrary he found times of tranquility to write his Talmudic thoughts./the *ɔn kodesh* in the great *beyss medrash./Right page, above:* That great udy Hall in early morning. *Below:* As the model of the Temple took ape, religious journalists came to report on it. *Right:* the talented ɛnach Weintraub, who built it.

At the funeral a Polish honor guard helped keep order, as the *talmidim* carried the coffin through the mass of mourners.

HisTorah citadel became Nazi quarters behind barriers when war brought the German kil

23

The second published volume

Not yet forty, he had a full, busy life by any standard. As a delegate to the Sejm, he was an outstanding politician. As a brilliant, charismatic speaker, he was invited and welcomed everywhere. As the Rav of Piotrkov, he stayed at the helm of his rabbinic office, controlling matters with a firm hand. Above all, he knew he carried the role and the authority of a first-ranking leader of the Polish Jewry that was loyal to the Torah; and he bore the burden with all the responsibility and concern that it entailed.

Yet there was still another side to him. Since his early years he had immersed himself in the Talmud and the literature of *halacha*; he had become "the *iluy* (young genius) of Shatz" and become known for his astounding Talmudic prowess. Now, in his years of maturity, the title had matured with him: Now he was regarded as *the* Talmudic scholar of the age.

His mind was forever busied with a variety of far-reaching, wide-ranging problems involving Jewry worldwide. In turn, Jewry worldwide did not forget that he was also a prime Torah authority. Throughout his adult years, both before the First World War and after, he was sent questions involving the Torah he knew so brilliantly.

Before the war the questions were rather mild-tempered: a matter of *pilpul*, a difficulty in a few lines of Rambam's code of law, a few unclear abstruse points in *kabbala*, and so on. After the war, the questions took on a troubled, turbulent tone, sometimes even a dismally tragic one:

People wrote to ask about *tum'ah* and *tahara*, ritual cleanness and defilement: Cannon fire left someone's body shattered as it killed him. A *kohén*, as we know, may not enter any area where he will become ritually defiled; and a Jewish corpse generates ritual uncleanness. May a *kohén* enter the area where the cannon fire did its damage?

A question came to him about an *aguna*, a woman whose husband was gone, and now she wanted permission to remarry. The man disappeared in the war, and evidence about the matter is meager and inconclusive. Could she have rabbinic permission to remarry? . . . And so other complex, difficult questions engendered by the frightful war — all, all were sent to him to consider; and his answers were decisive and authoritative, accepted without dispute.

It was known in the Torah world that such enquiries had been sent him, and he had replied. With time there was something of an outcry: For Heaven's sake, where were the responsa that he wrote? Where was the volume of *she'élos ut'shuvos* that would let the whole world of Torah study benefit from the questions he received and the learned answers he gave? So asked the letters that eventually began to reach him as the war receded further and further into the past.

Those who wrote these letters evidently knew little of the work load he carried, the duties he had to fulfill. All they knew was that he was the source of valuable new material in important areas of current *halacha*. Should he answer them that he was too busy? *Could* he answer them that? Those letters that demanded and importuned came from colleagues who were themselves scholars of first rank.

Somehow he found the time to prepare a good number of the *she'élos ut'shuvos* for the press, and in the year 5686 (1926) they were printed in Piotrkov as *Or haMé'ir* ("The Shining Light"), volume 1 of his responsa.

The many who had longed for it, who had demanded and insisted, were not disappointed. They found the contents richly satisfying. Where a decision in *halacha* is not involved, he lets his mind go with his own adroit and stimulating ways of *pilpul* — but always on a sound, consistent foundation of solid logic. Where a halachic decision must be reached, he becomes imbued with the profound earnestness of his task, and the sense of his responsibility can be felt in every word.

[Of separate interest, perhaps, is the ample material that he included from his correspondence with three luminaries in the world of *halacha*: the Chafetz Cha-yim, Rav Meir Arik, and the Rebbe of Ostrovtza. When he felt the need, he consulted them, and he gave great weight to their replies in arriving at halachic decisions.]

Especially moving, though, is the preface he wrote for the volume: As one reads it, what comes through is Rav Meir's extraordinary, blazing love of the Torah. Then his pen continues with the dream that was living in him then, night and day: to build a yeshiva that would serve as a world study center for the Torah. Out of the lines emerges the vision he had of structuring a new Yavneh — a re-creation of the vital, dynamic headquarters that Rabban Yochanan ben Zakkai made in olden times, directly after the destruction of the *beyss ha-mikdash,* the Holy Temple in Jerusalem. With his words he makes the reader see what it was he envisioned: to bring alive the great glory that the Torah had known in times long gone, and the high prestige that its scholars had enjoyed.

The preface ends: "Signed with a heart filled by a yearning love for our sacred Torah."

Here is the key to the man: His heart quivered and convulsed with anguish as he saw in what low, debased esteem the Torah's children were held as they studied with devotion in the Poland that he knew. With all his being he strove to find a way to make a drastic change in that miserable situation. This was the goal that he sought and aimed for with the construction of his projected *Yeshivas Chachmey Lublin.* . . .

****

One line on the title page, "Part One," indicated further hopes, if not further plans, of publication. For he did have in manuscript a great collection of many more responsa, written over the years in reply to questions involving religious law, that had been put to him. Nor was this all. There was a large written work on Rambam's code of law: a product of genius in its depth and range of Talmudic thought. He had writings on the Talmud; a collection of chassidic, homiletic essays; and more — and each of these works ran to several volumes.

Were any of these works ever brought to press, they would certainly bring new radiant light into the world of Torah study.

24

To build for Torah majesty

Yeshivas Chachmey Lublin ("the Yeshiva of Lublin Scholars"): those were the three words that brought a new conception, a new image, into the world of holy study. A fresh, radical approach to the very idea of a yeshiva emerged in the Jewish world, based on new axioms and new foundations. In its time and place it was a revolutionary change of direction, to open a new era in the history of yeshiva life. It quite simply charted a fresh course in the ways of Torah — a new path for Torah Jewry to follow.

Yeshivas Chachmey Lublin: In the years that it was destined to exist, it would gain world renown. It was to draw extraordinary attention to itself, as it became the focus of intense interest by Jewry everywhere. And this itself attested to the greatness and nobility of the idea and the goal that brought it into being.

Only a few years after it finally opened its doors to begin its life of dynamic vitality, the entire world could see the greatness of its achievements, the level to which it lifted the degraded and denigrated honor of the Torah. In those few years it gave the world hundreds of prime Talmudists, fine scholars, outstanding Jews of piety devoted to the Torah. From its doors came a new element into Poland's Jewry, that brought a hitherto unknown esteem and pride to our people as a whole, but especially to the folk that held to the Torah.

These were gifted and talented young men, very much aware of the world, with a well-developed sense of mature responsibility and concern for the community. With their readiness to undertake communal work, they were a type of Jew that the world about them had never seen.

[When he felt the time had come to concentrate his energies on it, Rav Meir knew that gradually he would have to reduce and terminate his activities as delegate to the Sejm and as the head of Agudas Yisra'el. Yet the leaders of that organization protested: "How can you leave us? What you've been doing with the Agudah in your work from day to day, is just revolutionary; *ir kerrt doch veltn* (you are overturning worlds)!" He replied succinctly, "If I, single-handed, am overturning worlds, let me have my way and in a few years I will raise up for you 200 *talmidim vos velln ibberkerrn di gantze velt* (who will turn over *the whole world)*!]

In the science of architecture there is a rule that the higher a structure must go, the deeper and sturdier must be its foundations. For years, then, the yeshiva existed only in the unresting mind and pulsing heart of Rav Meir Shapiro, as he thought, planned and dreamed.

Yet what were the foundations of *that* structure, in his mind? What made him conceive the edifice and build his plans and hopes for it for years on end? What drove him on relentlessly, till he could see the solid building standing and young scholars working away at their studies?

There was a conversation that we students once had with him about it. As he sat and thought how to answer us, his mind going back into the past, tears formed in the eyes that looked back well into the past, and they mingled in his mind with all the tears of pain and woe that he had seen from youngsters of all ages struggling to study Torah.

That was really all the answer we needed. There was hardly any point in asking for lengthy explanations. In the heavy sigh that came from his heart we heard a full description of the pathetic conditions which generally prevailed in the Polish world of Torah study. We knew those conditions ourselves, only too well. For so many precious youngsters, devotion to Torah study meant a life that bordered on martyrdom, as they struggled to subsist while they wore themselves out in study day and night.

He used to say: "There is flagrant cheating going on — robbery in open daylight — between the two eternal partners, Yissachar and Z^e^vulun. We learn from the Midrash (*B^e^réshis Rabba* 99:9) that in ancient times, these two tribes of Israel entered into a sacred partnership, and the Almighty confirmed the solemn agreement in the blessing that *Moshe rabb^e^nu* gave them (*D^e^varim*/Deuteronomy 33:18). By this contractual agreement, the people of Yissachar must study Torah faithfully, and the people of Z^e^vulun must support and sustain them, so that they can study properly. Then the two tribes can share the blissful reward in the Hereafter for all the holy Torah learning on this earth.

"In theory this is fine; but how is the partnership faring in reality? — miserably . . . very miserably. Yissachar keeps his end of the agreement quite faithfully. He even does more than his contractual obligation requires. And what does Z^e^vulun do? He cheats and robs. He does not even fulfill properly one single point, one detail, out of all the obligations that he accepted.

"Yissachar protests; he cries out, trying to awake the conscience of the world, trying to convey his poignant unspoken message: *Look; see how he is injuring me murderously — this contractual partner of mine. See how he oppresses me and debases me, how he tries to send me down to perdition!*

"And the world around him — what does it do? It remains silent and still. It makes not a move in response, not a gesture to interfere with Z^{e}vulun in any way. Not a word does it say to chide him or berate him. . . . In today's world, in the language of our time, this is fairness, decency, justice; and if the world insists on this, its will prevails. World power is nothing to be sneezed at, you know.

"So Yissachar cries out and protests — as he keeps sinking deeper and deeper into the ground; he is simply falling into oblivion. And all the while Z^{e}vulun keeps rising and coming up in the world — at Yissachar's expense!

"This is the situation of Torah study today!"

So Rav Meir Shapiro saw it: that by the Almighty's will, the Jewish people outside the boundaries of Torah learning owed the devoted scholars and students their sustenance and upkeep; and the dire poverty and misery in which Poland's world of Torah lived was therefore criminal. He simply knew that he had to do something radical and revolutionary about it.

****

In Rav Meir's memory lived an episode from his childhood that he linked directly with his determination to build the yeshiva:

In his childhood years, when he was studying happily in his native town of Shatz, there were eight other youngsters getting their schooling with him. Companionably, they studied together and played together, as young boys will. Some of them, as he recalled, had learning abilities in which they surpassed him. Their minds were sharper; they knew more.

The blissful, idyllic years of carefree childhood swiftly passed, however. All too soon his companions had to cross the threshold into the onset of maturation. All too early they felt the stresses and challenges of the need to grow up; and this meant fateful decisions on choices of direction.

Suddenly they took a different life-road, diverging sharply from the young Meir's path. They were simply swayed to the radical left of irreligiosity, and they left forever the pathway of the Torah which the young Meir had shared with them all through childhood. Other attitudes to life came along like winds in a gale, offering such poisoning delights as irresponsible, amoral liberty and free thought, and they were swept away.

Let no one think it was because they were searching for such ideas and were ready to welcome them eagerly. They were forced. Their parents were poor. He, young Meir, would be able to ride off to yeshivos, to secondary and more advanced Torah schools, and go further in learning and mastering his beloved Talmud. They would never have the means. Instead, they would have to enter the proletarian world of common labor, to help support themselves and their families. Whatever life-path they chose, further education in Torah was out of the question.

The grown, mature leader of his people remembered how he had reacted: His heart had wept bitter tears mingled with the blood of his soul. *Why did it have to be this way?* his young spirit stormed. Why weren't the leaders of Jewry concerned also about the children of the poor folk? Why should material considerations have to prevail over spiritual needs?

Rage, anguish, compassion — these were the emotions that woke and writhed in his storming sensitive heart. Now, in Piotrkov, he remembered how he had taken a secret vow then, in the town of Shatz: In silence he swore to the Almighty that if he should ever become a person of eminence in the Jewish world — with all the fire in his spirit, with the strongest passion of his heart, he would be concerned also for the poor ones among the youth of his people: He would build a yeshiva where the penniless, destitute young folk could be properly educated. Didn't the Sages of the Talmud teach (*bavli*, N^{e}darim 81a), "Be careful with the children of the poor, because from them shall Torah come"? He vowed that if he achieved a position of some authority, he would build a yeshiva where Torah could come from children of the poor.

Rav Meir remembered this one incident in his childhood, which he related to his *talmidim.* We students had witnessed hundreds of such incidents. We saw how Jewish hearts were ruthlessly lacerated and torn by a combination of bitter economic conditions and a powerful unclean spirit of the times. Gifted, sensitive souls were wrenched away from the Talmud study they loved, and their most precious feelings for the holy traditions of their people were systematically dulled and deadened. Every trace of our cherished age-old, authentic Judaism that lived in them was rooted out. Then, to fill the void they might feel, their spirit was clothed with various garments of atheism and Godlessness, which drew them ineluctably to the most vile and most dangerous Jewish enemies of our Torah: the Soviet élite in Moscow known as the *yevsektsia* — who did not hesitate to have the most learned Torah scholars arrested and exiled to Siberia, where they would have no chance to survive.

We students of Rav Meir watched so many that we knew, in their process of radical transformation and alienation from the *yiddishkaït* that sustained us. Our life spirit writhed with pain and agony; yet what was there for us to do? Had we seen some way to help them and turn them back to the Jewish way to eternal life, we too might have taken a vow, like Rav Meir, to do all we could and more. In our imaginations there were fantasies of great, noble actions that we took to rescue them from spiritual perdition; but reality was implacable. And so we surrendered to our own inevitable process:

First there was anger, rage, frustration; then came pity, empathy, and compassion for them; and finally there was apathy and resignation, followed by indifference. After all, we decided, we were not to blame for this appalling situation. The cruel realities of life had brought it. It was the world around us that demanded it and forced it upon us.

Then another thought came, that we had to consider: Could *they* be blamed — all the contemporaries and colleagues and companions who left the fold and turned alien to the Torah? But didn't they have a hard, bitter struggle to face? Didn't they find themselves in a twilight zone between life and death? In the mirror of their young life-spirits, didn't they see, perhaps, visions of dreadful tragedies that might lie ahead for them, till they decided that they *had* to take the fateful steps of leaving their true identity somewhere behind them?

In truth, didn't we come across young fellows here and there — in Warsaw and Lodz, Lemberg and Cracow — young Torah students who went wandering around, nestling against some wall for comfort because they were suffering from hunger and lack of sleep?

Weren't we ourselves, every one of us, living witnesses who could testify to the crude, brute denigration that the average member of a community displayed toward yeshiva students? As our great Rav indicated, the Sages of old envisioned a historic, timeless partnership in Jewry: Some, like the ancient tribe of Z^{e}vulun, would engage in commerce and industry. Others, like the tribe of Yissachar, would stay in the House of Study and work to gain a viable mastery of the Torah. Z^e^vulun would share its profits with Yissachar, giving its scholars and students enough to sustain them. In return, part of Yissachar's reward in the Afterlife would go to Z^e^vulun.

In the partnership that our Sages envisaged, as a pattern for ongoing Jewish survival, the average, ordinary member of a Jewish community in Poland had to be considered metaphorically of the tribe of Z^e^vulun; and the yeshiva *bochurim*, certainly of Yissachar. Then the treatment that a yeshiva *bochur* received in any given community was enough to make him cry aloud to Heaven. Was that how a full and equal partner should be treated? — a partner in a compact that had to provide for both of them a bridge between two worlds?

For what was the system like? For meals there was the standard arrangement of *ess'n teg* ("eating days"): every day of the week, a student went to different householder, for his one good meal of the day. At night he would sleep in somebody's little retail store. In any case the shop owner needed a watchman to guard the place against thieves; so he did the yeshiva *bochur* a "favor" and let him sleep there. Well, those Torah students proved to be faithful, reliable watchmen. In time they came to be in demand.

Consider then, if you will, the mental state of the yeshiva student. Have a look into the deeper corners of his heart. The food he received was, as it were, thrown at him with an attitude of disdain and insult by a householder who regarded him, more or less, as something between a parasite and an unaffordable luxury. It never occurred to the man to wonder if perhaps he was making the young guest's blood boil, or if, perhaps, he was making him feel that the vital red liquid was pouring from an open wound in his heart. What? — did a yeshiva *bochur*'s blood also course and function normally, like everybody else's?

Does it have to be explained, then, why a Torah student never felt nourished and sustained by the food he received? — why he always felt a gnawing hunger? Is it hard to understand why, as a rule, he felt nervous, shattered, vulnerable? And then he was expected to sit and study for hours on end, zealously, assiduously, to absorb the lesson material faithfully, so that he could retain it well.

So much for the food that the members of Z^e^vulun provided for the young scholars of Yissachar. Now let us consider further the matter of sleep. When a young student had a retail store to sleep in, he was quite content. What would he do if he had not even this? He would have to sleep somewhere in the street; or at best, on a hard bench in a *beyss medrash.* A store was better:

At night the shopkeeper let him in and left, locking the door behind him. Now the yeshiva *bochur* was imprisoned for some twelve hours, under lock and key — till the businessman rose in the morning at a fine leisurely hour and came at last to open the store.

As a rule, the young Talmudist was cold in the store. There was nothing he could do to warm himself. So he shivered, till his bones practically rattled. He sat down and opened the volume of Talmud he had brought with him, and spent the next few hours studying intensively, striving to warm himself by the "light of the Torah." Perhaps, eventually, he would telephone a friend who was similarly imprisoned in another store, and the two could discuss some fine points in the Talmud study that had occurred to him..

At last the hour grows late and the time comes to lie down on the pallet prepared for him and to get some sleep. Hardly has he closed his eyes, however, when he thinks he has heard a rapping sound somewhere. Could it be thieves? In alarm, he goes to investigate — and finds nothing. It must have been a gust of wind working on a loose shutter. . . . One way or another, he would never get a full night of sound, restful sleep. There was always something to make him wake and wonder in fear-ridden doubt.

Yet the conclusion had to be that this too was for the best. As our immortal Rav Meir Shapiro once put it with his wry humor, "The Talmud states (*bavli*, K^{e}subos 68a), 'Come, let us be grateful to *rama'im*, swindlers.' In a loose, general sense the term can include thieves also; and the yeshiva *bochurim* can be grateful that they exist: Otherwise, the young scholars would not be invited to sleep in the stores."

Now, what "lovely treat" might await the yeshiva student in the morning, when the well-fed owner came at last to open the place? Most likely, he would turn to his young guest, exhausted after the few snatches of sleep that he had been able to get during the night, and the man would grunt or growl out, "You there: take a brush in one hand and a pail of water in the other, and give this place a good scrubbing" (or it might be some other chore that he thought of). "Come on: get up and get busy."

Wouldn't the exhausted young fellow be justified if he lost his temper and exploded? Wasn't the owner going a bit too far in demanding this demeaning labor from someone who had gotten hardly any real sleep because he had served as a watchman without pay? A sharp, biting retort probably sprang to his lips, but he did not dare utter it. It was unthinkable for him to rebel against this "minor despot" though he saw him as a crude, sadistic exploiter. For what would the young fellow gain by rebellion? The man would dismiss him at once from his "position" as watchman. He would simply throw him out, barking as he left that there was no need for him to come back. And who knew how soon the young Talmudist could find another place?

So he carried out the owner's orders. He did the chores with such strength as he had, while he nursed the emotions of revenge that surged within him helplessly. He suppressed his feelings, kept them in and kept his tongue, waiting, hoping and dreaming of better times.

Yet the better times never came. He could only feel captured and enslaved, till he gave way to feelings of resignation and despair. And in this psychological state he would come to the *beyss medrash*, to begin another day of "scintillating" Talmud study.

Out of this type it was expected — no, demanded — that a religious leader should emerge: out of this type, whose innate natural self that had to develop and grow was enslaved and enmeshed in bonds of suppression and suffering; out of this type, who felt so dependent on others, so vulnerable to them, so greatly at the mercy of the folk who held power over him.

Of him it was expected — no, demanded — that he should be able to gather courage and take a firm, fearless stand on various religious matters. It never occurred to anyone to consider that this type was almost frightened to death by an angry frown or a cross look from a householder who gave him food or lodging. How in the world was he to emerge as a religious leader who could fulfill the command of the Torah, *You are not to be afraid before any man!* (*D'varim*/Deuteronomy 1:17)?

And yet, under such circumstances, in these miserable, deplorable conditions, the young *bochur* sat and studied steadily through the best years of his growth to maturity. Willingly, knowingly, he offered his heart and energy as a sacrifice on the altar of Torah learning, accepting it as a sublime ideal worth the sacrifice. He came and studied with an honesty that spurned any ways of evasion or deceit. In his own way, anguished or bedeviled as he might feel, he took a path of heroism for our sacred Torah.

After so much selfless devotion and sacrifice, was it any more than elementary justice to ask and expect that the community of religious Jewry at large should welcome him with the greatest honor? Surely his way of self-sacrifice deserved recognition and appreciation? Surely he earned the right to be placed at the forefront of Jewish society!

To our sorrow, nothing of the sort happened or could be expected to happen. For we came to live in a time when a virtually idolatrous respect developed for secular education that could lead to an academic degree. It became a time when any Jewish student who gained admission to a Polish secular school was almost revered; and if someone attained the degree of doctor, he was practically worshipped. In our Jewish world the ideal became to study in a Polish *gymnasya* (high school) or university. This became our Jewish dream, the great longing and hope even in a great many religious families.

How happy and fortunate a Jewish father felt when a son of his brought home a diploma, a certificate attesting that the boy had finished his course of studies in some secular school, Jewish or Polish. The family felt that the greatest, most radiant joy had come into their lives.

A great illusory rule developed in our Jewish world, as a guide to life: *Secular study will bring happiness and good fortune; Torah study will bring sorrow and misfortune.* For there was a groundless certainty that worldly study was sure to lead to material gains, while a young man devoted to Torah learning would be unable to earn a living. He would become and remain a useless person. He would be an other worldly ascetic, living in a misty aura of holiness and knowing nothing practical and useful about the earthly world of reality.

Hence only the secular, enlightened and educated student should be wreathed with a garland of admiration and adulation. He was (supposedly) a polymath: he had a full, rounded education and knew everything.

Needless to say, as such naïve, unrealistic myths became the firm, unshakable convictions of the society of our time, the prestige of the Torah's devotees fell to the uttermost abyss. They became regarded as persons of absolutely no account, who would be cast off into some dusty corner and completely disregarded. They ceased to be considered a meaningful part of Jewish society.

The accumulating effect of this state of affairs was disastrous. As the attitudes toward Torah learning grew steadily worse, whole masses in observant Jewry were suddenly wrenched out of the matrix of the Torah. Some of our best forces, our most promising young elements, veered off sharply, without warning, into the camps of the radical, alien ideologies. Day by day the ranks that held fast to the Torah shrank in number. The young learners simply deserted us in droves. We lost one group after another.... *Yet, could we blame them?*

****

This, dear reader, was the situation in the Poland of our time: in the years known in the civil calendar as the twenties, the third decade of the twentieth century. Such was the acrid, bitter atmosphere produced by a vile mix of economic and political conditions, fermented by winds of new and radical ideologies.

In that situation of utter pathos and misery, when despair could come so easily with a total loss of hope, we, his devoted *talmidim*, could look on our illustrious instructor and mentor, Rav Meir Shapiro, as nothing less than a rescuing angel. We saw him come and spread wings of compassion over us in our plight — over the entire youth of Poland that remained, even if in desperation, studying away at their volumes of Talmud.

With his actions that spoke louder than words he proclaimed a message of liberation: "You will be released," came his wordless message, from his heart to ours. "Your esteem will be lifted up. You will no longer have to slink through life, derided, beaten, cowed. You will walk and act in self-reliance. The chains in which the men of commerce and trade have kept you enslaved will be broken. I will shatter them for you. Only one belt will remain to gird your loins and keep you lithe and supple: the girding and fastening of the Torah. In its domain, under its wings, you will find your protection.

This is what it meant for us when a new star rose in our sky: a star that bore the words *Yeshivas Chachmey Lublin*.

25

To set the foundation

All things considered, it was not a long period that ensued from the announcement to the foundation stone. Rav Meir exemplified a short, pithy saying of Polish Jews: *geredt un geton* ("said and done"). Having declared an intention, invariably he went into action.

In Elul 5683 (August 1923) he broke new ground in the thinking of the Torah world when he proclaimed in Vienna his vision of a new yeshiva — at the first *K'néssiya G'dola* ("Great Assembly") of Agudas Yisra'el. Some eight months later, on *Lag ba'Omer*, 5684 (May 22, 1924), the foundation stone was positioned into the ground, in a festive, fiery ground-breaking ceremony.

It was the historic city of Lublin that was privileged to be the setting for this memorable event. And almost of itself the question came to a great many lips: *Why Lublin?* Would it not have been more felicitous and appropriate to locate the yeshiva in the holy Land of Israel rather than Poland? — in Jerusalem rather than Lublin?

And the questioning went further: Would it not be better to take the money that such a structure of splendor would swallow up, and share it out, so that a goodly number of small, modest yeshivos could be built, for every group and circle in Poland's Torah Jewry?

Such queries came pouring in, addressed to the creator of the yeshiva. People analyzed and discussed the matter with all the subtleties of *pilpul*, and each individual mind seemed to read a different intention or meaning in Rav Meir's plans. The plain truth of the matter, though, was quite simple: Certainly the most suitable, desirable and holy setting for the yeshiva was Jerusalem. One needed, however, to understand the broad, all-encompassing view of the matter that informed the Rav when he formulated his large-scale plans — and then all became clear.

In the years when the idea of the yeshiva wove and spun in his creative mind, the economic condition of the world at large was good. The prosperity that prevailed had not yet been broken or smashed by recessions or depressions. And so the overall financial situation of world Jewry was equally sound and healthy. There were enough men of wealth in the world community who had felt nothing as yet to make them fear a crisis. In general, the warning signals of impending crisis were hardly registered anywhere.

Assuming, then, that the funds for it could be found, this is how Rav Meir conceived his masterplan to rescue Torah education in Poland from perdition: *A network of yeshivos would be spread across the land.* Such was the plan he presented at the great rabbinic convention that was held later, in 5686 (1926): "To found a *yeshiva k^e^tana* (a secondary Torah school) in every town and small city; in every major, central city, a regional yeshiva; and for the entire country, a *yeshiva g^e^voha* (a learning center for advanced study)."

To us, the *talmidim* who were close to his operational headquarters, this is how he described his original masterplan: In every small town (*shtétl*) there should be a small yeshiva, which would supply pupils for the larger yeshivos. In the large, historic centers of Polish Jewry — Lublin, Brisk (Brest-Litovsk), Cracow, Lemberg, etc. — great, major yeshivos should be established; and the greatest yeshiva of all should be constructed in Jerusalem. That should be the destination of the most gifted *talmidim*, the greatest of the young scholars, who will emerge from these yeshivos. There they should go to complete their Torah education, learning the Talmud and *halacha* that apply to the Holy Land.

This was no pointless dream, no idle, empty speculation by a mind lost in fantasy. The times were ripe for it then. In later years, when the yeshiva was a living reality in Lublin and he had to strain and struggle to keep it alive, he said, "I didn't fool myself; I'm not at all disappointed about my great plans. I see what is going on in this land. The situation is catastrophic. Every possible means for Jews to earn a living and exist here is being systematically torn from us and made to disappear. The ground for survival is being pulled away from under our feet. And yet Jews give such handsome contributions, far more than they can afford. Had I made the yeshiva right then, when the idea was born, they would have showered me with money. . . . It just came into existence a bit too late."

For the first great learning center in his all-encompassing plan, the most suitable top-ranking location was indisputably Lublin. From there came the very conception of a yeshiva in Poland. It was there the idea had sprouted and blossomed; from there it developed and spread. And in that city some of the finest yeshivos in the world had flourished.

Having been carved up into three parts that were ruled for centuries by foreign powers, Poland was again united now into one land; and thus Lublin was again located most favorably at the country's center, as it had been in a much earlier time. Long before the land had ever been partitioned, Lublin became the natural setting for the periodic conferences of the *va'ad arba aratzos* (the Council of Four Lands), the supreme authority over the Jews of Poland in the areas of autonomy and self-government that they were granted.

More to the point, perhaps: In that urban center, some three centuries earlier, had lived and worked historic personages who could truly be called *chachmey Lublin*, the great, wise scholars of the city: There had been Rav Ya'akov Pollack, the founder of the first yeshiva, who originated the approach of *pilpul*; the immensely learned Rav Shalom Shachne [he and Rav Ya'akov were the great mentors and instructors of Rav Moshe Isserles — *Rama*]; Rav Sh^elomo Luria, *(Maharshal)*, the author of *Yam shel Sh^elomo*; and the noted *rosh yeshiva* Rav Meir ben G^edalya (*Maharam* of Lublin).

On the other hand, in the chassidic world Lublin was renowned as the site of the illustrious Rav Ya'akov Yitzchak Hurvitz, the youngest of the thirty-nine disciples of the Maggid of Mezritch, who became known for all time as "the *chozeh* (Seer) of Lublin." It was he who brought *chassidus* to the whole of Congress Poland about a century before Lublin acquired Rav Meir's great yeshiva.

In consequence, the most appropriate location for the yeshiva, planned as a creative, dynamic synthesis of Torah and *chassidus*, could only be Lublin, where the greatest masters of both that Jewry had ever known, lived and flourished. They had brought lasting pride and honor to our people in the past. Here, then, arose the yeshiva that would bring us, hopefully, new pride and glory in the present.

What a tragedy it was, though, that in the years when Rav Meir Shapiro's far-reaching plans developed and matured, the economic situation in Poland and everywhere deteriorated so disastrously. So many Jewish men of substance became impoverished and ruined. And thus Rav Meir's great, all-encompassing plan had to remain no more than a plan that lived in his heart of hope, with a dynamism of its own. All that came into reality was *Yeshivas Chachmey Lublin*, built to be a world center for Torah study. And even this was achieved only by a miracle, that will now be recounted. Such is the pure, unvarnished truth behind the yeshiva's construction.

****

The longest street in Lublin was named Lubartovska, and most of its inhabitants were Jewish. On that street, a renowned philanthropist named Sh'mu'el Eichenbaum made a most unusual donation: a tract of land that he owned, which measured 52,000 square meters (35,000 acres).

Eichenbaum was a historic type: one of the old style Russian Jewish men of means and generosity — good-hearted, good-natured souls from the vast domain of age-old Russia. In the years before the great World War he made a resolution that he would divide his large fortune in half: One part he would keep for himself; the other he would share out among the poor and the indigent who had to live in distress. In the years that followed, he continued his policy of benevolence and generosity. And evidently our Divine providence ordained that the plot of ground for the great yeshiva of Rav Meir should come from him — a large piece of land worth a small fortune under the conditions of the times: thirty thousand dollars.

This is how it happened:

[As recounted in an earlier chapter, early in the year 5683 (late 1922), Rav Meir decided to run for election to the second Sejm (the Polish parliament), as a candidate of Agudas Yisra'el. On the fifth of Tishri, 5683 (September 27, 1922) the first Sejm was dissolved. On the fourteenth of Cheshvan (November 5) the general election for the second Sejm was held. In that interval it was imperative for him to make journeys through the major cities, to arouse the devout Jews to join in the forthcoming election and give their vital support to the religious candidates.]

As part of his campaign plans, Rav Meir wished to visit Lublin and gain the strong support of its large number of observant Jews. The good-natured Sh'mu'el Eichenbaum put one of his coaches at the Rav's disposal, so that he could be driven about through the city and do "a thorough job" of campaigning there. Then the philanthropist went further: He offered to accompany the Rav and show him the historic sites of Lublin in what would amount to a "guided tour" — dovetailed and harmonized with the campaign.

As the two were riding along, Eichenbaum pointed to a plot of land: "Do you see that empty ground? I just bought it a short while ago."

"Why did you buy it?" asked Rav Meir; "for what purpose?"

"I really don't know yet," replied the philanthropist. "I had a chance to get it for a good price, so I bought it."

"In that case," said Rav Meir without hesitation, "I know why you bought it: for a great, holy purpose; but now it is still too early to talk about it." The conversation took place over a year and a half before the ground-breaking ceremony would mark the formal beginning of the yeshiva's construction. Already then, however, in the Rav's dynamic mind the resolution had firmly formed to anchor his dream in that historic city.

More than a year after this conversation in the coach, the idea was solidly on its way to becoming reality. A building committee was in existence, with Rav Meir at its head; and it duly published a formal report:

"We lift up our eyes to the time of old, to the golden age when the *va'ad arba aratzos* (the Council of Four Lands) was a living force, and a yeshiva of world importance functioned here as a center of Torah study in the land of Poland — from which Torah learning and Torah instruction went out to every Jewish home. Here have we met today to raise up anew the holy mandate of the Torah, so that we can affirm our submission to it. We call for the revival of the historic world center of Torah study, to be known as *Yeshivas Chachmey Lublin*; and for this purpose we have resolved to erect a stately building that will contain study rooms, dormitory and dining rooms, which can offer accommodations for five hundred gifted, capable students, with all their spiritual and material needs provided for.

"However it will turn out, above all, be this man remembered for good: the philanthropic Reb Sh'mu'el Eichenbaum, whose heart was moved by generosity to grant us as an absolute, permanent gift a plot of land suitable for the project.

"And may the blessed Divine Sovereign bestow His lovingkindness on us all, so that the object of our desire may succeed by our efforts — to return the crown of the Torah to its pristine glory of old, by establishing this holy, precious institution as an academy for the development of Torah learning and piety. Then may Torah study flourish here in great splendor, for the glory of the world community of devout and reverent Judaism.

"Signed in the week of the Torah portion in which it is written of the

Almighty that *He made houses for them* (*Sh^{e}mos*/Exodus 1:21), the sixteenth of Tévés, 5684 (December 24, 1923)."

In the presence of the *beyss din* of Lublin (the judges of the religious court), the deed of the land was formalized, and it became the property of the building committee, in which Sh'mu'el Eichenbaum held a prominent place. At the same time another magnate and prince of philanthropy made a major contribution: Tz^{e}vi Zilber, president of the Lublin community, promised to donate half a million building bricks — a tremendous start toward the realization of the project.

It is worth going back in time, however, to record the conversation between Rav Meir and Sh'mu'el Eichenbaum in which the "deal" was "made": When Rav Meir felt the time was ripe, he remarked to the magnate, "I want to offer you a really good business proposition. Since you became a wealthy man of property and business interests, I don't think anything as splendid as this has ever been offered you."

Reb Sh'mu'el looked at him in surprise: "Indeed? Since I've been in business as a man of property, *never* before have I been made such an offer? Is it really possible, that in all my dozens of transactions, involving enormous numbers of rubles, I've never encountered until now a business proposition like this? And now, honored Rabbi, you are prepared to close such a deal with me? Well, I'm certainly ready to listen." For he was definitely curious to know what in the world Rav Meir meant.

Came the reply, "I want the front part of your tract of land, to build a yeshiva on it."

Reb Sh'mu'el looked at him thoughtfully, and stated calmly that he would need half an hour to think the matter over; and away he went to the privacy that he needed. When he returned, he had his answer ready: "I'm sorry, but I cannot give you the front part of my piece of land. I can only give you the whole lot!" And his face was radiant with happiness. . . .

There was, however, an unexpected sequel: Sh'mu'el Eichenbaum's wife had not been there at the time, and when she learned about this "splendid business transaction," in which her husband had gone and given away the large piece of land for a yeshiva, she came along and imperiously demanded a *din torah* — a court hearing on the matter!

What could Rav Meir think? He feared the worst: that someone had persuaded her to go and void the whole transaction — reduce it to nothing. Yet what could he do? A demand for a *din torah* had to be honored.

On a set day, she duly appeared in the Lublin community's religious court, to present her case. A small throng of strangers gathered to fill the room and mill around outside, out of curiosity to know what she would demand and what the verdict would be.

To everyone's amazement, she expressed her deep satisfaction and great pleasure at what her husband had gone and done: that he had donated the large plot of ground for the great mitzvah of having a yeshiva of world importance built on it. There was one thing she wanted, however: that the gift should be made in her name as well, and it should be so recorded: as the deed of both Mr. and Mrs. Eichenbaum. She wanted an equal share of the tremendous mitzvah.

The *beyss din* duly gave its verdict: The document that recorded Sh'mu'el Eichenbaum's gift was declared null and void. In its place another document was to be written, containing the names of both him and his wife.

In the presence of the couple, the official *sofer* was called — the court scribe; and he rewrote the document as required. "Well, then," exclaimed the good lady, "now the costs of the case have to be paid!" But the judges were stymied: what sort of fees could they ask of her in such a peculiar case? She, however, helped them out of the dilemma: "In payment of the court fees," she declared, "I donate all the milk that will be taken from the hundred milch cows we have on our farm. It is to be used for the provision of food for the young learners who will come to study at the yeshiva."

Such was the generosity of this unusual couple that shared a common, harmonious interest in truly Jewish philanthropy.

****

As the time approached for the ground-breaking ceremony, major articles appeared in the Jewish press, that gave prominence to the idea of a yeshiva that would command worldwide acclaim, as they sang the praises of the mind which had conceived the plan. More than a little criticism, however, was also directed at the originator of the idea, mainly in the form of questions beginning with the word *Why?*: Why Lublin of all places? Why not Warsaw? Why not Jerusalem? . . . and so on.

In addition, there was one signal article in the press, written by Rav Meir himself, that bore the heading, *zeh ha-yom she-kivinuhu*: "This is the day for which we hoped!" (*Eycha*/Lamentations 2:16). With his gifted pen he conveyed to the entire Jewish world, for all to read, the full range of hopes, expectations and desires that for him, were bound up with the planned world center for Torah learning. He delineated all that he anticipated from it, all that he looked forward to seeing in consequence of its viable existence and dynamic activity. "The yeshiva," he wrote, "must animate anew the acclaim of the Torah in times of old. This learning center must draw and concentrate within its boundaries those highly gifted souls, those richly endowed spirits, who are capable and likely to become the pride of Torah Jewry. The young learner who comes here must find himself in a trustworthy, fatherly, protective atmosphere, where he can develop fully in a knowledge of Torah and a genuine reverent piety, to the greatest possible extent."

26

The ground-breaking ceremony

As the time approached, Lublin took on a festive appearance, as though it were decked out for a Jewish holiday. The streets were simply teeming with people. Tens of thousands of new, unfamiliar faces could be seen, all pulling and streaming toward one corner on the road called Lubartovska Street.

What was happening here? What was urging and driving them all toward that plain, nondescript corner? This question any number of voices were prepared to answer: "It is a festive day for the authentically Jewish world. A global study center is to be built here, that will lift high the prestige of the Torah. It will bring back to Lublin the splendor of Torah learning that it knew long ago. And this is the day set for the ground-breaking ceremony — over there, at that ordinary, insignificant corner."

****

Eminent rabbinic figures began arriving, along with rabbinic delegations from various institutions located both in Poland and in other lands. [From far-off Bukovina in northern Rumania, a mass of excited, enthusiastic visitors came streaming in. From Vienna came "troops" of *chassidim*, to accompany the Rebbe of Tchortkov. When the Rebbe of Ger let it be known in Warsaw that he was going by train to Lublin for the occasion, more thousands of *chassidim* were drawn as by a magnet to make the trip with him.]

On a specially constructed platform a whole group of revered chassidic leaders could now be seen: the august Rebbe of Tchortkov, with his sons, and nearby, the Rebbe of Ger, along with the Rebbes of Sokolow, Slonim, Kozhnitz, Novominsk, and so on. The venerable Rebbe of Belz sent his son-in-law, the Rav of Ustilla, as his personal delegate. In addition, on that platform were some fifty truly distinguished rabbis from all over the world.

In all, it was estimated that some fifty thousand people were gathered at the place.

****

The time came for the ceremonies to begin, and all grew still. A sense of holy ardor bordering on ecstasy seemed to hold everyone in thrall. In the sight of everyone, the originator of the idea stood on the platform now, ready to speak.

As might have been expected, he began with a passage from the Talmud (*bavli*, B^erachos 63b) that was astonishingly apt: "When our Sages came into the vineyard in Yavneh [where they were able to establish their Torah headquarters after the Temple was destroyed and Jerusalem demolished] . . . they all opened their discourse with words about the eminence of the populace that gave them hospitality, and then spoke on. Then Rabbi Yehuda, chief of the speakers at every occasion, began about the eminence of the Torah, and discoursed further."

[This is how Rav Meir Shapiro saw the event: literally as the genesis of a new "vineyard in Yavneh" to restore the majesty and authority of the Torah in Jewish life in the Diaspora. Perhaps there was added poignancy in this passage because, while he was known as Rav Meir, his parents had named him Yehuda Meir. At any rate, for him the ancient event in Yavneh was graphically returning to life.]

So moved by ecstatic emotion was he that tears filled his eyes and choked his voice. It took a few minutes till he could gain control of himself. And then he continued, "Now is not the time to hold lengthy sermons. We must get to work at once on this building that we need, and set the foundation stone. In the distant past Lublin was the Yavneh of this region of the world. Thus we have to rebuild it!

"Our human speech is too limited, too poor to describe and express the feelings that flutter and pulse through a true Jewish heart now, at this moment, when the foundation stone for the great edifice is to be put in place. We are bringing back to Polish Jewry the pride that it knew long ago. . . . Let it be enough to recall that this day is *Lag ba'Omer*, the *yortzaït* of Rabbi Shim'on ben Yochai, the day of the year when he passed on from this earthly world to his eternal reward; and as the Talmud relates (*bavli*, Shabbas 138b), 'Rabbi Shim'on ben Yochai rose up on his feet and said, *Perish the thought that Torah will be forgotten in Jewry!* We too can declare today confidently: Perish the thought that Torah will be forgotten in Jewry!"

The entire mass of people seemed to be swaying and floating in the air, inspired by the vision of the promised future, inspired as they had never been before. The throng felt palpably that they themselves were a living demonstration, for all the world to see, of the unalterable truth of those words that Rabbi Shim'on ben Yochai had spoken so long ago.

"Today," continued Rav Meir, "today is also the *yortzaït* of the *Rama*, Rav Moshe Isserles — and he was a *talmid* at the very first yeshiva in Lublin. We have to remember, then — all of us — that we are performing a deed today whose meaning will live for generations to come. At this place we shall rear and develop the future great authorities of our people, the spiritual leaders of Poland's Jewry. . . . "

Rav Meir then expressed his appreciation to all the distinguished visitors, all the eminent men of Torah learning and chassidic piety, who did not spare themselves the wearying toil and trouble of making the journey to Lublin, to participate in the celebration of this singular mitzvah. He paid a special tribute of gratitude to the remarkable philanthropist Sh'mu'el Eichenbaum, noting that thanks only to him could he, Rav Meir, have begun bringing into reality the dream he had held for so many years.

[In the course of the proceedings, the Rebbe of Tchortkov told Eichenbaum privately, with a smile, "Over this mitzvah that Heaven will credit to your account in eternity — that this tract of ground is being consecrated to build the yeshiva on it — over this mitzvah, I am not jealous of you. Here it is being proclaimed publicly, and it brings you great honor. What I am jealous of is the mitzvah you did originally, when you made Rav Meir a present of it discreetly, ccnfidentially. Not another soul knew about it, and you gained nothing whatever from that personally. And that led to your great 'public' mitzvah today. Over that mitzvah I feel jealous. . . . "]

Among all the revered and eminent guests, Polish Jewry tended to regard two as the very greatest of their time in Torah and piety: the chassidic leaders of Tchortkov and Ger. These two descended carefully now into the cavity that had been dug in the ground, as space for the foundation. First, the Rebbe of Tchortkov set the foundation stone in place. Then he took three coins and wrapped them in a silk cloth, and thus he placed them beneath the stone; and he quoted a few words from the Torah's Book of *B'réshis*: "How awesome is this place! This is nothing other than the House of God" (Genesis 28:17).

He continued: "When *Ya'akov avinu* (our Patriarch) came to the spot where his fathers had prayed (*bavli*, Sanhedrin 95b), he said, *How awesome is this place!* This place is fraught with an awe-inspiring atmosphere of sublimity since time immemorial. Not I engendered it, but my fathers. So *this is nothing else but a House of God*; as our Sages noted (*bavli*, P^esachim 88a), Ya'akov saw the Almighty's Divinity in the image of a house. Therefore a person who finds himself here need do nothing more than convert this place into a House of Divinity.

"This," concluded the Rebbe of Tchortkov, "is how I see the *Yeshivas Chachmey Lublin.* The site is historic; it is infused with holiness since time beyond memory. What is there for us to do now? — to build a House on the site. To paraphrase our Sages (*bavli*, Chagiga 3b), the first consecration [by Lublin's Torah scholars of the far past] hallowed it for its own time, and hallowed it for a time to come in the future [meaning for us here, today]."

Now it was the turn of the Rebbe of Ger. He took up the foundation stone and set it reverently in place. Then he cited words of the Almighty from the Torah's Book of *Va-yikra*: "And yet, with all that, when they are in the land of their enemies, I will not have despised them" (Leviticus 26:44). With the words of the Midrash (Sifra, *b^echukosaï parsh.* 1 *perek* 8, version of Yalkut Shim'oni I:675) he continued: "What, then, has remained for the Jews, so that they should not become despised [in Heaven's sight]? Surely all the good gifts they were given were taken away from them? What has remained for them? — the scroll of the Torah: for if Jewry had no Torah, it would be no different at all from the nations of the world."

"This," said the Rebbe of Ger, "is a Divine promise for the time when Jews will find themselves in a land of enemies, in a situation where, in their life of the spirit, literally nothing is left of them. Then, when it is a question of rescuing the Torah of the Jews, no sacrifice is too great. This day itself, as we stand here, bears witness. When Ya'akov and his father-in-law Lavan made a pact of peace, a mound of stones and a stone pillar were set up to mark the pact for their future generations. And Lavan said, 'This *gal* (mound) shall be witness, and this pillar shall be witness' (*B^eréshis*/Genesis 31:52). Today is *Lag ba'Omer*, and the same Hebrew letters are in both *lag* and *gal.* As they had a stone pillar set, so we have set this foundation stone today. 'This *gal* shall be witness': The letters of *gal* denote for us *lag* — this day of *Lag ba'Omer*, the *yortzaït* of Rabbi Shim'on ben Yochai, who said, *Perish the thought that Torah will be forgotten in Jewry!* 'And this pillar shall be witness':

"This foundation stone is a testimony to the certainty of Rabbi Shim'on ben Yochai that Torah among the Jewish people will never be forgotten: for we see here that, as the Talmud assures us (*bavli*, Bava M^e^tzi'a 85a), Torah returns to its setting of hospitality!"

****

In behalf of the venerable Rebbe of Belz, his son-in-law, the Rav of Ustilla, spoke at length to give the Rebbe's blessings and to convey his great hope that the entire Jewish community would participate to the fullest possible extent in the construction of this great Torah edifice. In addition, the Rebbe's written response to the invitation to attend was read aloud: "Your letter reached me, bringing me great pleasure and happiness. Thank Heaven, Jewry is no bereaved, grief-stricken relic. May it strive to grow strong and strengthen the cause of our holy Torah, so that Torah and piety may be imparted among our holy flocks. May the blessed Almighty help that your Divine purpose will succeed through your actions, to go higher and higher in your holy work and produce good *talmidim* who will be true scholars and men of piety. . . . May you be privileged to make a good beginning with the foundation stone, to meet with success and complete the task swiftly. . . . And may the merit of the mitzvah cast its protection over you and over all who assist you in this great blessed undertaking, so that all may be blessed in their every heart's desire, for good."

Many hundreds of blessings and greetings arrived by telegram from all over the world; but Rav Meir made a brief statement that it would not be possible for him to read them out. Particularly interesting, though, was the telegram that came from Jerusalem, from the great, renowned Rav Yosef Cha-yim Sonnenfeld. He sent word that he had sent a number of venerable Torah scholars to the *kosel ma'aravi* (the Western Wall), to pray there for the success of the project.

As for the "elder statesman" of the Torah world, the venerated Chafetz Cha-yim, he sent word that to his deep regret, on account of his feeble health, it was impossible for him to take part in this great, historic event, but he wished it full success.

****

Now Rav Meir stood again, prominently, on the platform — ready to address the massive gathering once more. His voice thundered, reaching not only the ears of his listeners but their hearts as well.

"Dear Jews of Lublin," he exclaimed with fervor, "at the same time that my colleagues and associates went to invite, formally and officially, the proper government representatives, I went to invite the great, immortal Torah scholars of Lublin who flourished here in the distant past — to ask those unforgotten, unforgettable discarnate beings to take part in our festive celebration. And they are here — on this site!"

He ended with a heartfelt appeal to the entire Jewish world to support this great undertaking that was, necessarily, of prime importance to the entire Jewish world — and to grant it support enough so that they could be privileged to celebrate soon the *chanukas ha-ba-yis*, the dedication of the completed House of Study, with the proper glory and splendor.

The festive event continued late into the afternoon hours; and when it became necessary to attend to *mincha*, the afternoon prayers, the throng of many thousands went *en masse* to the famed *Maharshal shul* (the synagogue that bore the historic name of Rav Sh^{e}lomo Luria), the largest and most beautiful Jewish House of Prayer in all of Poland.

Then the celebration went on for yet more long hours, as entertaining and inspiring addresses were given by various rabbinic personages and representatives of the many delegations. At the end, the names of all the patrons and donors were recorded by a *sofer*, a trained scribe, on a roll of parchment; and this was cemented into the ground area where the foundations would be set, as a record for posterity.

****

At last the impressive historic event drew to a close. Now would have to come the days of hard work, wearying toil and intensive effort, to make a reality out of the plans for the yeshiva building. First, however, there were to be some unexpected developments, disquieting and worrying, that would have to be dealt with.

27

Growling dogs, howling wolves

When the news of the grand ceremony and the imposing plans spread through Lublin, it brought a reaction that caught us by surprise. An ill wind came brewing up on the horizon of Lublin, spewed out from some dark barbaric age, as all kinds of self-appointed enemies of our faith sharpened their teeth and claws to spring to the attack.

Thus the radical socialist Jews of the *Bund*, who hated the Torah and its adherents with a rare passion, mounted a screaming propaganda campaign "Concerning the Resurrection of the Shtreiml." Actually, it had begun agitating neurotically well in advance, fully in the open, warning the Jewish populace in alarm not to let itself be deluded and misled about some sort of nondescript, insignificant, flyblown yeshiva in Lublin. However, when a mass of 50,000 people understood the global importance of the occasion and turned out for the ground-breaking ceremonies, to the *Bund*'s consternation it was only too obvious to everyone that all its nagging advance agitation and propaganda had been worth less than a rubbed-out kopeck.

In its rage of frustration, the *Bund* turned up the gas: *"Gevald,"* screamed its Yiddish headline, *"di cleric* [the Jewish clergy]! *Oy vey, di shtreiml!"* And to ensure its place of infamy in our future history, it ran special feature articles in its journal, the *Folkstzaïtung*, under such headings as *"Five-story monstrosity being built in Lublin."* In that piece of elegant literature, the journal went on to weep crocodile tears as it worked to warn and alarm its devoted readers of the great dangers that this yeshiva could bring.

Yet all the Marxist propaganda in the Polish Jewish world could amount to no more than the yipe and bark of a small dog against a large, full moon sailing in the sky. Not a fragment of damage could it do to the Heavenly plan, the sublime vision of the yeshiva, which now had the support, admiration and respect of hundreds of thousands.

A really dangerous threat, however, came from the entrenched, bitter Jew-hatred of the Polacks. Up rose the Endeks, members of the *Endecja* party — mainly middle-class and petty bourgeois citizens who paraded their antisemitism with a fierce national pride. Through the *Rozvoy*, their fanatic, fulminating propaganda organization, they agitated and clamored for action, till a major conference was convened, to devise ways to eradicate all hope and thought about this yeshiva in Lublin.

In the course of the "noble, eloquent" addresses at the conference, the declaration was made by important men of influence that it would be a dishonor to the sovereign Polish government to have a "Jew university" erected there, on their holy Polish soil. A firm and forceful resolution was adopted to oppose by every possible means, with every available strength, any chance of constructing the yeshiva.

This protest action evoked strong support against us, and in fact, work on the building was eventually stopped three times by the Polish government. Yet that could certainly not be enough to satisfy a vengeful hunger to hurt the Jews. Scenes came alive that seemed to have been exhumed from the buried past of the Middle Ages.

Thus, one day, a group of Polack Catholics suddenly proclaimed, perhaps under the mellow influence of alcohol, perhaps on the basis of a revelation in a dream, that once upon a time, that plot of earth had been their possession, in their absolute custody. For many long years, they insisted, they knew it as hallowed ground, consecrated to the Catholic faith since days of yore. Therefore, they howled, under no circumstances would they allow that holy ground to be desecrated by a yeshiva.

Nothing was of any avail: no arguments, no firm, indisputable proof that the piece of land had been Jewish property for as long as they could remember. No matter what, those fine, devout Polacks would never allow their holy ground to be defiled by any yeshivos. This was their undeviating reply, that they kept shouting and ranting with never a stop.

What happened next? The next morning, a huge cross many yards or meters high blossomed out of the ground at the place for the yeshiva, and it stood there, tall and imposing, for all to see. Hundreds of Poles, from the entire region, came to look.

Now it was no longer a laughing matter. The anti-Jewish incitement had turned serious and worrisome. For all we knew, that plot of ground might already be a lost cause for us. Heaven only knew if there were any means that could still help us counteract and overcome the black, poisonous hatred which those Polacks had generated. Perhaps that entire gathering of thousands upon thousands for the ground-breaking ceremony would turn out to have been for nothing?

Whatever would happen, however, we did not dare draw back. It was vital to take vigorous action against these lethal enemies. We had to mount a legal process of some kind against this virulent hatred. . . . Well, this we did, and we won the case. The plot of ground remained ours.

We won . . . and still we were stymied. In the course of the legal battle, the official permit to build there had been rescinded. We needed a new permit to be able to resume construction work — and the government officials were in no hurry to stir. The cross still stood there, as immobile as the government officials; and masses of Poles felt drawn to come and gaze at it.

In the Polish legislature there was an upper house, the Senate, in addition to the Sejm. And in it there was a delegate of Agudas Yisra'el named Asher Mendelsohn. It was this Senator who went to work for us now, vigorously interceding on our behalf in the right government circles and exerting influence where it was needed. The upshot was that the relevant government ministry set its seal of approval to a new building permit. In fact, to everyone's surprise, the ministry turned quite favorable and sympathetic to the whole idea of the planned yeshiva.

When the bitter Jew-haters realized that their campaign of hostility had failed and nothing further that they could do would be of any use to influence people in power, suddenly, in the middle of one night, the tall, huge cross upped and disappeared. Just as no one ever discovered who had set it up there, so no one ever knew who removed it.

Yet there was one thing, at least, that they felt impelled to do, in the nature of a retaliatory attack: They set to work on a Catholic theological seminary not far from our site, thinking that this would frighten off our building committee and make us abandon our site. The ploy, however, gained them precious little. Once the cross was removed, construction was resumed, and it went ahead at a rapid tempo.

The foundations, strong as iron, were duly finished; and there, one day, the first brick sprang up on ground level. Another while went by, and the first floor was done. . . .

But the costs, alas, were colossal. The work simply absorbed enormous amounts of money. The financial reserves became depleted. Income and donations tended to be small. And then came the infamous so-called "Grabski crisis":

[In all the time since it gained independence, Poland had failed to set up a government that could deal adequately with its financial problems and achieve a workable economic policy. Burdened with enormous debts from the wars it had to wage after it gained independence, it was never able to raise enough tax money from its population. Inflation kept rising at a disastrous rate, because the only way that any Polish government could raise enough money was to print it. With severe chronic disagreement among the political parties, the country's financial condition went from bad to worse, with no way to a workable solution in sight.

[While he was Minister of Finance for a second time, Wladyslaw Grabski became the new President, with dictatorial powers, at the end of Tévés, 5684 (early January, 1924). Till the autumn he did remarkably well, and the country's financial condition improved. Then he failed to raise the money he needed from his property tax and from a loan by the United States, and the government faced a new crisis. At the end of the civil year, the zloty was worth half the value it had held six months earlier. So began the "Grabski crisis" — which sent the standard of living sharply down and made every sector in the country poorer. However, while all in the country were hit hard, the Jews felt themselves lambasted by the notorious Grabski and his infamous cohorts.

[In the face of its "crisis" the government quite simply decided, openly and blatantly, to squeeze the lifeblood out of the Jews. Various kinds of new taxes were dreamed up particularly for this purpose, aimed with a sharpshooter's skill at the world of small trade, including the merchants and shopkeepers, the owners of the little stores. By and large, it was the Jewish population in Poland that depended, virtually exclusively, on small retail commerce for its livelihood; and with the new, fancy taxation that came with the "Grabski crisis," in general they were left impoverished.]

****

To interrupt with a wry note, as a member of the Sejm and a foremost Jewish leader in Poland, Rav Meir was once asked how he saw the economic situation of the country's Jews in general. He replied by citing a few words from the Book of *Eycha*: "the princess among the states has become *la-mass*, tributary" (Lamentations 1:1). "In ancient times," he explained, "we had a regal status in our homeland, like a princess; and then there was such a thing as Jewish capital and Jewish wealth. Here in the Diaspora it's all gone, vanished. Such a concept doesn't exist any more. When are we reminded of such ancient glory? — *la-mass*: when it comes time for us to be tributary and pay our *mass*, the heavy tax burden that is placed on us. For we are taxed as if we were still a sovereign people in ancient times, enjoying wealth!"

****

Inevitably Rav Meir experienced now the fate of every creative human being with the gift and the initiative to set a visionary project in motion. In the early times the whole Jewish world seemed to be filled with deep interest and warm encouragement for the planned yeshiva. Now he could still find great admiration for his grand plan; but when it came to the practical, realistic aspects, by and large everyone kept his distance and proffered no help. In the new, disastrous economic situation, so many sources of generous charitable help in the Jewry of Poland simply dried up. . . . For the first time he felt the full impact of his position and his task. With his whole being he realized what it meant to have embarked on so great a project, of such vast dimensions.

There was only one thing for him to do: to employ the age-old Jewish approach of asking for funds — appealing for help. He would cry out to awaken the Jewish conscience and arouse Jewish awareness. And thus, with delicacy and tact, the first appeal for support duly appeared in the form of an article in Piotrkov's *Unzer Lebn* ("Our Life"). It declared:

"The name *Yeshivas Chachmey Lublin* is known so well by now that in retrospect it can only be regarded as a matter for surprise. Stirring addresses to arouse interest in it have been given through all of Europe. Only one year has passed since it began to come into existence, and yet it has brought reactions from the entire world of Torah learning. By now it is already engraved in every Jewish heart. What many believed to be a pure fantasy, what others saw as paradoxical absurdity, is today a burgeoning reality. . . .

"There hovers yet before our eyes that majestic scene at which fifty thousand people attended, with our great exemplars of Torah learning and holy piety, the supreme authorities of our time; and we recall the sublime exaltation of the spirit which prevailed there. Whoever did not see that spiritual joy has never seen true exalted joy in his life. . . .

"The need of the yeshiva is so burningly urgent that every day is like a year for us. Hundreds of young Talmud learners wait in hope, with the greatest impatience, for the moment when the yeshiva will be able to open its doors to them. They simply ask, *When shall we go to the House of* haShem *(the Lord)?*

"And so we turn to you: In your hands lies the fate of this great Torah center. Come and give us your help in our great undertaking. And then we will answer their poignant plea directly: *Come and let us walk in the light of* haShem*!" (Y^eshayahu*/Isaiah 2:5).

28

The "grand tour" in Europe

No matter how well he might write his articles to plead for help, no matter how brilliantly he might speak to arouse his listeners, Rav Meir had to realize and accept that from Poland he would never receive the money he needed to complete the yeshiva building. As one might say, with the "Grabski crisis" any and all hopes of that became ***bagrubbn***: buried in the ground.

Without hesitation, he decided to travel abroad; and to publicize his move, he gave an interview to members of the press.

Said he: When he set to work on the project, he never in the least imagined that he would have to travel out to other lands to gather the money to complete it. He was quite certain then that Poland's Jewry alone would have the financial power to accomplish the task. To give one characteristic example for his optimism, the community of Lodz promised to contribute forty thousand dollars for the yeshiva. "The crisis came, however," he continued, "and it disrupted my plans."

[It might be noted in passing that Lodz was known as "the Manchester of Poland": In the course of the industrial revolution, textile factories developed in Manchester, England, till that country became a supplier of machine-made cloth to the whole world. Similarly, Lodz became Poland's center for the manufacture of textiles; and much of that manufacture was in Jewish hands. A further point: in those years, the buying power of an American dollar was immensely greater than it is today; and evidently forty thousand dollars represented a small fortune.]

A long while later, when he was in America, Rav Meir spoke again, in an interview with a newspaper reporter, of the belief he had at first that there would be no need for him to travel out of Poland, and certainly not all the way to America — because he felt certain he could raise in Poland itself all the money that was needed. Then too he mentioned the Jewry of Lodz, and gave more details: They had raised their commitment to a firm promise of fifty thousand dollars, but on condition that he, Rav Meir, would work with them for two weeks to publicize the campaign, after which they would go to work to amass the full amount.

As Rav Meir told the reporter in that later interview in America, in Lublin he received likewise a firm promise of a total of fifty thousand dollars, from the community as a whole and from certain wealthy individuals who made separate commitments. Then, unfortunately, came the notorious "Grabski crisis," and as the broad masses of Polish Jewry feared a future of imminent and permanent poverty, a stream of migration to the Land of Israel developed. It was known officially as "the Fourth Aliya," but unofficially as "the Grabski Aliya." Evidently, a great part of the funds that might otherwise have come to Rav Meir for the yeshiva, went instead to finance the flow of migration.

Afterward, when the hubbub died down and there might have been hope of an economic recovery among Poland's Jews, it became evident that the situation had deteriorated hopelessly, and no such recovery could ever be expected. Thus, as Rav Meir explained much later to the reporter in America, all hope of finding the money he needed in Poland alone — was gone forever.

"And so," Rav Meir explained now, while still in Poland, as he spoke to the reporters, "I have two intentions behind the long trip that I am planning — two reasons for it: *one*, to gather the funds we must have to finish the building; and *two*, just the news that I have gone traveling out to other countries — including America — will infuse new courage and resolve into our people here. It will inspirit them with fresh energy, to carry on with the work!"

It was no easy pleasure jaunt that he meant to undertake, but a long, bone-wearying journey which would take him westward through the European continent and on to the United States and Canada. Yet the strength in his indomitable spirit impelled him. Not for a moment was there a twilight zone of hesitation, uncertainty or doubt in his mind, whether he should travel out or not. For to question whether or not to go would have meant to ponder whether to construct and build or, instead, to resign and surrender to defeat — to lift up the Torah's prestige or let it go on sinking.

He was not the man to cogitate and ponder such a question philosophically. There was one clear resolve in him: *Yeshivas Chachmey Lublin* must be created; it must be; it must live. And from that resolve all his subsequent work followed. No thoughts of disbelief, no feelings of doubt, were allowed to crystallize and form. They dissolved and vanished before they could appear. In this principle lay the strength of that phenomenal man of action.

****

The first major full stop on his international journey was Berlin; and there, in Germany's capital city in the middle of the century's third decade, he found a warm, pulsing response from hearts with a sensitive understanding of the Torah's importance. The fund-raising campaign took on a communal folk-character, as rabbis, people active in the community, and personalities from all the levels and sections of the Jewish population, participated readily.

It was wonderful beyond anyone's expectations that in Germany there would be such an enthusiastic response, with so much ardor and empathy. Apparently the old, historic aspirations of Ashkenazic Jewry for Torah knowledge in times long gone were reawakened, and sparks of an ardor for Torah kindled and flared into new life, to gather into a splendid blaze.

The Jews of Germany took to their hearts the simple thought that the entire motive behind his travels was the Torah, and nothing more. The idea touched them deeply, and in their response they showed how moved they were.

In addition to the three addresses that he gave in Berlin, he spoke twice in Leipzig and twice in Frankfort, then once in Hamburg and once in Halberstadt. There, in those historic locations, his impassioned oratory evoked an unexpected heartfelt response of German Jewry. (Of the numerous discourses in Talmud and *halacha* that he gave, merely for the pleasure and the merit of sharing his immense Torah learning with others, no record was kept.)

From that country the railroad trains took him to the Austrian capital, Vienna, where he spoke twice. He traveled on to Czechoslovakia's cities of Pressburg (Bratislava) and Prague, where he spoke once in each. Next came Strasbourg in northeastern France, and the Dutch city of Amsterdam. His destination after that was London, in the far-off English isle, where he spoke no fewer than five times. From London it was a short trip to the English city of Manchester, and there the Jewish community listened to three addresses from him.

When he gave his talk to a Jewish audience in Strasbourg, a curious thing happened. Since the purpose of his campaign was to complete an important building in Poland, the Polish consul came to listen to his oratory, accompanied by other members of government circles. So impressed was the consul by the eloquent, inspiring address that he sent off a correspondent's report about it to the Polish telegraphic news agency, and the report duly appeared in all the Polish newspapers.

To return for a moment to his visit to England, at the start the campaign seemed headed for failure — as this little episode can demonstrate: Shortly after his arrival, Rav Meir was taken on a short railroad trip by a representative of the British Jewish communities, to see a man of great wealth on his country estate — although the man was known to keep a tight grasp on his purse strings and a tighter lid on his generosity.

The Rav's escort duly presented him to this tight-fisted money-bags as a most distinguished visitor from abroad, and he explained the noble, lofty purpose of the visit — the reason why the Rav had come to England. Rav Meir himself then took over and did his best to explain the great benefit to Jewry that the planned yeshiva could bring — how greatly it could contribute to the future of the Jewish people.

The man of wealth just shook his head: "I'm sorry," he replied with an icy coldness that certain Britishers could show to perfection. "I cannot give anything for purposes like that."

Having sized the man up and seen just whom he was dealing with, Rav Meir retorted, "Do you know? I never imagined that the British empire would be so hospitable." The wealthy Britisher could only look at him in astonishment: "Why, what do you mean? In what way, for example, do you find it hospitable?"

"In Poland, only a member of the parliament, a delegate to the Sejm, may ride the railroad for nothing. Here in England, where I am no sort of representative or delegate to anything, I find that I too have ridden the railroad for nothing. . . . "

This was a further incident: The time came for him to visit another man of great wealth. As he entered the door with his escort, the man caught sight of him and realized that if he invited this unusual visitor into his living room or his study, the matter would cost him dear: for it was obvious that the purpose of the visit was to ask him for a large, sizable contribution.

Convinced that there was not a moment to lose, the man went swiftly to his money chest and drew out a piece of paper currency worth a few

British pounds; and waving it grandly, he came to greet Rav Meir in the entrance hall. "Here you are," said the man blithely. "I'm sure you have come for charity; so I've brought you this."

Rav Meir looked at the amount being proffered, and he shot back, "A pregnant woman needed two *kapporos*" [two animal offerings to be sacrificed for her on the Temple altar in ancient Jerusalem for atonement, at a set time after she gave birth: *Va-yikra*/Leviticus 12:6-8]. "I don't!"

The British Jew could only look at Rav Meir in astonishment: "Now, what in the world do you mean by that?"

In his rich, fluent Yiddish (which the man understood), the Rav told him: "Sometimes I may come to a man of means for a contribution, and he receives me with a fine courtesy, even cordially; but he gives me only a small donation. Then I tell myself silently, *a kapporeh di gelt*" [let the money go for an atonement; so he didn't give me much; so what?]; "at least there is honor for the Torah here — in the way he welcomed me. On the other hand, if a person receives me without any proper courtesy and esteem, but he gives me a right handsome donation for the yeshiva, I tell myself silently, *a kapporeh der kovod*" [let the honor — its striking absence — go for an atonement]; "at least there is money here for the yeshiva!

"With you, dear sir, I find myself presented with both *kapporos* together. You receive me in the hallway as if I were some shabby salesman, and you offer me a pittance. Two *kapporos*, my dear sir, are fine for a pregnant woman after she gave birth — not for me!"

Eventually, however, Rav Meir's ebullient, fiery warmth, with his ringing oratory and sparkling humor, broke through even the frosty reserve and icy aloofness of the Jews in England, and his visit there too went well enough to meet with gratifying success.

Throughout the journey, since his departure from Poland, Rav Meir had the companionship, moral support, and added prestige of the president of the Lublin community, Reb Moshe Eisenberg, who held the position of honorary secretary in the Building Committee. When their travels in Europe were over at last, the two made their plans to cross the Atlantic and go on with the campaign in the United States.

29

America: the "grand tour"

With Rav Meir's arrival on the North American continent, destiny evidently ordained a glorious chapter all its own for the history of the Jewish people in the United States and Canada. To their lot fell the privilege of crowning his journey with success and taking the lion's share of credit for the completion of *Yeshivas Chachmey Lublin.* The Jews in the "new world" — largely immigrants from "the old country" — understood its purpose and appreciated its importance. They grasped its historic meaning for Torah Jewry everywhere; they realized its significance for the entire Jewish community, worldwide.

His words were heard: "How great a disgrace it would be for us Jews, everywhere in the world, if not even one institution of higher Torah study existed anywhere that would be comparable at least to some sort of university! Don't our people have the means to establish it? Aren't there enough great men of wealth with the ability to create such a vitally needed institution entirely at their own expense?"

With questions of this kind Rav Meir bombarded the American Jewish community. And its leaders found no words with which to answer him. They had to acknowledge that it was an outrage which cried aloud to Heaven — a dishonor of historic proportions for the Jewish people. Could it be that "the People of the Book" did not have this much understanding for the importance of the Book — the Torah — and the necessity for its study at the university level? *In truth?*

Consider! (so went the relentless argument of Rav Meir, that was given wide publicity): Within the last few years before his arrival, the prestigious *Yeshivas Rabbénu Yitzchak Elchanan* was established [with its eventual adjunct, Yeshiva University]; and authentic, age-old Judaism was given new life in America. Excellent! Admirable! But what of Poland, the historic "old country" of the Jewish people, where a community of over three million still lived? Did American Jewry feel no sense of responsibility? Was there something wrong with its conscience?

His call struck home, and it struck a responsive chord. Jews in the New World understood him, and with open-hearted goodness they contributed generously to his great historic undertaking: the creation of a world center for Torah study. The great Talmud scholar and religious leader received full, warm support for his noble vision and hope. [In retrospect, the Rav was to write about the Jews of America: "The most beautiful page in the historic development of *Yeshivas Chachmey Lublin* was written by them, thanks to their way of responding to the project."]

****

If the truth must be told, however, it was not a story of immediate, overnight success. His first few months in the United States were a very difficult and trying period for him — a time of ordeal, when he saw only dismaying signs of apparent sunset for his glorious dream — an approaching nightfall presaging doom for the whole project. The American tour seemed headed for total failure, to leave him with the simple conclusion that his long, wearying travel by ship over the Atlantic Ocean had been for nothing.

[There was only one bit of easement that he found in those bleak few months at the start. Soon after his arrival, the Days of Awe arrived, and one congregation asked him to serve as their cantor — *ba'al mussaf* — on Rosh Hashana and Yom Kippur.

[In the heady, not-too-religious atmosphere of America in those years, the aspect of Jewish life in Poland which transferred perhaps most superbly to this new world was the love of listening to a *chazzan* at a prayer service. The great cantors were probably the "stars" then in the religious immigrants' "entertainment world." And Rav Meir was gifted with a beautiful lyric voice and an astonishing creativity in chassidic melody. So in return for his "cantorial art" he received a donation of a thousand dollars for the yeshiva — a superb fee for a *chazzan* in those times.]

As he took stock of the American scene, the initial impression he formed was that for the Jews in America, "business is business," with a complete dissociation from the Torah. Such words as *Torah, ideals, spirituality* seemed alien to them. They simply showed no interest in the eternal values that historic Jewry recognized and cherished since time immemorial. In their world, everything was appraised and evaluated through a businessman's eyes, and beyond that — nothing.

It took Rav Meir a good few months to become acclimatized enough to this radically new environment to be able to put his finger on the nub of the problem: He had not given enough attention to the matter of publicity. He had to learn, slowly and painfully, that America was a land of publicity and propaganda — which meant a need for hype, bigger hype, and superhype. In short, the means he employed at first to bring his message and his call to American Jewry had been too diffident and low-key, too modest and shy. Instead of talking in a soft, well-modulated voice, one had to declaim in strident tones, and also "turn up the volume." Then the people would hear the message, in a language they understood.

Almost the instant that Rav Meir grasped the essence of what had been lacking, once he had the problem diagnosed accurately, the campaign entered a new phase immediately. The work of reaching the Jews of America took on a new dynamism and vitality — and the response was truly gratifying.

Be it recorded to the eternal credit of this community that even the extreme left, the most radical elements, which had reacted quite coldly to the idea of the great yeshiva, eventually came to understand and accept it, and they gave it their good cooperation — not only their ordinary members but even the representatives of their press.

The long and short of it was that once the campaign began to evoke some warm reactions, it accelerated into the standard American tempo of the times: the tempo of "hurry up." Everything went ahead "loud and noisy," at a rapid pace — and with good results. Having learned to understand something of this New World, the Rav spoke to his American brethren with the language of the heart:

"In Poland and America we have the two greatest communities of our people, and these two Jewries must help each other. There must be mutuality between the two. Between us must be built a bridge of common concern and shared responsibility *for the individual Jew.* American Jewry has attained, by Heaven's grace, to a life of affluence and esteem; Polish Jewry remains the custodian of a love of Torah and a Jewish awed awareness of Heaven. The two must merge and blend into one shared lifeway. One must enhance and complement and complete the other. . . .

"The United States of America was graced by Heaven to be dragged into the [First] World War only to a moderate extent; and consequently, it was left quite undamaged and unharmed. Now, in the aftermath, it has developed into a mighty empire, towering over the ruins of the other empires. Let our brethren in America remember well this most significant point. . . .

"Standing before you now is not the Rabbi of Piotrkov, not a deputy of my people to the Polish parliament, but a member of our people, trying and struggling to help our people. And so I call and appeal to you to help me in the task I have undertaken."

History should record a few separate words of praise for the "fourth estate" — the journalists and gentlemen of the press. With their "power of the pen" they promoted the campaign for *Yeshivas Chachmey Lublin* out of a laudable mature sense of responsibility. The entire American Jewish press ran lengthy articles to depict the character and personality of this man of eminence, the great Talmudic scholar, Rav Meir Shapiro, who was now the Rabbi of Piotrkov. Illustrated with a camera portrait of Rav Meir, the articles went on to explain to their readers the great, visionary goal that he had set for himself as the creative, initiating force behind *Yeshivas Chachmey Lublin*. And interestingly enough, all titled him "the Jewish minister of education in Poland."

Foremost in this respect was the Yiddish newspaper published for the observant Jews, the "Jewish Morning Journal." It was outstanding in its work to publicize the idea of the yeshiva. A leading journalist of the paper met with Rav Meir for a long, wide-ranging interview shortly after his arrival, and then he wrote it up, giving the whole matter very full and very positive, supportive coverage.

In the course of that article, the journalist reported something further, that was probably of particular interest to his readers. After describing the fascinating educational ideas that Rav Meir planned to put into practice at the yeshiva, the reporter gave yet more details that Rav Meir had imparted to him:

The visionary Rav intended to have a separate department in the yeshiva devoted entirely to Torah matters concerning the Holy Land. And in connection with this, directly after his campaign in America, the dynamic educator intended to travel on to the Land of Israel, to make a special study of the situation there, expressly for the study program that he planned to have at the yeshiva. For as Rav Meir saw it, the Holy Land was developing slowly but surely as a center of Jewish life, and it would continue to develop, at an accelerating rate: which meant that it was bound to become an important source of problems and questions in *halacha*.

Hence, Torah scholars and authorities could no longer treat such matters as hypothetical topics of theoretical interest. They would also have to become thoroughly, directly familiar with the practical aspects, with the actual state of affairs in real life.

Here was a clear, prime indication of this visionary builder's approach to the problems of the Land of Israel in the year 5685 (1925) — to build a bridge of healthy linkage and relationship between the Diaspora and the Holy Land — the Land of ultimate Jewish longing and hope, toward which (needless to say) his heart yearned.

And here, in turn, is a pen portrait of this distinguished visitor's character, as another journalist attempted to describe him:

"He makes a deep impression on everyone who comes to visit him. You see a lustrous, dignified countenance framed in a black beard, with a pair of knowing, sagacious eyes that make a profound impression: for out of them shines an openhearted friendliness along with unmistakable qualities of wisdom and understanding. Add to this a pleasant, unassuming smile, and a high forehead with sunken temples that denote earnestness. So taken all in all, you have an imposing personage. . . . "

During his stay in America, the Rav visited fourteen states, and in every one he received the cooperation and help of rabbis, members of the press, and people involved in social and communal activities — people from various parties and political shades and hues. Whatever the bent or nature of their politics might be, it had not extinguished or dimmed the warmth in their hearts, in their positive attitude toward the entirety of eternal Jewish values.

In the course of the trip, an International Committee was formed for further work on behalf of the yeshiva. It consisted of a hundred members, chosen in all of the fourteen states that he visited — especially selected individuals who included members of the distinguished rabbinic organization *Agudas haRabbonim*, United States Congressmen, editors of Jewish journals, and a series of foremost men of distinction in American life.

A count was kept of the number of times he spoke in public, and the total came to 242. This was how many times he addressed audiences, invariably infusing them with his own electrifying vision and enthusiasm and spurring them on to respond with positive action. He spoke always with heart, as he worked unflaggingly for the success of the venture. There is an old saying in our Tradition that "words which go out from the heart enter the heart." Whenever he spoke, the impression he made on his listeners was immense, and the contributions which were made in reaction were, relatively speaking, very satisfactory.

In all, the sum of fifty-two [or perhaps fifty-three] thousand dollars was raised in America — a colossal figure, amounting to a right tidy small fortune in those times — and this, in response to the 242 dramatic, electrifying addresses and sermonic talks that he gave.

Since Hebrew letters also denote numbers, Talmudic savants in America noted that the number 242 equaled the Hebrew word (from Talmudic times), *b^e^ram* ("truly, indeed"): for *beys* = 2; *résh* = 200; *mem* = 40; total, 242. And this brought to their minds a noted statement in the Talmud (*bavli*, Bava Basra 21a) about a Sage named Yehoshua ben Gamla: "*b^e^ram*," the Talmud declares, "Indeed, be that man remembered for good — because if not for him, Torah would have been forgotten in Jewry." This became the statement they cited about Rav Meir Shapiro, to sum up his historic visit to the United States.

30

America: a few highlights

It was noted in the previous chapter that at first the campaign in the United States went rather poorly, and it took a while to get the venture off the ground and make it gather momentum. Once it got going properly, however, the popular appeal of the venture grew from day to day, and the response from good Jewish hearts kept growing accordingly.

Unfortunately, another delegation of people from Poland was visiting in the States at the same time, to raise money for a certain existing yeshiva which they headed. When they saw how well Rav Meir's campaign was going, they grew alarmed that his success would inhibit and cripple their efforts and might even doom them to failure.

In an attempt to improve their chances, they spread reports that Yeshivas Chachmey Lublin was no more than a dream, like a vision of a castle in Spain, with not a thing to show for itself in reality. Not the least bit of construction work, they intimated, was being done. Thus they left an implication that all the money gathered for it was probably disappearing into certain pockets.

Rav Meir went about his own work calmly. He ignored all the adverse publicity by this other delegation and took no firm stand of any kind to counter it and stop it in its tracks. When he was asked why he kept silent while those others kept spreading their lies, he answered them by citing the Rebbe of Sadiggerr: "In the Book of *Koheless* there is a well-known phrase: God seeks the pursued person (Ecclesiastes 3:15). But the Hebrew word for 'seeks' is *y^evakkesh*, which can also mean 'asks, requests': The Almighty asks a pursued, oppressed person: Please wait patiently and don't do anything — because in the end all will be well for you."

And so it was in this case. In the long run, all the negative propaganda had no effect.

****

As a rule, the money he collected came from modest and middle-range donations. Some donations, however, were unexpectedly large. For example, there was one woman who gave five thousand dollars — but a little story went with it:

Having been advised that she was able and willing to help generously, Rav Meir went to visit her; and no sooner was he there, seated in the parlor, than she took twenty-five hundred dollars and set it on the table before him. The Rav, however, gave a slight frown. Sensing a certain displeasure in him, she asked for the reason. Was the amount not enough, perhaps?

In reply, Rav Meir told her a of small incident that happened with him back home, in Piotrkov: A certain beggar made his rounds in the city every week, to gather the money he needed to sustain him. Once he knocked on Rav Meir's door too, and he walked in to hold out his hand. Without much thought the Rav took out a coin of fifty kopecks and gave it to him — an amount that the beggar could collect ordinarily from perhaps twenty other people.

Well, said Rav Meir to the woman, that indigent beggar didn't take it, but began to argue and bargain instead. He insisted that fifty kopecks was too little.

Continued Rav Meir: "So I asked him: 'In the city, you get from one person a twentieth of what I'm giving you, and you take it well enough; you're satisfied. And here you go and tell me that this is too little?' He upped and answered me: 'Honored Rabbi, when I bargain and argue with you, it's worth my while: because I may get another fine, large coin like this. In town, if I go and argue for more, what will I get? — another kopeck or two? I save my breath and stroll on to the next person. I might as well get my next kopeck from him. It's easier and quicker than trying to extract it from the first man.'

"You see, then," Rav Meir explained, "I learned the lesson from that shrewd old beggar: Where I get a small, modest donation, I take it and make no effort to bargain for more. Here, however, I find a dear lady with a Jewish heart that understood my project well enough to give such a large sum directly, as soon as I came in. So it pays for me to try to argue and bargain for more."

Her response was to take another twenty-five hundred dollars and add it to the first.

****

While he was in the States, one of his American co-workers asked him, "Dear Rabbi of Piotrkov, against whose account did you undertake this enormous project, to construct such a huge building that has to cost heavy thousands of dollars? Where can you be sure you will get all the money you need? Weren't you ever afraid you might fail? Wouldn't it have been more sensible not to get involved in such a precarious, risky venture?"

"Let me explain it to you," said Rav Meir, "with a point from the Midrash. The Midash relates (Yalkut Shim'oni I:684): At the time that the Children of Israel received the Torah, the nations of the world became envious of them [and wanted to know], 'What reason did they see to draw nearer [to Him] than the [other] nations?' The Holy One, blessed is He, thereupon shut their mouths; [how?] — He said to them, 'Bring Me your genealogical record' — for Scripture states, *Bring to* haShem *(the Lord) the family lines of the people* (*T*e*hillim*/Psalms 96:7) — 'just as My children did bring [theirs' — as we read], *and they gave their pedigrees by their family lines* (*B*e*midbar*/Numbers 1:18).

"At first glance, the Almighty's response makes no sense: What link is there between the Torah and a fine, distinguished lineage? On the contrary: in *Pirkey Avos* (2:17) we read: Prepare yourself to study Torah, for it is not bequeathed to you as an inheritance. In other words, everyone has to labor and toil over the Torah if he wants to gain any mastery of it. The erudition that a learned father or grandfather attained is of no help at all.

"We can resolve this difficulty, though, with an illustrative little story: A young man once came to a chassidic Rebbe, to ask his advice about two business propositions that were being offered him. One proposition was very risky: there was a good chance of losing one's entire investment all at once. Yet, alternatively, one could succeed with it and become really rich in a short time. Now, from the second proposition no dazzling great fortune could be expected; but on the other hand, there was no danger of any great losses in it; and the capital invested could always be taken out.

"Which of the two proposals, asked the young man, would the Rebbe advise him to accept?

"Well, the spiritual leader told him, it depended: It depended on whether the young man had a rich father-in-law and perhaps rich parents. If he did, he could go ahead into the risky offer: because if, Heaven forbid, the business venture failed, his father-in-law and his parents would have to provide him with new money to invest so that he could support a family;

and of course, they would have the means for it. If those relatives of his were poor, however, let him not dare go into anything with a high risk. Let him embark only on business dealings without any threat of losing money.

"Now," said Rav Meir, "with the Rebbe's answer we can understand the Midrash: The Torah, with its 613 mitzvos, is a high-risk business indeed. We can win enormous profits and earnings if we keep the mitzvos and observe them faithfully. But we can suffer enormous setbacks and losses if we fail to keep the many mitzvos properly. By contrast, the rest of mankind were given only seven mitzvos to keep. That is certainly a low-risk business. They are easy to keep, and there is no serious danger of damage or loss. But the gains that it can yield are quite small.

"Now, then: When we, the Hebrews, the Israelites, the Jewish people, accepted the Torah, we reckoned it out: If we keep the Torah well, we'll be gaining tremendous reward; and if (Heaven forbid) we don't, with our prayers we can always fall back on the great Heavenly merit of our Fathers, the Patriarchs Avraham, Yitzchak and Ya'akov.

"What, however, could the nations of the world possibly do, when they didn't have any ancestors like ours, with powerful merit in Heaven that they could fall back on? . . . This, then, is exactly why the Almighty told them, *Bring me your genealogical record.* 'Let Me see if you have any fine, distinguished forebears in your family line, from whom you are descended. If you don't, how can you dare enter into such a business, where you will face such enormous risks?"

Rav Meir came to the end of his answer: "I made the same sort of reckoning when I decided to embark on this high-risk venture of mine: to build the *Yeshivas Chachmey Lublin.* Should I succeed in amassing in Europe the whole amount that I need, well and good. If not, we have a rich uncle in America. The Jewish people here are fine, upstanding citizens of the USA; so they are fine honorary nephews of your Uncle Sam; and that might entitle us to consider the American Jewish community our honorary uncle. That is not a bad *yichus* at all for us — not really a bad lineage. So as you see, here I am."

****

In New York City, he stayed for a brief period at one of its rather resplendent hotels. To his surprise, one evening the owner of the hotel came into his room in a rather nervous state, with an anxious, worried look on his face, and asked if he might speak with the Rav. "People have told me," he said, "that you are a very wise man. I'm in a very serious dilemma now, and I wonder if you could help me." Genially, the Rav invited the man to tell him what the trouble was, and prepared himself to listen:

A short while ago, three guests at the hotel came to him with a request: They wanted to give him a very large sum of money (dollars) to keep safe and sound for them, till they would come for it. There was one condition that they stipulated firmly: The money was to be given back only when all three of them were there.

Well and good: the hotel owner took the money and, in their presence, stowed it away in his iron safe.

Alas, said the man, yesterday one of the three came when he was away and only his wife was there. She knew nothing of the condition, and the guest simply asked for the money back, giving her a very clear description of the way the dollars were packed in piles and exactly where and how they had been placed in the safe. Suspecting nothing, she went and opened the safe and gave him the money.

"Now," said the hotel owner, "the other two have come, and they demand that I must give them, out of my own pocket, the full amount that they entrusted to me. They protest that my wife had no right to hand over the money, because they stipulated very clearly that it was to be returned only when all three were there. . . . What am I to do?"

The Rav replied instantly: "There is a very simple answer that you can give them: Tell them that you are prepared to hand over the money just as soon as they will produce the third gentleman. Until then, by their own condition, you owe them nothing. . . . "

****

At one time he found himself in a provincial town, where he had been invited to come and speak. When he was done with his fiery oration, the people in the audience all came bustling and moving toward him to shake his hand and exchange a few words; and to his surprise, he noticed a young boy among them, resolutely pushing his way through the tight press, till he reached the Rav.

Of course, Rav Meir had spoken in Yiddish, the only language he shared with all the members of the Jewish community in America who had migrated from Eastern Europe. He greatly doubted if this fairly small boy standing before him had enough of a command of this *mammeh loshon* to have grasped anything much of his long, rousing talk.

"Tell me," said the Rav: "Did you understand anything much of what I was saying? — enough to make you push through this tight-pressed crowd to talk to me?"

"No," the rather frightened lad shook his head. "I only grasped that the Rabbi was talking about *money*." (While he knew enough Yiddish to manage the brief conversation, the word "money" came out in the purest American English.)

"In that case," said the smiling Rav Meir. "you may have understood my talk better than all the grownups. . . . "

****

In that same small town, a rather curious thing happened: When the community heads invited him, they described the Jewish inhabitants as great, unlearned boors, who knew virtually nothing of the Jewish tradition; and they emphasized that he would have to speak in plain, simple language that they could understand. As they explained, he would have to refrain from citing Torah and rabbinic interpretation — because quite certainly he would not be understood.

Tailoring his talk to his audience, Rav Meir decided to tell a "Bible story": he merely related how the daughter of Par'o [Pharaoh] found the infant Moshe in a special box in the Nile River, whereupon she pulled him out of the water and decided to bring him up (*Sh^e^mos*/Exodus 2:5-10). Then the Rav made a simple point: When she made her decision and acted on it, she didn't know how the child would turn out, what he would be when he grew up. There was no way she could guess, much less foresee, that he would become the virtual king of the Israelites and the greatest of prophets, who would give them the Torah. And still, nevertheless, she took him and raised him.

How great would have been her happiness, declaimed Rav Meir, how blissful her joy, if she could have known then the future life of this little infant that she took. How elated she would have been, how readily would she have devoted herself completely to the little boy.

And so today, the Rav continued, when someone is asked to give money for a yeshiva, let him stop and think: How much would he — or any Jew — be willing to give if he knew for certain that his money would help sustain a boy in that yeshiva who would grow up into a world-renowned scholar like the Chafetz Cha-yim, a great international spiritual leader!

It was a perfectly simple talk, he believed, that even the greatest ignoramus could understand. Yet afterward he overheard a conversation between a father and his son, which made him realize that even this talk of his never got off the ground for his listeners, to get through to them.

Said the boy to his father, pointing a finger at Rav Meir, "Papa, he was in a special box in the river?"

"Sure," answered the father. "You heard him, didn't you?"

"And he got out of the box all by himself, safe and sound?"

"Well, there you see him, standing before us, and he's perfectly all right."

"If that's so, Papa, for a trick like that he deserves a ten-dollar bill."

****

At another time he found himself in the home of a very wealthy man in New York, who had become, however, so completely American in his way of life that not a trace of a Jewish identity could be discerned in him. Nevertheless, in the hope of obtaining a substantial donation for the yeshiva, the Rav decided to invest time in a visit. The man came from a German background; and since Rav Meir spoke the language fluently, the conversation went in German.

Carefully, the Rav outlined his plans for the yeshiva at length, trying to make his host see the nobility of the conception and the lofty ideals behind it.

All the man could say in response was that he had been an assimilated Jew for many long years, and in fact, neither his grandfather nor his father had ever had anything to do with anything really Jewish. So he was sorry, but he would not give anything for the yeshiva.

"*Sagen sie mir,*" said the Rav: "*Haben sie immer die heilige Bibel gelesen* (Tell me: did you ever read the Holy Bible)?"

"*O ya ya,*" came the answer. "Certainly."

"Do you remember, perhaps, the name *Haman* in the Book of Esther?"

Now the wealthy assimilated Jew was in a small quandary. As an apparent man of culture, he could not dismiss the Bible in haughty disdain as something Jewish; and he began racking his brains — till at last he remembered: "*O ya ya!* That was the wicked man who wanted to destroy all the Jews."

"Well, do you think that you are worse than Haman?"

"*O nein nein!* Whatever I may be, that certainly not."

"Let me cite for you, then, something from the Talmud: Some of the descendants of Haman, a few great-great-grandsons perhaps, studied Torah in B^{e}ney B^{e}rak" (*bavli*, Gittin 57b). "Somewhere down his family line there was a conversion to Judaism, and a direct male descendant came to a yeshiva in the Land of Israel to study Torah. It is not impossible, then, that one day your grandchildren will be studying Torah in *Yeshivas Chachmey Lublin.*"

This "attack" from a direction he had never expected left the rich man in confusion, with no answer to give. Somewhat abashed, he gave Rav Meir a handsome contribution for the yeshiva instead.

****

On one Shabbos the Rav was invited to a certain *shul* to speak about the yeshiva, and he was promised that the appeal would raise a good two hundred dollars. He would have to be, however, "the second speaker on the program": There was a boy becoming *bar mitzvah* in the shul that morning, and before the Rav spoke, the young lad would give his short prepared speech.

Ignorant of the "normal practice" in American Jewish life in those times, Rav Meir was dismayed to hear the boy make a solemn promise in his speech that he would be loyal to the Torah all his life. Why was the Rav so troubled by this? — because throughout the prayer service he could see cars arriving to bring the invited guests to the celebration. In fact, one car had brought the boy himself, together with his parents.

To see such open, blatant desecration of the holy day of rest, and then to hear the boy give his word, in what amounted to an oath, that he would keep the Torah and its mitzvos faithfully — this was more than the Rav could stomach. He decided to forget the promised money and speak out in protest. He simply had to react to this tragi-comedy before his eyes, to cry out sharply at the solemn promise that the boy was made to give in his innocence, even as the desecration of Shabbos and Heaven only knew what other violations of the Torah were going on right there.

When the time came for the Rav to talk, the president of the synagogue asked him what his topic would be, so that he could introduce him properly. The topic, said Rav Meir, would be: "In Poland, Jews are dying of hunger, and here, from the freezing cold" [meaning the absence of any warm, impassioned loyalty to authentic Judaism].

From the pulpit he lashed into the boy's parents for giving their young, impressionable son such an outrageous upbringing. How could they rear him, right from the start, with falsehood and lies? They bring him to his bar mitzvah celebration and have him take what amounts to an oath, and they never give him a chance to keep that oath.

The Rav went on to describe and explain the enormous crime before the Almighty of desecrating and violating the holiness of Shabbos; and therefore, how serious the consequences of such a bar mitzvah celebration could be.

As this "sermon" came to an end, he heard some sort of commotion in the women's section, and then he saw the reason: A group of women were coming toward him. *Nu nu,* he thought, prepared for the worst: They were probably the boy's mother and family relatives, coming to retaliate: to lash into *him* now, for having disturbed and spoiled their "simcha."

To his complete amazement, he heard them asking him to please give the boy a blessing. And they explained: Having heard now how dreadful was the sin of violating Shabbos, they were frightened that the young lad might die. . . .

A situation like this, the Rav knew how to handle: He asked the parents and the boy to give him their word that the boy would keep Shabbos and would put on *t'fillin* faithfully every normal weekday. When the promises were given, the youngster received a moving, heartfelt blessing from him.

There was, however, another astounding surprise in store: Afterward the president of the shul went up to the pulpit to thank the distinguished visitor for having made the congregation aware of what this great man saw as a grave wrongdoing, instead of flattering them with empty honeyed words, as other learned visitors did. For this, concluded the shul president, the contribution promised him for his yeshiva would be doubled!

With Heaven's help, he had been able to bring a Jewish soul to the observance of Shabbos, and incidentally to receive a larger donation for the yeshiva than he had expected.

****

In his American travels, Rav Meir came once to a small rural community, only to find himself listening to complaints by the people about their *shochét*: This ritual slaughterer of theirs, they explained, was evidently something of an amateur: When he finished dealing with their chickens, many times the fowl continued strutting around for quite a while. They asked the Rav if perhaps he could find a solution to the problem.

That same day, seeing that his pocketwatch had stopped, he brought it to the only watchmaker in the town, who repaired it. Five minutes later, wanting to know the time, he had a look at it — only to find that it had stopped again.

"Well, well," said Rav Meir to the local Jewish folk, "I see that you've gotten things mixed up here. If you had your watchmaker do your ritual slaughtering and let your *shochét* do watch repairs, all would be well: After the watchmaker finished with a chicken, it wouldn't run; and after the *shochét* finished with a watch, it would. . . . But so poor is your providential luck that each of them took to a trade that he wasn't suited for. . . . "

****

While he was there, one of the local inhabitants poured out his tale of woe that few customers came into his shop to buy his wares, and he was having trouble trying to make ends meet.

"What do you do in your free time," asked the Rav, "when there are no customers in the store?"

"I read a book."

"Listen to me," said the Rav: "In the free time that you have, say *t'hillim* [Psalms] or read a volume of Torah learning that it pays to study. I'm quite sure the devil won't be pleased by that, and he will send you customers steadily, to bother you and interrupt you. On the other hand, when you waste your time reading a book, he is quite pleased with that, and he will just persuade the customers not to go in and bother you."

****

A day came when the Rav had a group of visitors sitting with him, including a correspondent from a major American Jewish newspaper. This man wanted to hear what the Rav thought about the organized Orthodox Jewry of America, the population whose label meant that it was supposed to observe the Torah and the mitzvos properly. And with that the journalist made a strong effort to seek out and drag up out of a long past a whole list of all kinds of sin and wrongdoing that (as he saw it) Orthodox Jewry in America had become given to perpetrating.

For Rav Meir it was highly unpleasant to listen to this: What was the point of it? Was there anything he could do to improve matters if the man's information was correct in whole or part? America was a different world, about which he knew little. . . . The Chafetz Cha-yim would probably label the harangue as *lashon ha-ra*. . . . So he cut the harangue short:

"Can anyone tell me," he asked the people in the room, "where a journalist or correspondent is mentioned for the first time in the Torah?"

The answer he received was pure silence: no one there knew what to say.

"Then I'll tell you," he continued: "It's in connection with the *seh la'azazel*" [the goat that had to be sent off into the wilderness on Yom Kippur, taking with it all the sins of the Israelites, so that it could be hurled down a precipice to bring atonement for the people: *Va-yikra*/Leviticus 16:21-22]. "The Torah states that it has to be sent off *b^{e}yad ish itti*" [by the hand of a time-appointed man, someone appointed for that time]. "That term, *ish itti*, really means a journalist," insisted Rav Meir.

[Note that in the word *journalist*, the root *jour* means "day" in French, and so similar words in all the Romance languages. Thus "journalist" carries the sense of time: he brings the news of the day, of the present time. Again, the Hebrew term, *ish itti*, can be literally translated as "a 'time' man"; in English and other languages, newspapers around the world are called *The Times*, while an American news weekly bears exactly the title *Time*.]

"Now," continued the Rav with irony, "why should only a journalist have to carry out that task on Yom Kippur? Before that goat was sent off, the Torah tells us that the *kohen gadol* had to place his hands on the goat's head and confess the sins of the people. Well, our *halacha* states that in a confession of wrongdoing, the sin has to be specified" [Rambam, *hilchos t^{e}shuva* 1:1 — 'I did thus-and-thus']. "So, on Yom Kippur, the transgressions of the Israelites had to be listed in the confession over the goat before it was sent off. If any sin or wrongdoing was not enunciated in the confession, it would not be atoned.

"Well now, where could we find a person who would be able to list, for the benefit of the *kohen gadol*, *all* the sins of our people, omitting not even the slightest misdemeanor? As I understand the Torah now, they sent a correspondent, and probably a real crackerjack from a major American newspaper."

****

[While he was in the United States, two people who were Italians by birth were sentenced to death in Massachusetts, and the verdict brewed up a storm of controversy not only in America but throughout the world. The two were named Sacco (a shoemaker) and Vanzetti (a fish peddler), and the case was to become a part of American history.

[The crime for which they were put to death was an armed robbery in which two people were killed. However, all over the world people argued, with a good deal of justice, that Sacco and Vanzetti were found guilty not on the evidence, which seemed quite inadequate, but because they were Italians who held radical, anarchist views; and this was a time of violent anti-alien and anti-racial hysteria, especially about people with an anarchist philosophy. And so, bitter controversy about the sentence raged everywhere.]

As it happened, Rav Meir was in Paterson, New Jersey, at the time the verdict was given. Intrigued by the fact that this was a great Talmudic scholar who was also a member of the Polish parliament, a group of reporters from English-language newspapers came buzzing around him, to see if they could extract from him some piquant, newsworthy opinion about the double execution.

Rav Meir, however, knew when and how to stay out of needless trouble, and he replied gently, "In principle, we Jews are against the death penalty. According to the Talmud, if a death sentence was given and carried out once in seventy years, our religious courts would regard it as a catastrophe . . . " (*bavli*, Makkos 7a).

****

He was once asked how popular the planned yeshiva had become in Poland itself, how strongly had the idea been welcomed by the people there. He replied with a fact: A wealthy Pole, not Jewish, made an application to the yeshiva's directorship to have his son admitted into "the Jewish university"!

The answer Rav Meir gave him was that anyone who could meet the entrance requirements would be accepted. What were the requirements? The applicant had to be able to know from memory 200 *dapim* (double pages) of Talmud, with the commentary of *tos*^e^*fos*. Needless to say, no non-Jew ever applied and found himself accepted; but this *was* an indication of how well the idea had been received and accepted among the Polish population.

****

At the same time that Rav Meir was in the States on his campaign to gather money for *Yeshivas Chachmey Lublin*, the great Torah scholar Rav Meir Dan Plotzki (of blessed memory) was also there traveling about, to raise funds for another Torah institution in Poland.

Once, as it happened, the two met, and they were able to discourse and talk on matters Talmudic for a few enjoyable hours. When their discussions in the world of Talmud ended, Rav Meir Dan remarked in admiration and respect, "I think your great success in raising funds here in America must be on account of your powerful mastery of the Torah. I," he added modestly, "I don't seem able to gather as much money as you do."

"No," replied Rav Meir with a reciprocal modesty: "It proves the opposite: Your immense knowledge of the Talmud is the reason why you gather less money than I do. I recall that when I was living with my wife's parents, my father-in-law was the toll collector over a large number of bridges. He paid the government a lump sum, and then he had the right to collect a set toll from every person who wanted to ride his vehicle over any one of those bridges. Of course, he appointed people as tollkeepers, to stand at one end of every bridge and collect the fees from the endless flow of travelers.

"I remember how he complained once, in talking to me, that one of his collectors, a relative who was a learned scholar, always brought in small sums, while another tollkeeper, a Jew who was a complete ignoramus and completely deaf as well, brought in large, hefty amounts. My curiosity was aroused: What in the world could the reason be? What sort of talent did the deaf ignoramous have which the Talmud scholar lacked?

"I soon had the answer to the puzzle. I went to see the learned family relative at his place of work, and I struck up a conversation with him. 'Did you know so-and-so perhaps?' I asked him; and he livened up: 'Did I know him? We studied together under the famous author of *Beyss Yitzchak*! I remember even the splendid *pilpul* that the two of us evolved.'

"Off he went into a complete recall of the fine skein of Talmudic thought that the two young budding scholars had thought up together years before. Meanwhile, one vehicle after another went rattling over the bridge, as the horses harnessed to them never slackened their paces . . . and he was too busy to notice. He had to make sure to clarify every beautiful detail of his lovely *pilpul*.

"That done, he was still not ready to let me go. There was a wonderful way he had found to resolve a particularly difficult thing in Rambam's code of law, and he simply *had* to tell it to me. And he did — while another few wagons rolled past us, without a penny in payment from the drivers. He just went on with his *pilpul*, happy as a lark. . . .

"Eventually I managed to get to the other tollkeeper, and I asked him the same sort of question: *Did you ever know so-and-so?* Not a word did he hear. His only reply was, *A vehicle with two horses, a six-penny coin; with one horse, a three-penny!*

"As we were having this peculiar 'conversation,' a coach came riding by, drawn by two fine horses. I wanted to continue with him, but it was no use. He just left me standing there and went running after the vehicle. *Hand over a six-piece,* he bellowed; *do you hear? You're not going to sneak past me! Do you hear?*

"I wanted to try again to start up some kind of conversation with him; but I might as well have spoken to the wall. He knew only one answer, nothing more: *With two horses, a six-penny coin; with one horse, a three-penny.*

"This," the Rav told Rav Meir Dan Plotzki, "is exactly what is happening with us. When you come into a rich man's home to ask for a donation, as a rule he is something of a *talmid chacham*, a learned Talmudist of the kind we have back home, who migrated here and became wealthy. So he probably invites you to have a seat — and you sit; and then he probably asks you about a difficult matter in Rambam's code of law — whereupon you give an answer to resolve it.

"Then a whole discussion and debate develops over it, and from the man's private library a whole dozen volumes of learning get taken down to look into them — till they make a fine pile on the table. This is how half a day goes by till you receive the man's donation.

"When I go to see a man of wealth and he wants to get into a splendid discussion with me on some fascinating point in the Torah, I become as deaf as the wall. I get right to the point and explain that I came for money; this is all I know now, and nothing more. As soon as I have my donation, I am already gone — full speed on my way to the next visit."

31

America: retrospection and aftermath

He spent thirteen months in the United States — quite a large chunk of time. Yet in looking back, he knew it had not been a purely materialistic expedition — to gather the dollars and nothing more. If anyone thought so, he would be making a serious mistake; and it would prove that he knew nothing of this great, noble soul — nothing of his basic character or of his inner thoughts. Whoever knew him well could not make such a sorry mistake.

The facts on the surface are true enough: Without the material help that American Jewry provided so generously, *Yeshivas Chachmey Lublin* could not have been built — which means that had this alone been the purpose and goal of his lengthy travels through the States, it would have been idealistic and noble enough: to bring that edifice of Torah study into existence.

To all who knew him, however, it was clear as daylight that a deeper motive also went with that extraordinary Torah genius on his historic expedition. He went to make the Torah manifest to the Jews in America: to make them aware of it as a palpable reality of the first magnitude and the greatest importance.

This is probably how he would have put it into words: "The concept of the prestige and honor of the Torah must become a common, natural, familiar idea, flowing deeply into the minds and hearts of the whole Jewish people — both here and there, on both sides of the Atlantic Ocean." This was the hidden, inner side of his mission, which gave him an iron core of strength, an unquenchable flame of faith, on which to draw. It was a purpose that always animated that prodigious soul with new vitality and good cheer.

In the years that followed, the same fundamental idea was to sustain him more than once. Many a time then, beads of sweat would appear of themselves on his forehead as he was seized by anxiety at the dismaying deficits and debts that the yeshiva incurred regularly. At such times, as often as not, he would have to leave the yeshiva that he cherished and loved, and go traveling off to various cities and towns on a "rescue campaign" to keep his bastion of Torah in existence. Moments could come then when the roots of despair crept dangerously close to his ever-cheerful, ebullient, hope-filled heart.

Then he found consolation in this basic thought: "One satisfaction remains with me: Every visit I make in a town, every talk I give, every appearance before an audience — leaves behind an input of new spiritual life. People are awakened to sudden moments of spiritual stocktaking, to an unexpected accounting of their relationship to their Maker. Let this, at least, be my reward for my hard, relentless labor."

In those years to come, his heartening, inspiriting appearances within the borders of Poland never failed to make a profound impression. They were always immensely influential: for every instance was an emotional spiritual experience.

Realizing this, we disciples in Poland could extrapolate and understand what an extraordinary effect his visit in the New World must have had on American Jewry: how much spiritual animation, how much sublimity of vision he must have awakened in the hearts of listeners there. Beyond any doubt he aroused in many a yearning to renew their bond with the Torah and their loyalty to the authentic Jew's way of life.

Here, for example, is prime evidence of our assumption and conviction about Rav Meir Shapiro's odyssey through America — taken from an article in the Yiddish newspaper *Canader Odler* (Canadian Eagle) in the year 5687 (1927), about his appearance at the Young Israel synagogue in Montreal:

First the article describes the powerful interest that his spirited address aroused in the community, and it cites a few salient highlights from the singularly effective and impressive talk. Then the article concludes: "For a long time to come we will yet remember the spiritual pleasure we had from the brilliant *pilpul* thoughts and homiletic interpretations that we were privileged to hear from this great Talmudic mind of our time."

Quite characteristic of the reactions to Rav Meir's appearance in America is this citation from a letter by the renowned Rabbi Dov Aryeh (Bernard Louis) Levinthal of Philadelphia, one of the most esteemed spiritual leaders in American Jewry: "The historic visit of the great Torah scholar of Piotrkov in the United States has lifted high the prestige of the Torah, unfurling its banner as an ensign of Jewish majesty. The great, mighty influence of that visit is still to be felt today in our land. His name has remained venerated, recalling this extraordinary personage to whom every sensitive soul felt drawn. . . . "

Yet all this reflects only a small part of the full impact that his visit had. For it was a triumphant "victory march" that this great soul made in the New World [a world that was well described in his time as the land of bluff and sports activities]. It was the singular achievement of this great soul, through his relentless work, to make American Jews aware of the crucial importance of his mission to rescue and raise up a new generation of devotion to Torah study.

Everywhere, in every city where he appeared, he visited all its institutions that worked for Torah learning, for worthy Jewish social purposes, or for the distribution of charity. And everywhere he left behind him flaming sparks from his great spirit, memorable fragments of his great animation and warmth. As he felt it appropriate, here he gave a few inspired homiletic thoughts, there a small lively discourse in *halacha,* elsewhere a bit of scintillating conversation, and at times a piece of sparkling wit and humor, that left everyone in high spirits — both the people who received him and the people who came along as escorts, helpers and co-workers.

To be received and welcomed so cordially by every circle in American Jewry, by persons and groups of every sort — this was something to which only a few rare individuals attained — only emissaries sent by Divine providence to fulfill a holy mission. One personage of this kind was Rav Meir Shapiro.

And he never forgot the generous help and understanding that he received from American Jewry. At every opportunity he found, he mentioned them favorably, with a word of blessing. The "American chapter" brought pages of glory into the history of *Yeshivas Chachmey Lublin.*

****

Immediately upon his return from the States, he rode on to Lublin. In its expectancy and readiness to welcome him back, the city took on a festive holiday appearance. There was a heightened air of anticipation as all looked forward to the arrival of this distinguished guest after he had been away from Poland for well over a year.

At last he was there in their midst, gazing at the building and drinking in the hard, unalterable fact of its growth. There had been one floor when he left. Now five were all finished and done, and all was ready for the sixth and last, which would then be topped with a fine, sturdy roof.

In abstract theory he had known all along of the building's progress. As he kept sending "home" the money he raised, he had been kept informed of the continuing stages of construction for which the money paid. But to stand and see it there was a different experience for him. He was overwhelmed by emotion, till tears of pure joy came to his eyes.

In his happiness, he decided to delay his return to Piotrkov and to spend Shabbos in Lublin. On that holy day of rest, he went to pray in the *Maharam shul* [the historic synagogue named after Rav Meir ben Reb G^e^dalya, the illustrious scholar who had taken charge of the renowned yeshiva in Lublin at the age of twenty-four and served as its *rosh yeshiva* between the years 5342 (1582) and 5347 (1587)]; and there the present Rav Meir delivered the first of two memorable sermons. Later in the day he spoke again, in one of Lublin's great halls. Both times, he described the general life of American Jewry and its colossal achievements (with its generosity) for authentic, timeless Judaism.

The structure stood, completed. Now the hour of destiny came for the Jewry of Poland: The time had come for this sector of our historic people to show if it had the understanding and resolve to contribute its share to the edifice of Torah splendor that was being created in its midst.

Rav Meir focused first on Lublin itself, the city to which its olden glory as a historic Torah center was now to return. A campaign was mounted to raise the costs for the doors and windows. And the response came in the main from truly Jewish hearts that were rich in spirit and faith — a response that opened an amazing range of purses and pocketbooks. Even the poorest among a generally impoverished population gave their pittances toward putting in at least one window in the structure: For the building would be filled with Torah study and prayer, and perhaps through *their* window the sounds would reach the Almighty's Throne of Glory. These were the kind of words that were heard everywhere as people gave the amounts needed for a door or a window.

In the other large cities of Poland, the response to the campaign was generally quite cold at first. Then his fiery call went out to the cities, in a circular that was printed up and distributed everywhere:

"Dear brethren in Jewry: A full year and more I labored with sweat and toil in the countries overseas, the United States and Canada, to bring blessing to this land, by completing the great House where Torah learning and Jewish piety will be nurtured: *Yeshivas Chachmey Lublin.*

"My labor bore fruit, by Heaven's blessed help: When I left our land, we were up to the second floor in the construction of our edifice, and now we have reached the sixth, with the roof ready to be added, to make the building complete; and a good sum of money remains yet with us to finish some further part of the great edifice.

"But even if our people in America undertook to have all the construction work completed, you are not free to evade all obligation.

"You, the Jewry of our land, were privileged to be able to attend the ground-breaking ceremony here, in your land. You are privileged that out of this land of ours, a mighty voice of Torah shall resound to the entire Diaspora. Now a holy obligation lies upon you to go forth to the help of *haShem* valiantly, to muster the last of your strength, and to provide at least enough to move ahead to the completion of the construction work, and to create some basis for the yeshiva's upkeep.

"I therefore call to you now: Let not one of you fail to take into his home the *pushke* of Yeshivas Chachmey Lublin. That holy charity box shall be the firmest basis for the maintenance of our Institution in the future as well. . . .

"Know that our brethren in America are paying good attention to all that we are doing here. If they will only see your selfless devotion for our holy Institution, they will increase their donations over and over. . . . "

With this public call went the *pushke*, the new charity box that was carefully designed and produced for mass distribution. The front side showed the huge handsome building. On one of the side panels there was a portrayal of a small, attractive Torah scroll, while the opposite panel carried a specially composed short prayer. Beneath that, a warning was added that no one should lessen (on account of this new charity box) the amounts that he or she was accustomed to put into the *pushke* of *Rabbi Meir ba'al ha-ness* (Rabbi Meir, Master of the Miracle — an old fixture in every devout home in Eastern Europe), which had to go for the upkeep of indigent families in the Holy Land.

This firm warning was printed at the request of a few great spiritual leaders; but unfortunately, it was not enough to calm the fears of the custodians and managers of the *Rabbi Meir ba'al ha-ness* charity fund in

Galicia. Evidently their minds conjured up lurid pictures of drastic losses of income if a new, attractive ***pushke*** was allowed into Jewish homes to stand beside their old reliable source of funds. And so a storm of protest arose, complete with imprecation, malediction and anathema on all and everyone who would dare take into his home the ***pushke*** of Yeshivas Chachmey Lublin.

In response to this small tornado of hostility by the managers of that charity, whose narrow personal interests were so painfully obvious, a public call was issued by 300 great Torah scholars and devout models of piety — among them the famed authority Rav Yosef Cha-yim Sonnenfeld of Jerusalem, whose abounding love for the Holy Land and its pious Jews was well known. The purpose of the public call was to proclaim as a decision in law that according to the ***halacha*** it was perfectly permissible to take the ***pushke*** of the new yeshiva into one's home. Then the public call continued, in the wake of the decision:

The purpose of the charity box of *Yeshivas Chachmey Lublin* (said the proclamation) was to help it lift up the dignity of the Torah — but not that alone. It also had a particular educational significance. From his earliest years, a child would learn to know the building of the yeshiva as a familiar, beloved part of his life, linked with the charming picture of the small *séfer torah* at the side. Thus, in his young heart a great love would form and solidify for the Torah, and for the yeshiva, where he would hope and yearn to be accepted one day.

Directly after this proclamation by the great, authoritative scholars of the time, a massive ***pushke*** campaign was gotten under way, to give it the widest possible distribution and have it accepted by the people at large. And the campaign was blessed with success, so that a foundation was established for the institution's eventual support in later times.

For the present, however, there was still a painful lack of thousands of dollars to get the building finished, to make the interior as suitable and imposing as the exterior was impressive, so that it could truly serve as a world center of Torah study. The Rav continued his work without a let-up. He stormed and demanded, proclaimed and aroused, to waken and move Jewish hearts to help him again and yet again, till he could open the doors of the institution to the many thousands who were waiting in longing for the day they could enter.

****

[Ever prone to optimism and hope, he kept seeing the goal in sight. Thus, at one point in the year 5687 (1927) he announced in a public letter which received wide distribution that he confidently expected the doors to be opened at last in the summer of 5688 (1928). Perhaps, however, when the time came, he could only recall the doleful words of the prophet Yirm^{e}yahu: *The harvest is past, the summer is ended, and we have not been saved* (Jeremiah 8:20).

[The dismaying fact was that the odious, pitiful economic policy of the Polish government, mainly intent on squeezing blood from the Jewish minority, continued to impoverish the soil of human activity that might have yielded some decent harvest of charity. As the incomes of the relatively wealthy and middle-class Jews declined, so did the donations they gave as Rav Meir came visiting them.

[This, however, the Rav might have borne with equanimity. What bore down on his nerves and heart was another phenomenon: Certain elements in the Jewish population took to hampering and obstructing his activities. Whatever they might have gained by it, psychologically or financially, they decided to contribute to his campaign what was evidently the only thing they could: their nuisance value. Thus such a type might have held out an opened hand and said, "Do you see this palm? When grass will grow here, that's when he'll open that yeshiva."

[The result was an accumulating bitterness and anger in his heart, especially when the year 5689 (1929) came, and the opening of the yeshiva was still a good while off.]

In that year, the third *K^{e}néssiya G^{e}dola* (Great Assembly) of Agudas Yisra'el was convened in Vienna. Here again, Rav Meir Shapiro rose to address the delegates; only, this time his voice was suffused with a profound sense of sorrow, verging on tragedy.

Once more he unrolled before his listeners a poignant, heartrending portrait of the young Torah learners in his land. He depicted graphically how they languished from hunger and need, grew weakened and feeble, and at the same time they had to suffer untold derision and scorn. Then he went on to describe how their suffering was mingling and merging together with his own:

He recalled the immense enthusiasm that had prevailed during the ground-breaking ceremony. What fervent, impassioned promises of help he had received from certain individuals and from whole communities!

How earnestly they had obligated and committed themselves! And then what? All remained promises that would never be fulfilled, empty checks that could never be cashed at the bank. The fiery enthusiasm came in words, not in practical actions. . . .

"And today" (he continued) "nobody is interested any more. It bothers nobody, it troubles nobody. But the tragedy has gone even further: Not only will no one help me; people actually hinder me. Stones are put in my way . . . stumbling-blocks . . . obstacles to hamper me." There were people who knew exactly where his words were aimed — at certain elements whose efforts were indeed obstructive or destructive, aimed at him quite deliberately.

"In the Book of *Koheless* the wise King Sh^elomo (Solomon) tells us, 'The fool folds his hands together, and eats his flesh' (Ecclesiastes 4:5). But did anybody ever see a fool eating his own flesh? What does it mean, then? It denotes a fool who has no sense, no initiative, no ability or method to go and create anything. So he folds his hands and sits complacently, doing nothing. But there is one thing that he does: 'he eats his flesh.' The Hebrew does not state that he eats his *own*, but just that he 'eats his flesh': whose? — the flesh of anyone around him who succeeds in doing something creative and producing something positive and worthwhile. Then that fool goes to work gnawing away at this person's flesh, trying every which way to bedevil and annoy the life out of him."

Rav Meir's voice rose with his passion: "Why do I deserve this? — for my 'great sin' of trying to create a great mansion of Torah study? Is it for this that I have to suffer the tribulations of exile, travel about endlessly to raise money, work alone to the point of exhaustion with no one to help me? — only to find that not only will no one help me, but on the contrary, people simply want to stone me? They just want to eat my flesh! — those fools, those eternally obstructive, destructive fools!"

For a moment he paused, and then he continued more calmly: "And yet, the more I suffer for that structure, the more precious and vital it becomes to me. A child would not be so all-important to its mother if not for the labor pains she suffers when she brings it into the world."

Again he paused . . . then went on: "The Torah calls our Divinely promised territory 'a land of milk and honey' (*Sh^emos*/Exodus 3:8, etc.); why specifically milk and honey? When we reflect well, we can find the symbolic meaning: Honey comes from a bee; milk, explains the Talmud (*bavli*, B^{e}choros 6b), is derived in the cow (by an internal process of transformation) from its blood. Sometimes you have to be prepared to give your blood again and again, and to suffer poisonous bee stings any number of times, before you can reach your goal and find yourself at last in your promised Holy Land.

"This is how I feel about my *Yeshivas Chachmey Lublin*: Let them buzz around me and sting me as much as they want. It will avail them nothing! I am ready to shed blood, to give blood, to lose blood; I am ready to accept every persecution, every insult and derision. One thing alone remains clear and certain to me: In spite of everything, *Yeshivas Chachmey Lublin* will come into existence!"

Once more he paused, and once more his voice rose: "How greatly we have sinned toward our religious, observant youth; and for this, our Orthodox Jewry will have to give an accounting — for its stultifying indifference. . . . And what, when all is said and done, has Polish Jewry done for that building in Lublin which has already cost close to a million zlotys? True, when I returned from America, I was given a most impressive welcome. Yet, dear Polish Jewry, have you fulfilled your obligation with that alone? Did you end your participation, your helpful actions, with that alone? Do I have to go on traveling out forever on my own private journeys of exile, to keep knocking on the doors of people of means? Why will no one ever come forward, by his own initiative, and volunteer to join in this labor? Why?"

Under the impact of his scorching words, the conference voted into the record several strong and pungent resolutions that were designed to help with the completion of Yeshivas Chachmey Lublin. The resolutions were adopted by such a great assembly, with such ardent enthusiasm. Yet in retrospect, could it be said that they saved the situation? Were they a significant spur to positive action?

The answer must be left for later pages.

32

To create a library

We have jumped ahead to the year 5689 (1929). Only then would the sense of frustration, the feeling of exhaustion to the point of despair, grow truly strong. In 5687 (1927) he was still his cheerful, ebullient, optimistic self. And his effervescent creative mind stayed open for ideas to advance the progress of his "yeshiva in the making."

The idea of the Library seemed to come naturally, almost inevitably: to establish at the yeshiva a great collection of holy volumes of Torah learning, as a prime necessity for the world study center that he envisioned.

Thus in 5687 (1927) he issued a printed call to the entire Jewish community, worldwide, demanding every single individual to help as he could, so that an immense "Central Torah Library of Lublin" could come into being. The goal that he proclaimed was an assembled treasure of a hundred thousand volumes, to form an all-encompassing repository of Torah learning for the Yeshivas Chachmey Lublin: For he looked forward to the opening of its doors in the summer of the following year, and he saw the projected library as an absolute necessity. He wanted that Library (housed in the yeshiva building, of course) to contain every single printed work of Torah literature, from the very first to the very latest.

In his printed circular he called on every individual community, in every town and townlet, to form a "Lublin Library Committee" for the specific purpose of collecting items for the project. . . . And like other ideas of his, this one too found its targets and struck home.

Poor as the Jews in Poland might be in kopecks or zlotys to spare, they were not poor in the holy books of learning, large and small, that had been produced through generations of study by devoted scholars and devoted work by printers. An immense number of these volumes had even migrated to America with their owners.

As the positive reactions began to gather momentum, a good number of individuals took their fine private libraries and donated them. A great many others, wanting to go on enjoying their printed treasures while they lived, left them to the projected Library in their wills. Thus, in his last will and testament, a noted philanthropist in America named Benjamin Gut, himself the author of a few volumes, bequeathed his valuable collection of some 4,000 titles.

Slowly and steadily the Library took form, as thousands upon thousands of volumes came in; and among them, even rare printed works and valuable manuscripts could be found. Eventually it achieved the stature of one of the greatest libraries of Torah literature in the world.

As the treasure took form under his eyes, Rav Meir linked a new, inspired thought with it. As a rule, an individual learner in the world of Torah study had only a few meager volumes at hand: a few modest tractates of the Talmud, perhaps the basic commentaries, and in general, that was all. If someone felt a yearning to find some new explanation or thought on a Talmudic text, perhaps a fascinating comment or insight that he could ponder, he had nowhere to look for it. He would have to make his way to one of the larger towns to find a volume that he sought.

To answer the problem, his fertile mind proposed a novel solution. In the world of Talmudic study, one of the most novel and popular works of commentary is a series of volumes titled *Shitta Mekubetzess*, by a mid-sixteenth-century Talmudist in Egypt named Rav Betzalel Ashkenazi. He was obviously thc owner of a priceless collection of commentaries on tractates of the Talmud by a large number of *rishonim* (Early Scholars — some of whom are otherwise unknown); for he gained his immortality in the annals of Torah study by compiling long extracts of explanation and commentary on four important tractates.

What Rav Meir Shapiro proposed now was this: With the new, splendid Library at hand, let the young Talmudists destined to study there compile their own new series of volumes, on all the tractates they studied, that would be worthy of the name *Shitta Mekubetzess.* Let them follow in the path that Rav Betzalel Ashkenazi had created, and gather in order every worthwhile passage of novel explanation, interpretation and commentary that they would find in the vast rabbinic literature on the library shelves. With the cooperation of understanding philanthropists in the Jewish world, the results could be published in a series of attractive low-cost volumes that all, rich and poor alike, could afford.

What a tremendous spur this would be (argued the energetic, persuasive Rav) to Talmud study by people everywhere. And think of the side-benefit: a first-rate source of material support for the young scholars and students working on the project, as they received a proper salary for the many years of intensive study and labor that the project would require.

To move ahead again in time, as soon as the yeshiva opened, the project was initiated under his personal supervision, and the work went ahead at a good rate of speed. A first volume was made ready for the press, and it was about to appear in print, when the life of the great creative spirit behind it was cut down; and in the wake of the calamity, as the entire Jewish world, stunned in disbelief, mourned his death, the project had to be abandoned before it could even make a proper start.

Now, however, all that existed was the hope and the plan. And even that had to be left for a while, as a side matter, to make way for a more central concern that needed his attention: the spiritual content of the yeshiva when the eager young Talmudists would come there.

What, in short, should be the method of study? What path should they take to learn and to master the pages of the Talmud?

It was a question that vitally interested not Rav Meir alone, but the entire world of Talmud study: Should the new institution seek out one of the traditional pathways that existed in the world of the yeshivos, where each had its well-trodden road? Or should it create a fresh, original method that would really suit the fresh, original idea of a world study center?

The problem was indeed very much in the air. People at large pondered and cogitated, and it held a central place in the alert concern of Rav Meir himself. For he himself was by no means decided as yet: Should he indeed merely transplant out of the past the way of study that had existed in a Lublin yeshiva long ago?

That, however, provided no simple, single answer. He knew well enough that then too, centuries earlier, there had been no single, uniform method through all the years, accepted and followed by all the scholarly heads of the yeshivos which they maintained. In every period of time, the study method had taken on a different form.

Take, for example, the pioneering founder of focused, regular yeshiva study in Poland: the illustrious Rav Ya'akov Pollack. In mid-sixteenth-century Lublin, he created the method of *pilpul*: to juxtapose citations from different places in the Talmud, perhaps also from the commentaries, or from Rambam's code of law; to find difficulties or contradictions; and then, by keen analytic reasoning, to find ways to resolve and remove the difficulties.

This was the approach he took, to stimulate his *talmidim* to livelier study, to arouse and develop their interest. And this was the approach his disciples took in their adult years, when they took positions as Talmud instructors in yeshivos throughout Poland.

Yet the great scholar known as the Maharam of Lublin took a diverging approach in his time. Between the years 5342 (1582) and 5347 (1587), Rav Meir ben G^e^dalya was *rosh yeshiva* (head of the yeshiva) in the city, and he instituted a different method of study: for his goal was a firm, sound knowledge of the plain, basic meaning of the Talmud text. He wanted no part of the dazzling heights that a keen intellect and insightful mind could attain by *pilpul*; for he greatly preferred a simple, direct understanding of the contents, which could make Talmud study accessible to everyone.

Somewhat later there was Rav Sh'mu'el Eli'ezer Edels, known in the world of Torah study as "the Maharsha," whose commentary can be found in the back of virtually every volume in the standard editions of the Talmud. Any serious study of his commentary makes his own approach of penetrating analysis quite apparent.

Finally there was Rav Sh^e^lomo Luria, better known to Talmud learners as "the Maharshal": For the last fifteen years of his life, from 5320 (1560) to 5334 (1574) he was the Chief Rabbi of Lublin. He too was firmly opposed to *pilpul*, and he too developed an approach of his own. And like the Maharsha, he too merited to have his Talmud commentary printed at the back of virtually every volume in the standard editions.

Open, then, just about any large, thick volume of Talmud in a standard edition, and in the back sections you are quite certain to find all three on a single page: on the upper part, Maharsha (*chiddushey halachos va'agados Maharsha*); and below, side by side, Maharam and Maharshal (*chochmas sh^e^lomo*) — three commentaries from Lublin with three ways of study: *Maharsha* — a quiet thoughtfulness and a clear, penetrating understanding in depth (the approach is apparent in virtually every line); *Maharshal* — to derive the essence of the *halacha*, the normative, definitive law, that can be found in the Talmud text (this approach emerges more emphatically in his *Yam shel Sh^e^lomo*); and finally *Maharam* — a simple insistence on the plain, basic meaning of Talmud text.

Thus Rav Meir could find three *chachmey Lublin*, three great scholars of the city's illustrious past, with three discrete ways of Talmud study. And so the question remained: What method should be adopted for the new, modern Yeshivas Chachmey Lublin? And indeed, who was truly competent to reach a verdict and announce a decision with authority on the one system that would hew most closely to the truth, that would best elicit the eternal verities of the Talmud, because it would prove to be the most consistent internally?

On the other hand, could there be any one certain answer? In at least two instances (*bavli*, Eruvin 13b; Gittin 6b) the Talmud relates that when there were two opposing views and there was a need to know which of the two Heaven considered right, to be accepted as *halacha*, a Divine echo was heard: "Both these and those are words of the living God." Perhaps, then, here too, all three approaches could lead equally to Divine truth, to "words of the living God."

Unable to decide, Rav Meir decided instead that it was time for him to go traveling, in search of an answer.

33

Into the Lithuanian yeshiva world

In Eastern Europe, most of the yeshivos were situated in Lithuania. Rav Meir felt the need now to meet with their venerable, seasoned *roshey yeshiva* and talk the matter through with them. With thoughtful consultation and wise counsel, he knew he would find the right way of study to implant in Yeshivas Chachmey Lublin.

In its own way, the journey through the yeshiva world proved to be yet another "triumphal procession" for him. At every destination he was welcomed with the utmost enthusiasm. There were those who had, initially, various doubts and misgivings, questions and misconceptions about his projected yeshiva; but afterward they accepted it wholeheartedly, along with his perceptive plans for it.

Not too much was ever reported or told afterward about his visits, but from the few facts we have, a picture emerges of the strong impact that this great Talmudist of Poland made on the yeshivos of Lithuania.

As the Rabbi of Piotrkov, it was from that city that he set off; and his first stop was a nondescript little town named Radin, a place of utter insignificance that might never have featured on any map, but for one fact: The oldest and most important yeshiva in Lithuania was located there, having been founded many long decades ago by a learned man named Rav Yisra'el Meir Kagan (the local variant form of *kohen*), whom the entire Jewish world knew as the Chafetz Cha-yim.

Old and feeble though he was, probably well past his ninetieth birthday, this acknowledged dean and Elder Scholar of the great masters of Talmud and *halacha* was still in residence there as the yeshiva's guiding spirit. And so the journey from Piotrkov by railroad brought Rav Meir first to Radin.

Before his arrival, however, there were preliminaries — a whole week of them. From the time the Yeshiva of Radin learned of his intention to visit, a week was devoted to making proper plans and preparations. And when he arrived, accompanied by the silver-haired *parnas* (titular head) of Lublin's Jewish community, Reb Moshe Shtcharansky, an august and auspicious welcome awaited him.

There were representatives of the small Jewish community, delegates of the *talmidim* (the yeshiva students), and delegates of various social institutions. By each group in turn he was greeted with warm, hearty words of cordial welcome. And then there was one more message. At his age, in his state of health, it was out of the question for the Chafetz Cha-yim to come in person. Instead, there was his personal representative, with full "power of attorney" to greet Rav Meir Shapiro in his name.

When all the greetings were over, the first move of the visitors in the little town was to the Chafetz Cha-yim's home. And there Rav Meir was welcomed with an unusual warmth and affection by the venerable sage himself, as he lay resting on his couch.

One part of this old world-renowned scholar had not aged: his mind. As people filled the room to the last inch, trying to overhear, he began questioning Rav Meir in detail about the program of study and religious activities planned for the Lublin yeshiva. As the questions and answers continued, at one point the hoary sage's eyes seemed to light up with an inner smile: when he learned from his visitor that there were plans at the yeshiva for a program of intensive study in *kodashim* ("holy things"): the tractates of the Talmud dealing mainly with offerings and animal sacrifices at the holy Temple, the *beyss ha-mikdash*.

It was evident that this bit of news made the Chafetz Cha-yim especially cheerful. Raising his weak, hoarse voice a bit, he began citing (by heart, of course) a series of passages from his published writings in which he offers textual proof that the study of *kodashim* will bring closer the *g'ula*, the ultimate, messianic Redemption of the Jewish people. For then the third and final *beyss ha-mikdash* will become more likely to arise, with Heaven's help, so that all the devoted study and mastery of *kodashim* can be put to sacred practical use.

As their conversation continued, the venerable sage learned that the people currently participating in the *daf ha-yomi* program, studying daily the same scheduled double-page of Talmud around the world, now numbered a quarter of a million. He then asked his visitor for a favor: As Rav Meir informed him, in a short while the *daf ha-yomi* program was due to get to *kodashim*. When the time came, the Chafetz Cha-yim wanted to be told of it. Once it was a fact that a quarter of a million were studying this part of the Talmud regularly, said he, there was not the slightest doubt that the time for the *g^eula* would move considerably forward.

Being very feeble at his advanced age, the Chafetz Cha-yim had been lying prone on his couch the entire time. Now he gathered his strength, and with an energetic effort he sat up. "The *daf ha-yomi* deserves this," he said: "that I should receive him properly." (As the Jewish world had decided long ago to call him the Chafetz Cha-yim, so he decided, evidently, that thenceforth his name for Rav Meir would be the *daf ha-yomi*.)

With their "private" conversation at an end, in his weak, low voice the Chafetz Cha-yim bade Rav Meir, "Say something now" — some brief Torah thought — "for the people assembled here."

"I came here to listen!" replied Rav Meir, in the same especially loud voice that he had used all along — because advanced old age had left the great scholar with very impaired hearing.

"But I am weak and ill," came the soft, barely audible answer. "I cannot give any proper talk."

Half turning with a smile to their audience, Rav Meir had his own kind of rejoinder ready: "When a man would bring his *bikkurim* (first-fruits) to the *beyss ha-mikdash*, he was instructed by the Torah, 'Then you shall come to the *kohen* who will be [there] in those days' (*D^evarim*/Deuteronomy 26:3). Well, in Midrash Sifre, Rabbi Yosé of Galilee finds the wording puzzling: 'Would it occur to you to come to someone who is not in your time?' In Rashi we find that Sage's answer in its clearest form: 'You have only the *kohen* in your time — as he is' — whatever his limitations. So I have come here, to the prime *kohen* of our time, because, as the prophet Mal'achi said (2:7), *the lips of a* kohen *will keep knowledge, and let Torah be sought from his mouth.*"

[It is told that old and feeble as he was, the Chafetz Cha-yim was so taken by this that he mustered his strength and voiced a brief bit of original, insightful Torah thinking that was suitable to the occasion. It might be guessed that, standing close to him, Rav Meir listened carefully, and then repeated it aloud for all in the chamber to hear.]

However it was, Rav Meir then set off on his brilliant, stimulating style of *pilpul*, through the highways and byways of Talmudic thought, enthralling and fascinating the yeshiva students who had gathered to listen. It might well have been the first time they heard such dazzling profundities and flights of incisive, insightful thinking. He roused them for a while from their placid, static, rather monotone way of study, to make them share his inner world of dynamic joy, the effervescent, cheerful liveliness that could always well up and surge in him.

[A record remains of something else that he told the group of young scholars at the Yeshiva of Radin, in the study hall (perhaps at this time, perhaps on another occasion): He recalled his first days in New York, before he learned the proper techniques and approaches to gather funds successfully in America. He kept meeting nothing but difficulties and failures, and managed to raise not a penny. And so (he told the young people in Radin) he sat in his hotel room one morning, feeling nothing but the acrid sense of failure.

[As he sat helpless in his valley of despair, said Rav Meir, the first part of a melody — rather melancholy in mood — came to him for the uplifting words in the Book of *T'hillim*: *im amarti mata ragli* ("If I said my foot is tottering" — Psalms 94:18). In the study hall in Radin he sang it for his listeners; and as they shared the scene and the mood with him, tears came flowing from their eyes. Not one person there listened with dry cheeks.

[Then Rav Meir continued: He told how he was "hired" to serve as a "cantor" in a synagogue on Rosh Hashana and Yom Kippur for a fee of a thousand dollars (a stupendous figure in those times; this incident was related above, in chapter 29), and how his fortunes changed after that, till he found himself receiving sizable and hefty donations, thick and fast. And so — he told his listeners — one morning he sat in his hotel room, feeling at last that the Creator was not only in His heaven but also on earth, and all was right not only with the world, but also with him. And then — he related — as of itself, without any conscious act or thought on his part, the second part of the melody came to him, joyful and exultant, for the second part of the sentence in *t'hillim*: *chasd'cha haShem yis'adéni* ("Your lovingkindness, O Lord, sustains me").

[Once again he sang, and as of themselves, the young Talmud scholars of Radin sang with him. And then they were dancing, like the most fervid, devout *chassidim*, as the words rang out with his *niggun* to avow to the Almighty that "if I said my foot is tottering, Your lovingkindness, *haShem*, sustains me!"]

When the time for it came, there was a *m'lavveh malka*, a modest meal on a Saturday night after Shabbos had ended, in which he joined the young Talmudists again. As they recalled it later, it was an experience whose like (to cite Yeshayahu) "no eye had ever seen" (Isaiah 64:3). He began truly to reveal his creative gifts, till he emerged as an absolute revelation. They had never known that such a giant of the spirit and the emotions could exist, with such a capacity to cast a spell over his listeners and raise them to such powerful responses of religious joy.

One of the *talmidim* in Radin found the right description for the inner essence of their incredible visitor: Rav Meir Shapiro, said he, was "the lively *niggun*": It was not that he sang a lively, uplifting, heartwarming chassidic melody. It was not that he had a certain singular capacity to bring happiness to a person's heart. He was himself the melody, the happiness itself.

Such was the impression that he left with the students; and this is how they summed up his visit: "The great, brilliant Talmud scholar spent only a few days in Radin, but those days remain inscribed in everyone's memory: For he transmuted our weekday, workaday environment into the festive atmosphere of a *yom tov*. Into melancholy he infused a pulsing, living *niggun*. . . ."

When Yeshivas Chachmey Lublin was able to open its doors at last, a brochure was issued in his honor, giving a brief account of his life and achievements till then. There, these enthusiastic words of one *talmid* in Radin were cited: "It was a great day when we set eyes on him in holiness, when we were privileged to see his spiritual might and majesty. With the Divine luster of his seraphic countenance, he would infuse so warm a spirit of sublime, noble, holy life."

In general, the visit to Radin became an occasion to demonstrate the power and glory of the world of Torah study; and it forged a bond of heartfelt friendship between Rav Meir and the Chafetz Cha-yim, which would continue as a firm, living link in the years that followed.

****

From Radin he rode on to Baranowitz, where he visited the two yeshivos, *Toras Chessed* and *Ohel Torah*.

[Though no more than a fairly small town, Baranowitz had a dynamic, lively community of chassidim who were devoted to the wondrous, inspiring Rebbes of Slonim. It was they who built and maintained *Toras Chessed* as a *yeshiva g*e*dola*, where hundreds of adolescents received their Torah education. This place of education blended the Lithuanian approach to

Talmud and *halacha* with worship and prayer in the finest chassidic tradition.

[The other yeshiva, Ohel Torah, was founded around 5667 (1907) by none other than the "grand old man" of Novaradok, Rav Yosef Yozel Hurvitz, and it was originally headed by a son-in-law of his (the son of the local *rav*) who had been born and raised there. Thus it became a typical *litvishe yeshiva* of the Novaradok type, devoted to Talmud and *mussar* (the self-analytic study of ethics and morality).

[After the First World War, making his way back from Russia, the Chafetz Cha-yim's great disciple Rav Elchanan Wasserman stopped off at Baranowitz, and he was persuaded to stay and take charge of it. Under his energetic leadership, *Ohel Torah* finally acquired a building of its own, so that it could end its peripatetic existence in the various Houses of Prayer and Study.]

After Baranowitz, Rav Meir's next destination was the famed Yeshiva of Mir, where he spent a considerable amount of time in consultation and discussion with the *roshey yeshiva* and its great master of spiritual influence, Rav Yerucham Levovitz. Unexpectedly, he found Rav Yerucham full of boundless admiration for him and for the creativity in his great project, Yeshivas Chachmey Lublin.

[In his itinerary he made sure to include the renowned yeshivos at Kletsk and Slobodka. At each stopping he was received with great acclaim and enthusiasm, as the figure he had become beyond all doubt: the unanimously acknowledged leader of Poland's Torah Jewry.]

****

All his traveling to the yeshivos of Lithuania was done at last, and Rav Meir returned home. Then he gave a historical survey of the rise and formation of the two groups of yeshivos in the two lands: Poland and Lithuania.

He described the substantive differences between the two, and showed how the variations in their lifeways had arisen out of the differences in the conditions of life between Poland and Lithuania. Because of the conditions in Poland, said he, from a pupil's earliest years of Talmud study the emphasis had always had to be on a clear understanding and retention of the textual material, and hence, not enough time could be spent on attention to profundity in the study and to comprehension in depth. This, said Rav Meir, was the historical reason for the formation and development of what came to be known as Polish *pilpul*.

In general, the Rav brought back with him a very favorable impression of Talmud study in Lithuania, with its characteristics of strong discipline, persistent, assiduous study, and an essential inner love of the Torah for its own sake.

One day, though, he was asked if he had found some basic characteristic difference in the ways of study between Poland and Lithuania. "Of course," he replied with a twinkle: "the same difference that exists between a *chassid* [a devoted follower of a chassidic spiritual leader] and a *misnaggéd* [one who rejects the way of the *chassid* and finds his life goals in the pure study of Torah and *halacha*]. . . . Here," he asserted with his facetious wit: "let me explain what I mean with an illustrative example:

"One day a *chassid* and a *misnaggéd* were sitting together and studying some of the tractate Sukkah, and they duly came to the well-known account: It was told about Yonasan ben Uzzi'el: During the time that he sat and become involved in Torah study, any bird that flew over him would be burned up immediately (*bavli*, Sukkah 28a).

"At that the two fell silent and became lost in thought; whereupon the *misnaggéd* asked the *chassid*, 'What have you become so thoughtful about?'

"Replied the *chassid*, 'I'm just meditating about the extraordinary, paranormal, superhuman degree of holiness that this Talmudic Sage attained — enough to make such a profound physical change in the atmosphere over his head. And I keep wondering how a person can get to such a great level of sanctity. What is the way that leads to a holiness like that?'

"Then, however, the *chassid* noticed that the *misnaggéd* was also away off somewhere in the realm of pure thought; and so he asked in turn, 'What are *you* pondering?' And the other replied, 'I was wondering what the law should be about the bird. According to the Talmudic laws of damages, if that bird belonged to somebody, would Yonasan ben Uzzi'el have to pay him for it? Is this a case of *grama b*ᵉ*yada-yim*, in which he caused the bird's death as directly as if he had killed it with his own hands?'

"And there," concluded Rav Meir with an elfin smile, "you have a clear illustration of the difference between the Polish and the Lithuanian way in Talmud study."

****

The time came when he had to decide at last on the system of Talmud study that should prevail at the yeshiva. After his travels to the known study centers in Lithuania, would he indeed adopt their way of learning?

Evidently the time had come for him to decide; and yet he let the question continue hanging in the air. Only later, as the date of the opening drew closer, did he let the answer become known — the solution he reached as his thinking crystalized:

Yeshivas Chachmey Lublin would formulate and follow a way of its own: an eclectic approach combining the best elements of the existing methods. It would strive for the penetrating thought and depth of understanding that could be found in Lithuania. It would feature strongly the keen intellectual approach of ***pilpul*** for which Talmud study in Poland was noted. And from the Torah learning in Galicia it would take the way toward a clear command of Talmudic text and a clear approach toward ***halacha*** to deal with questions in law. . . . Espousing these three ways, the new yeshiva would work toward a synthesis, to develop at last into its own singular path.

With this answer, Rav Meir considered the question of approach and method resolved. He was free to take up now the question that followed: a detailed daily learning program. He produced a tentative schedule of study, and sent it to all the great Talmudists in Poland, asking for their reactions and thoughts, inviting criticism and constructive suggestions for improvement.

When their answers arrived, he carefully chose a number of these foremost scholars to serve as a collegium that would arrive at a final decision. And so, in time, the yeshiva came to have a clear line to follow in Talmud study, and a clear study program to schedule into the daily routine of activities.

The preliminary work was all done. Nothing remained but to find a way to get the last of the construction work finished and to let the yeshiva come alive.

On toward the opening

How many years of work had he invested in the dream? How much thought and planning had gone into it? How much painful effort, how much wearying toil had it cost him to raise thousands upon thousands of dollars, so that the dream might be actualized in the poverty-stricken, faith-filled world of the pious Polish Jew?

Now it was the year 5689 (1929); and what was there to show for it all? A handsome, impressive building stood on Lubartovska Street in Lublin. And the interior was not finished. The building was not ready for the small multitude of young, budding Talmudists who wanted to fill it with the sound and fury of their animated study.

Rav Meir knew the solution to the problem; the Book of *Koheless* told it exactly: "and money answers everything" (Ecclesiastes 10:19). When it was there, it was the eternal solution. When it was not, it was the eternal obstruction.

He had the figures. He knew how much was still needed to get the interior completed. It was a worrying amount indeed, and when he looked about him, there was not a ray of hope to be seen. No men of spirit were moving about energetically, with élan, to gather meaningful donations. He could expect nothing from that direction that could get the edifice "open for business" soon. Yet for him the yeshiva was an imperative, burning necessity that could brook no delay.

Where should he turn? Perhaps he recalled an old, time-honored maxim of the Sages: *eyn tzibbur 'ani*, "There is no such thing as a poor, indigent public." He decided to demand once again, in the strongest possible terms, the help of his people in Poland, refusing to believe they would fail him altogether.

Dated the first of Adar I (February 11, 1929), his printed public call bore as its heading the words of Yosef (Joseph) when his father sent him to find his brothers: *I am looking for my brethren!* (*B'réshis*/Genesis 37:16).

"Only a few months remain until the day set for the opening of our World Torah Center in Lublin — and the monetary fund [for its completion and upkeep] has not been created! . . . My brethren, *where are you?*

"Here one brother of yours, one fellow-Jew, is collapsing under the burden before your eyes. Are you just going to look on calmly? — with indifference? *Where are you?*

"Capable, gifted youngsters from every corner of the world are virtually writhing in their longing [to come and begin their studies at the yeshiva]. *And you keep still?*"

He continued with the words of reproach that R^euvén (Reuben) hurled at his brothers when he felt that their crime in selling Yosef into slavery had caught up with them: *Did I not tell you: Do not do wrong to the boy!* (there, 42:22). . . .

"In this critical hour, when the final hammer blows must fall [to finish the building], let no one fail to appear at the front. [Let our emissaries] come forth valiantly to the help of the Almighty . . . to raise money . . .

"And to you, dear generous brethren among the people, I call: Know what you have to do . . . for if not now, when? . . . Give with hand and heart to our worthy delegates who will call on you to ask your help. Just one more step with vigor on your part, and Yeshivas Chachmey Lublin will be all complete, from the foundations to the roof. . . . "

Such were the words that came from his heart to the people, to stir their obdurate hearts and rouse them from their torpor. And their degree of response indeed rose and grew warmer. A large, respectable amount of money was amassed; and the rest, that he still needed, was borrowed from Poland's national bank. He was able to get the loan only by expending enormous efforts and bringing powerful influence to bear in the right quarters.

One last detail remained: The great men of piety and learning who constituted the *mo'etzess g^edoley ha-torah* (the Council of Torah Authorities) of Agudas Yisra'el were assembled to decide on the date for the opening. The time they chose was Tuesday the twenty-eighth of Sivan, 5690 (June 24, 1930).

The Rav announced the planned opening, to let the news be spread around the world; and at the same time he proclaimed a new, original project: to have a *séfer torah* written on behalf of *k^elal yisra'el* — a Torah scroll to bring merit to the Jewish people in entirety.

[Perhaps behind the idea was a wish to bring the great community of Poland a greater measure of Heaven's protection and grace than it could ever have earned before — by a new approach: With the *séfer torah* under way while the day came closer for the opening of the yeshiva, Polish Jewry might earn some sorely needed Heavenly merit both through the Written Torah in the scroll, which he planned and hoped to keep inside the *aron kodesh* (the holy Ark), and through the Oral Torah that would be studied intensively, in the yeshiva's great Hall of Study and Prayer.]

At any rate, this was something that had never been done before. Until then, in Jewish history, the initiative for writing a Torah scroll would come from a wealthy individual seeking merit in Heaven and able to afford it, or from a congregation in need of one for its Shabbos prayer service; and then the congregants would bear the costs. Never, though, had a *séfer torah* been produced by and for a country's entire community — because no one had conceived the idea before. And the genius of the idea, eminently suited to Rav Meir's mind and temperament, lay in its simplicity. It was the kind of project that was certain to evoke the response, "Yes! Of course! Why did no one think of it before?" It was the kind of idea that could enter with the greatest ease the heart of virtually everyone in the broad spectrum of Poland's Torah Jewry.

In publicizing the plan, Rav Meir noted that according to certain Early Authorities (*rishonim*), it was a mitzvah (one of the 613 mitzvos ordained by the Torah) for every Jew to write his own Torah scroll. Then he went on to demonstrate conclusively, by his way of thought among the halachic sources, that by participating in this project, any and every ordinary Jew would carry out the mitzvah!

As explanatory background, he added a most intriguing point: In a truly singular way, olden tradition links the Jewish people to the *séfer torah*, the most sacred object it has in the world: By the teachings of the Sages, 600,000 souls were present at Mount Sinai for the Revelation, and these souls animate the Jewish people in every generation. Likewise, the Written Torah is held to contain 600,000 Hebrew characters. Thus it is believed that each individual soul is linked to one particular character.

Hence, Rav Meir insisted, when Jewry participates in the writing of a scroll by having one letter written for one soul, the linkage becomes objectified in the act of the writing, for that writing becomes a palpable act through which the people receive and accept the Torah.

Thus the idea was publicized and "marketed"; and it was welcomed with true ardor and warmth. The greatest men of learning and piety, the foremost spiritual leaders, sent in their money for their letters — for example, the illustrious Rebbes of Tchortkov, Belz, and Ger. Such people, in fact, readily paid for their letters much more than the set rate, and added messages of blessing and encouragement, stressing the great value and importance of the enterprise.

In his earnest desire to reach the ordinary, everyday members of his people, he set the rate at the Polish equivalent of a dollar per word; and knowing only too well how many would find even this beyond their means, he emphasized that it would be equally meritorious to pay for just a letter. So it truly became a broadly based folk action, with the fervent participation of the whole community. There were a great many payments for whole words, and many more for single letters. And a great number of people paid for the letters in their individual Hebrew names, wherever those characters might be found in the Torah.

Everyone felt the privilege that it was for him to take a share. Everyone experienced the deep satisfaction of finding a way to join the great spiritual leaders and Talmud scholars of his time in one Torah scroll. A person could live with the inspiring thought that right next to his word (or letter) in the *séfer torah* was, very possibly, the word of an illustrious *tzaddik* of the age.

In brief, the whole idea generated a tremendous interest and enthusiasm, and the result was a widespread keen, animated desire to "buy" letters and words by paying the cost of their production by the scribe. In a short time, enough money came in to acquire the necessary parchment and set a first-rate *sofer* to work. Soon enough, the Torah scroll of *k^{e}lal yisra'el* would exist.

****

At the same time that the scribe sat down to his labors as a result of Rav Meir's initiative, as the result of another inititative by him, two eminent Talmud scholars set out as a delegation of the yeshiva, to examine candidates worthy of admission to the great study center. The minimum requirement was a competent knowledge, by heart, of at least 200 double pages (*dapim*) of the Talmud, with the commentary of *tos^{e}fos* that was printed alongside the text. It could be confidently assumed that any youngster with such a store of learning in him had an adequate background and an adequate capacity for study to be worthy of admission to Yeshivas Chachmey Lublin.

When the delegation of two went traveling about for their extended series of interviews and oral examinatons, they were pleasantly surprised to find some youngsters with a solid mastery not of 200 double pages but of 500 — and sometimes even more. Yet perhaps they should not have been so surprised: The news had been spread about a good year in advance that such examinations would be held, and literally everywhere, in every town and townlet, young budding Talmudists set to studying on their own initiative with a feverish zeal and intensity that people around them had probably never seen before.

In every young heart burned the longing to be accepted as a student at the yeshiva. The youngsters could only imagine the "room and board" that the yeshiva would provide; but they knew full well the conditions (bordering on nightmare) under which *yeshiva bochurim* lived everywhere else. Add to this the prestige that a *talmid* at the yeshiva was certain to enjoy, and it is easy to understand why it became the greatest longing and dearest dream of every lad with a capacity for Talmud study to gain admittance into the new learning center.

For a good year or more the intensive study went on all over Poland, everyone intent on reaching the goal: 200 *dapim*. That became the magic number, 200, which rang out and echoed in every youngster's heart in Poland's world of Torah. That was the number in their dreams and hopes, the number toward which they strove and struggled, studying away through the hours of day and night.

Then, when young learners knew at last that they had this amount of Talmud safely in the grasp of the mind, entrenched well within the memory, they knew they could relax and breathe more easily.

At the proper time they set off from their home towns, to arrive at one of the designated places of examination. There they were duly tested by the two men of eminence, the yeshiva's delegation, so that the two could determine the fate of the incipient Talmud scholars.

It was no secret that at the time of a youngster's examination, his father was very likely occupied in saying a great deal of *t^ehillim*, one Psalm after another, in fervent prayer to Heaven that the boy should receive a passing grade. And when a father learned that his youngster had actually been accepted, he knew it was no small boon of grace which Heaven had bestowed on him. Most likely an outburst of tears came from his eyes, as a feeling of gratitude filled his heart, once he knew, beyond all doubt, that his son would be studying in Lublin.

Then he had to steady and ready himself to receive the flood of felicitations and good wishes that were showered on him from all sides. Everyone congratulated him on his great good fortune, on the signal privilege granted him by Heaven, that a son of his was found gifted and capable enough to be suitable for Yeshivas Chachmey Lublin. . . .

[In the world of secular education, it has long been known that students always "cram" for an important examination: They store and stuff into their minds all the knowledge they will need to answer the kind of questions they expect. Then, once the examination is over, they are likely to relinquish the stored information with startling speed and let it flow away into oblivion. How different it was with the students who eventually entered Yeshivas Chachmey Lublin:]

Interestingly enough, once the youngsters were all there, settled in and embarked on their learning program, they came to know one another, and only one conclusion could be drawn: Taken all together, they constituted a complete living Talmud: For, in preparing for the critical entrance examination, each had studied thoroughly and intensively one particular tractate. And in each one's mind that tractate stayed!

Thus, one particular young fellow became linked in their minds with *Massechess Shabbos*; another, with *Massechess Eruvin*; and so on. And this had an important practical effect: As they pursued their ongoing study, when a youngster found it necessary to check something in another tractate, he thought it would be a pity to take the time to walk to the bookcase where the volume was kept, take it off the shelf, and open it to the page he needed. It was so much easier and faster to find the fellow-student who had mastered the tractate in preparing for his examination, and to ask him. Invariably, the answer he received would be accurate and complete, including full information, as necessary, from *tos^e^fos* and the later commentaries.

So the young learners at the yeshiva contained their own "living Talmud," ready to supply one another with clear, sound, accurate information from and about the Talmud as the need arose.

35

To impress the Press

The days moved on steadily, till only a few weeks remained before the scheduled day of the opening. Soon the doors to this envisioned citadel of Torah would have to move, to admit its eager young prodigal learners. And so the time had come to inform the world that a good long while ago, Yeshivas Chachmey Lublin had left the realm of hopes and dreams and taken on a real, physical form. The world had to be told, further, that in its real, physical form it was about to waken into dynamic spiritual life.

It was time, Rav Meir decided, to hold a major press conference in Lublin, to be attended by a considerable number of journalists and reporters, from all the periodicals and newspapers in Poland.

The reporters were seasoned, cynical veterans in the world of journalistic publicity. They were quite expert in the art of puffing, huffing and bluffing, blowing up facts and statistics till something appeared larger than life. So they discounted heavily all they might have heard or read about the yeshiva. They simply never expected to see any true grandeur or majesty in the finished structure. They looked forward to seeing another typical yeshiva building in Poland, that had been given some unusual publicity. The last thing they ever expected to find was that in this case the publicity they had seen was not unusual but altogether amazing: It was simply the truth.

Had they not come to see the edifice with their own eyes, they would never have believed it: Not one word in the publicity was an exaggeration.

Interestingly enough, shortly before the formal opening, Rav Aharon Ashinsky, the eminent Rabbi of Pittsburgh, Pennsylvania, came on a visit from the United States, and he went to look at the building. When he was done with his thorough, careful inspection, he realized, to his belated astonishment, that when Rav Meir had made his lengthy tour of America, in all that he had said about the yeshiva, in every bit of description he gave, no single detail had been exaggerated. It was as grand, as majestic and imposing, as the Rav had said it would be!

Thus the Rabbi of Pittsburgh had been struck at the time by the Rav's statement that the yeshiva would have a hundred rooms. Now, he went through all the floors systematically, and realized there actually *were* a hundred rooms! He found the sheer honesty of Rav Meir overwhelming: The Rav had refrained completely from using the American language of hyperbole and exaggeration. . . .

On his return to Pittsburgh, the Rabbi of the city wrote an article for the Yiddish press giving the impressions he had carried away with him. One prominent paragraph read: "Since there really are a hundred rooms, why did the Rabbi of Piotrkov say only a hundred? The language of the publicity should have been in the American style. At the very least, he should have said: *Yeshivas Chachmey Lublin has a thousand rooms!* "

The thinking of the journalists invited to the press conference underwent a very similar process. They came with their minds set in their usual working order — and thus they discounted heavily everything they were told about the yeshiva in the advance publicity.

Then they saw a truly grand, imposing structure before their eyes; and they could not help being impressed. They had never imagined that the publicity could be the plain truth — and they were deeply moved. In consequence, when they wrote up their impressions for the newspapers, there was an unusual enthusiasm and warmth in their articles.

In the reception he held for them, Rav Meir unfolded the entire history of the yeshiva. He gave a description of the long road he had been forced to travel — a road strewn with obstacles and thorns — till Heaven granted him the sight of the edifice in its finished state. Then he dwelt on the historic importance of Lublin for Polish Jewry — the pride of place that the city had always held in the life of Poland's Jewry, with its yeshivos of renown.

To illustrate his point, Rav Meir gave some fascinating facts from the country's history: There was a time when Poland closed its borders to all foreigners. No aliens were allowed entry; none could obtain visas even to visit. Yet King Zygmunt (Sigismund I) made a singular exception for members of the Jewish people who wished to come to the Yeshiva of Lublin! For it had an extraordinary reputation, that reached to every corner of the Jewish community in the Diaspora. And thus it was known that the renowned learned savant and rabbinic leader Menashe (Manasseh) ben Israel sent his sons from Amsterdam to receive their Torah education in the Yeshiva of Lublin.

Rav Meir went on to list the illustrious Torah scholars and authorities who emerged from the historic city's yeshivos. It was enough, said he, to mention Rav Shalom Shachne, his son Rav Yisra'el, his son-in-law Rav Moshe Isserles (*Rama*), Rav Sh^{e}lomo Luria (*Maharshal*), and so on. They were the learned masters of Talmud who spread a knowledge of Torah and religious law throughout the Jewish world. In fact (Rav Meir continued), so advanced and important were the city's yeshivos that by government rule, their heads, the esteemed *roshey yeshiva*, enjoyed full autonomy in Jewish life and were made independent of the authority of the rabbi of the city.

It was in the sixteenth century that a fierce controversy developed between the rabbi and the *rosh yeshiva* in the city. King Zygmunt August [Sigismund Augustus, son and heir of Sigismund I] took the trouble to intervene personally and get the matter smoothed out; and it was then he issued a decree that the *rosh yeshiva*, in his person and in his activities, was to be wholly autonomous and outside the rabbi's jurisdiction. Thus all future quarrels between persons in these respective positions of authority were liquidated before they could arise and turn serious.

With this, Rav Meir's short journey into history ended. In the name of the journalists, one of them, named Stupnitsky, responded with a formal greeting of good wishes. Then he continued: "When I set eyes on this building, I became filled with both joy and fear: joy — because such blessed initiative can still be found within the Jewish people; and fear — that this wondrous, inspiring edifice may suffer some day, Heaven forbid, the same fate that befell all the great historic structures that Jews erected — in the countries of Spain, Portugal, and Holland . . . in the city of Posen. Jews built them, and today non-Jews possess them. I pray, therefore: May it be the will of our Father in Heaven that this building shall remain in Jewish hands."

The noted Hillel Zeitlin [a gifted writer in Yiddish and Hebrew with a strong interest in the mystic and poetic side of authentic Judaism] wrote an article in the Yiddish newspaper *Moment*, in which he deplored the fact that it was found necessary to bring the yeshiva into being with so much publicity and notoriety. What need was there, he asked, to hold press conferences, at a time when only a soft melody should have been heard within the structure, accompanying the study of a Talmudic controversy between two Sages, such as Abbayé and Rava — the melody of a soul yearning for its reunion with Divinity through the holy study.

Unfortunately, wrote Zeitlin, they were living now in a time of utter superficiality, entirely on the surface of life, so flooded by publicity and propaganda, that a soft earnest voice suffused with a sublime intensity would never be heard. It would just be utterly lost, drowned out completely.

He could only hope that when all the present storm and tumult died down, eventually it would bring in its wake a flow of Heavenly light, so that the yeshiva could truly became "the factory of the nation's spirit" — where the soul of the people could be formed and forged anew, in its pure age-old form, as it was in the historic yeshivos of Lublin through the earlier centuries. And thus let its rays of Heaven's radiance spread throughout the world. . . .

Needless to say, the criticism that Hillel Zeitlin expressed could not be disputed. In essence he was absolutely right, of course. Yet what he really did, probably without realizing it, was to point up sharply the enormous difference between the time of the olden, historic yeshivos and our own ongoing present. Then the Houses of Study could be established and opened without a breath of publicity. In our time it was heartrending to see how necessary it was to use the same methods for the yeshiva as those that the advertising industry used to promote a household product! It showed what Jewish life had come to in the "modern" world.

The core of the problem was that without such methods of propaganda, those who could help the project and promote its progress — communal workers, rabbis, eminent men of learning — did not seem to understand of themselves how vitally necessary this yeshiva was, as a setting for a heartwarming, uplifting melody to accompany the intensive study of the Talmud. There was an incredible indifference, an immovable inertia in the Jewish world that made such press conferences and publicity campaigns unavoidable and inevitable.

We saw this so plainly as the tragedy of our people: that the crystal-clear truths of our age-old way of life could not reach the ears of the community unless they were converted first into some alien form. It was a saddening, disheartening fact that the Torah, however they saw it, no longer made any impression on them. They could no longer be attracted by its inner light, but only by an ephemeral, temporary glamor glittering over its surface.

It was a condition that had become entrenched, and no one had the power to alter it. The interest of people at large would not be drawn to the true essence of the matter but only to the fancy, dazzling trappings that might be contrived around it. Whatever had to be done for the sake of the yeshiva, it would have to be done by adopting the current methods of superficial publicity and empty propaganda. It seemed the only way in which the radiance of the Torah might yet be able to reach a broader range of the Jewish people.

****

Interestingly enough, linked to this problem, a difference of opinion developed between the venerable Rebbe of Tchortkov and his ardent *chassid* Rav Meir, the founder and creator of the yeshiva. The Rebbe believed that the opening of the yeshiva should take place without any fanfare, without any dazzling manifestations of publicity. He pointed to a striking lesson in the Midrash (Tanchuma, *ki sissa* 31): The first tablets of stone with the text of the Ten Commandments were given to Moshe in the course of the Revelation at Sinai, following a tremendous display of awesome splendor, amid bolts of thunder and flashes of lightning (*Sh^emos*/ Exodus 19:16, 31:18); and so eventually they were smashed to pieces (there, 32:19). On the other hand, the Sages note, the second tablets that Moshe received were given him in complete privacy (there, 34:1-4, 28). They were given no chance to be exposed to evil influences. And they remained.

Nevertheless, his chassidic disciple disagreed. [Two rejoinders that he gave remain on record. This is the first:

[Since all the past, the present, and the future are known perfectly to the Almighty, ever and always, He certainly knew in advance that those stone tablets would be smashed. Why, then, did He go ahead and give them, nevertheless, amid the great lightning and thunder at Sinai? The answer has to be (insisted Rav Meir) because at that time the whole world was sunken in a baleful darkness, immersed in the dimwitted delusions of idolatry. It was imperative to arouse the world from its stupor and lethargy in the most clamorous, jarring way possible. Said the Almighty, "Let Me give the tablets even so, even if they will be smashed to bits, as long as they will shake up the world and make mankind learn about Me!"

[Similarly, said Rav Meir, all the clamorous publicity around the opening of the yeshiva will sanctify the Divine name of Heaven and will bring a revolutionary improvement to the prestige level of the yeshiva student — the esteem in which he is held. The honor of the Torah will be raised. . . .

[Then there was another thought that Rav Meir put to his great mentor, the Rebbe of Tchortkov:]

He pointed to the description in the Mishna (M^e^nachos 10:3; *bavli*, 65a) about the elaborate preparations, before a great throng of onlookers, for bringing the *omer* offering at the *beyss ha-mikdash* on the second day of Pesach — *so that the matter should have wide publicity! — so that people should talk about it everywhere!*

Well, asked Rav Meir, why the radical difference in approach between the two instances? Why did the second stone tablets need privacy and isolation, whereas, nevertheless, the omer was given strong publicity?

The difference, he explained, lies in this: When the first tablets with the Ten Commandments were given, at the Revelation, the entire people committed themselves to accepting and obeying them. In passionate ardor they exclaimed, *na'asseh v^e^nishma* (We will do and we will heed! — *Sh^e^mos*/Exodus 24:7). Hence, later it was enough to provide a second set of stone tablets in total privacy, in the aftermath of their sincere declaration of loyalty.

When the *omer* offering had to be brought, the Sages had it done according to their ruling: on the second day of Pesach — in full, open opposition to the view of the *baïsussim* [quite possibly the Essenes, linked today with the sect of the scrolls of Qumran], who held that it should be brought only on a Sunday. As the Mishna itself explains, this was the reason for giving the preparations maximum publicity: to impress on the people the authority of the Sages and their Oral Torah: It was this Torah that must be followed, and not the doctrines of a divergent sect. And since there had never yet been a firm, clear acceptance by the Jewish people of the authority of the Sages (the *p^e^rushim*), the procedure on the *omer* was given the strongest possible publicity.

The Rebbe of Tchortkov listened to his disciple thoughtfully, and he realized that Rav Meir was right. They lived now in a turbulent world of conflicting ideas and ideologies that struggled endlessly for the mind and heart of the Jew. No *a priori* bond of loyalty to the Torah could be taken for granted. Here was a chance to draw people closer for a moment to the world of Torah and its supreme importance — through all the trumpets and instruments of publicity that they were able to command.

The Rebbe of Tchortkov consented.

****

Ever ready with questions that might sting and annoy (like journalists in every time and place), some reporters with a bit of learned background came at him with a prime query: How could he go ahead and build a yeshiva like this? Wasn't he going against the grain of devout Jewry, against its fundamental, age-old way of Torah study? Wasn't he overlooking an explicit teaching in the sixth chapter of *Pirkey Avos* (6:4)? "This is the way of Torah study: A piece of bread with salt shall you eat and water by ration shall you drink, and on the ground shall you sleep — and in the Torah shall you toil."

How, then, could the Rav go and construct such a large, impressive building where its young budding Talmudists would live with full creature comforts, perhaps even in the lap of luxury! Wasn't that in direct contradiction to the words of the Sages?

"Well," replied Rav Mcir, "this is a question that we hear quite often. Let me make it understandable by a little story out of our historic past." This is the incident that he related:

It was the time of severe conflict between *chassid* and *misnaggéd*, when the Gaon of Vilna became known as the implacable foe of the way of *chassidus* which Rav Shné'or Zalman of Liady (author of the *Tanya*) was developing. According to the story, Rav Shné'or Zalman came once to a very small town near Vilna, to spend Pesach there. In those early times, the people who had adopted the chassidic way followed it as discreetly and unobtrusively as they could, having no wish to arouse the wrath of their neighbors, and especially not the anger of the Vilna Gaon. They had never even dared think of forming a small separate congegation of their own, to worship in the chassidic way. All the Jews of the *shtétl* prayed together in the local *shul.*

On the first night of Pesach, as they chanted and sang through the prayer service to welcome in the beloved festival, the *chassidim* (with Rav Shné'or Zalman in their midst) had a powerful longing to chant *hallél* toward the end of the service — the joyous Psalms of praise and thanksgiving (113-118) in which the liberation from Egypt is mentioned: This was a firm, accepted practice of *chassidim* everywhere. Yet as long as the whole congregation was present, they did not dare: They had been severely warned against it.

And so they bided their time in patience till the prayer service was over and all the others went off to their homes. Then they firmly locked themselves in and sang the *hallél* to their hearts' content. . . .

Yet how could they keep such a thing secret in the little *shtétl*? Soon enough, everyone knew of this "crime" that had been committed.

The man who reacted most sharply to the news was the *shammas* of the *shul*, whose job it was to take care of everything in the local synagogue. He knew it could cost him his position: the "crime" could well be blamed on him. He could simply be accused of having failed in his duties.

There was only one thing for him to do: He would not let the matter fade into the past. He ranted and demanded and insisted: the *chassidim* must go to the Vilna Gaon and confess to their great misdeed.

Seeing how distraught the *shammas* was, they agreed readily. They went and stood before the Gaon, and admitted to having said *hallél* as part of their prayer service on Pesach evening. But, they added, in doing so they relied on the Rav Yosef Caro, the author of the *Shulchan Aruch*: for he cites this custom; and hence it has a valid basis in *halacha*!

At this (it was told) the Vilna Gaon struck the table in anger. "Yes," he exclaimed; "but doesn't Rav Moshe Isserles (the Rama) add, 'We, however, do not have the practice of saying *hallél*'?"

When he saw how enraged the Gaon had become, Rav Shné'or Zalman spoke up: "Honored Rabbi, please calm yourself! If I may dare ask, were you there at the time, standing and watching how the Rama struck the table and declaimed in anger, *We, however, do not have the practice of saying hallél*? I believe he said it in an entirely different tone of voice, with a feeling of great regret and sorrow: *We, alas, do not have this precious, beautiful custom of saying hallél*!"

"In the same vein," concluded Rav Meir, "I would answer this question: That great Sage of olden times really meant to say, *Alas, this is the way of Torah study*. So tragic and miserable is the situation of old and young who would study Torah. They receive only bread and water for their sustenance and a piece of hard ground for their rest at night! But I tell you: *This must stop!* We have no right to let it continue. . . . And so the corrective answer is *Yeshivas Chachmey Lublin*."

****

There was an alternative answer which he gave sometimes, when this taunting, provocative question was thrown at him:

In that noted teaching by the Sages, there is a sentence which follows: "If you do so, happy shall you be, and it will be well with you." Well, this applies only if you take this ascetic path of your own free will, because at the level of spirituality that you have reached, you find this necessary for your further development. In other words, you have all the amenities you need to study Torah in comfort, but you choose deliberately to live on bread and water. A good bed is available, but you choose to sleep on the ground. Then indeed "happy shall you be, and all will be well with you": happy in this world, and all well in the World-to-Come.

Perish the thought, however, that we should arrogate to ourselves the right to *compel* a yeshiva student into so high a spiritual level. Who made us so absolute a master over a young scholar's physical existence, to deal with that as we like?

We have to hold only one thought in mind about Torah study: "It is a tree of life to those who hold fast to it, and happy are those who support it" (*Mishley*/Proverbs 3:18). For anyone who upholds and supports those who study Torah, it must bring happiness and fortune in life.

****

[Time and again he had this well-known passage in *Pirkey Avos* flung at him by people of wealth, when he came to demand donations for the yeshiva from them. Finally the time came when he stood up and answered boldly: "It is an error — an egregious error that the rich people in Jewry make. Many a time the Midrash explains something with the word *asm^eha* — 'question mark'; or Rashi explains something *bismiha*: 'with a question mark': A sentence that we read must be understood not as a statement but as a query, given in wonder. . . .

["And this is how I understand the passage in *Pirkey Avos*: Is that the way of Torah study? — you are to eat a piece of bread with salt? . . . you are to drink water by ration? . . . sleep on the ground? Under such conditions shall you toil and struggle to learn the Torah? No, no, and again no! This is not the way of proper Torah study!"

[Still another answer came from him at times, from his alert, creative mind: That passage must be understood only in the sense of "even if": Even if you are fated to live under such stringent conditions of privation, even then should you toil away at Torah study; and then, ultimately, all will be well with you. . . . Moreover, said Rav Meir, at the beginning of that chapter in *Pirkey Avos* (6:1) we read, "Whoever studies Torah for its own sake merits many things; and not only that, but the world is worthy for him" — which means (Rav Meir explained) that by his dedication to Torah study he merits to deserve to get from the whole world whatever he needs to be able to study properly: adequate food and clothing, a comfortable, relaxing physical setting, and so on.]

****

[Two days before the yeshiva was to be opened (Sunday, 26 Sivan 5690/June 22, 1930), he set out for Lublin, accompanied on the railroad journey by a group of outstanding *talmidim* who had studied with him at his yeshiva in Piotrkov. They would form the nucleus of the student body at the new yeshiva.

[As he chatted with them amiably, at one point he struck a wry note, as he cited a line from the *z^emiros* traditionally sung Saturday night at the meal called *m^elavveh malka* (sung in the hymn that begins *ish chassid haya*). "At the start," said he, "I used to pray with its plain meaning, *borey olam b^ekinyan, hashlém zeh ha-binyan*: 'Creator of the world by acquisition, complete this structure.' I implored Him to help me get the building finished. Now I still say those words to Him, but at the word *hashlém* I think intensely that it is from the same root as *shalém*, 'pay': I keep praying to Him to help me pay off the heavy debts that I had to take on to get it finished. . . ."

[For a short while he sat silently, lost in thought; then he gave the bit of a smile that generally indicated a flash of wit which had come into his mind. "If there is any one person who should be thanked for the construction of the building, it is none other than Chaïkl the water carrier." All the young Talmudists perked up their ears, eager to hear the explanation of his enigmatic words about Chaïkl (a Yiddish nickname derived from *Cha-yim*) that was sure to follow:

["Our Sages taught that a person is judged by Heaven every single day; yet they also taught that Rosh Hashana is a human being's judgment day for the entire year ahead. How can we accept both statements? Either they hold that a person is judged every day, or they postulate that his judgment is given once a year. Surely they cannot expect us to accept both teachings?

["Well, Rav Yisra'el Ba'al Shem Tov replied with a little story about Chaïkl the water carrier. By that bit of a story, said the Ba'al Shem Tov, the difficulty can be resolved: One morning, Chaïkl came passing by his window, whereupon the Ba'al Shem asked him how he was feeling. Chaïkl gave a deep, bitter groan: the work was just back-breaking, said he: It took all his strength away, and sometimes it left him with aches and pains; and all he could eke out of it was barely enough money to live on. The next morning, Chaïkl came passing by again, and the Ba'al Shem asked him once more how he felt. 'I thank the Holy One, blessed is He,' said Chaïkl cheerfully, 'that an old Jew like me still has enough strength in the body to go and earn an honest living'!

["Said the Ba'al Shem Tov: 'From this we learn that while a person's earnings (for the whole year) are allotted to him (by Heaven) on Rosh Hashana, or at most, by Yom Kippur (*bavli*, Bétzah 16a), he receives a judgment from Heaven every single day on what mood he will be in for the burden or the lot that he must bear that day. So one day he will groan, and the next day he will be bright and cheerful.'

["Well," Rav Meir told his students, "I wobbled about just like Chaïkl: There were days when the burden of getting that building done pressed down heavily on me. There were so many stumbling-blocks and failures and defeats, till, time and again, I went weak in the knees and felt no strength left in my hands. Then another morning came, and I felt a new strength and courage just from the fact that I was building something with a new, unprecedented importance: *Yeshivas Chachmey Lublin.* And a new happiness kindled with a great light inside me. . . . "

[When the train arrived in Lublin, heads of the community were there as a welcoming committee, waiting to receive him with honor. Now they greeted him with a happy enthusiasm; and once he was with them, a spirited chassidic dance started up, as if of itself. . . .

[On the day of the opening, he took the time to travel out to the old, historic Jewish cemetery. There he went from one hallowed gravestone to another, to give a formal invitation to the holy discarnates whose names were inscribed there, who had been the great Torah scholars of Lublin in their mortal lifetimes.

[Back at the yeshiva, he met the new *talmidim* who had come from near and far. When the youngest of them stepped forward, Rav Meir placed both his hands on the boy's head. Briefly he kissed him on the forehead, and as tears glistened in his eyes, he blessed them all. It was a moment when the young hearts trembled and beat a little faster.]

36

To open the doors

It was a national day of Jewish festivity, through all of Poland. There is no other way to describe the atmosphere that prevailed. On the windows were pasted stickers with the picture of the yeshiva building. Everywhere festive lights were lit to heighten the scene and to enliven the sense of celebration. Assemblies were organized, so that suitable people could give talks about the occasion, and discussions could be held about the significance of the event. Otherwise it would have been a plain, ordinary Tuesday: the twenty-eighth of Sivan, 5690 (June 24, 1930). What, exactly, was happening, then, to change it so dramatically? It was a question that one asked another here, there, everywhere. They wanted to know: What was going on? What was the occasion? And the answer that rose and coalesced from all the answers was: It is a Jewish folk holiday, an extra day of *yom tov*, another *Simchas Torah* — because the Torah has been liberated and redeemed from its exile. It has its own royal mansion now, its own palatial home. . . . Where? — in the prominent, historic city of Lublin. Who built it? — the great Torah authority, the world-renowned Rav Meir Shapiro, the Rabbi of Piotrkov.

Special telegrams appeared, with prepared messages of congratulations and good wishes, out of which a person could choose one and send it for a few kopecks. Thus anyone and everyone could share in the celebration by adding a message of cheer that best expressed the feelings in his heart about the historic opening. Afterward these messages were given permanence in special bindings, as lasting mementos of the event.

Such were the ways of activity and response in the country at large. What, however, was going on in Lublin itself? What appearance did the setting for this unprecedented event take on? With what sort of feelings and emotions did the city itself receive this radiant day of festivity? And what of the suburbs and surrounding regions?

The city was literally drowning in decorations. There were huge signs reading *baruch ha-ba* (Welcome), or *t'nu kavod la-torah* (Give honor to the Torah), and so on; and the letters appeared on transparent material, through which light could shine. The streets were teeming with thousands of human beings, from all the corners of the land.

The night before the opening could only be described as a vigil. An endless line of buses, taxis and horse-drawn vehicles kept coming in from the surrounding regions and riding through the streets, filling the air with singing. Throats poured forth their Jewish melodies to such words as *v^e^tahér libbeynu l^e^'ovd^e^cha b^e^'emess* (and purify our heart to serve You in truth); *ha-torah, ha-torah hi cha-yeynu* (The Torah, the Torah, that is our life). The very air of Lublin seemed to breathe and come alive with the singing.

Then there were the railroad trains. Every hour they arrived to deliver hundreds of disbarking passengers. The Ministry of Transport added on extra trains, too, on account of the celebration; and they kept arriving, to discharge people by the thousands. There were learned rabbis and devout spiritual leaders. There were delegations from every Jewish community in the land. And there were distinguished visitors in general, of every kind and description.

Packed with teeming humanity, Lubartovska Street seemed to have turned dark at midday. Estimates of the number that made up this mass of humanity came up to the figure of a hundred thousand. The density of the throng was very great, and the crowding threatened to become unbearable. A few hundred policeman were organized to maintain order, under the personal direction of the city's chief of police.

And then there were the hundreds of journalists, from Poland itself and from other countries, who came to give the event full coverage not only in the land itself but worldwide. There were respresentatives of such news agencies as United Press and Reuters. From Poland's national news agency, none other than the managing editor came.

As time moved on, from moment to moment the throng grew yet greater; and the price for a ticket of admission to the area directly before the building skyrocketed.

While they were waiting for some sort of activities to begin, the gentlemen of the press managed to obtain an interesting statement from none other than the venerable Rebbe of Tchortkov. Said he: "The purpose of the yeshiva is the study of Torah, to provide our Jewish youth with a religious education. It was especially important to establish this educational center here, in Poland, because we have as our neighbors the Bolsheviks" [the radical Communists in the Soviet Union] "who try in every possible way, direct or devious, to destroy the Jewish religion. How vital the yeshiva is for our life as a people, we can gauge from the fact that all the Jewish factions and parties consider it important (whether or not they themselves are religious): because the Torah is the best guardian and protector of the Jews in Poland. . . . "

****

Amid all the tension and excitement, suddenly there was a fragment of silence, and then a great sigh rose from the density of the throng, as all eyes turned to watch: Over the great balcony appeared the official ensign of the yeshiva, designed for its exclusive use by its founder and director — Rav Meir himself.

It was all in black and white, the only appropriate colors (or rather, non-colors), according to the Sages, that could symbolize a world center for Torah study. For the Midrash taught (Tanchuma, *b^e^réshis*, beginning) that "the Torah was written in black fire on white fire"! On the ensign, then, there was an embroidered representation of a Torah scroll. Above it, the embroidery showed two hands holding a crown: to denote the tribe of Z^e^vulun (merchants in the world of trade) giving the Torah its sovereign status in Jewish life by supporting its study. Beneath it another pair of hands was shown, upholding the Torah: to denote Yissachar, the tribe of scholars that holds the Torah high in Jewish life by studying it.

It should be noted, too, that when the Israelites journeyed originally through the wilderness, from Egypt to the Promised Land, each of the twelve tribes had its ensign; and the color of Z^e^vulun's was white. Then again, the white hue was meant to bring to mind the parchment on which a *séfer torah* is written.

As the immense gathering realized what this was, and as the word spread that it had been designed by Rav Meir himself, a great wave of ovation broke out. The sustained applause was deafening. (It might be added that if imitation is the sincerest form of flattery, Rav Meir had reason to feel highly flattered in the months that followed: Virtually every Torah institution in Poland made an effort to produce something similar.)

There was an excitement of delight in the air now, that almost crackled in its intensity. Continually, tens of thousands broke into sustained bouts of chassidic dancing, linked together by hands on shoulders as they sang for joy. Even the thousands of Polish onlookers became caught up in the contagion of the atmosphere. . . . The heat was intense, yet no one seemed to feel it.

One thing had to happen yet to set the ceremonies in motion formally — one thing for which all were waiting: the appearance of Rav Meir Shapiro, to give his greetings and blessings. . . . And then the moment came, and there he was — the man of Talmud, the man of vision, the man of action — standing on the balcony between the revered Rebbes of Tchortkov and Ger, with a host of other personages of Torah and piety around them.

A mighty outcry came from the great throng below: the single word *y^e^chi!* (Long live!) And it became a part of a ferocious ovation. Then, evidently, there was a sudden realization that the serious moment had come: the moment of awe: the moment to give way to the true, exalted meaning of the historic occasion.

Silence came, and stillness prevailed . . . and in soft, solemn unison, all sang the thirtieth Psalm from the Book of *T^e^hillim*: *mizmor shir chanukas ha-ba-yis l^e^david* (A hymnal song for the dedication of the House, by David). Then they sang the Polish national anthem [as the country's norms required]; and finally the voices rang out in another product of Rav Meir's creative mind: the yeshiva anthem. Into its inspired words he wove his thoughts about past, present and future; the melody was one of the very many heartwarming small pieces of chassidic music that he composed.

At last he stood ready to speak. [Now he seemed like a person renewed, with the lithe animation and vitality of a lion. Fallen away from him, vanished, was all the weariness and fatigue from the seven years of heartbreaking, soul-breaking toil that it had taken to reach this day. Paraphrasing David in the holy Scriptures (*Divrey haYamim*/I Chronicles 22:14), he declaimed in a moving, emotion-laden voice, "So I, in my poverty, have prepared a House for the Lord of Hosts!"]

Then, as the great audience listened, the people heard him speak first in Hebrew (the sacred language), then in Polish, and finally in Yiddish.

In Hebrew they heard him say, "Blessed be those who have come in the name of *haShem* (the Lord); we do bless you from the House of *haShem*: you great men of our nation, luminaries of our exile, *tzaddikim* of our time, rabbis of our people; you children of mine, students of the yeshiva, with whom God has thus favored us; you representatives of the exalted national and local governments; you delegates of our people, deputized emissaries of Jewish communities; you writers of the Jewish press; and you, the entire House of Jewry that has gathered here to give honor to the Torah. Be you blessed, all of you. Blessed be all who have come in the name of ***haShem.***"

The message thundered out into the air, every word sharp and clear, weighed and uttered in total solemnity. And again there was a response of stormy applause.

When silence reigned again, it was time for him to greet all the government officials, with his elegant command of the Polish language. In the course of his greeting he told them: "Yet before the time of the early King Zygmunt Stari, the first Jewish religious council was convened in this city of Lublin — in the year 1033. By meeting here it set the foundation for the forceful organization with strong internal authority which became known in Poland's later history as the *va'ad arba aratzos*, the Council of the Four Lands.

"In the year 1567, on the basis of a *privilegium*" [a royal document or charter defining the rights, privileges and duties of certain subjects of the monarch] "granted by King Zygmunt August [Sigismund Augustus], the opening of the first major intitute of Jewish education took place here in Lublin. On the tenth of May, 1571, King Zygmunt August invested the Rabbi of Lublin, Rav Sh'lomo Luria [the *Maharshal*], with full legal and jurisdictional rights over that educational institute, the Yeshiva of Lublin.

"Now we live in the Republic of Poland, which has arisen to a new, independent life after centuries of division and enslavement. It has renewed the splendid traditions of the past by helping to build Yeshivas Chachmey Lublin!"

With his Polish declamation done, he continued in Yiddish: "Now a word to the great numbers of my brethren who are gathered here: What was it that moved me and drove me to this enterprise? What was the background of the idea? — the soil in which the roots of this blessed, happy conception formed and developed? I will tell you: If any of you ever watched and saw how the *yeshiva bochurim* in this country sleep in the stores and shops as night watchmen; if any of you ever observed well the conditions under which they live — for you that won't be a question at all. You know the answer."

In full voice he recited the *b^e^racha* of *sheheche-yanu*, complete with the Divine names in it: a benediction to express his gratitude to the Almighty "because He has given us life and sustained us and brought us to this present time." Then he went on to paraphrase it in Yiddish:

"Be You praised and blessed for the Divine inspiration, for the conception of Yeshivas Chachmey Lublin that You infused in me; *sheheche-yanu* — for the strength and endurance to accept and persevere through all the difficulties, to ovecome all the obstacles, on the road to the realization of this conception: Yeshivas Chachmey Lublin; *v^e^kiymanu* — and be You praised and blessed that I have been privileged to be sustained and kept in existence to reach this day, when Yeshivas Chachmey Lublin is opened at last: *v^e^higi-yanu la-z^e^man ha-zeh*, and You have brought us through to this time!"

Now it was indescribable — the rousing ovation, the absolute fury of applause that broke out in response. On and on it went, till it gradually subsided and ended with the greatest reluctance.

The program continued with the formal greetings and good wishes of the government representatives, including a telegram from the Foreign Minister, Zaleski, that was read aloud.

After all the Polish messages, the Rebbe of Tchortkov rose to speak in the name of the World Council of Torah Authorities. He began with a sentence from the Book of *T^e^hillim*: "This is the day that *haShem* made; let us exult and rejoice in it" (Psalms 118:24). He continued in Yiddish: "Today's dedication of this House, Yeshivas Chachmey Lublin, is a great festive celebration for the entire Jewish people." Then the Rebbe of Ger spoke, with the greatest warmth and fervor. After him came Rav Aharon Lewin, the esteemed Rabbi of Reisha (Rzeszow), who served for over a decade, with distinction, as a deputy in the Sejm. He spoke in two roles: first, in the name of the rabbinic organization, *Agudas haRabbonim*, in which all the spiritual leaders of the Jewish communities were joined; and then he brought his blessings and good wishes as the representative of all the Jewish communities and political organizations that placed themselves under the banner of the Torah.

The greetings, the blessings, the hopes and the wishes were all over at last. Sedately and reverently, the Rebbe of Tchortkov took the prepared *m^e^zuza* and affixed it to the right doorpost — the small case that enclosed a piece of parchment with the proper words of the Written

Torah. Thus it would always be there, to remind anyone entering of the Almighty's immanent presence everywhere in general, and in this House in particular.

With the *m^ezuza* in place, the moment had come for the yeshiva to be opened, at long last. . . . And at that instant, overcome by his great happiness, Rav Meir Shapiro fainted. "The fervent yearning of the soul," said the Rebbe of Tchortkov, "the longing to experience the Divinity which is here with us now — from that came the momentary weakness."

This too passed, and the youngest of the young, budding scholars waiting to enter the yeshiva to study there stepped forward now with a golden key in hand, to unlock the doors. "As the portals of the yeshiva have been opened here," declaimed Rav Meir, "so may the Divine Master of the world open the gates of rescuing help and consolation for the Jewish people!"

[The mighty roar of *omeyn* from the tens of thousands thundered through the air, to set a sublime confirmation of Amen upon the blessing. . . . In retrospect, how poignant those words of prayer were, less than a decade before the Germans came to bring their Final Solution.]

****

As a postscript, it might be worth noting that in the course of all the greetings and blessings, one rabbinic personage decided, as he spoke, to bestow on Rav Meir a new title of honor: "the second Maharam of Lublin." [The first one had also been named Meir, and he was an immortal part of the Torah study in historic Lublin: Back in the sixteenth century, at the age of twenty-four he had become the head of the noted yeshiva, where he taught for five years, to contribute his share to the development of Torah study in Poland.]

Once this particular greeting was over, Rav Meir asked for the right to reply: "We know that the great conqueror Napoleon was made king of France as Napoleon I — the First. His son was called the Second, but he never sat on the throne in France, and so the title meant nothing. When the grandson, Louis Napoleon, became king of France, he could and should have been enthroned as Napoleon II — the Second. Instead, he insisted on the name of Napoleon III — the third — because he considered his grandfather unique: To a first like that there could be no second, who might be considered comparable to him. So he became Napoleon III.

"I say the same thing to you: If you wish to give me a fine honorary title, perhaps it could be *Maharam the Third*, but never the Second. To the first Maharam there could be no equal."

****

On the illustrious day of the opening, an article by Rav Meir was printed in the Polish Jewish press. He wrote it in advance and got it into the proper hands in good time, so that it could appear concomitantly with the great ceremony and celebration. There he expressed a main thought about the yeshiva that he wanted to leave with the people:

"With the passing of this day, the great enterprise and achievement that is Yeshivas Chachmey Lublin goes over into the hands of *k^{e}lal yisra'el*, the Jewish community at large. The individual in charge withdraws from the charge and transfers it to the public.

"Now, what about this public? In its entirety, today it stands enthusiastically united. In its heart it feels that this is the happiest moment of its life. But it was a heavy burden that the individual who built it had to bear. He became tossed about from one land to another. Many a time he was driven to the limits of despair. . . . Yet how light the task can be for an entire community at large. When all Jews join hands to act as one hand, then, said the Maggid of Kozhnitz, that hand is great enough to reach Heaven.

"Dear brethren, fellow-Jews, into your hands I entrust my one and only child, Yeshivas Chachmey Lublin; and I give you my heartfelt wish that you may live to derive great *nachass*, great spiritual happiness from him. . . ."

37

The palace of Torah

Now that the gates and doors of the yeshiva had been opened, people were free to come in and see it near at hand. And a most imposing sight it was. Once a person passed through the gates, an edifice of classical elegance met his eyes, while on the grounds before the building grew an enchanting grove of pine trees.

Before a visitor went further, he might wonder how those handsome tapering evergreens had come there. The answer is a story worth recounting. Not only is it interesting in itself, but it also reveals the great impression that the yeshiva could make even among non-Jews.

In the course of the construction, the yeshiva's board of directors contacted a Polish noblewoman named Countess Roland, who owned farmland not far from Lublin, and asked if she would sell them several hundred small trees from the woods on her land, to beautify the grounds in the yeshiva's forecourt. The reply of the countess was that the yeshiva was well known and highly esteemed in certain circles of Polish society. Therefore she wanted no payment for the trees that she intended to give. On the contrary, she considered it a privilege to be able to make a contribution of this kind. All she asked in return was that she should be permitted to pay a visit to the yeshiva. She wanted no more than that as her payment.

A short while went by, and the clatter of horses' hooves heralded the arrival of a few wagons, laden with twelve thousand young pines. With them came a number of her gardeners, whom the countess sent along to attend to the planting. And from those small trees grew the pine grove that beautified the yeshiva grounds.

Past the trees stood the building. Two elevated plaques that caught a visitor's eye recorded the dates of the ground-breaking and the opening; and between the plaques, at the very center of the front, letters of a golden hue proclaimed words from the Book of *T'hillim*: *Come, children, listen to me: an awed awareness of* haShem *will I teach you* (Psalms 34:12). Above, at the top, the name could be read: *Yeshivas Chachmey Lublin.* With its six stories, the building rose indeed to an imposing height.

The broad regal doors would admit the visitor into wide corridors, from which he could descend to the quarters below. There he would find glistening hygienic baths, including a *mikveh* (a facility for ritual immersion of one's body), and dressing rooms; a laundry with facilities for washing clothes and drying them, all electrically operated; the yeshiva's own bakery, with mechanically operated machinery, that turned out its fragrant, oven-fresh products three times a day. Then there was the dining room, over thirty meters (about 100 feet) long. Adjacent to it were the two large kitchens, one for meat dishes (*fleyshik*), the other for dairy (*milchik*).

The rest of the space on the lower level was taken up by storage quarters at normal temperature, and special cellars for cold storage. From these a way led out to the garden: a large area, long and broad, that served as a park or nature reserve. A variety of trees grew all about, and every few feet there were tables and benches, where the young scholars could pursue their studies in the open or merely sit and rest to refresh themselves.

Past the garden a visitor would find another part of the basement level, which contained the administrative offices of the yeshiva, the infirmary, and special rooms for special students: the *masmidim* who wanted to devote as much time as they could to Talmudic study and found themselves able to function well with only an hour or two of sleep at night. When the lights were turned off in the rest of the building, in those rooms they stayed on.

[Somewhere on this floor, below street level, there was also a room planned to serve as a Jewish scriptorium: Potential and budding *sof^{e}rim* could study, learn and practice the age-old craft of the scribe, till they could produce the accurate texts on parchment for *m^{e}zuzos*, *t^{e}fillin*, and even entire Torah scrolls.]

Finally, in those basement quarters below the entrance level, there was the small-scale model of the *beyss ha-mikdash*, the holy Temple, as it had appeared in ancient Jerusalem in the time of King Herod. It was located in a separate large chamber, with enough spacc all around so that young, budding scholars plunging into the Talmudic topics of *kodashim* could see before their eyes a clear representation of the realities to which their abstract textual study related.

The hands that had created this miniature masterpiece belonged to a highly talented *chassid* named Chanoch Weintraub, who drew the data for his careful, accurate work from the printed literature of our Oral Torah. As he pursued his researches relentlessly, he went eventually to the Library of the Vatican in Rome, to consult some of the rare volumes in its possession. When he believed he had all the data he needed, or all he could obtain, he set to work with his great craftsmanship and skill. As he used the colors of gold and alabaster most capably, the final result was truly impressive: a faithful, captivating reconstruction out of ancient history.

As this singular work of artistry became known in the world of Polish Jewry, it became a "tourist attraction" of first rank, that drew thousands of visitors from all over the land. In the time that they gazed at it, they had a rare chance to glimpse or sense some of the splendor and glory that the Jewish people had known in its ancient times.

On the first floor there was the large lecture hall for major *shi'urim* (Talmudic discourses); and then the immense *shul*, the great Chamber of Prayer that rose to a height of three floors. At a casual passing glance, it might have seemed only another large, impressive synagogue, of the kind to be found in many large cities of the world. There was, however, an atmosphere of freshness and youth within, that made it distinctive.

Around the three sides ran an unusually broad and handsome gallery. Then there were the magnificent carvings in the decorations and painted embellishments, and the Chanuka menora made of brass, that rose to a height of three meters (ten feet). The community of Przemysl, Galicia, purchased it and presented it to the yeshiva, to commemorate a visit that Rav Meir had made there. The whole great Chamber of Prayer seemed to have been formed and fitted expressly to blend with the unmatchable gestalt that became our Yeshivas Chachmey Lublin.

Adjacent to the *shul* was the great Library with its many thousands of volumes and its valuable collection of rare old editions. (Its conception and formation were described in an earlier chapter.) Going on, a visitor would come to the Auditorium or assembly hall, where all the large gatherings and important receptions of the yeshiva took place. It was the plan of Rav Meir to make this the recognized, acknowledged place for all the important gatherings of the religious community, all the rabbinic conferences, and so on. The rest of the floor contained the hundred rooms that the Rav had publicized, which served as the comfortable dormitory for the young Talmudists.

Such were the lower levels of this immense, majestic new citadel of

Torah study, which became revealed to the great stream of visitors once the doors were opened. [It should be noted for the record that interior construction work on the sixth floor remained undone; but the five completed floors were more than adequate for the flourishing, dynamic life of the yeshiva, and more than adequate to impress and even awe the flow of people who came to feast their eyes and their souls.]

****

Lengthy articles appeared in the entire Jewish press, to report the auspicious opening in full. A typical banner headline [in Yiddish] was: *Old, historic Yavneh blossoms into new life.* [When the second Temple was destroyed in ancient Jerusalem, Rabban Yochanan ben Zakkai was granted the right to go safely to the city of Yavneh and establish a new center there for the study and authority of the Torah; and thus authentic, historic Judaism survived and continued. Here the newspapers expressed a people's yearning and hope that in the deep insecurity of their Diaspora, this new, magnificent yeshiva would achieve the same purpose.]

In the rest of the world as well, articles of greater or shorter length appeared in the press, sent by the journalists and reporters who had come to cover the event.

With a significance all their own were the many hundreds of congratulatory telegrams that arrived from near and far, from personages of international eminence. Thus, in the message that came from Rav Yosef Cha-yim Sonnenfeld, the august rabbi of the devout community in Jerusalem, Rav Meir read: "... and I am confident that the holy yeshiva will prepare the way for the future [messianic] Redemption."

Rav Yitzchak Isaac Herzog [destined to become the second Chief Rabbi in the Holy Land] was Chief Rabbi of Ireland at the time. In the message that he sent from Dublin, he stated, "This holy, sublime House shall bring a refreshing dew of revival, to infuse a spirit of enduring, eternal life in the entire Jewish community."

From the renowned, creative Rav Yehuda Leib Zirelson (Tzirelson) of Kishinev, Rumania [who had once been the Chief Rabbi of Bessarabia] came a singular greeting: "Spirits [contained] in physical bodies shall experience bliss for a whole day in a [spiritual] realm that is wholly good — a whole day from the [destined] days of the World-to-Come. The great illumination that will appear from Yeshivas Chachmey Lublin shall shed light on the darknesses of this earth, and will prepare the way for the righteous [messianic] Redeemer, who will [now] hasten his footsteps."

Then there was a telegram from Dr. Nosson Birnbaum [the man who had been born with a gift for inevitable profundity of thought and charismatic leadership, who had started out as an influential heretic — Mattisyahu Achér — then turned full circle and became a leading figure in Agudas Yisra'el.] His message was: "May it be the will of *haShem* our God that from the holy yeshiva, generations [of students] may emerge, learned in our sacred Torah, loyal to our religion, and fit to rise and ascend in the realm of Jewish holiness." Such, in general, were the contents of the messages, with their heartening and inspiring good wishes.

****

On the very day of the opening, Rav Meir gave a *shi'ur* to his new body of *talmidim.* He was insistent that the entire day must not be "frittered away" on ceremony and good wishes. He had to give a proper discourse, so that there would be Torah study immediately in the new edifice.

He began with a preliminary talk about the problem of *chinnuch.* Drawing deeply on homiletic sources in the Oral Torah, he pondered and analyzed what could be considered a valid, authentic education for Jewish youth. Then came the *shi'ur* proper, in which he handled his Talmudic subject matter with his legendary brilliance.

[Both in his talk on education and in the *shi'ur*, there was one definitive thought that he stressed, as a firm, immutable conclusion in *halacha*: A first, initial consecration bestows a permanent holiness for both its own time and for the future. With passion and fervor, he declared that now Lublin lived again in the same holiness that irradiated it centuries earlier, when it had blossomed as a world center of Torah study. After an interruption of hundreds of years, he declaimed, Lublin would become again the Jerusalem of Poland.

[To the education of the young learners in this new yeshiva, he applied the same thought, as a veritable principle in *halacha*: The Torah they would learn there would hallow them both in the present and in their future — for the rest of their lives — as a foundation for a timeless, eternal Jewish identity.]

In the wake of the Talmudic *shi'ur* came the arguments and discussions [customary in matters of *pilpul*], as the young fellows considered and digested what they had heard.

At last the time came when they could go to their dormitory rooms and relax, after this long, full day. And now, when they were free to reflect and express their feelings, one main thought emerged: *It had all been worth it.* All the years they had dreamed and yearned to be accepted into this incredible, revolutionary yeshiva — they had not been wrong. Whatever they had hoped for, whatever they had imagined in their fantasies, they did not feel disappointed now. In fact, they agreed, it was really better than what they had expected.

One student told another (a newly-made friend) how enormously difficult it had been for him to prepare adequately enough till he could pass his examination and be accepted, how many dozens of nights he had gone without sleep, struggling to absorb what he was studying, till he could feel himself in possession of the required 200 double pages. Now he knew — now they all knew — that it had truly been worth it!

One happy boy felt so moved by his emotions that he was unable to contain himself, and he recited aloud the *b^e^racha* of *sheheche-yanu.* He simply had to say the full benediction to thank his Maker for having brought him to this time and place in his young life.

Another boy sat down to write a letter home. "Now I understand at last," he informed his parents, "what *Moshe rabbénu* meant when he said, *you should choose life.*" (*D^e^varim*/Deuteronomy 30:19) . . . And a third felt so elated at actually being in this fabulous yeshiva, really and truly, that he simply had to keep talking, not caring particularly if he made any real sense or not. . . .

****

The next day, when the grand opening was already part of history, was Wednesday the twenty-ninth of Sivan (June 27, 1930). The Thursday and Friday after that would be days of *rosh chodesh* (New Month days), to mark the beginning of Tammuz. By the norms of our circles, that Wednesday was therefore designated as *yom kippur katan,* "a minor Yom Kippur," to be observed with some of the characteristics of the great Jewish fast day. Hence we all fasted that day; and many thousands who had attended the opening ceremonies went to Lublin's old, historic Jewish cemetery, to stand at the graves of the holy men of the past and offer up prayers to Heaven for the yeshiva. They prayed earnestly that the newly opened citadel of Torah should endure and flourish, to succeed in its purpose.

Among the throng Rav Meir Shapiro was also to be seen, accompanied by his new *talmidim*, to add their voices to the solemn prayers. As might be expected, the Rav rode to the cemetery in a carriage (a droshky) drawn by two horses, while the students made their way on foot. The driver and horses waited patiently with the vehicle, till the Rav declared himself ready to go back. When he left the cemetery, however, to take his place again in the droshky, something quite unexpected happened: A fair number of burly, well-muscled Jews deftly released the horses from their harness and took their places. Substituting manpower for horsepower, they pulled the vehicle back through the city streets to the yeshiva, accompanied by the lusty singing of all who marched along. The whole became a kind of triumphal parade on the route that only Jews could create and enjoy.

****

[In connection with Lublin's old Jewish cemetery, let it be mentioned that there was another time in the year on which Rav Meir went there, regularly, to offer up prayers. The day before *rosh chodesh Kislev* is likewise observed in certain circles as *yom kippur katan*; and hence on that day too, many in Lublin would always fast and go to the cemetery, to pray at the graves of its great immortal souls.

[In the few years that Heaven granted him to head the yeshiva, Rav Meir would always take *talmidim* with him and head particularly for the grave of Rav Shalom Shachne, the main disciple of the pioneering Rav Ya'akov Pollack, who thus became the second great scholar who made Lublin an important Torah center in Jewish life. There Rav Meir would always stay long at the tombstone, praying intensely that the Talmud study at the yeshiva should be fruitful and successful, so that the *talmidim* would make good progress and achieve their goals.

[It should be noted that in the local community there was a tradition that in his lifetime, Rav Shalom Shachne forbade anyone ever to say, at any time after he was gone, that he was no longer the Rabbi of Lublin! This was evidently the reason for a subsequent community rule: Anyone chosen to the rabbinic post had to go first to his grave, to earnestly ask his permission. A second tradition originated with the great Rebbe of Lublin (the *chozeh*, the Seer). When someone was in great trouble and distress, the Rebbe would direct him to go and pray specifically at Rav Shalom Shachne's place of burial. And the Rebbe would explain: All the other great holy souls whose bodies lay buried there, migrated to the Holy Land. Only the holy discarnate Rav Shalom Shachne remained, to give his protection to the community of the living.]

The full model of the holy Temple, the *beyss ha-mikdash*, in the Yeshiva's basement.

38

Into the rabbinate of Lublin

On that same Wednesday, directly after the opening of the yeshiva, the Jewry of Lublin proceeded to celebrate another dramatic event, born out of the community's initiative. [A good while past, the venerated Rav Eliyahu Klatzkin left the position, which he had held with distinction for many years, to spend his last years in the Holy Land; and since then the post had remained vacant.] Now, by the community's unanimous decision, Rav Meir Shapiro was appointed to the rabbinate of that city. He would be Lublin's supreme religious authority.

The good Jews concluded that if the great founder and director of the new, illustrious yeshiva in their city remained the Rabbi of Piotrkov, he would have to split his life into two divergent paths. And so, by the decision of one and all, the very day the yeshiva was opened in such great ceremony, he was chosen by acclamation to become as well the Rabbi of Lublin. [The result was that in the great hall of *Yeshivas Chachmey Lublin*, when he was done with his first brilliant *shi'ur* to the students, he was handed the document of his formal appointment.]

Years earlier he had proclaimed it as his dream and goal in life: to become a full, proper spiritual leader among his people by bearing the dual title of *rav* and *rosh yeshiva*: as the great Torah scholars had done in earlier centuries, to serve as guide and mentor to the adult community, but also as educator in the full sense of the word to the next generation in its formative years. And now he found himself arrived at his goal in the important historic city of Lublin.

As the news of his prestigious appointment spread, masses of people, from the city and beyond, streamed to the yeshiva to give him their sincere congratulations and to wish him *mazal tov*, the best of good fortune in his new position. Among themselves too, the people shook one another's hand warmly, exchanging congratulations and feelings of good cheer out of the happiness they felt. All shared in the sense of their own good fortune at having him now for their spiritual head.

Among the community leaders, official reception committees were organized immediately, to formulate plans for a proper, imposing welcome with due honor and esteem, after he would formally accept the position.

On the very next Shabbos, in just a few days, it was expected that he would give his introductory sermon in the *Maharshal shul.* And so, on Shabbos morning, he was escorted to that historic synagogue by the *parnassim,* the official heads of the community; and in solemn, sober ceremony, they led him to the "Maharshal chair," where none but the Rav of the city was ever permitted to sit.

Before the reading of the Torah, Rav Meir went to the pulpit, amid a tense, expectant, absolute silence. There was an excitement in the air as all waited to hear his very first sermon.

This was its central thought: "From the wisdom of the Book of *Mishley* we learn: *In the place of great men, do not stand* (Proverbs 25:6)." Continued Rav Meir: "If destiny has brought me to the place where such great rabbinic authorities, such great Talmudic masters and Torah luminaries stood and held sway in our revered past, the order that I must obey is: *do not stand!* I must not be an *oméd,* content to remain on my feet in one static position, basking in the glory of imagined achievements. I must rather be a *holéch*: one who keeps walking and moving on. Upon me lies the duty to go further, from one step to the next; to mount ever higher, from one level to the next, striving and striding ever upward in religious leadership . . . and together with myself I must elevate spiritually this entire community of Lublin. . . .

"The Midrash relates (Tanchuma B, *va-yéra* 46): When Avraham (our Patriarch) went with his son Yitzchak to the *akéda,* to bind Yitzchak on the altar and offer him up as a sacrifice in obedience to the Almighty (*B'réshis*/Genesis 22), Satan made great efforts to interfere and prevent him. Thus Avraham suddenly found his way blocked by a river, that Yitzchak and he would have to cross; and it was deep and dangerous enough to drown them.

"Yet Avraham was not daunted. He knew the river was an unnatural phenomenon. He knew it was the Devil's work: Satan was making a great effort to prevent him from passing this last great test of his life by obeying the Almighty. At all costs he crossed the river with Yitzchak, and they pressed on.

"We all know how the matter ended: we read this part of the Written Torah every morning in the preliminary pages of our prayer service: After an angel called to him to stop and do nothing to harm Yitzchak, he saw a ram caught by its horns in a thicket; and without delay, he offered that up as a sacrifice in place of his son (there, verses 11-13).

"Something seems puzzling here, though: Why didn't Avraham suspect that the ram might also be no more than the work of the Devil? What made him sure about it?

"The answer lies in two Hebrew words: *ne'echaz bas*^{e}*vach*, 'caught in the thicket' (there, 13). This was not a smooth, simple matter: the ram's horns were caught in a tangle of branches. By contrast, the river he encountered had been a smooth, simple, commonplace phenomenon. So he knew it was the work of the Devil.

"The same holds true about this rabbinic position that has been accorded me." He had no need to explain. His listeners knew what mighty efforts the accursed *Bund* had made to prevent his appointment, once it became known that the religious community leaders planned to give him the post. From attacks in their newspaper to political ploys in the community council, the *Bund* leaders tried by every possible means to keep him out. They were afraid that under his brilliant, inspired rabbinic leadership, the political strength of religious Jewry in Lublin would grow — at the expense of the *Bund*. Mercifully, their efforts failed.

"My appointment to this position, likewise, was no easy, simple matter. There were devious entanglements as efforts were made to prevent it. And so this is the proof that my appointment was not (Heaven forbid) the work of the Devil but, instead, the gracious will of Heaven."

Reactions of great satisfaction and pleasure at the appointment came, in fact, not only from the local population but from Jewry worldwide. . . . And new festive plans were made, to give the Rav a suitable royal welcome as the new Rabbi of Lublin. A special planning committee was chosen, which proceeded to work intensively on the preparation of a program that would combine dignity with popular appeal.

As the day arrived, so did Rav Meir, on the railroad line from Piotrkov, accompanied by all the eminent heads of Piotrkov's Jewish community as well as a variety of prestigious rabbinic figures. At the station, waiting to give him a rousing royal welcome, many thousands stood gathered, ready for his descent from the train. And behind them, it seemed as if the entire Jewish population was out in force, arranged in two rows along the route that the Rav was to take in the horse-drawn vehicle of reception.

On everyone's face a smile of pleasure and satisfaction was spread wide. There was a genuine happiness in the air, to which everyone contributed, from which everyone drew.

Puffing and hooting, the train belched and snorted its way into the station. The car doors opened; and then he was there in the doorway, dressed in splendid rabbinic garb, and holding a small *séfer torah* snugly in his right arm. By word of mouth, the fact spread rapidly through the attending throng: It was a miniature Torah scroll that Rav Meir himself had written.

[Let it be noted that while every qualified, capable *sofér* has the ability to write a normal-sized scroll that will meet the requirements of revered Jewish law, only a select few could ever undertake to write one small enough to be carried with ease in the crook of an arm. For this an innate calligraphic skill is needed, that enables a scribe to handle his quill with unusual deftness. In his arm, then, Rav Meir carried evidence of one more talent in his range of creativity — a talent that let him fulfull the mitzvah that every Jew ought to write a Torah scroll for himself.]

All eyes were drawn to that little Torah, which he evidently held with a symbolic meaning; and he spoke to explain it: "From the Talmud we know that a worthy, law-abiding king of our people had to carry a small scroll on his arm 'that would go out and come back in with him' (*bavli*, Sanhedrin 21b). Why? — so that when he appeared in public and saw people paying him great regal honor, he should not be carried away helplessly by feelings of haughty, overwhelming pride: for he could keep in mind that all this great honor and homage was properly going, in Heaven's view, to the Torah he carried, and not to him. The Torah deserved it, not he."

As he descended from the train, he was met by a tumultuous ovation. Over the sounds of thousands upon thousands of hands clapping, rose the repeated mighty roar of *y*e*chi rabbénu* ("Long live our Rabbi!")

Now came the majestic parade through the streets of Lublin. In a splendidly decorated coach the Rav rode in sovereign state on the prepared route, as hundreds of droshkies and hire-vehicles followed. Directly behind him rode the yeshiva students, and after them came the community heads and all the various delegations. All along the route, on every street, people could be seen on the balconies and at opened windows; and wherever the coach appeared, new mighty ovations resounded in the air.

It was a day of great honor for the Torah, in the purest and fullest sense of the term.

Thus Rav Meir arrived at the yeshiva; and there, in the great lecture hall (*ulam ha-shi'urim*) he gave his inaugural address, to mark his formal acceptance of the rabbinic mantle. The gallery that ran along the three walls was filled to the brim with the *talmidim*. Below, on the floor level, the seats were taken by worthy members of the religious community and by guests who had come for the occasion. In the heightened, soul-stirring atmosphere, Rav Meir spoke:

"It was a grand, exalted moment in my life when I learned that I was to be intrusted with this position, to become the spiritual leader of the great community of Lublin while serving, simultaneously, as the head of the world-renowned Yeshivas Chachmey Lublin.

"In our remote, ancient past, when our people of old had to go into exile, they took an oath that on every great, festive yet solemn occasion, they would remember Jerusalem: *If I forget you, O Jerusalem, let my right hand forget its power* (*T^ehillim*/Psalms 137:5). Even if anyone wanted to forget Jerusalem at this moment, by its very existence this community of Lublin would remind him of it. For two citics in this region of our exile merited to be designated as Jerusalems: Lublin became known as the Jerusalem of Poland, and Vilna as the Jerusalem of Lithuania. In our continuing history, these two cities came to serve the Jewish people as substitutes for the genuine, original Jerusalem. For they became focal centers where Torah study flourished, to burgeon anew in our Jewish life.

"In its time of glory, Lublin was the greatest citadel of Torah study in the Diaspora. When masses of Jews were expelled from cities and towns in Germany, Poland opened wide its gates; and then Lublin became the Torah center of all Jewry. For some two hundred and fifty years there was one double title of authority that was heard and echoed in Lublin: *av beyss din* [head of the religious court, i.e. the Rabbi] and *résh m^esivta* [head of the advanced-level yeshiva]. The two ranks went together in a single position of eminence.

"Then, some three hundred years ago, the community of Lublin committed a historic wrong against my forefather Reb Heshl, of blessed memory. While his father, Reb Ya'akov, lived, that man of learning held the double position: *rav* and *rosh yeshiva*. Yet when he passed away, the worthies of the community decided that this double title could not be bestowed on Reb Heshl. They argued that two positions of grave responsibility were at stake here, and more than one could not be intrusted to Reb Heshl, since he was only a young man of twenty at the time. And so they gave the choice to him: he could decide which of the two positions he preferred; but he could not have both.

"With his longing to be involved in the spread of Torah, my forefather chose the post of *rosh yeshiva*, and was content with that. Four years later, however, the traditional double position of *av beyss din* and *résh m*e*sivta* became vacant in the city of Cracow, and it was decided there to appoint Reb Heshl to it.

"So soon as the worthies of Lublin learned of this, they held a meeting, and it was decided to give both positions in the city to Reb Heshl, so that he could assume the double title right there and remain with them. . . . When they came to him, however, to bring him the good news, he merely replied that they were too late by a few hours: He had already given his word of acceptance to the delegation from Cracow which had come to bring him the offer.

"Now the community of Lublin is making amends for that historic wrong: It is uniting the two positions back into one for a direct descendant of Reb Heshl. In the air that I breathe, in the atmosphere wherein I move, both areas of activity will be for me as one: the rabbinate and the directorship of the yeshiva. And this yeshiva, which has justly won fame worldwide, will yet have much to contribute worldwide.

"Now, when I was informed that I had been chosen unanimously to become the Rabbi of Lublin, I took account, spiritually, of my whole being. I examined myself critically, to decide if I had the right to take on two positions of such great responsibility. As I sat pondering and reckoning and wondering, I opened a small *chumash* idly, at random; and [there in the Written Torah, in the Book of *B*e*midbar*] I came across these sacred words: 'to do the work of the *mishkan* (the abode) of *haShem* (the Lord), and to stand before the community to serve them' (Numbers 16:9).

"So there was my answer: In the first part of that text was my directive to lead and administer this resplendent yeshiva, where the best young Talmudic minds are gathered. In the second part I saw a pointer to the rabbinate in this community. Here was a message for me from Divine providence that I was chosen for both positions. And thus I present myself, ready for my duties in both dimensions of holiness: to serve both my community and my beloved *talmidim* — who, for me, stand on a higher level with their Torah study.

"At this moment, then, as I accept both positions and assume both mantles, I would wish to give my greetings and blessings to both; and I don't know which of the two to address first. . . . Well, a few days ago, in the *daf ha-yomi* program, we studied *daf* 8 in the tractate B^{e}choros, and we read something quite interesting there: By his great cleverness, Rabbi Yehoshua ben Chananya managed to gain entry into the sacrosanct academy of the elders of Athens, and there he saw young lads seated above, on an elevated level, while the old men sat below, on the ground level. He stood still and thought, 'What shall I do? If I greet the elders first, the others will kill me: they will say: We are greater than they are — for as you see, we are seated above, while they are below. If I greet the young ones first, the old men will kill me: they will say: We are senior to them; they are mere children.' So he looked straight ahead of him and exclaimed, *Peace to you!* (*bavli*, B^{e}choros 8b).

"Let me do the same now: to the worthy members of my community, and to my cherished students: *Peace to you!* We are going to rebuild Lublin together. We must go hand in hand, the leader and the conmunity, to attain our holy goals. Together we shall awaken and invigorate the old, historic spirit of Lublin, as we work to build and regulate the present Jewish life in this city.

"May Heaven help me to achieve my goals in these two highly responsible positions, so that I may bring back to Lublin its great aura and name in Jewish history, so that it may become again, truly, the Jerusalem of Poland!"

****

Y^{e}chi! Y^{e}chi! Again there was a tremendous ovation, as the heartfelt outcries long resounded and reverberated in the great lecture hall, to wish him a long life. And when the cheering and the shouting subsided at last, he went on to appropriate Talmudic and homiletic thoughts, in honor of the occasion.

Later, in his chamber, the Rav received a delegation that appeared in the name of the city's entire Jewry, to bring him their congratulations and felicitations on his entry into the rabbinate. . . .

And then, as in the communities he had headed in the past, the days of celebration inevitably ended; all the festivity receded and faded away — to make room for his hard, unsparing application to the practical tasks that the rabbinate involved.

Now came the working days for which many in Lublin had long been waiting. Now it was time for him to examine the conditions and arrangements for proper observance of the law in the community's religious life. And alas, he found the same sort of conditions and problems as in his previous communities: dilapidation and neglect in virtually every area of religious observance.

With his penetrating gaze and unflinching mind, he grasped quite clearly what had to be done; and he set in motion the necessary processes to repair and correct matters. Soon he began to see the blessed results of his strenuous, unremitting efforts.

Looking back a few years later, it is quite impossible to give any clear, proper accounting of all that he accomplished in the first short period of his rabbinate in Lublin. From his mind, with an authority that no one opposed or questioned, came new enactments and preventive measures, some major and important, others rather minor and supplementary. And religious life in Lublin took on a fresher, livelier look. Especially noticeable and significant were the changes and improvements that brought new life and vigor into Jewish education.

[He made sure to let no area of public religious activity escape his attention. Thus he took upon himself the direct supervision of the *chevra kaddisha*, the Burial Society which dealt with all aspects of burial, from the ritual preparation of the body to the final act of interment. He involved himself in the problems of the *bikkur cholim* Society, which had to deal with the sick; and when that Society ran a campaign to raise money, he participated energetically.

[In the main address that he gave for the campaign, he said: "In the Mishna we learn of three mitzvos that should be observed without any set limit or measure: visiting the sick, accompanying the dead, and studying Torah. Here in Lublin, the hospital is near our great yeshiva, and the cemetery is behind the yeshiva. I hope and pray and trust that the hospital will not supply any material for the cemetery, because the yeshiva, with the voices of Torah study resounding within it day and night, will serve as a mighty, effective barrier between the two. . . . "]

All in all, the net effect of his substantial practical labors can be summarized, quite succinctly: In place of the dull, static, listless religious life in Lublin, the religious quarters began to pulsate with a new vitality. The work that he set in motion went ahead with a robust energy that began, soon enough, to bring immense results.

39

At the helm of the yeshiva

Once the pressing rabbinic duties in community life were behind him, and he knew that problems in public religious observance no longer needed his personal involvement, he followed the same path that he had taken in the other communities: He turned his attention to his first and truest love: giving the young a sound and thorough Torah education. Here, however, there was no need to build any new structures or create any new facilities. The great yeshiva was there, the splendid product of his years of toil, ready and waiting for him.

He returned to it gratefully.

With living conditions that made history in the world of Poland's yeshivos, with Rav Meir's ebullient, lively warmth to encourage them, the young Talmud scholars bent to their work with a will. They persevered and plowed on with a mighty zest, as the chanting sound of their study resounded in the yeshiva twenty-four hours a day. . . . And soon the results began to appear, as the young folk made prodigious strides in their learning.

All, without exception, developed a keen understanding and appreciation of the ways of *pilpul*, and gradually began producing their own contributions to the genre. From time to time, various Torah scholars of first rank came to visit, and they were both amazed and delighted at the mastery and the keenness in Talmud that these young learners displayed. Some of them, with phenomenal memories, could recall at will a thousand *dapim* (double pages) of Talmud text, with the commentary of *tos^e^fos* — which could comprise at least one complete order (great section) out of the six that make up the Talmud.

The young scholars knew how fortunate they were. Materially they lacked for nothing. They had every comfort. And they felt the loving presence of the Rav watching over them with a fatherly concern for their welfare. Without any other pressing care in the world, they could devote themselves entirely to their study, with a rare zeal and intensity. And they did.

It was left to Rav Meir alone, however, to see the other side of the picture also — and a grim, bitter side it was. As he looked at it, he knew just what he saw and what it meant for him: a sentence of continual relentless exile for the rest of his years. He was one of the great Talmudic scholars of his time; he was probably the most gifted educator in Poland's world of Torah study; and he would have to go out traveling, again and again. He would have to go rattling around from one tycoon to another, from one man of wealth to another, to keep pulling and extracting money from them. Otherwise a catastrophic danger could always loom up and face the yeshiva: the nightmarish prospect that the yeshiva would be closed down, Heaven forbid.

So he became again a traveling fund-raiser across the length and breadth of Poland. Only when he knew that there was enough money to cover the running expenses for a while — only then could he allow himself to return to the yeshiva for a short respite, a brief oasis in time.

Back with his cherished *talmidim*, he felt veritably back in paradise. Welling up from his heart and mind, as though from a fountain, came an outpour of dazzling, inspiring thoughts on Talmudic topics and texts, which the young scholars absorbed eagerly. The *shi'urim* that he gave were discourses of the purest genius. And always there were his apt, witty flashes of interpretation on phrases and sentences in the Written Torah, that were so enlivening and heartwarming. . . .

Yet time moved on inexorably, and the money supply dwindled all too rapidly, as the debts mounted again at an alarming rate. He would have to go back into his dismal solitary exile, to raise money. There was no way to evade it. . . .

Thus a morning came when he appeared in the *ulam ha-shi'urim* apparently as usual — and yet the atmosphere was altogether different. By their sixth sense or invisible antennae, or else by the school grapevine, the *talmidim* knew; and they murmured and whispered among themselves: He had come to say goodbye again; once more he had to leave them.

Then he began speaking, and they knew it was true. He was bidding them farewell for a while, charging them to continue studying well without him, till he could return. Tears stood in his eyes, and he tried to brush them away. He saw no need to make his beloved spiritual children share the anguish that he had to bear. . . . Yet they saw it all in his face. Behind the cheerful smile that he showed them, all the fearful pain he felt was reflected in his countenance. They could read his thoughts so clearly — the thoughts that came of themselves out of the unavoidable embitterment in his heart:

"Why is Fate tearing me away from my cherished *talmidim*? Why can't I be allowed to stay and breathe the clear, pure air of Torah study within the walls of this yeshiva? Why can't I go on giving those young learners their daily due, their daily adventure in creative Talmudic thought that I owe them?"

In the silence that he kept, they heard his soundless outcry of protest. Yet there was nothing they could do. He had to carry the enormous burden alone. The Jewish world acknowledged him as a foremost Talmud scholar. As an educator in the Torah world he probably had no equal. And now, for this unique yeshiva that he created, he had to be not only the *rosh yeshiva*, principal, director and administrator, but also the publicist and publicity man, and finally, even the fund-raiser. The financial burden fell squarely on his head — and there it stayed.

Once the chef, in charge of the kitchens, raised something of a rumpus because Rav Meir was unable to pay him his salary for a while. Ruefully, Rav Meir responded, "I'm already a one-man staff here: I do just about everything here myself. One thing is still lacking in my scope of duties: I don't do the cooking. Now, the way things look, I may have to learn to do that too. . . . "

It would have been a prime piece of wit, an excellent joke, had it been anything other than the plain, dismal truth.

He called out to the Jewish people, tried in every way he could to rouse the public from its lethargy. In one printed circular that mirrored his emotions of pain, he began with words from the Book of *Sh^{e}mos*: *azov ta'azov immo*, "you must help [deal with the burden] with him" (Exodus 23:5). Then he continued: "On a day of great despair I began to wonder: For the sake of a mitzvah [to uphold Yeshivas Chachmey Lublin] is it permissible to develop a hatred of Jews, Heaven forbid, [because they won't help]?

"A volume of Torah learning was lying on the table, and I opened it; and there I found a thought by the holy Rebbe, Reb Bunem of P^{e}shis-cha. In the Book of *Va-yikra* we are told, 'Do not hate your brother in your heart' (Leviticus 19:17). Said Reb Bunem: This means, rather, ***with your good heart***. Have you brought any cheer yet to your fellow-Jew? — not yet?

Find some way to cheer him up, and don't withhold it from him! This is the Torah's command to your heart. . . . With that thought I calmed myself a little. Perhaps I must only find a way to bring my people good cheer, and then they will help me with my burden. . . . "

He calmed himself a little with a chassidic thought; yet how much could that help, and for how long, when the drastic financial problems of the yeshiva wrenched him away mercilessly from the beloved soothing atmosphere of his oasis, in his citadel of Torah?

In his constant attempts to generate further publicity for the yeshiva, to keep it from being forgotten, he sat once talking to a journalist who wanted to help. And the journalist asked: "So much has already been written about the yeshiva. So greatly have its praises been sung. What more can I do now?"

"Go and bewail it," answered Rav Meir dolorously. "Weep and lament over it." Perhaps that would arouse some living response.

He could not stop. He could not desist and give up. He had to storm and shout and raise a cry of alarm. Again he called, in a printed circular: *It is my brothers I seek!* And he continued: "Where are you, all my fellow-rabbis, communal workers, men of means? All of you who sang the praises of the yeshiva in the past: where are you now, when there is work to be done? Why are none of you to be seen?"

The tragic fact was that this outcry reflected a new, dismaying truth. Many a time he went looking for men of means, to try to elicit some funds from them — and they actually hid from him! How often it happened that he went to see one of the wealthier members of Jewry, and as soon as the man learned that the Rav had arrived and was waiting for him in his office or reception room — the man found some way of concealing himself. He simply left Rav Meir sitting and waiting — till Rav Meir realized, in bitter disappointment and humiliation, that he might as well leave.

Afterward he would have to find the strength to carry on with his usual cheerful spirit and sparkling flashes of wit, so as not to discourage or dishearten the people who worked with him. To find some relief, however, he would allow himself to reveal his feelings when he thought it would do no harm. Late one night, then, as he sat in the company of a few chosen *talmidim* who were close to him, he remarked, "Maybe you think that when someone hides from me and leaves me sitting there in his office — as it happened today — I don't really suffer? I don't really feel the anguish?

. . . the blood pouring from my heart? I just keep it well covered inside me. I don't want to dishearten the people working with me. I hope I'll gain enough merit in Heaven to be able to tell about this some day amiably and calmly, as a piquant little incident that we took in our stride."

[Having come from a family of great wealth, his devoted wife, Malka Tova, had a sizable collection of jewels and ornaments, and a good number of *objets d'art* of great value. By Heaven's inscrutable, inexorable will, the years of marriage had brought them no children, to whom she might leave these small treasures. One day, then, she took the lot and sold it all, and the money went immediately into the yeshiva's account. She found solace enough in the firm promise that Rav Meir had given her in a letter he wrote while he was in America: that she would have a full half of his share in the World-to-Come, as a completely equal partner.

[Yet even that could relieve his plight for only a short while. . . . With time, small wrinkles began etching their way into the visage that had always radiated such joy of creativity, such ebullient cheer in living with the Torah. The lines of worry appeared in his face like small clouds gathering softly in a clear blue sky, till they were enough to presage a coming storm.

[One day he declared bitterly, "Once I used to be a *soney betza*: I hated the very idea of money and its incredible importance; I spurned people's ill-gotten gains; I scorned their filthy lucre. Now the yeshiva has wrought havoc with my life. All day long, all I can think of is money, money, money — nothing else!"]

Yet despite everything, he never stopped hoping for better times, when he would be able to look back on his achievements with cheerful satisfaction. But alas, those times would never come. For the rest of his all-too-short life he would bear this tragic burden of a struggle to maintain the yeshiva — the kind of tragic burden, perhaps, that may have been ordained for the singularly great men of every age.

****

With the heavy load of responsibility and galling worry, however, Rav Meir showed a new facet of his greatness, as it developed now almost before our eyes: an ability to put his cares aside and continue to lead and inspire with his amazing fund of optimism and good cheer.

As the seventh of Adar approached (February 24, 1931), the Rav decided to make it the yeshiva's own special holiday: First of all, as any proper Jewish calendar would show, it was the birthday of Moshe ***rabbénu*** (as well as the day of his departure from earth: ***bavli***, M^e^gilla 13b). Then it was the birthday of our own Rav Meir. And so Adar 7 took on a festive character, as a time for celebration.

The entire Talmud was parceled out among the ***talmidim***, so that every one could study through his part during the night; and then, on the festive day, all together could celebrate a *si-yum ha-shass*: the conclusion of the study of the entire Talmud.

Anticipating in advance that the occasion would become genuinely, rapturously happy, in good time Rav Meir invited to Lublin the most eminent members of Polish Jewry — among them rabbinic figures, heads of communities, and religious political personages.

Once he had them all together, convened within the walls of Yeshivas Chachmey Lublin, he proceeded to work astutely for the yeshiva's future. Out of all the distinguished guests who came, he chose one hundred men from all parts of Poland, and organized them into an Administrative Council of the yeshiva. At their head, as its president, he placed Reb Elya Mazur, the president of Warsaw's Jewish community — since that was the largest of the communities (***kehillos***) in all Europe. And the Rav explained: It would be the holy task of this Administrative Council to see to it that the material upkeep of the yeshiva was assured.

There and then a fair number of people pledged large, sizable contributions and promised to work actively for the yeshiva. Thus, at the moment, it seemed that this particular undertaking by Rav Meir had been a good, felicitous idea, which could be expected to lead to favorable results.

For a good while afterward, the optimism and the hope continued. And then, alas, eventually it became all too clear that both the new organization and the good promises would remain no more than fine achievements on paper. Nothing substantial could be expected to follow. And thus the burden of responsibility for the yeshiva's upkeep returned in full to its original resting-place: Rav Meir's shoulders.

Any dependable long-range solution was still nowhere in sight. The situation continued to be an ongoing series of impending catastrophies, one alarming emergency after another: and hence, for Rav Meir, only one endless struggle after another.

Finally, somehow, somewhere, he was able to obtain a sizable loan, which gave him full relief — for a while. None knew as well as he did, however, how temporary the relief would be. Eventually it only made the yeshiva's affliction of debt all the worse — and prospects for repayment were, as far as could be seen, non-existent.

****

At a certain gathering around meal tables, he allowed himself the relief of giving vent, at least, to some of the inroads of despair that he could not fend off. Said he: "When Moshe *rabbénu* found that the burden of dealing with the people had become too much for him, he cried out to the Almighty, '. . . did I give birth to them, that You should say to me, *Carry them in your bosom, as an* omeyn *carries a suckling infant*?' (*B'mid-bar*/Numbers 11:12).

"Well, this is puzzling. The word *omeyn* gemerally denotes a mentor or tutor of an older child, who has left infancy behind to enter his juvenile period, when some sort of schooling must begin. Yet in his complaint, Moshe compares the people to a *yonék*, a nursing infant. Then surely he should said 'as a *meynekess*,' a wet-nurse, instead of *omeyn*?

"This, however, was the very point of Moshe's plaint to the Almighty: You tell me to bring up this people, to give them an education in the Torah and a grounding in the mitzvos; and at the same time You tell me that I must concern myself with supplying them with meat! I must be burdened with their physical needs! Isn't it, then, exactly as if an *omeyn*, a tutor and educator for older children, has been given a nursing baby to care for, when he obviously has no way of coping with the baby's needs?

"Well, I am in the same dilemma," continued the Rav. "At the precious time that I need to devote myself to education, to the proper study of our Torah, I am told that I must gather money to pay for bread and meat, to cover the expenses of the yeshiva. What greater woe could befall a spiritual leader than a situation in which he cannot fulfill his Divinely ordained obligations?"

He kept hoping and hoping for "better times," when the financial situation and physical maintenance of the yeshiva could be put on an even keel, and he could find deep spiritual gratification as the ebullient, dynamic head of the resplendent educational center that he had created. To his misfortune (and ours), those times never came. To the end of his shortened life, he was destined to bear the kind of burden that Providence seems to allot to men of true greatness in every generation.

40

Within the oasis

If a dark night of unremitting financial burdens was ordained for him, the way of the world is, however, that night should alternate with day, when the sun can shine. Whatever ordeals were ordained for him so that he could maintain the yeshiva, there remained the times that he could spend within it, to cast his own unique influence on the young scholars, in his dynamic interaction with them.

There were aspects of his great, sublime spirit that inevitably molded and forged the masterly development of the yeshiva; and past any doubt, the most significant aspect was his abounding love for the *talmidim* who lived there.

Probably in every language, the word denoting love is generally greatly misunderstood and greatly misused. Thus, for example, in our Torah world the term *ahavas yisra'el*, "love of Jews" or "love of Jewry," tended to be bandied about till it became a fairly meaningless stereotype or platitude. Similarly, in our world of ordinary yeshivos, it was taken for granted as a standard norm that a *rosh yeshiva* was always "devoted" to his *talmidim.*

Were we to use such terms to describe Rav Meir's unique way of relating to the students, we would only make a travesty of that unique, exalted spirit. We would convey not even a poor small copy of all that he was when he could interact with us with all his dynamic spirit.

[One clear indication of his relationship to the young learners is the plain fact that whatever time he had now, free from the endless worries of financing the yeshiva, he devoted entirely to the students: to give his incomparable *shi'urim*; to look after their concerns and needs, like a father; above all, to set them a living, dynamic example of how to serve the Creator by scintillating Torah study and heartfelt worship, by a personification of holiness in an endless spirit of joy.

[Even the night that marked the start of *Tish'a b^{e}Av*, the night of annual mourning in the Jewish year, when ordinary Torah study was forbidden, he sat on the bare floor and the *talmidim* gathered around in a circle; and for hours he told story after story about the *chozeh* (the Seer) of Lublin, the great chassidic Rebbe whose life on earth ended on that very day of the year.]

The best way, perhaps, to indicate the kind of love he bore his *talmidim* and to gauge its intensity, is to describe the response and the reaction that he received from us. The simple fact was that every single one of us was ready to do and to give for the Rav all he could, in pure *m^esirus nefesh*, in utter devotion.

This powerful bond of fatherly affection between the Rav and the learners became an essential, inseparable element in the entire learning program. It was a verity that he experienced and lived — so much so that once, in a moment of unrestrained candor and truth he exclaimed, "If any *talmid* doesn't feel my love for him, like a father's love for his child, for him the Torah will be an elixir of death!" [No one had to tell these young scholars where the phrase "elixir of death" came from. All knew the teaching in the Talmud (*bavli*, Yoma 72b): If a person gains merit, it — the Torah — becomes an elixir of life for him; if he does not merit it, it becomes an elixir of death for him.]

It was one brief sentence, without too many words; but those sublime, moving, deeply felt words said it all. We felt the truth of it.

One unforgettable incident happened there, by which Heaven may have wanted, perhaps, to confirm the reality of his striking words:

In the second *z^eman* (semester) after the opening of the yeshiva, one of the youngest of the *talmidim* fell ill. The malady was deadly serious, and the doctors who examined him could only shake their heads. . . .

The entire time that the young scholar lay in bed with his illness, the Rav stayed at his side watching. At night, when Rav Meir retired to his own bed, he would get up a few times and go to ascertain the patient's condition. His waking hours, night and day, he filled with prayers to evoke Heaven's mercy and Divine compassion. He wept and wept as he prayed and implored Heaven, chanting through the entire *séfer t^ehillim* over and over again.

At last it was clear that the illness had reached a crisis point. A professor of medicine who was attending the case was called to the patient's side. Once more he examined him; and when he left the bedside, he whispered to the Rav, "The end is near. The case is hopeless."

The tears came from Rav Meir's eyes as they had never poured before. His outcry was heartrending. And he went running about in the corridor as if bereft, wringing his hands in anguished despair.

A while later, he calmed down; and he told the *talmidim*, "Go and say *t'hillim* steadily; we need more. But I swear to you: he is ours now! Our prayers have prevailed to get him back!" He was right: so it was. In a short while the boy was fully recovered and back with us. Three days after his last visit, the professor was asked to come and examine the patient again — and he was simply amazed: "A miracle," he murmured; "he has returned from the dead!"

One thought hovered in the air among us, as we mused and pondered about it: Who knew how much of his own Heavenly merit the Rav had given away for the life of the *talmid*? In those few moments of utter, terrifying despair, when his grief-stricken outcry was enough to tear your heart, who knew how many years of his own allotted life the Rav gave away to that dying patient, so that he could be certain enough to guarantee that the stricken boy would live?

****

One further fact attests to his unique relationship with his young scholars. If anyone in the community at large, in the world beyond our yeshiva, wanted a favor from him, the surest way to get it was through a *talmid*. If the "outsider" knew one of the *talmidim* and could get him to speak to the Rav in his behalf, he could be quite certain that he would get what he wanted. Rav Meir would simply never refuse a *talmid* a request that he was able to grant.

[His perceptive concern for his *talmidim* was, if anything, only too obvious. If he showed any favoritism, it was perhaps to the extent that the more a student excelled in his studies, the greater grew this educator's loving care for him. It should be added that the majority of students came from poor, indigent families; and when he learned of some particular distress or trouble that beset someone's family, invariably he did what he could to help. Such was his sensitive heart that he could not do otherwise.]

****

There was so much that he wanted to teach the young Talmudists at the yeshiva who became his pupils and disciples. There was so much that he wanted to convey by instruction and by example, in the few years that it was granted him to be with us — when he wasn't torn away to go looking for funds to keep the yeshiva going.

In so many ways did he influence us, by instruction and by example. Yet of all that he wanted us to learn in our preparation for life in this world, the most important thing was designated by one word: *simcha*. In our Yiddish-speaking milieu, it denoted a joyful cheerfulness. And beyond any doubt, through all his life, this was the outstanding characteristic of his multifaceted spirit. Moreover, when his tragically short life had to end, the last words on earth that his holy spirit whispered were, *nor b^e^simcha* — "Only with joyous good cheer!"

Two kinds of supernal influence evidently nourished his heart while he lived: One inspired him with *simcha*, and the other with *bitachon*, a singular mixture of Divine trust, faith and confidence. And in this way he was *chad b^e^doro*, unique in his generation. . . . For time and again, the dismal tragedy of the burden he bore plumbed the depths of his soul, till he reached an ultimate level of despair. Yet with his power of *simcha* he could throw off the entire mood heroically and shut it altogether out of his consciousness.

"I've been laden with a hefty pack of *tzoress*," he would often say, "and people think, *Nu, let him be stuck with them; let him carry those bitter troubles of his.* Well, instead of worrying and agonizing over them, I decided to be happy with them and sing for joy over them. I decided to say fine bits of *d^e^rush* over them — a few little homiletic thoughts. And if they really start to annoy me and get on my nerves, I sing my 'theme song': *im amarti mata ragli, chasd^e^cha, haShem, yis'adéni* (If I should say my foot is tottering, Your loving kindness, O Lord, will sustain me! — *T^e^hillim*/ Psalms 94:18). For the blessed Holy One helps only in *simcha*, only through a cheerful spirit."

[It should be noted that this sentence from the Book of *T^e^hillim* to replenish optimisim and faith, with the melody that he composed to it, became quite well known in the world of Rav Meir Shapiro.

[On one occasion he spoke out not so much in regard to his own, personal pack of troubles, but rather with his mind on the drastic economic conditions in which the Jews of Poland had to try to survive, between a boycott and a ruinous tax policy. The whole situation could only be described as an unending state of crisis.]

Said Rav Meir: "I am certain that the state of crisis in which we find ourselves does not pose as great a danger for Jewish existence as does the sense of deep grief and melancholy that results from the state of crisis. Jews have lived through crises which were far worse, far more severe. But deep grief and melancholy pose a danger of becoming lost entirely, of letting our Jewish identity disintegrate into oblivion, Heaven forbid.

"With the help of the state of crisis, the *yétzer ha-ra* [the Devil at work in us, individually and collectively, as the Evil Temperament] seeks to drive Jews into utter sorrow and bitter despair — and that's it: With that his work is finished. Why should he bother to work on every Jew separately, if he can do the job wholesale, *en masse,* and mislead *k^{e}lal yisra'el*, our Jewry in entirety, all at once? If he succeeds with that, Heaven forbid, then *presto!* — it will mean an end for *yiddishkaït*: Every last trace of authentic, historic Judaism will vanish from the face of the earth.

"I therefore say to you, dear brothers, don't listen to him. Live only in *simcha*, in the cheerful, optimistic certainty that you will overcome every single crisis and will outlive every single trouble. Above all, our Jewish leaders must live steadily in *simcha*: [There is a teaching in our Oral Tradition to explain why the Torah forbade the *kohanim*, who ministered at the *beyss ha-mikdash*, to become involved in burial and mourning for the dead, except in a certain few cases:] 'Once the *kohanim* are in grief, the result is that the altar remains idle and useless.' If our rabbinic and national leaders — those who stand today in place of the Almighty's holy servants who ministered at the holy Temple in times of old — will give way to grief and despair, the entire altar of Judaism, all that we do to worship and serve the Almighty today to invoke His protection and grace, will become idled and will disappear."

****

There was a memorable story that the Rav used to tell:

The great gift of *simcha* (said he) is something I acquired from one particular source. To my forefather the hallowed Reb Pinchas'l Shapiro of Koretz, a single son was born: a most gifted and talented boy, who was named Meir'l. The youngster was a gem, in truth a precious rare stone, blessed with a sharp intelligence and abounding grace, who attained a mastery of greatness in Torah and *chassidus.* It was only natural for my forefather to expect this precious son of his to take his place when he himself would have to go to his eternal reward.

The time came, however, when a dread plague broke out and spread through the town, and it carried off a great many victims. The terror and confusion were overwhelming, as people perished in droves. The Houses of Study and Prayer were filled with worshippers night and day. They prayed ceaselessly for Heaven's mercy, with wailing outcries that were enough to tear heaven apart. Yet alas, from day to day the plague only grew worse. People from the entire region of Koretz came to the Rebbe with broken, pain-racked hearts, to implore Reb Pinchas'l as they wept: "Holy Rebbe, holy tzaddik and scholar, arouse Heaven's mercy for us and save us, before we all perish!"

And so Reb Pinchas'l began praying with a fervor that became ever more intense as he continued. He sensed that his prayers were penetrating and agitating every division and level of the Heavenly realm; and yet he discerned that the evil decree remained: It could not be nullified....

At last Reb Pinchas'l went to the *aron kodesh*, swept the velvet *parochess* aside, and flung open the doors. Before the Holy Ark, with the Torah scrolls visible to all who filled the chamber and listened, he exclaimed, "Divine Master of the world, I have only one son, one precious child whom I treasure like the apple of my eye. Herewith I give him to You. Take him. Let him be an offering, to bring atonement for the Jewish people!" No one could doubt that this final outcry of Reb Pinchas'l had been heard in Heaven — and heard well. As mysteriously as the plague had come, now it disappeared. Yet the same day, Meir'l, the Rebbe's child, fell deathly ill. And through the town a new wave of tumultuous agitation spread: Once again something would have to be done. All knew how precious Meir'l was to the holy tzaddik. He would never survive it if the child were taken from him. And surely Meir'l deserved Heaven's mercy in his own right: he himself was so dear and holy.... Yet whatever was to be done, it would have to be done swiftly. As the whole town knew soon enough, the boy was already at death's door.

Once more the Jewish inhabitants came running to the tzaddik, in grief and lament. "We don't want it!" they shouted. "We don't want such a great sacrifice. We want that the great light in his soul should shine upon us, as he grows up and lives among us!"

Once more the harrowing wails of the people penetrated his heart; and so once more Reb Pinchas'l went to the *aron kodesh* in his prayer chamber, to open its doors. "Divine Master of the world," he cried out, "You heeded my prayer before, because I gave You my Meir'l as a holy offering for the community. But now the community won't agree to it! What am I to do now? How can I find a way out of the perplexity?" He put his head inside the holy Ark, close to the Torah scrolls, and wept steadily for a long while.

Suddenly he lifted his head and began aloud the standard prayer of *mi shebeyrach l^e^choleh*, that asks the Almighty's blessing and healing for someone who is seriously unwell. When he came to the middle part, where the invalid's name must be uttered, Reb Pinchas'l chanted, "may He bless, may He heal the sick one, *Yehuda Meir*" . . . and continued on with the rest.

This done, he exclaimed, "Divine Master of the world, my Meir'l I indeed gave You; but the people redeemed him and took him back by adding the name *Yehuda*. I did this just now in their behalf. With his new name, then, he no longer belongs to the Angel of Death but to the Jewish people!"

The boy who was now called Yehuda Meir duly recovered and returned to health. When he grew up, this son of Reb Pinchas'l, Reb Yehuda Meir Shapiro took his place as a spiritual leader among his people, to spread the light of Torah and *chassidus* for many long years; and the teachings that he conveyed lived on among the Jewish people for many generations. . . .

****

This was the story that the head of Yeshivas Chachmey Lublin told more than once. Then he would continue: "That name in full, Yehuda Meir, was given me when my life on this earth had to begin. I must complete, then, the work that he began on this earth; and this means that I am living through years that were granted me as a gift. Had I not been given years of life from that illustrious great-grandfather of mine, I could never have come into this world. Well, then, a person like myself must always be in a state of *simcha*, knowing as he does that his years have been granted him as a gift which in no way could he deserve on his own merit. Therefore I have to be *nor b^e^simcha*, only in a cheerful state of optimism!

"And how right our Sages were when they taught us (*bavli*, Shabbos

30b, etc.): The *sh^e^china* will not abide — we cannot become receptive to the warming, sustaining grace of the Divine Presence — out of a state of indolence, nor out of a state of melancholy . . . but only out of the *simcha* of a mitzvah, the cheerful contentment we can get from doing a holy good deed that the Torah commanded."

41

In the chassidic dimension

Through the years that *chassidus* developed in the life of Polish Jewry, it became accepted as a firm rule, almost an axiom, that if someone was a *gadol*, a truly great Talmudic scholar, necessarily he would be a *misnaggéd*, an "opposer," with no sympathy for the chassidic world, who rejected it quite entirely.

Greatness in Talmud study and acceptance of *chassidus* were held to be two diametrically opposed, mutually exclusive ways of life and development, that could never be united. *Why?* (it was asked); *because that's how it is* (came the answer): It lay in the very nature of every great Talmudist (so it was argued) to turn aside from the chassidic way.

[For as a rule, the Talmudist had to develop a hard commanding intellect, which would dominate emotions and heart, so that he could serve his Maker through a clear knowledge of *halacha*. On the other hand, the *chassid* sought to serve his Maker primarily through the heart and its surging emotions, under the spiritual guidance of his Rebbe.]

Along came Rav Meir, by any standards a supreme master of Talmud, and he showed how harmony could prevail between the two realms, how *chassidus* could actually be the diadem that adorned the spirit of a great scholar, adding grace to his image, so that he acquired the gestalt of a whole human being.

It was to one path in *chassidus* that Rav Meir felt drawn from early years: the way that derived from the kabbalistic concept of *hod sheb^{e}tif^{e}eress*, "glory in majesty." It was a path that Reb Yisra'el, the founder of the dynasty of Ryzhin, had taken. In Rav Meir 's lifetime, the successor in the dynastic line who followed in this path was the venerated Reb Yisra'el, the Rebbe of Tchortkov. And the fact was that so soon as Rav Meir saw him, for the very first time, he felt drawn to the great spiritual leader, and became attached to him. His spirit recognized at once that in that realm of Ryzhin he truly belonged. Under this Rebbe's influence, psycho-emotionally, he began to live indeed with the visions and conceptions of "the glory of majesty" as a supreme way in service to the Almighty. . . . It might be added that in our world, there were a wealth of stories and traditions about

Ryzhin which we absorbed in our earliest years: fabulous accounts and fragments of tales about the great Rebbe who lived "once upon a time" and wallowed in a treasure of gold and precious gems, with a three-pointed crown, studded with diamonds, on his head. We heard how all would bow down to him as to a Jewish sovereign.... All was so fascinating and breathtaking as we listened. In this world we knew, where Rav Meir had grown in his time as we in ours, a foundation of awe was implanted in us toward the chassidic dynasty of Ryzhin.

In the later adult years of Rav Meir, a spark of the way of Ryzhin was there in him, glowing so brightly in his fiery, tempestuous spirit — so plainly there for all to sense and to see. And so it was that over a period of years, sensitive and exalted feelings, visions and ideas accumulated in his great mind and heart, to gather ever more form and ever greater force, until the finished conception of Yeshivas Chachmey Lublin emerged to be produced in reality, as a true Torah palace of majesty.

On one particular occasion he indicated quite clearly how the idea and the form of the yeshiva developed out of his roots in *chassidus*. Another Rebbe of the line of Ryzhin came to visit the yeshiva, and in the words of greeting with which he welcomed him, Rav Meir expressed this thought:

In the realm of *chassidus*, the Jewish people could take pride in three pillars of learning and worship, three giants of spiritual leadership, who helped form and develop it; and all three were named Yisra'el: the Ba'al Shem Tov, the Maggid of Kozhnitz, and Reb Yisra'el of Ryzhin. Their ways were different from one another, corresponding essentially to the ways of our immortal Patriarchs: Avraham, Yitzchak and Ya'akov: *chessed* (lovingkindness), *g'vura* (sternness), and *tif'eress* (majesty).

The Ba'al Shem Tov represented the source of *chessed*. Apart from bringing the radiant light of *chassidus* into the world, he generated that quality and did acts of lovingkindness with each and every individual. He had the right words for everyone. If a country Jew came, he would speak with the man about his cow, about the milk it provided; and at the same time, through the conversation, his mind would focus on *yichudim*, mystic unifications in the Heavenly realm that would bring benefit to the world.

The Maggid of Kozhnitz was the pillar of *g'vura*, stern judgment. He meted out punishment to everyone, considering everything in the light of rigorous, razor-sharp justice. Not even the greatest person would emerge altogether blameless from his keen, critical scrutiny.

Finally there was the great Rebbe of Ryzhin, the pillar of majesty. He made everything appear resplendent to the great mass of Jewry — utterly, gloriously radiant. With physical grace and material splendor he made the Torah appear captivating and alluring, to the people, so that they could be elevated to a conception of Heaven's mystical majesty.

"And therefore," Rav Meir concluded his welcoming address, "this worthy guest, who derives from the root source of *tif'eress*, has an innate close link with our yeshiva, whose own origins lie in the Heavenly sphere of *tif'eress* and whose purpose is to project the splendor of our genuine Judaism."

****

At any rate, through the years of his life, a powerful bond of friendship formed and grew between Rav Meir and the great chassidic leader whom he took for his Rebbe: Rav Yisra'el of Tchortkov. And in fact, Rav Meir once remarked, "From the time I reached the age of sense, I have never lifted hand or foot, either in my private, personal life or in my social activities, without consulting the Rebbe first and talking it over with him. The Rebbe's advice is for me, axiomatically, like a source of Divine guidance.

The Rebbe, in turn, reciprocated his attitude by relating to him with the same devotion and heartfelt affection. Once, after Rav Meir had been appointed to the prestigious rabbinic post of Lublin, the Rebbe of Tchortkov found occasion to tell him, "Whether I am a great Rebbe or a small one — that makes no difference whatever; but just think back on all the blessings I bestowed on you, all the assurances I gave you: Every one of them was fulfilled; they all came true. A devoted friend to you, I most certainly am. . . .

"Well, the great Rebbe Reb Baruch of Mezhibozh said that it is not *a guter yid* [a "good Jew" — a holy tzaddik] who can really help a person, but rather a good friend. Why, then, does everyone travel to *a guter yid* in search of help, to ask for a blessing? The answer is that only *a guter yid* can properly fulfill the mitzvah, *'you shall love your fellow-human like yourself'* (*Va-yikra*/Leviticus 19:18)."

In all the years of their singular friendship, whenever Rav Meir found the need and the time to visit the Rebbe at his residence, invariably he received the chassidic equivalent of "red carpet treatment": The Rebbe always greeted him most cordially and had him sit directly near him at the table over which he presided.

Among the other *chassidim* gathered around the large table, while the great majority accepted this amiably enough, the older *rabbonim* felt pained by it — especially if they had to move to make room for him: Here they were, esteemed men of learning, lifelong devotees of the Rebbe, and quite a bit older than Rav Meir. Then along he came, and he received such preferential treatment!

Early in the relationship, the Rebbe sensed their pained displeasure, and he took the trouble to explain: "When a *lamdan* comes to see me — a learned Jew with a keen intelligence in Talmudic matters — I welcome him cordially, to honor the Torah that he possesses. When a rich man comes to visit me, I give him a most friendly welcome, because, as the Talmud teaches, *rebbi m^e chabbed ashirim*: Rabbi Yehuda haNassi used to honor men of wealth (*bavli*, Eruvin 86a). Again, when a truly Godfearing person comes to see me, I receive him warmly, because thus I pay honor to the ever-abiding, ever-present Almighty, of whom this man is so very aware. Then, if I see a visitor who comes from a distinguished family line, I give him a truly fine welcome, in honor of his fathers. If someone is a communal worker, active in good causes, I receive him well for the sake of the honor of the community....

"Well, now, what do you expect me to do when someone comes along who is all these rolled into one, embodying all these qualities in himself? How can I *not* give him such a special welcome?"

****

Strange, though, are the ways of Divine providence. Not content with his close, heart-bound relationship with the great Rebbe of Tchortkov, Heaven seemed determined, evidently, to develop Rav Meir himself into a Rebbe, a full-fledged leader of *chassidim* in his own right.

Without much choice, the time came when people began applying the title of Rebbe to him — although to many it could only seem paradoxical: Was it possible that this great Talmud scholar, a noted *rav* in all respects, serving with distinction as the Rabbi of Lublin, would suddenly put all that aside in order to become a Rebbe? Would he really devote all his time to chassidic study and meditation and guide his flock through his behavior and his Torah thoughts, giving them his blessings and advice when they came individually to consult him? It was incomprehensible! In fact, it even sounded rather legendary, as if some fragment of reality had been embroidered and embellished out of all proportion. . . .

Yet it was the truth: not something that happened overnight, but the result of a long-drawn-out process. And the process began shortly after the opening of the yeshiva.

One fine day, a dusty, tearful traveler came through the doors in search of Rav Meir. "Where is the Rav?" he asked the first person he encountered. "I must see him!" He was taken to the administrative office.

"Maybe somebody else could help you?" a member of the staff asked him. "The Rav is enormously busy right now."

"No!" — and he gave way to a fresh outburst of tears, like a small child, demanding to be admitted to Rav Meir at once. Before those tears, all obstacles had to be thrust aside: He was allowed into the Rav's "inner sanctum" without further delay.

"Holy Rebbe, save me!" exclaimed the man as soon as the door had closed behind him.

"What is the matter? Calm down." . . . It took a while for his emotions to subside, and then the man began to speak: For three nights in a row, Rav Meir's forefather, Reb Pinchas of Koretz, appeared to him in a dream and told him that he must travel to Lublin and see his descendant Rav Meir; it was imperative; otherwise, Reb Pinchas warned, he would regret it. . . .

Well, said the man, the first two times, he ignored the matter: those were just dreams, he thought. The third time, however, the tone he heard in the dream was downright menacing; and so he decided to travel to Lublin immediately, although the journey was rather a long one. . . .

Now he implored Rav Meir to pray for him. . . . And with that, the visitor wrote out a *kvitl*: on a small sheet of paper he wrote his own Hebrew name and the name of his mother, then a few words about his situation, and what he wanted and hoped for, through Rav Meir's intercession in Heaven for him. This he duly gave to Rav Meir, as any *chassid* would to his Rebbe.

In thoughtful silence, Rav Meir gravely took the *kvitl* and looked at it; and he assured the man that no ill would befall him: All would be well.

And this, evidently, was the prologue to what Heaven intended for him. By itself, it certainly did not amount to much. It hardly created any stir or aroused any comment. In the course of time, though, as the yeshiva developed, it became a common practice for many people to come and spend a Shabbos in the yeshiva, to enjoy, in the company of the young scholars, the indescribable atmosphere that was so redolent with echoes of lively Torah study and chassidic singing, interspersed with lively chassidic dancing.

However enjoyable all this was, the highlights of a Shabbos at the yeshiva were quite certainly the discourses of the Rav: the wondrous, mellifluous flow of his thoughts as his mind ranged over the treasures of the Torah. And the net result of a Shabbos at the yeshiva, the effect of the whole experience on a guest, was that he could only wait eagerly for a chance to come again.

So it was that when a wealthy man in Lodz felt a yearning for a Shabbos that would give him deep spiritual pleasure, he would turn up at the yeshiva, to be welcomed as a guest. With the passage of time, a spiritual bond tended to develop between the frequent or regular guests and Rav Meir. And then, somehow, the idea seemed to form and take shape in the air that he ought to begin functioning as a Rebbe, fully, openly, "officially." For the way he acted, the way he impressed those who came into his proximity and felt his influence, made people think in that direction.

Finally the idea was broached openly — but alas, only in the last year of his life. He was in the resort town of Krinitz [Krynica, in the province of Cracow] to improve his health, when a second strange incident, exactly like the first, occurred: Someone arrived from the far-off region of Volhynia, looking for him, so that he could make the same desperate, urgent request: Would Rav Meir take pity on him?

This man recounted exactly the same kind of dream: Reb Pinchas of Koretz appeared and told him that only Rav Meir, the direct descendant of Reb Pinchas, could help him. . . .

As this little story became known, it left everyone there musing and wondering. And at last Rav Meir himself had to suspect that something formidable was going on here, at Heaven's instigation: For the second time someone had been sent to him for spiritual help — and in each instance, from such a far-off location!

That year, out of his reflections, he made his announcement: "In the year 5697 (1937), when I become fifty, according to our Sages, I will reach the age for giving good advice and counsel (Pirkey Avos 5:24). Then I intend to resign from the rabbinic post of Lublin and devote myself completely to the yeshiva. And then I intend to become a Rebbe, and I plan to give the *pidyonos* to the yeshiva." [The word *pidyonos* is the plural of *pidyon*, which denotes the sum of money that a *chassid* would invariably leave for the maintenance of the Rebbe when he came to give him a *kvitl* and ask for a blessing.]

Apart from other considerations, in making the announcement Rav Meir simply yielded to a wave of pressure and pleading. By then he had been subjected to years of it by a host of good friends and pupils, acquaintances and admirers. They had begun their pleading and urging a long time past, and the pressure they exerted had simply grown stronger from one year to the next, till it became particularly intense in this final year, while he was in Krinitz.

In response to his announcement, he received an unusual document that was written to him on the *yortzaït* (anniversary of the departure from life) of his illustrious forefather, Reb Pinchas of Koretz. It was written at the initiative of a few eminent rabbinic personages and other worthies, and a number of disciples, who signed their names to it. The text read as follows:

"On the tenth of Elul, the day when the departure from this world by Jewry's holy one, luminary of the Diaspora, paragon of his generation, the Rebbe Reb Pinchas of Koretz (may his merit protect us) is celebrated: it has been resolved that his direct descendant Yehuda Meir ben Margulya shall be aided by a complete [Divine] rescuing help; and as the Almighty is pleased by his way of life, let him sit on the throne of his holy forebears as a Rebbe in the year 5697, if *haShem* wills it, in Lublin, after a journey to the grave of his holy forebear of blessed memory, Reb Ya'akov Shimshon of Shepetivka [Shepetovka] in Safed, in our Holy Land. To this we bear witness . . . " Then the series of signatures followed.

Thus the year 5697 (1937) became a time of great hope for all the *talmidim*, disciples and good friends of the Rav. It was a time to look forward to with the greatest anticipation. Only, alas, it was not to be. . . . By Heaven's decree, the future *chassidim* were destined to remain orphaned, without his shining, warming presence to guide them.

How keenly the loss would then be felt. We believed with complete faith that by his great power of Torah mastery, by his great merit as a leader of Jewry, he would be able to bring down a powerful help from Heaven for *k^{e}lal yisra'el*, for Jewry in its entirety. In the aftermath we could only conclude that the generation was not worthy of it. . . .

****

Of particular interest, perhaps, is a private, confidential conversation that the Rav had about the matter with his great mentor, the Rebbe of Tchortkov.

On a certain Shabbos toward the end of a Jewish month, Rav Meir was in Tchortkov, to spend the holy day of rest with the Rebbe. That morning, during the prayer service in his large *beyss medrash*, after the reading of the Torah the Rebbe decided to honor Rav Meir by inviting him to lead in the rest of the service, as the *ba'al t^{e}filla* (cantor): first would come the special prayer *(y^{e}hi ratzon)* for the new Jewish month that would begin in the coming week, and then *musaf*, the concluding part of the service, would follow.

After the prayers, the Rebbe of Tchortkov gave Rav Meir great praise for his talents as *ba'al t^{e}filla*: His voice, said the Rebbe, had been lyrical indeed, and his melodious chanting, exquisite. Afterwards, the Rebbe invited him to join him for *kiddush* (the prelude to the full Shabbos meal) in his private quarters; and there the Rebbe waxed enthusiastic again over Rav Meir 's talent and power as *ba'al t^{e}filla.*

Said Rav Meir, "Rebbe, if I really possess such a great force in prayer, perhaps I should devote myself only to this field of Divine work, exclusively. After all, I'm a direct descendant of Reb Pinchas of Koretz. To him all the gates of prayer were open in the Heavenly realm!"

For a full moment the Rebbe sat still, immersed in his thoughts. After a long silence, he said, "I am going to tell you a story about the illustrious Rebbe Reb Zyshe, may his merit be a shield over us." Rav Meir prepared himself to listen, and this is what he heard:

****

We know that there was a period in Reb Zyshe's life when he went off into a personal exile, to wander about from place to place, for the sake of the *sh^e^china* [the Divine Presence] and for his own spiritual development. Wandering about as he did from one province and region to another, in time he came to Galicia. There he heard that in the town of Zolkava [Zolkiew] there was a Rebbe named Reb Yuzpa [a dialectal variant of *Yosef*] who conducted a yeshiva; and by all accounts, he was a consummate master of Talmud. At that, Reb Zyshe decided to make his way to Zolkava.

So it was that one morning, as he entered the yeshiva, he found Reb Yuzpa in the midst of a *shi'ur*, a profound analytic discourse on one of the most difficult subjects in the Talmud. As this scholar's mind grappled with the subject, he managed to shed light on some complex passages in both *talmud bavli* and *talmud yerushalmi*. The young learners were entirely concentrated on the discourse, and they paid no attention whatever to the itinerant, wandering beggar, dressed in tattered rags, who came in with his sack over his shoulders and sat down in an empty corner. . . .

So there Reb Zyshe sat, quite still, never taking his eyes off Reb Yuzpa. When it was all over at last, Reb Zyshe went up to him to express his appreciation. "More power to you: *y^e^yashér ko-ach*," said Reb Zyshe. "That was a fine *shi'ur* indeed. . . . I was told in this part of the world that you give great *shi'urim*, and I came especially to listen to you. Well, I must tell you that it was well worth the trouble. You give a first-rate discourse indeed."

"Well," replied Reb Yuzpa, "that you found yourself pleased with me — this I can understand: You heard something from me, and you found it likable. But I see you now for the first time; I know nothing about you; and yet something about you seems so attractive to me, spiritually."

"What is there about me, for Heaven's sake, that you could possibly find pleasing? I have no abilities in Torah study . . . I know nothing."

"It isn't possible," Reb Yuzpa insisted, "that you have no true wisdom and holiness in you. I perceive that you carry within you some special, wondrous quality that makes you find favor with anyone blessed with Divine good sense."

"Well," said Reb Zyshe, "all I can do is to say the regular prayers, like any ordinary Jew — nothing more."

"Which plain, ordinary Jew doesn't know how to say his prayers?" asked Reb Yuzpa, surprised.

"I know how a Jew should say the prayers before the Creator of the world," replied Reb Zyshe, trying to make himself a little more clear; and Reb Yuzpa understood. "Well then," said he, "perhaps you would be willing to teach me the mystic meanings and implications of our traditional prayers?"

"Let us go into another room, that might perhaps be set aside for praying and beseeching, and I will open for you all the Heavenly gates of entreaty."

At that, the two went into another room, and now Reb Zyshe became the teacher, and Reb Yuzpa the pupil. With a flow of thought that brought clear perception in other dimensions of the mind, Reb Zyshe taught his host the hidden meanings in the regular daily prayers — to such an extent that at last Reb Yuzpa clasped his head in both hands and cried out, "Rebbe! Perhaps I should shut down my yeshiva and disband my body of pupils, and I'll go following you in the way that Elisha followed Eliyahu" [the prophet Elijah: *M^elachim*/Kings I 19:19-21]. "Then I could learn from you how to say one single word in my prayers properly, at least once in my life — to say it that one time perfectly, with full concentration and devotion, before the Creator of the world!"

"I will tell you," replied Reb Zyshe: "Our Sages taught us: 'Just as the faces of human beings are never exactly alike, one to another, so are their minds never exactly alike, one to another. Rather, each and every one has a mind of his own' (Midrash Tanchuma, *pin^echas* 10). There are so many millions of people in the world, and no one looks exactly like some other person. The cast of this one's face is quite different from the cast of that one's. Well, the same holds true about minds, perceptions, casts of thought: because the spirits and the souls are divergent and different.

"Thus, every person's precise purpose on earth is unique to him. Every individual is created by His Divine will to do the work of Heaven that was allotted to him. And for this reason each person receives his abilities, that will lead him to the purpose which Heaven allotted him. So this is why the Sages tell us, 'A person should always study at that place [in the Torah] where his heart desires' (*bavli*, Avoda Zara 19a). For if he decides to study something in particular, or to serve the Almighty in one particular way of worship, or to reach a certain level of holiness, it is a sign that this is what Heaven intended for him, and this is indeed the purpose of his life on earth."

Reb Zyshe reached his conclusion: "You, Reb Yuzpa, have strong abilities in teaching the Torah. Your purpose on earth is to maintain a yeshiva and say great *shi'urim* . . . and I will go on with my praying. . . . "

****

So ended the story that the Rebbe of Tchortkov related; and in the last sentence, Rav Meir realized that he had received his answer: "Your purpose on earth is to maintain a yeshiva and say splendid *shi'urim*; and I will go on with my praying." It greatly confirmed him in his own inclination to reject for now any thought of taking on the role of Rebbe; and as noted above, he firmly deferred it till his fiftieth birthday.

Still, as the news of his decision about the future spread, so did the interest and the anticipation. It became a focus of conversation and great hope.

One day a certain Rebbe who was related to him met Rav Meir, and he said in jest, to tease him, "You know, we had one decent Rav in the family — a proper Rabbi as a Rabbi ought to be" [meaning Rav Meir, of course]. "Are we going to lose him?"

Rav Meir returned the banter: "In return, you will have a decent, proper Rebbe, as a Rebbe ought to be!"

****

So the visions and beliefs, legends and hopes that were engendered and woven around Rav Meir Shapiro were richly enlarged and greatened. All looked forward to his fiftieth birthday as an epochal date in the life of this Rav of Lublin, when he would acquire his new, entrancing title, a veritable name to conjure with: the Rebbe of Koretz-Lublin.

And we did not have the merit to see our hopes fulfilled. The generation could not be privileged to have him for its Rebbe, with all that this role could mean for us. For this was a spiritual leader whose heart split and burst for his people. He saw Jewry spiritually in ruins, in an utter confusion of absolute chaos; and the scene inflicted such deep wounds in his heart, that could never be healed.

It was yet as Rabbi that he was taken from this world.

42

Toward the rabbinate of Lodz

Whatever his unknown, unforeseeable future held for him, however, in the early years of the century's fourth decade he was very much alive and busy in Lublin, in three main roles: (1) as the Rabbi of the community; (2) as the administrator and *rosh yeshiva* of Yeshivas Chachmey Lublin; (3) as a debt-ridden individual burdened with the enormous problem of finding ways to pay off what the Yeshiva owed, and the means to keep it going.

Into this three-faceted life situation, a new factor entered: The community of Lodz wanted him to leave the rabbinate of Lublin in favor of the rabbinic post that it offered him now.

Within Poland, the city was known as Little Manchester; abroad it was simply called the Manchester of Poland. For with the rise and development of the Industrial Revolution in nineteenth-century England, Manchester became world-famous for the great textile mills that sprang up. The deafening machines that worked there night and day, driven by engines that were powered by steam, turned out reams upon reams of cloth that were taken by ships all over the world. Lodz could not match Manchester in size, but the same kind of factories rose up there, likewise to produce endless reams of cloth; and as a great many of the factories were in Jewish hands, the community of Lodz was unmistakably wealthy.

Now, during the few years that it was granted Rav Meir to function so brilliantly at the head of the yeshiva, this community decided to try to tempt him away to the rabbinic position that it offered.

It could be argued that the Jews of Lodz were actually entitled to him. Lodz was the second largest city in Poland; only Warsaw exceeded it in size. [In the internal politics of Polish Jewry, the city's Jewish community might well have been unique. As a rule, the *Bund* was politically powerful; in an age when a horrendous number of Poland's Jews were living wthout any link to the Torah, the *Bund* persuaded great droves of them that their only hope for the future was with this Jewish workers' party, on the Socialist road to utopia. Hence, in a great many of the larger Jewish communities, the *Bund* was the dominant force.]

Lodz stood out as a striking exception: The Jews known as Orthodox, who lived in loyalty to the Torah and the mitzvos, were in the majority. It was, in fact, known as a stronghold of Agudas Yisra'el. It needed only a rabbinic personage of authority at its head, indeed someone like Rav Meir Shapiro, and he would be able to achieve wonders, quite certainly, in every field of activity. For it was clear as day that the city had an active, dynamic community, ready to cooperate with a forceful leader and obey his directions with enthusiasm.

[For almost thirty years now, the position had remained vacant.] The Jewish populace kept waiting in hope for an appropriate person to come and chart the lines of activity for them.

It was only natural, then, that they should turn to Rav Meir and invest great effort to prevail on him to take the rabbinic position. In fact, a strong effort had already been made a few years earlier. In the year 5688 (1928), when he was the Rabbi of Piotrkov, a special delegation of the Lodz community came to tender him the post, offering the most favorable conditions. Then, however, he absolutely refused to consider it. "But why?" he was asked. What possible reason could he have to reject so handsome and attractive an offer? In reply, he gave a parable:

A personable young man, evidently most suitable for marriage, was once offered a *shidduch*. The matchmaker went to great pains to describe clearly all the features of the *shidduch* that should make the match so suitable and attractive: The young lady in question was good-looking and was possessed of the social graces; she came of a fine and prominent family; there would be a most handsome dowry, and so on; in short, *mit alleh mailess (ma'alos)*, with all possible good features and wonderful advantages. . . . The young man listened to everything, and at the end he shook his end: He had to reject the offer; he could not consider it. So of course, he was asked, "But why?" And he replied, "There is only one small drawback: I happen to be married."

"You see," continued Rav Meir after the parable, "I'm in the same situation. Certainly Lodz has a large community, with a wonderful rabbinic position to offer, *mit alleh mailess* [with all possible advantages]. Only, I am already tied up with the community of Lublin, with the yeshiva." For in the year 5688 (1928) his mind was completely absorbed in his determination to find the means to make the six-story building a finished, existing reality.

In ancient times, Moshe *rabbénu* described the Hebrews as *am k^e^shey oref*, a stiff-necked, stubborn people (*Sh^{e}mos*/Exodus 34:9). As a predominantly Orthodox community, the Jewry of Lodz certainly had that characteristic; and this refusal by Rav Meir while he was the Rabbi of Piotrkov did little to daunt them. Instead, a common front was formed, representing all the chassidic groups and political parties, with a single purpose: to work unanimously to get him into the rabbinic seat of Lodz.

In the year 5693 (1933) the yeshiva was in full existence and in full operation as a dynamic center; and the Rav was in full swing trying to cope with the enormous financial needs of the yeshiva. . . . And so he came that year to Lodz, to mount a campaign for funds.

The formal message of welcome by the community was given by its president, a deputy to the Sejm from Agudas Yisra'el named Reb Leybl Mintzberg. Into the warm, cordial greeting he wove a clear, new invitation, in the name of the entire community, to the city's rabbinic post.

In the course of his lengthy, spirited address in response, Rav Meir made no direct reply to the offer. Instead, when he was done with his sermonic discourse, he suddenly went off on a wholly new tack:

"I always found it hard to understand a few certain words in our Book of *T^{e}hillim*: The Psalmist hymns to the Creator, 'my soul thirsts for You . . . in a parched and thirsty land without any water' (Psalms 63:2). What sort of metaphor is this? Why does the Psalmist conjure up the idea of a thirsty longing for water in a land where there just isn't any? In a deathly dry, sand-blown desert, of what use is it to long for water, something that cannot possibly be gotten there?

"The answer is that when thirst becomes too strong a need, it cannot be constrained by logic and reason. The powerful craving for water comes even when it is obvious that there cannot be any. . . . Well, I am now in the same situation: I want with all my heart that someone should come along and give me thirty thousand dollars for the yeshiva. Isn't an idea like that so much more impossible a dream than finding water in a parched, sand-blown desert? How, then, can I allow myself any hope like that?

"The answer is that the pressure on me is so powerful. The yeshiva's enormous burden of debt presses down on me, and it puts such thoughts into my mind in spite of me!

"Fellow-Jews!" cried out Rav Meir suddenly: "Give me thirty thousand dollars, and I'll give away to you my entire share of the World-to-Come!"

Thus he gave no clear, direct answer about the new offer of the rabbinate. Yet in his words there certainly was an implied, indirect answer: The community wanted to win him over by the powerful attraction of money that it could offer, which would enable him, finally, to cover the debts of the yeshiva. What he left them to understand was that he would rather sell his share in the World-to-Come and remain in Lublin with his beloved *talmidim*, sooner than go and take on the rabbinic duties in Lodz.

Yet not one person there was ready to venture forth and take him up on his offer. His audience merely sat there spellbound, amazed at how far this great Torah scholar was willing to go in his total dedication to the yeshiva.

The debt burden remained, however. If he could ease it a bit from time to time by raising funds here and there, the relief could only be temporary. The load he carried could only return, or indeed grow worse. And so, necessarily, the offer from the Lodz community had to be considered, and considered again, each time perhaps with growing favor.

The proffered position would bring him a net monthly salary of thirty thousand zlotys, with an added side income of another two thousand. Out of this, he reckoned, he would be able to set aside a few thousand every month for the yeshiva. One week in each month he would be free to spend in Lublin.

That was all very well as far as it went. Yet what of his own overriding concern, that gave him no peace by night or by day? And so he added an intractable condition: First, the community of Lodz had to make him an outright gift of a hundred thousand zlotys for the yeshiva. Only when that was done would he be ready to assume the rabbinic position.

To anyone who knew him it was clear as day that the rabbinate of Lodz in itself held no great attraction for him. The historic setting of Lublin was far more dear to him. He even rejected a proposal to become the Rabbi of Jerusalem! No considerations of advancing in his rabbinic career were involved. The only deciding factor was the sheer, brutal necessity to rid the yeshiva of its harrowing burden of debt.

For long months on end the negotiations went on. A hundred thousand zlotys was a formidable sum of money, and it was difficult to get the whole amount together in the city. "The trouble," explained the president of the community, "is that everybody agrees. If there were only some opposition to the whole idea, the conflict and argument would stir people to ambitious action, and the needed amount would be raised."

In the final month of his life, the prospects of his moving to Lodz began to appear more and more realistic. Public opinion became convinced finally that he was really going to leave Lublin very soon, to take charge of the Lodz community. Then, one day, an official delegation came at last to Lublin, consisting of the most eminent members of the Lodz community, to inform Rav Meir that to a considerable extent, the *k^{e}hilla* agreed to accede to his demands.

[It was directly after Sukkos, 5694 (mid-October, 1933) that Rav Meir gave his consent at last. With the authorized community heads of Lodz, over small glasses of liquor, he drank a toast of *l^{e}cha-yim*, as they wished him *mazal tov*.]

They went to see Yeshivas Chachmey Lublin for themselves, at first hand; and then they wrote in the Visitor's Book: "Fortunate are we that we have been privileged to see the holy yeshiva in its splendor and glory, and the triumphant banner of the Torah waving unfurled on high, under the leadership of His Excellency, the pride and splendor of Jewry, the Mentor and Educator, Rabbi Meir Shapiro. Even so may we be worthy to see him ministering in splendor in the Rabbinate of our city of Lodz, and may he lead our community over the flowing waters of our holy Torah until the advent of the Messiah. . . . "

[In Lodz the news brought a flood of happiness to the hundreds of thousands of Jewish inhabitants. It made no difference what type they were, or to what political movement they belonged. All rejoiced. And preparations were begun to be able to receive him properly. It was decided to rent a handsome, palatial building and to renovate it into a resplendent residence for him, that would reflect the wealth and importance of the community.]

So went the developments in the city of Lodz. [Meanwhile, Rav Meir did his best to reassure those in Lublin who were bound to him with the strongest ties of affection. He gave them his promise that he would not abandon and forget them. And to his close friends and associates he outlined concrete ideas and thoughts:

[In time his "exile" in Lodz would end, and he could return to his core interest and deepest love: the education of his *talmidim*. Now, however, he was able to feel the oppressive, crippling burden of debts and running expenses beginning to lift from him at long, long last. Finally, after harried years of endless worries, he felt free to start thinking and planning again.

Once more his creative mind visioned and soared:

[In only a few short years he would reach fifty, the age of wise counsel. Then he could dedicate himself entirely to a life of holiness and true spiritual elevation, as the heir and successor of the legendary Reb Pinchas of Koretz. He would enlarge the scope of the yeshiva, increase its grandeur and fame, to raise the prestige of all yeshiva students and Torah scholars. . . . And from afar, the Holy Land continued to draw him as with a magic allure, to Jewry's promised shores of enchantment where he had never been. . . .

[Soon afterward, the heads of the Lodz community came again, to discuss final arrangements for his move to their city. The news of the visit spread as if carried by the wind; and the Jewish inhabitants of Lublin became truly disturbed. An emergency committee was formed "for the sake of the Rav."] No longer could they remain quiescent and asleep. [Printed public calls appeared, along with releases to the press, about a concerted campaign to counter the plans of the Jews in Lodz, by raising locally the hundred thousand zlotys that the Rav demanded from the wealthy members of the other community. "We won't let our Rabbi leave Lublin!" shouted the headlines.

[The *chassidim* of the Rebbe of Kozhnitz, who had their own House of Prayer in the city, took the lead in declaring a firm resolve to raise fifty thousand zlotys to ease the yeshiva's burden of debt. And in response came the resolution from Lodz to raise twice the amount, or even three times as much.]

The conflict between Lodz and Lublin became a bitter one, as ambitions flared and resolutions hardened. The relatively poor community of Lublin set itself heart and soul to compete against the wealthy Jewry of Lodz. People went to work on the matter with the greatest intensity, and soon enough a "Special Committee for the Rabbi" became busy as beavers in Lublin, pursuing its goal of raising the needed amount.

The result was that the relevant people in Lodz speeded up their own efforts to close the negotiations with Rav Meir. They became apprehensive that if the Lublin community succeeded in raising the amount he wanted, he might find a way to dissolve his agreement with them. Feeling that there was no time to lose, the Lodz community sent word that a final delegation was being sent, with the community president himself at its head, which would bring at last the *k^esav rabbonus* — the formal, official document, duly signed as necessary, which would make him the Rabbi of Lodz.

The tragic fate that was ordained him decreed otherwise, however. When the document was brought, he lay on his bed stricken with the illness from which he would not recover.

He was never to read the *k^{e}sav rabbonus.*

43

Toward the end

As the time came near for the ordained end of his life, signs and indications began to appear. The final year, especially the last months, were full of singular, even extraordinary, things. At one point he arranged a life-insurance policy with a premium of thirty thousand dollars, and as beneficiary (to receive the money in the event of his death) he named the yeshiva.

[Actually, he took no initiative in the matter. It was handed him on a silver platter, as it were, and he accepted it as Heaven's will: In a move to enlarge its operations, the Prudential Life Insurance Company of America opened branches in Poland. Looking for a way to promote interest and sales, it was in desperate need of good publicity; and its chief agent hit on the idea of selling Rav Meir a policy for an unusually high premium, on unusually good terms. For it did not take the agent long to realize that Rav Meir was among the best-known figures in Polish Jewry. He was sure the resulting publicity would be invaluable.]

All at once Rav Meir developed an intense longing to travel to the Jewish homeland, and he firmly resolved that whatever happened, for next Pesach he would take a trip to the Holy Land. From the very best of the young Talmudists at the yeshiva he chose a few, whom he intended to take with him. Great plans began taking shape in his mind — practical, concrete, hard and fast — in connection with the projected trip: plans for a branch of Yeshivas Chachmey Lublin, to be established in the historic Promised Land.

There, in *eretz yisra'el*, the news that the illustrious Rabbi of Lublin planned to visit was received with great satisfaction. A variety of feature articles appeared in the press, offering commentary, conjecture and speculation. Some even declared that as a recognized Torah authority of the highest rank, he would be able to do significant work in the political hassles and party conflicts that prevailed among the religious Jews in the Holy Land. It was hoped and believed that he would be able to bring them all under his iron hand and make one party, one effective, united political force, out of them all. And then, the speculation continued, perhaps he would be able to set firm boundaries to the enormous lawlessness that reigned outside the religious camp, in regard to sacred tradition and common morality and decency.

****

It was the custom of Rav Meir during his years in the city that on the festive days of Pesach he always went for the prayer services to the *beyss medrash* that bore the name of the legendary *chozeh* (Seer) of Lublin. Now, however, as late autumn brought the festive holydays of Sukkos and Simchas Torah, he announced a change: "This year I plan to be in the *beyss medrash* of the *chozeh* for the *hakafos*" [the seven sessions of joyous dancing with the Torah scrolls, to celebrate the annual end of the weekly readings in the Torah], "since I intend to be in the Land of Israel for the prayer of *tal*" ["dew" — to beseech Heaven for a fertile season of summer growth] "on the first day of Pesach."

[In the non-chassidic world of the *misnaggéd,* the *hakafos* in the Diaspora take place only on the evening of Simchas Torah, and again the following morning. Among *chassidim* in the Diaspora, it became a firm custom to have them also the previous evening, on the night of Sh^{e}mini Atzeress. It was to these *hakafos* that Rav Meir referred now.]

So spirited was the dancing that evening, so dynamic with a holy joy, that all who were there were drawn in and carried along on the endless waves of happy rhythm and melody. [At the head, leading the festivity, was Rav Meir himself, with the little *séfer torah* (that he himself had written) carried in the crook of his arm. He danced in a fervor of happiness, as never before. Behind him came the regular *sifrey torah*, that had been taken from the holy Ark to be carried in the dancing. Volumes of the Talmud were carried too, with the same sense of exultant celebration — volumes of the rare and venerated Slavuta edition. This was Rav Meir's idea [that he had put into practice for years], so as to make it a complete celebration of the Torah: both the Written Torah in the scrolls, and the Oral one in a precious Slavuta edition of the Talmud.

[Toward the end of the eighteenth century, a quality press was founded in the small city of Slavuta by Rav Meir's forefather Reb Moshe, the son of Reb Pinchas of Koretz, and this was operated in later years by Reb Moshe's two sons. The volumes of Talmud that were printed there were handsome folios, produced with great care and devotion; and forever after, they were greatly prized in Poland's Torah world.]

As more and more celebrants joined in the fiery singing, as more and more pairs of feet moved and swayed in the ecstatic rhythms of chassidic, worshipful fervor, the evergrowing number of participants needed ever more space — till the festivity went in unbroken continuity from the *beyss medrash* of the *chozeh* through all the streets to Yeshivas Chachmey Lublin! And as the dynamic gaiety moved in tempo happily, the *chassidim* managed to find, entangled and swept along with them, an entire battalion of *B^erit haCha-yal* [the "union of Jewish army veterans" who had seen military action with European forces, mainly Polish, and who formed now part of the Revisionists!]

[The Revisionists were general, non-religious Zionists, but with a difference: They believed in putting great emphasis on military prowess, to create a Jewish army that could fight for the people's "national" rights to its ancient homeland. Hence the *B^erit haCha-yal,* keeping up appearances of military pride and might. Now a whole battalion of these war veterans — definitely not religious — had managed to become rather incorporated and amalgamated by the dancing and singing *chassidim.*]

At first thought, there was a strong impulse among the *chassidim* to oust these army veterans as an "alien" element. When the Rav learned about it, however, his unhesitating response was, "Let them be! A little fire of our happiness with the Torah has been kindled in them also!"

So it was, then, that as the "fire" of fervent celebration spread steadily through the streets and reached the yeshiva, a whole new "supply of fuel" was added to the "blazing festivity": The Torah scrolls of the yeshiva were taken out, and with them seven new *hakafos* were begun. The Revisionist battalion was thoroughly amalgamated into the non-military action by then, and its members joined in with gusto. For a brief while they had a chance to sense the power in utter unity with the Torah, as compared with the display of power in military behavior. . . .

****

The next morning, in the prayer service of Sh^emini Atzeress, *t^efillas geshem,* the annual prayer for rainfall, had to be included; and so Rav Meir went that morning to the *Maharam shul* (the House of Study and Prayer named after the Maharam — Rav Meir ben G^edalya — of Lublin), where he served as the *ba'al tᵉfilla* in the prayer for rain.

[The prayer of *geshem* on this day of the year was intended originally for the Land of Israel, where the annual rainy season is due to start soon afterward. In the Diaspora, rain in the following months is not such a vital necessity. The general tenor of the prayer, however, is a powerful plea for life (since the whole need for rain is to be able to grow an ample supply of food); and this is most clearly expressed toward the end, when the cantor chants, "For You are *haShem* (the Lord) our God, who makes the wind blow and the rain fall"; then the congregation cries out, "for blessing, and not for curse"; and again, "for life, and not for death!"]

Everyone felt the powerful emotions in the words that both the *ba'al tᵉfilla* and the responding worshippers sent up to Heaven.

[A strange, inexplicable height of intensity was reached when they came to one particular line of religious, prayerful poetry in the text. Referring to the twelve sons of *Ya'akov avinu* (Jacob), who became the founding ancestors of the people's twelve tribes, the worshippers sang to the Almighty of "their descendants, whose blood was shed on Your account like water." For some reason that no one could explain, that seemed to release floodgates of tears. All wept, even the children; and no one knew why. . . .

[Not an inkling was there yet on the surface that his life would end soon; yet some sense of foreboding could well have been in the atmosphere, beyond the reach of the rational mind. In the words of the Book of *Tᵉhillim*, "my soul knows very much" (Psalms 139:14). More important, perhaps, was that it was not long after Hitler had taken control in Germany, and the Jews in nearby Poland (just over the border, as it were) could not but sense the savage, terrifying threat of the Nazis and their own vulnerability and helplessness.

[In fact, only some two weeks earlier, as the awesome holy day of Yom Kippur loomed up on the calendar, there was almost an acrid smell of fright in the air. All felt it, and no one could offer any explanation.

[Late on the day before Yom Kippur, as evening began to fall and the time of awe approached, Rav Meir could be seen hastening through dark, narrow alleys and courtyards in his white *kittl* and woolen *tallis*, on his way to the *shul* of the Maharam of Lublin. Hundreds saw him as he sped on, and they called out, *"A gut yor!"* (A good year), or else, in Yiddish, "Give us a blessing, Rebbe." He said something in response, and hurried on, held in thrall by a sense of quivering awe, with not a trace of cheer or a smile on his somber face.

[Through the packed synagogue he made his way with difficulty to his place at the eastern wall. . . . Then it was time to open the holy Ark and take out the *sifrey torah*, so that respected elders could walk with them through the *shul*, as the cantor (walking before them) and the worshippers would take turns chanting *or zaru'a la-tzaddik* (Light is sown for the tzaddik, and joy for those who are upright in heart: *T^ehillim*/Psalms 97:11).

[A venerable man of hoary age went on forward to the *aron kodesh* to take a Torah scroll. Yet as he began to move with it, he struck against a projection and tottered and fell. From all sides people rushed to the old man, wanting to help him up. He had held on grimly to the scroll, however, to make sure that *it* did not fall; and now he thrust everyone away till he could get up by his own strength, the Torah still firmly in his arm; and in a voice that all could hear he exclaimed, *"or zaru'a la-tzaddik . . . "*]

Now, before the solemn prayer of *Kol Nidrey*, the Rav went to the pulpit to give a most moving, emotional sermon.

[He quoted the immortal words of Rabbi Akiva in the Mishna (Yoma 8:9): "Fortunate are you, O *yisra'el*: Before whom are you being cleansed? who is purifying you? — your Father in Heaven!"

["Divine Master of this entire world," he cried out: "We have all seen now how a man of eighty mustered his last bit of strength to hold firm to a *séfer torah* even when he fell, till he could get up with it. What is he, then, if not a symbol of this nation that holds fast to Your sacred Torah even when it falls!"]

With a burning grief he spoke of the sorrowful situation of the Jewish people all over the world. He described the accursed rise to power of the satanic Hitler, and the implementation of his Nazi policy. He told of the brutal wounds that had already been inflicted on the Jews in Germany. At the end, in great despair, he cried out the words of the prophet Yoel, "so tear your hearts, and not your clothes!" (Joel 2:13). "Tear your hearts in contrition and penitence before Heaven," he exclaimed. "Otherwise, Heaven forbid, we may have to do the tearing in our clothes."

All knew well enough the custom of *k^eri'a* — that a Jew makes a tear in an article of clothing as a mark of grief when he must begin mourning the loss of someome in the primary family. No one there, however, sensed the unwitting prophecy in his words — that they applied to *him* — that soon, all too soon, the hundreds of *talmidim* at the yeshiva would be "tearing *k*ᵉ*ri'a*" in a stunning stupor of grief over his departure from the world.

[Later that night, he sat in the great study hall as the young scholars listened, and he expounded on the concept in the Jewish tradition — linked to a teaching in *bavli*, Yoma 85b — that *itzumo shel yom m*ᵉ*chappér*: the strong essence of the day brings atonement and forgiveness. The word *itzumo*, said Rav Meir, connotes the word *etzem* in the Written Torah's phrase, *uch*ᵉ*etzem ha-shama-yim latohar*, "and like the very essence of the sky in purity" (*Sh*ᵉ*mos*/Exodus 24:10). The holy day has its own inherent purity and clarity, that serves as a wondrous cleansing force to bring Jewry its Divine atonement and forgiveness.

[In the first part of the day that followed, he was his usual optimistic, cheerful self again, with his radiant face and spirit. In the later hours he became the *ba'al t*ᵉ*filla* for the *mussaf* service; and when he came at last to the stanzas of the *assara harugey malchus*, the vision (condensed out of history into a heartrending drama) of ten great martyrs who were put to death by the Romans in ancient times, he wept like a child — as though he foresaw that the annals of Jewish martyrdom were far from finished.

[For *n*ᵉ*'ila*, the day's final prayer service, he was again the *ba'al t*ᵉ*filla*. And when all the praying was done and night had fallen, he gave orders that all the young scholars were to file into the dining room. They came walking in, and found him already waiting for them, with a pitcher of warm milk in hand, to pour a cupful for each one as he filed past.]

****

[A few days later, the festival of Sukkos came, and Rav Meir proceeded to spend it in immense happiness, imbued with the heightened spirit of *yom tov* as never before.] During *chol ha-mo'éd* (the Intermediate Days of the Festival), he chose one of the more senior Talmud scholars among the *talmidim* and appointed him *mashgi-ach*, spiritual supervisor at the yeshiva, to see to it that the study would go on properly; and as comment, he paraphrased a passage in the Talmud (*bavli*, Avoda Zara 8b): "From us will come the kings, from us the directors: The yeshiva will continue functioning by its own forces and resources."

Then the newly appointed *mashgi-ach* took over the discussion, and he developed his ideas for a detailed program of study in the new semester that would soon begin. When he was done, the Rav asked the people around him, "Well?—how do you like the presentation of my prime minister?"

****

The night of Hoshana Rabba, he had a rather awesome dream, which he accepted, however, quite equably and calmly: He found himself in the yeshiva, together with the previous Rebbe of Tchortkov, Reb David Moshe (who had passed on a long while ago), and with that Rebbe's son Reb Yisra'el (still very much alive in this world), whose devoted *chassid* Rav Meir had always been. Reb Yisra'el recounted to his father the greatness of this *chassid* of his, describing his formidable power in conveying and spreading a knowledge of the Torah; and he told to what an extent this Rav Meir had reinforced the prestige of the Torah and greatened the glory of Heaven in the world.

"If he is really so important and distinguished," replied the older Rebbe, "we ought to have him enter Heaven."

"He is much more needed here on earth," replied the current Rebbe of Tchortkov.

The next day, Rav Meir recounted the dream to one of his close associates, without a trace of sorrow. On the contrary, with a smile he added, "See how important I am in Heaven. . . ."

Yet who could know if this was not perhaps the cause of his unusual, even extraordinary conduct in the very last period of his life? Who could know if, with his own sensitivity and awareness, he did not perhaps understand the meaning of the dream only too clearly?

****

One of his former pupils, who was now in his adult years, came to the yeshiva on a visit; and as he sat talking with the Rav, the conversation turned to the topic that was then of great current interest: the intense desire of the Lodz community to have him as the city's Rabbi, and the attempts to raise the huge amount of money that he demanded.

"Of course I understand," said the visitor. "You want the funds to pay off the yeshiva's enormous debt."

"No," replied the Rav. "That will be only a way to ease matters. The debt will be paid off another way": and he cited something from a mystic text that devout Jews in the chassidic world would always say on the very threshold of Yom Kippur, just before the prayer of *Kol Nidrey*: "There is one who acquits himself of liability with his money, and there is one who acquits himself with his life-spirit" (*Tikkuney Zohar*, second series, *tikkun* 5, end).

Only considerably later, looking back in retrospect, was it realized that he had in mind the premium on his life insurance policy, to be paid to the yeshiva after his death.

44

The final week

A few weeks later, on the very last Shabbos of his life, there were strange occurrences that were striking. Various peculiar changes could be noticed in his conduct. Thus, Friday evening before ***kiddush***, as he chanted the words of *eyshess cha-yil* (*Mishley*/Proverbs 31:10-31), with tears in his eyes he repeated over and over the phrase, *va-tis-chak l'yom acharon* ("and she was cheerful toward the last day").

Through the years since the yeshiva had opened its doors, every Friday night, when the first of the three holy Shabbos meals was over, it was the custom of the young Torah scholars, invariably, to rise and set off in a cheerful dance inside the dining room, with the Rav joining them happily. That night it simply "didn't go": Somehow, there was something in the air that opposed their efforts. Over and over again they tried: they joined hands, placed hands on one another's shoulders, began swaying energetically to a spirited melody — and the enthusiasm flagged and sagged and petered out. And no one could say just what the reason was.

****

For quite some time now, following his firm decision to visit the Holy Land for Pesach, he had embarked on a new daily learning session. At five o'clock every morning he would meet with eighteen of the older students, and together they would study the agricultural areas of *halacha* concerning the Homeland. Punctually at five, every morning, the Rav would always be at his place, waiting for the *talmidim*, who tended to be late by a very few minutes.

At their last study session, they ended with Rambam's commentary on a paragraph in the Mishna tractate Pé'ah (4:11), where the last words were, "and the *halacha* (the definitive law) follows the view of Rabbi Meir." Only much later, in retrospect, would we realize that even in this small fact, Heaven intimated something for us to ponder about our Rabbi Meir.

Somewhere around that time, Rav Meir was asked point blank if he really intended to sail to the Holy Land. He gave the exact reply that the *chozeh* of Lublin had given well over a century earlier, when he was asked why he would not go to visit the Holy Land: "To travel to *eretz yisra'el*, I have enough strength; but where can one get the strength to travel back, away from *eretz yisra'el*?"

Tuesday morning came; and the Rav did not appear for the early morning learning session. It was five o'clock, then six, then seven . . . and there was still no sign of him. Evidently this was no simple, trifling matter; and so a conversation started up among the students: What could have happened? He was always there ahead of them, to await their arrival; and now it was so very late! Could he have merely overslept? No: that was impossible. Something serious must have happened. . . .

They waited another short while, and decided to investigate. In his quarters they found him lying in bed, suffering from a sore throat, with no wish to take anything to eat or drink. Instead, he told them to call a medical doctor immediately. It was evident that he was in the grip of a great fear. As the Talmud explains about such a phenomenon (*bavli*, M^e^gilla 3a), "Although he himself does not see [the reason for his terror], his guardian angel [the discarnate protective Heavenly being which accompanies him through his lifetime] does see it."

Thus, we realized afterward, he had an extraordinary power of premonition. For at other times, even if he had a seriously high temperature, he would not forego a *shi'ur* or a study session, and he would never ask for a doctor to be called.

Now his wish was fulfilled without delay; in fact, a few physicians were summoned; and when they were done with their examination, the ailment was diagnosed as an inflammation of the throat. It could be expected, the doctors said, that in a few days it would be gone. One of them then wrote out a prescription for a medicinal preparation to use as a gargle.

Nevertheless, Rav Meir remained restless and agitated. The doctors' reassurances were unable to calm him. And after a while he called two very young *talmidim* into the room and bade them sing, to the chassidic melody that went with them (which they knew), the words from the Book of *T^e^hillim* that he felt he needed: *ya'ancha* haShem *b^e^yom tzara* . . . (May the Lord answer you in a day of trouble: Psalms 20:2).

During the day a delegation arrived from the city's *chevras bikkur cholim*, the "Society for Visiting the Sick," whose purpose it was to look after people who fell ill. With no idea how seriously unwell he might be, they merely came to invite him to their local House of Prayer for a Shabbos morning that would soon arrive. By an old tradition in Lublin, the Rabbi of the city always joined the *chevra* for the prayers in its *shul* on the Shabbos morning when the Torah portion of *va-yéra* was read. [At the root of the old custom lay the meaning that the Talmud found in the first few words of the Torah portion, "Then *haShem* appeared to him" (*B*ᵉ*réshis/* Genesis 18:1). As the Sages interpreted it (*bavli*, Sotah 14a), the Lord came to fulfill the mitzvah of *bikkur cholim*, visiting the sick: for Avraham was recuperating from his recent circumcision, recorded a few sentences earlier in the Written Torah.]

At any rate, the Rav received their formal invitation courteously, and he assured them, "If *haShem* will grant me life, I'll come to you."

By Wednesday his condition had worsened, and he found it hard to talk. Unlike his regular daily custom, that morning he did not even ask to see the mail that had come. And that night he asked that a particular text from the prayers be sung for him, with the chassidic melody that went with it. The words meant, "that it may become known and revealed that He is King over all the earth"; it was with this singing that the *talmidim* would always be wakened on Yom Kippur, early in the morning.

That whole night, he was unable to sleep: he simply felt too nervous and disturbed — on edge. In the morning he asked for the physicians to be called again. They came and examined him, and had nothing new to add. When they left, he said in annoyance to the people in the room, "There is no time to be ill." Then he told the *talmidim* who were there: "Our Sages teach us, 'Afflictions cleanse away all the sins of a person' (*bavli,* Bᵉrachos 5a); and we have also an old principle in our Tradition" [derived from *yerushalmi,* Bikkurim 3:3, 68c] "that when a person is appointed a *parnas*, the managing head of a community, all his transgressions are forgiven him. Whatever sins, misdeeds or wrongdoings there may be on his Heavenly record, his slate is wiped clean. Both teachings came true for me."

As the hours moved on, he kept growing weaker. The students asked him if perhaps they should all assemble and say *t*ᵉ*hillim* for him, to beseech Heaven's mercy for him through the impassioned words of prayer in the Book of Psalms. With his usual irony and optimism still undiminished, he retorted, "Don't take me yet for such a fearfully serious invalid, that I need *t*ᵉ*hillim* said for me."

The last day, it was difficult for him to manage the morning prayers by himself. A *talmid* had to help him put on his *t'fillin*; and then it took him two hours to go through the entire service. For he kept praying with powerful *d'vékus*, with a mighty sense of unification with Divinity and the strongest yearning to keep the bond unbroken.

And his condition kept growing worse. His breathing became so labored and difficult that his efforts could be heard three rooms away. Eventually he became unable to talk at all, and to communicate, he wrote everything down.

The people around him asked him for permission to go to the cemetery and pray for him at the grave of the *chozeh* (the Seer of Lublin). He consented, and on a piece of paper he wrote the words that he wanted them to say in prayer: "that those who are healthy should not fall ill, and those who are sick should be healed." He still felt a primary concern for his Jewish people in general, that was greater than any anxiety about himself.

The doctors of medicine came to examine him once more. They did their probing, they checked the symptoms, and consulted together; and their conclusion was reassuring: The patient would begin improving quite soon. Those who were present could not be so easily satisfied, however, and they asked the physicians, "Perhaps you see some complications, some new factors or developments that have made his condition worse? Whatever the cost, we are prepared to pay: Perhaps we must bring in professors of medicine from Warsaw, or from Vienna?"

The doctors, however, continued to give their assurance: It was only a light inflammation of the throat that would soon be gone. . . . And since they were so certain in their heartening optimism, nothing of his illness was told the people in the city so that they might say *t'hillim* for him, to beseech and arouse Heaven's mercy.

When night fell, he was entirely unable to pray. He called in ten *talmidim* to form a *minyan* for *ma'ariv*, so that they could say the evening prayers as a congregation with the intention of worshipping also as his agents — and thus they would acquit him of his obligation.

Later that evening, Sh'mu'el Eichenbaum, the great philanthropist and good friend of the yeshiva, came to see the Rav — to observe the mitzvah of *bikkur cholim*. (It was he who had owned the large plot of land on which the yeshiva now stood, and had donated it for the yeshiva.) Now he brought news about the vigorous campaign that the Lublin community had set in motion not to let the Rav leave the city to become the Rabbi of Lodz. Rav Meir listened with interest, and then he whispered just one Hebrew-Yiddish word in response: *halvaï!* ("Would that it be so; how dearly I wish it.")

****

The hour of night grew later and later. On a piece of paper he asked that he be shown all the prescriptions which the doctors had written. When they were handed him, he went through them and selected the one for a preparation to cleanse the throat and the respiratory organs; and he asked that a new supply be gotten for him.

Every few minutes he kept washing his hands, while his mind was obviously immersed in distant thoughts. The evident struggle that he had to make to draw breath was heartbreaking. One could feel the frightful, racking agony that he had to undergo to try to get a bit of air into his lungs; and try as he would, he kept failing, because the channels were blocked.

On a piece of paper he scrawled a request to be carried into another chamber that he designated by its number ("Room number so-and-so"). Interestingly, that room had two doors, each with the name of an organization that had contributed money toward its construction. One door bore the name of the *Bikkur Cholim* Society (for care of the sick) of Chicago; the other, of the *Chessed shel Emess* Society (for proper Jewish burial) of St. Louis.

When the transfer was accomplished, he asked for a change into a clean undershirt and a fresh *tallis katan* (a four-cornered garment with *tzitzis*, ritual fringes, at the corners). Needless to say, his wishes were carried out. But then his wife, the *rabbaniss*, noticed a change in his countenance, and she began weeping emotionally. Rav Meir did his best to calm her, as he wrote the message, "Now the true *simcha* begins." . . .

In a broken, barely legible scrawl he wrote, *trinkt alleh l'cha-yim*: "All of you, drink *l'cha-yim*!" Some liquor was poured out into tiny glasses, and all who were there drank and wished him *l'cha-yim*, "to life!" Then he shook hands with them all, one by one, holding each one's hand in his for a long time. And now he gave his instruction, *macht a rikkud'l*: "Make a little chassidic dance — to the words, *b'cha bat'chu avoseynu* (In You our fathers trusted; they trusted, and You rescued them)" (*T'hillim*/Psalms 22:5). His wishes were obeyed: they joined hands, put hands on shoulders, and lifted their feet in rhythm as they sang the holy words to the melody they knew so well — the melody which he himself had composed.

How many times they had sung it in the past, when the lovely, inspired *niggun* could bring its cheer to their hearts. Now they glanced at him as they danced by, joined in their circle, and they saw how extinguished his eyes were, the light gone out of them; how sallow his complexion; how the tears kept falling and falling without a stop. . . .

And yet they had to dance. The Rav had ordered them. . . . Where are the words to describe the infinite tragedy in that scene? . . . the rhythmic motions of life and . . . death . . . the last chassidic dance that he would see on this earth?

It was clear that the end was approaching. Into the great *shul*, the Hall of Prayer, the young scholars came streaming now to say *t'hillim*, to implore Heaven's mercy for him. In the corridors the voice of a *talmid* could be heard rousing everyone with two simple words that he chanted over and over to a soft haunting melody: *ra-cha-mim g'do-lim*: "Great compassion, great compassion!"

The *talmidim* were woken from sleep — the great body of students who had gone to bed without any thought of a possible catastrophe looming: The verdict of the doctors had been so reassuring. . . . Now the sounds in the air hurtled them from their beds and sent them rushing through the corridors, unable yet to realize just how drastically fateful the present moments were.

In their bewildered disturbance they almost fell over one another. "What happened?" they wanted to know. "What's come up all of a sudden?" And in the great *shul* there was only stormy agitation: a heartrending tempest of attempts to tear through the heavens and bring down pure Divine mercy. Here and there young persons were beating their heads against the wall. There were outcries of *oy na lanu ki chatanu*, "Woe to us that we have sinned!" (*Eycha*/Lamentations 5:16). "It's all, all on account of our sins!"

One individual after another began crying out a donation of years, to be deducted from his allotted lifespan and given to the Rav, so that he could go on living. "I give five years," one voice called out; "I give ten," exclaimed another; and so on. And a short while later, one mighty declamation sounded and echoed in that great Hall of Prayer: "We give away all our remaining years to the Rav!"

An atmosphere of worldwide tragedy for the Jewish people filled the great hall. A sense of terrible destruction and devastation saturated the air. And the frightful wailing and lamentation reached his ears. . . .

Clearly and distinctly he pronounced two words: *nor b^e^simcha* ("Only with gladness!"); then he snapped his fingers — and expired. He passed over and away and out of his body. And he was gone from us.

****

With a wild scream a *talmid* came running into the great Hall of Prayer: *der heyligger rebbe iz niftar gevorn,* he cried out: "The holy Rebbe has died!" And the *talmidim* fell to the ground. Some tore their hair in grief. "Where were we?" they wailed. "How could we let this happen? Why didn't we know? Why didn't we do anything to stop it? Why? . . . Why did it happen?"

They seemed to be bathing in an ocean of tears — tears mingled with heart's blood. "Woe is us; *gevald!* What's happened to us? In whose care have you gone and left us? Why? . . . Why? . . . "

They remained lying on the ground, exhausted, all consciousness gone, till the fountain of tears ran dry and they could not weep any more. Only a quiet pain and prostration were left: an experience of abysmal tragedy that found expression in utter silence, amid a sense of pure, final helplessness.

Only time could bring us back to full reality, to face our situation and see what had to be done and what could be done.

45

Stunned reactions, initial responses

Whether we wanted to or not, at the yeshiva we had to learn to accept it: The great, holy light in our lives had gone out. The radiant, glorious sun that brought us guidance and hope, had suddenly grown completely dark.

We recalled something that we knew he had said in his very first rabbinic sermon, when he came to accept the post of spiritual leader in Glina — when he was a very young man starting out on his career: "In the Torah is my life, and with the Torah I will die." In every possible way, in every meaning of the term, he lived in the Torah; but more important: he lived for the Torah. And he died for the Torah: The first, immediate result of his departure from this life was that the yeshiva received the premium of thirty thousand dollars from his life-insurance policy, and it was able to pay off a heavy, pressing debt which hung over the yeshiva's neck like a millstone. Had the debt not been cleared, the building would have been put up for sale at public auction, and would have passed quite certainly into Polish hands. Thus it can be said that he offered up his hallowed body as a sacrifice on the altar of the Torah, for the sake of the Jewish people.

****

When the news reached the city of Lublin, it struck the population like a thunderbolt. No one was prepared to believe it. He was such a young man, barely forty-six years old . . . and already gone from the world? No one outside the walls of the yeshiva had had the slightest hint of his illness. As far as the rest of the world knew, he had been perfectly healthy. And suddenly such a bitter, devastating tragedy was hurled into the knowledge of the city.

Here is one indication of how utterly and absolutely the shocking news caught everyone by surprise: On the front page of the local newspaper of Agudas Yisra'el, *Dos Yiddishe Togblatt*, large announcements of his death appeared within heavy black borders — set hastily in type and inserted in time to make the morning edition. In that same edition, however, on an inside page a news item appeared: that in the following week, the Rav was to leave Lublin to assume the rabbinic position in Lodz!

This is proof indeed that no one in his own city, beyond his close associates, had any inkling of the illness and of how deadly serious it was. When the newspaper staff learned of the great tragedy, there was barely enough time to set the obituary announcements for the front page. No one had a chance to deal with the news item on the inside page, that had been set and put into position earlier — although obviously it had no meaning now.

Evidently it was the will of Divine providence to keep everything hidden from public knowledge till after the bitter end — for even as his condition was getting worse, the medical doctors kept giving their firm assurance that he would recover.

****

His death came toward morning, at half past three, on Friday the seventh of Cheshvan, 5694 (October 27, 1933): exactly ten years after he had taken his first steps into the city of Lublin. And as people began remembering and talking, there were some who told a strange tale indeed:

When Rav Meir lived in Tarnopol, he became deathly ill with a severe case of typhus, and the medical doctors held out no hope for him. Then some of his good friends announced to Heaven "donations" of years from their allotted lifespans, to be added on to his allotted years on earth.

According to those who remembered, the sum total of time "donated" for him came to eighteen years, and on the seventh of Cheshvan, 5694, the eighteen years ended exactly.

Others told another tale, out of Jewish folklore: For the past two hundred years, they said, no Rabbi of Lublin ever succeeded in leaving the city to take over the rabbinate in another community, except for those who set sail for the Holy Land. Thus, they noted, Rav Simcha Bunem Rapaport served as Rabbi in Lublin, and then accepted the rabbinic post in Lemberg; and when he set off traveling from Lublin to Lemberg, his life ended in mid-journey, at Shrebreshin — and so he was not even privileged to set eyes on Lemberg. . . .

[Actually, this was somewhat inaccurate. Rav Simcha *ha-kohen*, not Bunem, Rapaport, who lived around the start of the eighteenth century, served as Rabbi in Lublin, and then in Hurodna. From Hurodna he planned to transfer to Lemberg, but died on the way, when he stopped at Shrebreshin.]

****

The administration of the yeshiva proceeded to inform the entire world of the dire, drastic misfortune. The first step the staff took was to telephone to the newspapers to tell them that Rav Meir Shapiro, the Rabbi of Lublin, was no longer among the living. The typical response they received was something like this:

"Who? — the Rabbi of Lublin? — the one who was always so lively and full of vitality and youthful energy? Dead? *Impossible!* This must be a piece of imagination from some irresponsible person."

No one was ready to believe it.

Later that morning, the Polish national radio broadcast the tragic information; and thus the whole Jewish people in Poland learned of it. After that the telephone in the yeshiva office was not given a moment's rest. From all over Poland the calls came, and then from other countries. From as far away as Vienna and Frankfort people wanted to know: *Was it true?* Was he actually taken so young, so suddenly, from the people he led with so much valor and courage?

When the mournful report was confirmed, invariably there was an outcry of despair at the other end, and in the exhalation of breath that followed, one word could be heard: *ba'avonoseynu* — "for our sins."

All over Poland, the newspapers put out special editions with lengthy, detailed biographies of him, describing his many achievements. In Lublin, placards of mourning appeared all over, mounted on the walls of buildings. One heading read, "A diadem has been removed from everyone's head." Other placards designated him as "the heart of the nation"; "the Divine image"; "the noble Ruler of Jewry"; "the scholar of the world, exemplar of the generation, its pilot at the helm, the faithful servant, devoted to his flock." And one placard stated grimly, "We stand facing the fearful, awesome shadow of death. Banished is the glory from Jewry."

Yet it was left perhaps to the Polish press to describe him briefly and succinctly as the Poles in the country saw him. There he was called simply "the Jewish king."

****

By the formal decision of great men of Torah and *chassidus*, the funeral was not held that day, but was postponed to Sunday, to give a great multitude the opportunity to come and patrticipate. All agreed that beyond any doubt, the deceased deserved a final honor of magnitude.

While others dealt with arrangements about the burial, we went on with our usual preparations for Shabbos. Yet how tragically out of the ordinary this Shabbos would be for us — with him so painfully missing.

46

Shabbos without him

The very thought of it brought a frightful pall, such a terrible gloom to our hearts. The atmosphere of the Friday night *tish*, the atmosphere in the yeshiva dining room when he was there with us for the first of the three holy Shabbos meals, had always been so heavenly. There had always been a sense of elation and bliss that lifted us above and out of the ordinary, worrying world around us. And his was the dynamic energy that was responsible for it. . . . How lively and joyful that atmosphere of the *tish* had been — the sense of being at the Shabbos meal table with him.

Under his direction, with his participation, the air had filled and reverberated with chassidic melodies, which as a rule he had composed, that we sang with the words of the *z'miros.* In between there had always been his flow of thought: brilliant, sparkling ideas drawn from the Torah portion of the week or linked with it. The atmosphere was not of this world, and while it lasted it could lift us out of our mundane life to experience some tinge of Heaven on earth.

And now he was gone. This Shabbos, the second in the month of Cheshvan, 5694, he would not be there. He *could* not be there. . . . The very thought was too much for us to bear. The *talmidim* thrust it resolutely aside. . . .

What else could we do? The sun moved inevitably toward its setting to let evening approach. We had to change into our Shabbos clothing and gather in our place of prayer, just as usual, just as if nothing catastrophic had happened. In the approaching, arriving holiness of the Shabbos, all our grief had to be checked and restrained, to be kept under powerful control.

There was a singular courage in the behavior of his widow, the *rabbaniss.* Without any wavering or weeping, she took off her garments of mourning and put on her Shabbos clothes, and went with firm determination to light the Shabbos candles — in the room where the body lay — the body of her illustrious, world-renowned husband, that remained there now so still, wrapped in black cloth.

When the lighting was done and the small flames burned soft and clear, she went to stand by her husband's body, and she said: "*Heyligger rebbe,* I always hoped that when we would have to pass over to the next world, I would leave this world before you: for what, then, was my whole life ever worth measured against a single day of your life? Now, however, it happened otherwise. This is how Divine providence wanted it. I beg you, then, holy Rebbe: make every effort that the kingdom of Torah which you created should have a sustained, continued existence and should not be wrecked, Heaven forbid. That will then be my only consolation. . . ."

****

The *mashgi-ach* ("spiritual supervisor") gave a formal decision that under the law, the *talmidim* had the status of an *'onén*, a person in grief over the death of someone closely related, before the burial. This meant that we could not follow our usual practice and have one of us go up before the holy Ark and serve as the *ba'al t^efilla*, to lead us in the prayers. One of the men who came to join us was chosen instead.

After the evening prayers that welcomed in the holy day of rest, all the *talmidim* filed past the body, and each said in turn, *Gut Shabbos, Rebbe!* Would the greatest master of threnody be able to portray that short poignant scene for later generations?

At the tables, everything was set as always. In the kitchen, as always, the *rabbaniss* stood supervising the distribution of the portions — just as she had done every Friday night since the yeshiva was opened — just as if no calamity had occurred only hours earlier.

We sang *z^emiros* too, as the time came for them between courses; but try as we would, they could only sound pathetic. The mouth sang, and the heart wept. Every note of music was dredged through an ocean of tears that kept coming and falling. It needed only one glance toward the place from which the luminous visage of our great Rebbe had always radiated his cheerful optimism — the seat that was now covered with boards to mark his irreparable absence — and the tears came again.

We wanted to forget ourselves. After all, it was Shabbos now. We wanted to enter its holy atmosphere that would lift us out of the weekday world. Yet how to forget, for even a moment?

Some of the young *talmidim* got to talking among themselves: The Rebbe had not wanted to leave Lublin for Lodz. He wanted to stay and go down in history as the further (and last) Maharam of Lublin. And his wish had been granted . . . .

****

In all the Houses of Study and Prayer, it was proclaimed that on Saturday night, from the time that Shabbos ended, one and all could go and say *Farewell* to the great Rav, to take leave of him for the last time. And everyone was asked to sign a promise for a set sum of money, as a donation to the inheritance that he would leave posthumously (as it were) to the yeshiva.

Among themselves, the students divided up into groups that would keep the vigil: Every hour another group would take its turn to stay by the revered and to study chapters of the Mishna (*mishnayos*) for the sake of his soul.

That Shabbos, of the Torah portion of *lech l'cha*, drew to an end. The great, tall candles that had burned down steadily for over twenty-four hours began to waver and flicker. Stars appeared in the sky, and we held the evening prayer of *ma'ariv*. . . . And then the dam broke: All the grief and pain, kept under iron control through the whole of Shabbos, came pouring out now all at once. The yeshiva became covered again in its grey shroud of mourning, amid the incessant sounds of dolor and lament.

Inhabitants of Lublin began arriving with signed promissory notes in their hands. Small tables had been set out in the corridors, and on these the notes were left, as the people moved on to the chamber where the body lay. There the members of *B'rit haCha-yal* stood on guard to maintain order. It was their way of showing their gratitude, while paying their last respects, because this great religious leader had so genially included them in the happy, festive dancing with the Torah scrolls in the season of Simchas Torah, only two weeks before. It was his last season of such festive celebration on earth, and he had let them share it, although they were only a battalion of non-religious army veterans that belonged to the militant Revisionists in the Zionist camp.

With their military discipline they kept iron-firm order as thousands came to file through the chamber in a last somber act of reverence to all that the Rav had been, to all that he had done.

Late in the the night, *treyggers* arrived — ordinary observant Jews who earned their living as porters, carrying heavy loads; and with them came awe-stricken coach drivers, observant Jews who subsisted by driving their horse-drawn vehicles as needed. They came to ask a posthumous forgiveness of the Rav, if perhaps they had ever done anything in his lifetime to hurt him or injure his prestige in any way.

One of them said: "I'm a father of five children; but if I were told that I should go from this world in place of the Rav, so that he could go on living, I would do it directly. . . . Do you know what a tzaddik he was? It was once late in the afternoon before a *yom tov* was about to start, and the funeral of an important worthy man had to be held. We rode out with the coffin and the mourners to the cemetery; the Rav was among the people who came. The burial was duly done; but the people who had hired us stayed on at the fresh grave. I guess they had a lot more prayers to say, or something. We drivers kept waiting, so that we could take them back and get paid; but it kept getting later and later. There wasn't too much time left till the holy festival would start and we would be forbidden to drive. . . . So the Rav says to us, 'Ride home. Don't worry about us. We'll find a way to get back. And after *yom tov* come to see me. I'll pay all of you whatever you lose by leaving now.' We came to him, and he paid us in full what we asked for."

****

All was in mourning. Everyone, everything, everywhere, wept. The whole city was in lament: old and young, of whatever age; all the political parties, whatever their shade or hue in the Jewish spectrum — every heart felt broken by the stark calamity; and all came through the flowing hours of darkness to pay their last respects and take their final leave.

In the very late hours of the night, people began arriving at last from beyond the city limits: distinguished masters of Torah and piety, and various delegations sent by other communities. Everyone hastened directly to the chamber in the yeshiva, to cast a glance at the body draped in black, in which his great soul had lived; and then each one opened a small volume to study briefly a paragraph of the Mishna, intending every word and thought of the sacred text for the good of that great immortal soul — while tears wet the pages.

From every corner of Poland they came. Everywhere Jewish hearts had felt a tremor of anguish when the black news of his death came; and everywhere people felt it a holy duty to come and pay their last respects.

Once more masses of Jews assembled in Lublin — many tens of thousands — just as the great throngs had gathered for the ground-breaking ceremony, and again for the opening of Yeshivas Chachmey Lublin. Only, now there was no whisper of cheer, no trace of elation. Then they had come to a joyous celebration. Now they came to eulogy and lament.

In the long, great corridors of the yeshiva, eminent men of learning wandered and moved about, looking shaken and brokenhearted, wringing their hands: "*Gevald!* Woe is us: How could it happen? How was it ever allowed to happen, without anyone alarming the whole world?"

****

Right then and there, an assembly was convened, with the participation of all the attendant rabbinic personages and the presidents, *parnassim* and general heads of the Jewish communities in the whole of Poland. At the helm of the assembly stood the man who had once agreed to serve as president of the yeshiva's Administrative Council: Reb Elya Mazur, president of the Warsaw community. It was he who opened the assembly.

He began to speak, but tears came to choke him, till he was unable to continue clearly, without choppy pauses that he had to overcome. "We cannot say," he exclaimed, "*Our hands have not shed this blood* (*D'varim*/ Deuteronomy 21:7). We are guilty! So now we must keep watch over this yeshiva, to make sure it does not break down, Heaven forbid; to make sure this hallowed building never falls into non-Jewish hands — never this building that is so full of Torah study and holy prayer. . . . Dear brethren, by freeing the yeshiva from its burden of debts and ongoing expenses, let us try to atone and find forgiveness for the enormous crime we committed against the Rav and his sacred yeshiva. . . . "

A representative of the *talmidim* went to the rostrum and addressed the assembly in the name of us all. Every word he spoke was so imbued with a bitter, frightful despair that it struck home with the piercing stab of a sword: "For the third day now, in that other chamber our great father lies unmoving, and we have no merit left to see him any more, because he lies covered by black cloth. . . . Torn is the heart, dried out is the well of tears; and through the depths of our pain-racked, woebegone heart a mighty outcry erupts from the words of the Sages that we study: 'Rabbi Meir went to his eternal rest . . . What will become of the Torah?' (*bavli*, Nazir 50a). Who will educate us? Who will be concerned for us?

"We are certain that his holy spirit will continue to abide in this House. But we beg of you: Provide, however, the material needs of the yeshiva! If I may paraphrase from the words of our Sages (Mishna, Yoma 1:5): We impose an oath upon you by the soul of the one who made his name abide in this House, that you are not to alter anything out of all that we have said to you."

Afterward the well-known Rabbi of Kalisch spoke, as an old disciple of the Rav who had studied with him in Glina, where Rav Meir had held his first rabbinic post. Said he: "For twenty-two years the Rav was as a father to me. When I was twelve years old he found me in Glina, a complete orphan without father or mother. He took me into his home and brought me up, into the world of Torah and good deeds. And now he is no longer among us. . . . "

At the close of the assembly, all those with rabbinic authority issued a decree: No one from outside the city had the right to leave Lublin until he obligated himself to give a certain specified sum as a donation to the yeshiva. . . . In the shortest possible time, placards to that effect appeared in the city, headed by a phrase from the Book of *Daniyyel*: "This statement is by the decree of the guardian angels" (Daniel 4:14).

47

The burial

The time approached for the *tahara*, the solemn ritual cleansing of the body, so that it might be brought to burial without any besmirchment — compatible to the return of the spirit to the place it earned in the world of eternity. And now we simply felt as if we were living through a dark nightmare that pressed down on everyone's heart.

It was decided that after the ritual cleansing, the body would be immersed in the *mikveh* of the yeshiva, as a final act of ritual purification before burial. Before that, all the *talmidim* would immerse themselves, to become spiritually fit to participate in the interment. For a formal decision by the *beyss din* decreed that only they might take part in carrying the bier.

While the *tahara* was under way, fearful outcries could be heard from outside the walls; and among them the words of Rabbi Akiva (the holy Sage) came through clearly: "Fortunate are you, O Jewry: Before whom do you become purified, and who is it that purifies you? — your Father in Heaven" (Mishna, Yoma, end).

It was time now to dress the body in its shrouds: Only devout learned *rabbonim* and *talmidim* were permitted to perform the duty. Then *hakafos* took place in the great Hall of Study and Prayer, where the Rav had always given his brilliant *shi'urim* to the young scholars. The *hakafos* were solemn circular processions around the bier, done now in accord with venerated, time-honored instructions from the mystic world of *kabbala*, by the *talmidim* under the direction of the *mashgi-ach*.

With the Hall filled to capacity, the *hespédim* began — the stirring, heartrending eulogies that would move the immense audience to the heights of emotion. The first to speak was one of the world's truly great Talmud scholars: Rav Menachem Zemba.

He began with a citation from the Book of *D'varim*: "What man is there who has built a new house and has not dedicated it? Let him go and return to his home" (Deuteronomy 20:5). However, the verb *channéch* (dedicate) also means "educate, guide, direct into life." So Rav Menachem Zemba continued: "The Rav was not yet given the grace and merit to nurture and structure the education in the yeshiva, to guide it, shape it and form it into the dynamic, living mold that he wanted — and the imperious decree came from on high: *Let him go and return to his home!* Let him return his holy spirit to the Divine throne of glory from where it came. . . .

"Our Sages tell us," Rav Zemba continued: "When one member of a group dies, let the whole group be worried and concerned" (*bavli*, Shabbas 106a; Rashi explains: that death might perhaps strike further among them). "We need a whole group to be concerned for the yeshiva, to care and provide for it as he always did, all by himself. . . .

"Our Sages teach: When Rav Abbahu's spirit found its eternal rest, the walls in Caesaria shed water — they wept for grief (*yerushalmi*, Avoda Zara 3:1; 42c). So here," declared Rav Menachem Zemba, "do the very walls of the yeshiva shed oceans of tears in grief at the enormous loss that it has suffered. The pain is so great, because only six weeks ago the holy Chafetz Cha-yim was taken from us, and here the Jewish people brings to its Maker a new, further sacrificial offering.

"Divine Master of the world: In our preliminary prayers of the morning there is a paragraph from the Talmud (*bavli*, Yoma 33a), in which Abbaye lists the things that were done daily in the *beyss ha-mikdash* when the holy Temple stood. At the end Abbaye infers from a word in the Torah that with the second *olah* (burnt-offering) of the day, all the sacrifices and offerings of the day would be over and done with. Merciful Father in Heaven, we beg You: With these two great sacrificial offerings let us have done all that You require of us. No more!"

Certainly the most moving and unforgettable part of the funeral was the moment when the *talmidim* took their oath at the coffin of their great Rebbe: One of them, chosen as spokesman, stepped forward and spoke the words that left everyone's heart sobbing: "Into whose care have you abandoned this little flock? Holy Rebbe, with whom have you left us? We, your *talmidim*, were always with you like two bodies with a single soul. . . . Brothers, companions, let us cling together closer, and standing now before the sacred bier of our holy Rebbe, let us take a fervent oath that we will never abandon and reject the walls of the yeshiva. And you, holy Rebbe: do not forget us and lose sight of your loyal, devoted pupils. Remain our eternal head of the yeshiva, ever our guiding leader. Infuse into us the influence of your holy spirit. . . ."

****

The funeral cortège got under way. In the city, all traffic was halted, as the specter of death haunted the whole of Lublin. All the stores and shops were shut, as a mark of honor and mourning for him. Such were the throngs that the streets seemed blackened with humanity — an assembled mass estimated at seventy thousand.

At the government bureau of education, the Supervisor of Schools issued a formal order that all school children, non-Jewish as well as Jewish, were to take part in the funeral.

Close to the coffin, order was maintained by a first line of members of the religious organizations. Backing them was a second line, composed of members of the *B^erit haCha-yal.* [Still grateful for the genial friendship he had shown their battalion by including them in the happy dancing of his last Simchas Torah season, these war veterans of the Revisionist camp insisted on trying to give him something back, to the very end.] And behind them, a full battalion of Polish police was out in force.

Joined in the procession were official representatives of the Polish government, specifically delegated to attend: representatives of the Ministry of the Interior, the War Ministry, and the Foreign Ministry. Then there were the *Voivode* — the governor of the province; the city mayor; members of the Polish military élite, and so on.

Continually, words of *hesped* could be heard, as great men of Torah and eminent personages spoke to eulogize him and lament his tragic death. All along the way, as the procession moved slowly through the packed streets of Lublin, pitiful outbursts of wailing could be heard — spasmodic eruptions of sobbing and weeping — from all the houses and balconies. The atmosphere was frightful. . . .

[The coffin was carried into every House of Study and every House of Prayer; in every *shul* and *beyss medrash*, words of eulogy and lament were spoken. Time seemed to stand still, and no one paid attention to the passing of the hours. . . . When thought had to be given to the interment at last, the light of day had dimmed with the onset of evening, and great tapers and torches had to be lit.]

The final moment drew close, when the body would have to be lowered into the ground. One last glance could yet be caught of the luminous, radiant face that the holy personage had shown the world while he lived. Although it was three days since his mortal life had ended, the visage still seemed to glow with the light of the sun.

One more time the *talmidim* and disciples looked upon their beloved Rebbe: one more, final time on their fatherly educator and life guide. Then the closing of the grave would remove him from the waking sight of human beings forever. The very acme, the ultimate high point of the woeful tragedy could now be felt. Into the open ground were thrown thousands of notes imploring Heaven's help through his intercession, together with all the "promissory notes" that people had written, obligating themselves to contribute money to the yeshiva.

Over the coffin heavy clods of earth began to land now, as the *talmidim* performed on themselves the ritual of ***k^eri'a***, making a tear in a garment as a mark of grief in mourning. And then, like an elegy in a darkening night, the mourner's prayer of ***kaddish*** resounded from the hundreds of students: *Yisgadal v^eyiskadash sh^emey rabba* . . . (Greatened and hallowed be His majestic name . . .).

In the old, historic cemetery of Lublin, a new historic tombstone was added, to mark the grave of "the second Maharam of Lublin." Then a small structure, a mausoleum, an *ohel*, was erected at the burial place of this legendary, epoch-making master of Torah and piety.

Here many, many would come in the years that followed, from the four corners of the earth, to pour out their tears at his holy grave and to leave written notes with their impassioned pleas for Heaven's rescuing help. Here, they felt certain, was one of the most suitable focal points in the world to invoke Heaven's mercy: at the grave of a man with a boundless compassion and love for his people, who dedicated his whole life for Jewry. . . . For even at the end, when he sensed that he would have to leave the world, he managed to arrange an element of heroism in his death, that would save the yeshiva from imminent collapse and disappearance.

Directly after his departure from this earth, his image began to grow in the consciousness of his people. Remembered facts and reported incidents began to weave (almost of themselves) into colorful legends about him. And thus, after his death, Rav Meir Shapiro of blessed memory became at last, far more than ever in his lifetime, a name laden with great import.

In this sense, one teaching of the Sages came literally true for him: Greater are ***tzaddikim*** after their death than they were in their lifetime (***bavli***, Chullin 7b).

48

To preserve the spiritual estate

Ineluctably, inevitably, the mourning spread to the entire Jewish world. It was apparently the first time in our era that the death of one human being evoked such a sincere widespread response. To the student body came hundreds of messages by telegraph and by mail, offering heartfelt condolence and comfort. The greatest names in the Jewish firmament wrote to express their sympathy and their blessings and hopes for the yeshiva's future — among them the current Rebbe of Lubavitch, the renowned Rav Cha-yim Ozer Grodzinski of Vilna, the revered Rebbe of Boyan, and the venerated Rebbe of Sadiggerr.

More important, perhaps, were the plans for practical help that the great personages of Torah and piety in Poland promulgated for the material existence of the yeshiva. Taking concerted action, they proclaimed a campaign of *kofer nefesh* ("atonement for the soul"), to last for an entire year from the day that his life ended. During that year, each and every member of Polish Jewry would be called upon to "redeem" himself from whatever might be his share of guilt in the early demise of the great Rav.

No one in the Jewish community of Poland, declared the proclamation, had the right to evade this obligation and fail to "redeem" himself by donating a set amount. [By now it was widespread, common knowledge that the Rav had insured his life for thirty thousand dollars, naming the yeshiva as beneficiary, shortly before Heaven ended that life; and in the ears of those who had heard him, there still echoed the words he cited somberly from *Tikkuney Zohar*, words that all said in private prayer before *Kol Nidrey*: "There is one who pays off his debt with his money, and one who pays off with his body."]

Now, the proclamation demanded, when the great Rav (of blessed memory) had acted so clearly with his own physical body to help the yeshiva free itself from debt, let the Jewish community acknowledge that it failed to help him suitably in his sacred labor, and let each and every one act to help the yeshiva with his money, to acquit himself of whatever share of blame for the tragedy might be his. . . .

The plan required dynamic action: People would have to go to all the individual communities in Poland, large and small; to speak at assemblies and gatherings; and literally to collect the funds, in the manner of tax collectors, perhaps.

This program of action, the older ones among the young Talmudists undertook, with the help of the rabbis and communal workers in every city, town and townlet. And the result was a great stir of interest and spiritual arousal everywhere — not only in Poland but among the Jewish people the world over.

The most indigent, impoverished soul pinched off what he could from the money he had for food, so that he could bring it willingly to the delegation from the yeshiva that came visiting through the cities and the towns.

For their part, the older adolescents and young adults among the *talmidim* who went traveling around for the yeshiva proved unexpectedly equal to the task. They knew it was not enough to come pouncing at people with outstretched palms. They had to give warm, inspiring, stirring talks to assembled audiences; and when they did, it became evident how much their great educator had not only taught them but — more important — had influenced and formed them.

They gave *hespédim*. They eulogized their great, immortal mentor, describing how he had built the yeshiva and worked for it as his great dream and hope for Jewry. And in their talk, all his eloquence, all his power to hold an audience spellbound, came through. He had indeed brought them up, not only as a teacher but as a role model.

Now they proved that they were true and worthy heirs of what he left them to inherit. With their young, dynamic energy, they bent with a will to the colossal task of the *kofer nefesh* campaign. And how they worked — and succeeded — would have brought joy to his heart.

Eagerly, readily, they invested long weeks of sincere, unwearying, devoted labor to their mission, with never a thought about any strain or fatigue that they might feel. They simply kept going from one town to the next, from one community to the next.

Beyond expectations, their dedicated labor brought results. They succeeded in amassing a most considerable amount of money; enough to pay off a large part of the debt burden that still rested on the yeshiva's shoulders.

In consequence, as the world of Torah learning learned with relief,

Yeshivas Chachmey Lublin would be able to continue functioning in full. For a while now, there would be no need to worry about finances for the institution — but only for a while. Unless a way could be found to bring in continuing further support, all too soon the yeshiva would be back in the same desperate plight of pressing debts.

Something that the Rav had once written came back to the people at the yeshiva: It was his goal, his hope and wish, that out of his focused, ongoing relationship with his *talmidim*, one whole, harmonious family structure might form. In keeping with this thought, a new entity was brought into being: an alumni association.

It was quite certainly Rav Meir himself who had begun referring to Yeshivas Chachmey Lublin, in writing of it, by an abbreviation formed from the first Hebrew letters: *yod, chess, la-med.* This gave him *ya-chél*, a Hebrew word that could recall a phrase from the Book of *T'hillim*: *yachél yisra'el el haShem* (Let Yisra'el hope to the Lord: Psalms 130:7). The new organization was named now *achaï*, a Hebrew word meaning "my brothers," which was also an abbreviation from the letters *alef, chess, yod* — that would stand for *Agudas Chanichey Yachél*, "the Association of Alumni of Yeshivas Chachmey Lublin."

The first essential purpose of this new body was to form a strong organized force out of all who had studied and learned their Torah under this great, immortal *rebbe* — all who had been his pupils and become his disciples, to live by his teachings and his guidance. By linking firmly together, they could seek and find ways to realize, through the yeshiva, his timeless ideals.

In a sense, this new organization, *Achaï*, would provide a way to go forward with the impassioned, fiery oath and commitment that the *talmidim* had sworn at his open grave: never to leave the yeshiva behind them, abandoned and forgotten. Through *Achaï*, the alumni could stand ready to answer its every call for help. When and as they were needed, they would be prepared to gather their strength and make every effort to help the yeshiva continue its physical existence.

They knew how strong had been the hope of their unforgettable *rebbe* that as a result of his work with his *talmidim*, one harmonious family would coalesce in concentration around the yeshiva. Now the adults who had been his *talmidim* realized that when the head of a family like this is wrenched away by the merciless hand of death, the members of the family must indeed unite well and hold together strongly, so that they can assemble as their timeless legacy all the rays of spiritual light which they had received from him while he lived and taught. Having absorbed all that he had given them in his lifetime, they could then go on to serve as a mighty reflector, to spread their spiritual inheritance beyond the horizon of the yeshiva.

Above all, the alumni were determined that among themselves there would always live the brotherhood, the mutual loyalty and devotion that had bound them together. They were determined that if it had indeed been his dream for one family to emerge from the yeshiva, welded together for strength in unity, every one would hold every other dear in his thoughts, ready to offer help that might be needed among themselves, as much as any and every one could manage to give.

Thus *Achaï* came into being, its members ready to support one another and to ga p-1 ther material support for the yeshiva.

There was yet one more obligation that they took upon themselves: to tell the *talmidim* who would enter later, after them, just who it was that had conceived and created Yeshivas Chachmey Lublin. It would be for them to tell of the great, holy man who had lived among them; to describe how he had spent his life, and finally given it, for the sake of the Torah. They would show how he had not hesitated to offer himself up as a sacrifice on the altar of Torah study.

By such means, all the later budding, developing Talmud scholars would know — would absorb into their hearts, their minds, their bones — what enormous efforts had been needed to build the yeshiva. And thus they would understand how much they should try to give back, in devotion to their study in the learning years, and in loyalty to the yeshiva afterward.

[To move forward in time through the next few years, the fact stands on record that, evidently with the strong support of *Achaï*, the yeshiva was able to function at full strengh through the years that followed, as if there were no mounting, ever-increasing threats to Polish Jewry from the shrill ranting of Hitler that was broadcast over the air waves; as if there was no sense of unease, steadily growing stronger, from the animal actions of the Nazi forces in neighboring territories. The number of students, who could receive there not only their prime education but full room and board as well, indeed grew to about three hundred.

[At the start of the summer of 5696 (1936), with the support of a few benefactors, work was started on the interior of the sixth floor, which had been left untouched all the years for lack of funds. On completion, it would enable the yeshiva to accommodate still more students. For the desire of capable, gifted young Talmud learners all over Poland to be admitted had grown enormously with the years. The yeshiva was simply flooded with hundreds of applications. It was pathetic to have to respond negatively for lack of space and funds. Now the administration looked forward in hope to an improved situation.

[The burden of debt under which the yeshiva had to function was eased considerably. Payments at the national bank were put on a regular basis, to be spread over a number of years.

[In Tévés 5697 (December 1936 or January 1937) a "Torah Assembly" was held at the yeshiva, attended by great learned scholars and worthy men of eminence; and it was decided to organize a great convention at the yeshiva on the twenty-eighth of Sivan, 5698 (June 27, 1938). By the Assembly's proclamation, that day was to be marked by a great "Torah celebration" both at the yeshiva and by religious Jewry worldwide. For on that day, the learners of the *daf ha-yomi* all over the world were due to complete their study of the entire Babylonian Talmud for the second time.

[Furthermore, there was the Torah scroll of *k^{e}lal yisra'el* (Jewry in its entirety), which Rav Meir had gotten under way in his lifetime — described above, in chapter 34. The inspired idea of Rav Meir had been for every sacred letter and word in it to be paid for by some individual among the Jewish people. Thus a large part of the population would gain merit in Heaven, and the yeshiva (where the *séfer torah* was to be kept after it was completed) would gain sorely needed income.

[In Rav Meir's lifetime, the project was launched with immense enthusiasm and great initial success; but the scroll was not completed. In the course of the years, interest waned, and progress slowed to a crawl. Now, finally, it was moving toward completion; and on this target date, the twenty-eighth of Sivan, it was planned to finish the writing at last, and to bring the *séfer torah* into the yeshiva's holy Ark with great ceremony.

[Nor was that all. The day would mark the eighth anniversary of the yeshiva's illustrious opening. By then the construction work on the sixth floor was expected to be done, to make the Torah edifice truly complete; and so a new *chanukas ha-ba-yiss* (Dedication of the House) would be held.

[Evidently, then, with the full, active support of *Achaï*, the alumni association, the yeshiva was able to remain viable and to flourish, making plans for the future even in the year 5697 (1937). This could only indicate how well the Rav had molded his disciples in his image, how deeply he had inspired them with his own uncompromising, total dedication to Torah study.

[Let us return, however, to the time that followed the agonizing impact of Rav Meir's departure from the world.]

****

Clearly, the alumni association called *Achaï* set itself a demanding, formidable program when it was forged into being in the wake of Rav Meir's tragic death. From then till now, as I write these words, not too much time has elapsed; and yet, even in this relatively short time, there have been achievements to its credit that could be recorded with pride.

Especially noteworthy is the institution of the "Committee of Five" that the association created: Every month, five members of *Achaï* are designated to spend time at the yeshiva for one purpose: to focus their attention on young new students and give them private tutoring as necessary, so that their way of study, their grasp and absorption of Talmud text, can rise to a satisfactory level.

This activity has generated a spirit of lively interest among the young learners. For through the alumni what they could experience was just the kind of stimulating influence that the great, unforgettable Rav used to have on his *talmidim* in his lifetime.

At the same time, *Achaï* has paid close attention to the financial situation; and as necessary, various actions have been taken and campaigns carried through on behalf of the yeshiva. In addition, as a kind of by-product perhaps, a "mutual aid society" was formed under the name of *va'ad ezra* (Help Committee), to come to the rescue of individual members if and when they have needed help.

At the time of this writing, *Achaï* is considering and studying ways of developing and expanding its areas of contribution to the welfare of the yeshiva. There is every hope that it will succeed in finding its way to new, splendid achievements on an ever-widening scale.

****

Primarily, necessarily, the alumni association focused first and foremost on the finances to ensure the yeshiva's continued existence. Yet their unforgettable Rav had also been their educator, the life-spirit of the yeshiva's educational program. It was he who had worked in his inimitable way to move the yeshiva toward the level of a true world center of Torah study. And in this all-important role, he was also gone forever. In this area too, as the heirs to his spiritual estate, his grown pupils and disciples had to take action.

As a first step, a "spiritual governing board" was formed, called in Hebrew the *Shilton Ruchani.* The members who would serve on it were the greatest Talmudic scholars in Poland; it would be their task to conceive and direct the spiritual image and configuration of the yeshiva. To function at its head, the great Rav Moshe Friedman, the Rebbe of Boyan who lived in Cracow, was chosen.

Each and every member of the board agreed to come to the yeshiva for four weeks in the year and stay there. Thus, throughout the year, some member of the *Shilton Ruchani* would always be present as a figure of authority and inspiration [and perhaps also as a kind of "scholar in residence"], in addition to the regular *roshey yeshiva* (instructors) and *mashgichim* ("spiritual supervisors"), who were themselves among the foremost Talmud scholars of our time.

****

Exactly four months after his life ended, the date on the Jewish calendar was 7 Adar, 5694 (February 22, 1934). In his lifetime, taking into account that it was his birthday (as well as the birthday and *yortzaït* of *Moshe rabbénu*), the holy Rav Meir had made it a special holiday of the yeshiva. Under his direction, it became the practice for the *talmidim* to study through the entire Babylonian Talmud during the night [by parceling out the pages and the chapters among themselves], so that on the following day they could celebrate a *siyyum ha-shass* ("Completion of the Talmud").

For this "special holiday," the entire *Shilton Ruchani* came to Lublin. The full "spiritual governing board" assembled at the yeshiva, to assess the progress and achievements of the young learners. As they conversed, questioned and listened, they were profoundly impressed by the sheer amount of the Talmud that the young folk knew fluently — and how keenly they understood it.

The assembled board decided to go ahead and carry out a plan that had formed in Rav Meir's mind while he was alive. It had been his idea to bestow a special title taken from the Talmud (*bavli*, Megilla 28b) on a select number of *talmidim.* The title was *tzurba d'rabbanan*, used in the Talmud to designate a brilliant young student of the Oral Torah with an incandescent mind. The young learners in the yeshiva who would receive it, according to Rav Meir's plan, would be those who mastered two of the six sections of the Talmud: the orders of *Mo'ed* and *Kodashim*; in addition, they would have to know well certain parts of the *Shulchan Aruch.*

Among the Rav's papers, a list of fifty young learners was found in his handwriting — those whom he had found fully eligible for the title. Now the *Shilton Ruchani* made the whole matter public knowledge, and it announced its intention to go further with the program.

Throughout Poland there was a response of great enthusiasm and interest. And inside the yeshiva it stirred the young learners to an enormous will to study, propelled by a keen sense of competition. Meanwhile, a suitable document was prepared, that would serve as a kind of diploma. It was a handsomely designed certificate, of great esthetic appeal, that was printed by lithography on a large sheet of impressive size. A few lines duly noted that the first fifty to receive formally the title of *tzurba d'rabbanan* had been chosen by Rav Meir himself, of blessed memory.

When the *Shilton Ruchani* decided that a young scholar was eligible, a certificate was taken and his name was imprinted on it. Then all the members of this "spiritual governing board," the greatest minds in the world of Torah study, signed it individually, by hand. [Needless to say, the first fifty scholars were those on Rav Meir's list.]

This is how the text of the certificate began: "Yeshivas Chachmey Lublin remains the monument for the everlasting memory of its great creator and founder. The voices of Torah study that resound there day and night, the many thousands of pages of Talmud that are learned there every day — all and everything is reckoned for the merit of this great Torah genius." Then it gave the notable dictum of the Sages (*yerushalmi*, Sh'kalim 2:5; 47a), "Tombstones need not be made for tzaddikim: their words are their memorial."

****

[So ends the biography that a main *talmid* and disciple, himself a most gifted Torah scholar, wrote of his master quite soon after Rav Meir Shapiro's tragic death. In an era ordained for a multiplicity of Jewish tragedy, the great, unique yeshiva that he bequeathed to his people survived the Holocaust no better than the people itself. Once the bestial "conquering heroes" of Nazi Germany were in control of Lublin, they made sure to act like the ancient savages of Rome. As the Romans destroyed the *beyss ha-mikdash* in the far past, so the Germans gutted with fire this sanctuary of Torah.

[By the written testimony of a Nazi participant, they took a particular pleasure in emptying the famed library of its hundreds of thousands of volumes. There was a deep, keen joy in their animal hearts as their well-muscled hands piled the volumes in the city square, so that kerosene could be poured over the lot and then the whole could go up in flames. For some twenty hours the volumes burned, to provide the sheerest pyromaniac delight to the "conquering heroes" that Satan had spawned in Nazi Germany. (A small number of precious volumes, however, did survive the Nazi pyromania somehow, and found their way out of the country, complete with the yeshiva's stamp and the library shelf number.)

[Afterward, whatever survived of the building was converted into a Gestapo center; then it served as military quarters, until it became a hospital for wounded German soldiers. After the war, along with so much other property, holy or profane, that the Polacks appropriated eagerly and greedily in the wake of Polish Jewry's disappearance, the structure that Rav Meir struggled so hard to build and maintain was taken over without question and made into a school for nursing.

[And yet, no matter how much of his hopes and dreams died with him when his mortal life ended, no matter how much destruction the Germans could wreak afterward (with eager Polish help) on the accursed anti-semitic soil of Poland — the essential thrust of his life and purpose on earth could not die with him, nor could it be destroyed by the Holocaust.

[There is a strange historic fact which Heaven may well have ordained to indicate just this. Anyone at all familiar with the norms and ways of Polish Jewry in Poland knows what an important, integral part every hallowed Jewish cemetery played in the life of that people of faith. Whenever a crisis came to a family or a group, whenever an urgent, desperate need was felt for Heaven's rescuing help, it was a normal practice to go to the cemetery and offer up special prayers at certain gravestones. Heaven's special, exceptional aid was implored through the merit of the immortal soul of the great person buried there — the merit he had gained in his lifetime — and (it was hoped) through that immortal soul's intercession, by virtue of the prayers.

[Perhaps nowhere in Poland was this practice observed more strongly or more faithfully than in the old, historic city of Lublin. At any rate, the Nazi animals evidently knew or sensed this: for in their program of total Jewish destruction, they made sure to include the hallowed gravestones in the cemetery. *And yet, for some reason that no one has ever been able to explain, one was spared:* the stone at the grave of Rav Meir Shapiro!

[If the tombstone survived, all the more certainly did his hopes and dreams, that gave purpose and meaning to his foreshortened life of dedication and sacrifice. In the year 5694 (1934) a *chassid* of Tchortkov named Reb Ya'akov Halperin built a large religious suburb of B^{e}ney B^{e}rak in the Jewish homeland, safely out of the reach, forever, of all Nazi-type talons and claws; and he named it *Zichron Meir* — so that the name of the dedicated visionary would live on in the Holy Land that he yearned so strongly to reach and could not.

[The neighborhood of *Zichron Meir* is religious. For the holy day of rest, the streets are closed to traffic, so the heavenly spirit of Shabbos may prevail without any raucous violation. In the heart of the suburb, a handsome structure stands in stately dignity, bearing the name of *Yeshivas Chachmey Lublin*; and over it presides the suburb's Rabbi, a main disciple of Rav Meir named Rav Sh'mu'el *ha-lévi* Wosner.

[Toward the end of the year 5718 (1958), by the decision of the supreme rabbinic board (*Mo'etzess G^{e}doley haTorah*) of Agudas Yisra'el in the Holy Land, the mortal remains of Rav Meir were taken from Lublin and reburied in Jerusalem. Once again, and for the last time, the Jewish people had a chance to honor this imperial soul for the way he had fulfilled his destiny of leadership in the Diaspora. Funeral processions were held in both Tel Aviv and Jerusalem, and huge masses joined. Great men of Torah recalled him in their eulogies, as his remains were brought to their final resting-place in the Holy Land, so that he may await the great day of Resurrection.]

****

[In retrospect, then, when our Sages stated that for tzaddikim there is no need for any tombstones, evidently the thought must also extend even to so grand and impressive an edifice as the one that Rav Meir built in Lublin. Not in its walls and floors did he leave his people the unforgettable legacy of his life. "Their words are their memorial": not mere words and phrases that can be recorded for others to read, but the spirit, the courage, the inspiration that he infused into the Jewish people when he acted and spoke — this is his living memorial.

[Wherever disciples of his have gone on to teach the Torah and to inspire others to learn, with his living memory to guide them; wherever people participate in the daily Talmud study program of the *daf yomi* — the simple idea that was born in his mind and traveled from there forever into the Jewish soul — there "his words are his memorial": The words of Torah that are heard are a living testament to a great soul that found its unique place in the religious life of the Jewish people.]

Bibliography for the translation

The manuscript that has been rendered here into English was written in Poland in 5694 (1934), not long after the tragic death of Rav Meir Shapiro, of blessed memory. It was intended for serial publication soon afterward, in a Yiddish newspaper in New York. One of Rav Meir's main disciples, very possibly *the* main one, the author (of blessed memory) was evidently as much confidant as *talmid* of this phenomenal religious leader, and thus he probably absorbed a full measure of valuable information at first hand from Rav Meir himself, from reliable friends, acquaintances and contemporaries, and from Rav Meir's published writings.

Necessarily, he wrote of the world he knew, as he knew it: mainly Poland in the lifetime of his illustrious teacher and educator. He could assume that the readership he envisioned, the Yiddish-speaking population in America, also knew that world well: the overwhelming majority had migrated from there. Hence he simply recorded what the great leader did and said, without any need to explain terms or describe events that have become by now, some sixty years later, a part of forgotten Polish Jewish history.

For this English edition, however, time and again it became vital to provide background information so that names and happenings would make sense to a reader of our time. Hence a variety of sources were consulted, and explanatory material was added wherever it was considered essential. All such additions in this volume are indicated by the standard use of brackets: An opening bracket appears at the beginning of every inserted paragraph; and where a short or lengthy addition ends, a closing bracket appears at the end of the last paragraph.

Now, beyond any doubt, this is the richest and fullest biography of the almost legendary leader of Poland's Torah Jewry that has ever come to light. It is, however, not the only one. Shorter, occasionally less accurate, Hebrew accounts appeared in the past; and here and there they contain valuable additional or supplementary information which remained, apparently, outside the author's range of knowledge or interest. Those accounts have been read and culled with care, so that material of value could be incorporated into the English edition, to give us a more complete life-story and a fuller life-portrait of its immortal subject.

Insertions from these sources have been similarly indicated by brackets: In each insertion, an opening bracket appears at the start of every paragraph, and a closing bracket at the end of the last one. Those sources are also listed below.

It should be noted that in addition, relevant articles in the Jewish encyclopedias were consulted as necessary, for background information; but it was not felt necessary to list them here.

My thanks are given to the *béth ha-s^{e}farim he-l^{e}umi*: it was there I could find and consult all the sources, some of them very rare and not otherwise accessible.

All titles that are not in English are in Hebrew, unless noted otherwise.

Baranovitz: séfer zikkaron (Hebrew and Yiddish). Tel Aviv 5714 (1954).

Raymond Leslie Buell: *Poland: key to Europe.* London 1939.

Chagigas haTorah: 28 Sivan 5698 (Yiddish): [Lublin 5698/1938].

Henoch H. Halpern: *M^{e}gillas Glina* (Yiddish): New York 1950.

Asher Korech: *K^{e}hillas Glina.* Jerusalem 5710 (1950).

Luach daf ha-yomi, machzor sh^{e}mini. B^{e}ney B^{e}rak [5735/1975].

R. Binyamin Mintz: *Meir b^{e}ahava.* Tel Aviv 5703 (1943).

R. Meir Z^{e}ev Nistempover: *haYotzér viYtziraso: maran ha-ga'on Rabbi Meir Shapiro* . . . Przemysl 5697 (1937).

Piotrkov try bulanski v^{e}ha-s^{e}viva: séfer zikkaron (Hebrew and Yiddish). Jerusalem [5725/1965].

R. Tovia Preschel: *Rabbi Shalom Shachne miLublin* (monograph), in *Sinai* v. 100. Jerusalem [5747/1987] pp.682-700.

Maurice Samuel: *Blood accusation: the strange history of the Beiliss case.* New York 1966.

Sanok: séfer zikkaron liK^{e}hillas Sanok v^{e}ha-s^{e}viva (Hebrew and Yiddish). Jerusalem [5730/1970].

Séfer haYovél lichvod . . . Rav Meir Shapiro . . . Lodz [5690/1930].

Simon Segal: *The new Poland and the Jews.* New York 1938.

N. Shemen: *Lublin: shtot fun torah, rabbonus un chassidus* (Yiddish). Toronto 1951.

Di Yidn in poyln, v. 1 (Yiddish). New York 1946.

Appendix

****

the author, as a friend remembered him

In its original form, this recollection about the author appeared when he was no longer alive. It is an account by a writer who knew him well, who had served as one of the editors of Dos Yiddishe Togblatt, *the daily newspaper published by Agudas Yisra'el in Warsaw, in the thirties. It is given here in English, so that we may read what one friend and colleague remembered about him.*

The foremost, outstanding *talmid*

a remembrance of Rav Yehoshua Baumol
OF BLESSED MEMORY

by Shmuel Rotstein

I know I must write something — something to perpetuate the name and the memory of this young, dynamic scholar who excelled among the excellent, till he was cut down in the frightful Holocaust as he was blossoming into his full powers of manhood. But a tremor seizes me. I can only quiver and hesitate.

Who am I to dare approach so holy a subject? — to try and evaluate his lustrous, radiant image? And yet I am among the survivors who were privileged to live and work with this singular group of exalted souls that were destined to leave us in their ultimate sacrifice, in those horrific, demented days.

I knew him; and now, however I can, I must write about him. . . .

****

Yehoshua Baumol was a prodigious Torah scholar, who stood out among the outstanding, who clearly excelled among the best of us. His brilliant personality already shone in his earliest years — to such an extent that everyone predicted how surely he was destined for greatness.

I came to know him when we were both very young, as we became friends in the Carpathian mountains of Galicia, near the border of Czechoslovakia. The region was famous as vacation land, a destination for masses of people in the summertime, where they could breathe the fresh air and enjoy the invigorating atmosphere.

His father was the local rabbi, and as young boys, we two became fast friends. Every year, we spent several weeks together, walking among the ridges and the hills, as we talked and talked about the mighty matters that dominated our world — the world of Torah and its loyal, faithful adherents.

At that time Poland's religious Jewry was attempting its first tentative steps into the arena of organized public life. Our devout people now had a religious daily newspaper, to defend and protect all we held holy and dear; and in the Jewish ranks a spirited battle was flaring between the loyally religious and the cynically secular. Every good, capable member of our camp readily "girded his loins" to join in the "holy war" to defend our authentic faith and to demonstrate that our observant, believing Jewry was nowhere near the end of all hope, but was was still firmly, totally committed in its devotion to its Maker.

The result was that those who had decided to throw off all traces of the Torah and mitzvos, to see the Jewish people as essentially secular, like any other nation, found themselves confused and bewildered. They had never imagined that there was still such energy and force in the ranks of the faithful, especially among the youth. They never expected that the young would react so vigorously and join together in defense of the Torah's own people.

Among the many vacationers who came to those hills and mountains in the summer were a great number of devout folk from the chassidic Torah world, who used to spend time with the local rabbi, Rav Yoel Moshe Baumol. So he paid attention not merely to the spiritual needs of his local, year-round community, but also to the pious summer visitors. His residence was always a wide-open house, ready to welcome all who came; and people of spirit and vision came annually to renew their bonds of friendship with the rabbi and his family.

With his sparkling traits of character, it was especially the younger of the Rav's two boys, the alert and lively Yehoshua, who drew the visitors' attention. Already then he had a good store of Torah learning and chassidic sense, and everyone enjoyed his pleasant, well-mannered ways and his captivating words of wisdom.

****

Let us begin at the beginning: Yehoshua was born in 5673 (1913) in Butchatch [spelled in Polish *Buczacz*], a fairly large and important city in Galicia that had become known in the Jewish world for its numerous men of learning. He received his Torah education from the best of teachers, who saw in him a shining light for the future. In the path of his father and grandfather, devoted followers of the famed Rebbes, R. Cha-yim of Sanz and his son R. Yechezkel of Shinyeva, the boy was drawn into the chassidic world. From his early years he basked in radiant chassidic warmth, and this remained a powerful influence on him for the rest of his life.

In time his grandfather, the Rabbi of the small town of Shtchevnitz-Krushtchenko, near the Carpathian mountains, passed away; and Yehoshua's father went to take his place, moving the family with him. The change of location, however, brought not the least change in the gifted youngster's education. He continued studying zealously, night and day; and soon he became known as an *iluy*, a young prodigy with a depth of knowledge in Talmud. At the same time, with his fertile, dynamic mind, he worked to gain an ample knowledge of classical religious philosophy and thought.

His father was a profound Talmudic scholar, from a distinguished, wide-branching rabbinic family line. As Yehoshua grew, the man gave his young son his ongoing attention when he could. In the summer months, as the resident religious authority, he was fully occupied with rabbinic duties, especially the supervision of *kashrus* and Shabbos observance in all the hotels and lodging houses; and he had to take the time to receive the many worthy and important visitors who came to pay their respects. The quiet winter months, however, remained serene and peaceful; then he could devote most of this time to the holy studies of his two beloved sons, Yosef and Yehoshua. It was then that this local rabbi could formulate his own *chiddushim*, his own original thoughts in every branch of the Torah. Virtually all of them the gifted younger son absorbed.

* the bond with Rav Meir Shapiro and the yeshiva in Lublin

About this time, a radiant new star loomed in the skies of Polish Jewry. Rav Yehuda Meir Shapiro was a direct descendant of the holy Rav Pinchas of Koretz, the legendary disciple of Rav Yisra'el Ba'al Shem Tov, who became one of the founding luminaries in the chassidic world. An immensely learned Torah scholar, in a meteoric rise to fame, Rav Yehuda Meir served successively as spiritual leader in Galina, Sonik, Piotrkov, and finally in Lublin.

This dynamic leader of our time had already gained renown with his singularly original idea of the *daf yomi*, a daily study program of a double page of Talmud for the whole Jewish world. Now he planned to restore the crown of Torah study to its full ancient luster, to magnify the glory of Heaven in the world, by establishing a yeshiva in Lublin which would be a world center of outstanding Talmud learning.

In the city of Lublin, on *Lag ba'Omer*, 5684 (May 22, 1924), in a ceremony of great splendor and majesty, in the presence of masses of our people and their most eminent spiritual leaders, the cornerstone of *Yeshivas Chachmey Lublin* was set. Then the call went out for all capable young Talmud scholars to prepare themselves for examination and acceptance in the great Torah edifice that would arise there under the leadership of Rav Meir Shapiro.

Everywhere, keen young minds took to studying with a vengeance. For by the rules, only those with a sound, thorough mastery of at least two hundred *dapim* (leaves, two sides of a sheet) of Talmud, with the standard commentaries, would be accepted into the yeshiva. And among the many who studied away diligently in preparation was my childhood friend, Yehoshua.

In 5690 (1930), when the time approached at last for the yeshiva to open its doors, Yehoshua was among the first two hundred candidates for admission who passed the examinations, as the testing was done by a panel of distinguished rabbis and scholars appointed by Rav Shapiro. My childhood friend did not merely pass, however; he displayed so much knowledge and learning that the examiners could not find words enough to praise him.

Within the walls of *Yeshivas Chachmey Lublin* Yehoshua's development reached its fulfillment. The essential factor was the amazing power of Rav Meir Shapiro. There seemed to be a magnetism in this great educator which cast a spell over everyone who came in contact with him. Invariably, the living dynamics of his character evoked vibrations of holiness, self-effacement, and spiritual ascent — the kind of responses which had occurred in masses of Jews when they were exposed to the influence of the great founding fathers of the chassidic world. Time and again those legendary figures thawed and warmed Jewish hearts and souls which had become frozen in the great spiritual wasteland of their time. Somehow, they had had the power to draw Jewish hearts to a genuine worship of the Creator in a blazing enthusiasm that transcended boundaries.

Rav Meir personified the earliest, most authentic chassidic doctrines: faith and trust in the Almighty, unmitigated cheerfulness, and a boundless enthusiasm and longing for an infinitely remote yet all-encompassing Divinity — a way of belief and existence that could best be characterized by the words in *T'hillim*, "If I thought my foot would slip (falter, collapse), Your kindly grace would sustain me" (Psalms 94:18) — words that he would often sing with the melody he had composed for them.

Even before someone succeeded in getting spiritually near to him, the very atmosphere around Rav Meir would exert its influence. A person would find himself acquiring new conceptions about the world, human beings, and a genuine Judaism that was unadulterated, undistorted, and unreformed.

Through this singular individual who became his revered educator, Yehoshua found himself drawn to the regal chassidic realm of Tchortkov, to which Rav Meir Shapiro, the great Rabbi of Lublin, was himself entirely devoted. Thus the young gifted pupil of Rav Meir became in turn a devoted follower of Rav Yisra'el of Tchortkov, and afterward of his son and successor, Rav Nachum Mordechai (be their memory for a blessing). He joined and absorbed the great chassidic way of Ryzhin.

Within the yeshiva, once Rav Meir realized what sort of *talmid* Yehoshua was — a likable young vessel, able and ready to receive, absorb and retain every kind of goodness and blessing — he never let the bond between them go slack. He was forever urging on the young fellow to go further in his development, as the great educator transmitted to him freely, generously, a bountiful abundance of his own Torah knowledge and body of thought. So in time Yehoshua became like a great, sturdy tree of Torah learning and devoutness.

Sometimes literally, sometimes figuratively, the two seemed to spend the years at the yeshiva together, hand in hand. Occasionally Rav Meir would actually take his pupil by the hand and go off for either a short walk or a very long one; and he would talk with him about matters of the highest importance in their Jewish world. It was as if the great master's holy spirit sensed that a weighty, responsible mission awaited this gifted adolescent approaching manhood, and it was necessary to fill him with courage and prepare him for what the future held in store.

Only rarely can a spiritual leader of stature infuse into his students a great, full measure of his own mighty spirit. Only rarely can such a heroic figure cast his influence upon them so strongly that they receive and integrate a lion's share of the qualities and traits that their teacher possesses. With this great Rav of Lublin, we saw it happen; his work as a master educator was not in vain. A considerabe number of *talmidim* who listened regularly to his discourses and *shi'urim* internalized successfully a major portion of his redoubtable characteristics. And among them, his faithful, devoted pupil Yehoshua Baumol stood out. At the very first glance it was so evident that this was one of the foremost disciples of the great master of Lublin.

* the campaign to save the yeshiva

This fact became unmistakably obvious after the sudden, tragic death of Rav Meir on that bitter day, the seventh of Cheshvan, 5694 (October 27, 1933). It was a calamity that shook the entire world of devout, observant Jewry, but most poignantly in Poland, where the entire religious community had placed so much hope in this spiritual giant who towered over his people, who shone like a star lighting the skies of Jewry in its most troubled days. Everyone there had believed that he would lead his people to a time and clime of serenity and calm, across the channels of the two great institutions he founded: *Yeshivas Chachmey Lublin* and the *daf yomi* — institutions that would return to their full prestige and glory our venerated Torah and all who studied it. O how strongly they had all believed. . . .

After only a few short years of tentative, precarious existence, the young, fledgling learning center suddenly remained without its leader at the helm; and there was serious danger that it would collapse and fall under its burden of debt. The élite of the senior students, the very best among them, mobilized a rescue campaign that reached across the length and breadth of the land; and with this initiative, they did more than lift the yeshiva out of danger. So successful was the campaign that the institution was put on a sound financial base, which could assure its continued existence. Moreover, by their action they were *m^ekadésh shém shama-yim*: they hallowed the Divine name of Heaven — as well as the name of their venerated Rav whom Heaven had taken from them. In sum, they simply enhanced the prestige of the Torah everywhere.

Among the stalwart spirits who enlisted in the ranks of the rescue campaign, our Rav Yehoshua Baumol was most certainly included — by then a young man of ability and talent, with a growing reputation as a rising force in the Jewish firmament. His remarkable oratory could strike a fire of holiness in the hearts of his listeners, that would inspire his sizable audiences to make their contributions, over and above their means, to rescue the yeshiva.

So moved were they by this young man and his harmonious flow of words that it seemed almost as if the great Rav of Lublin was speaking to them through him. And they concluded that if the Rav was able to produce *talmidim* like this, then the Jewish people was in no danger of being left without leadership. Through such *talmidim* they felt that the spirit of the Rav was very much alive among them.

Traveling around on his campaign trail to keep the yeshiva alive and well, my old childhood friend landed one fine day in Opotchna [officially spelled *Opoczno*], in the central Polish province of Kielce. It was a town with a sizable Jewish community that formed at least forty percent of the town population. Well, there the local rabbi took a particular interest in him, and the interest led to the young man's marriage with the rabbi's daughter, an educator in the *Beyss Ya'akov* movement. The young couple went on to build a fine home of faith among their people.

It should be noted that while still studying at *Yeshivas Chachmey Lublin*, Rav Yehoshua had taken to writing Torah thoughts, *chiddushey torah*, which appeared in appropriate periodicals and publications — and his *chiddushey torah* drew the attention of *g^edolim*, great Torah scholars, with some of whom he also corresponded. From time to time he also published articles in the newspapers of religious Jewry, especially the main paper, *Dos Yiddishe Togblatt* in Warsaw. These articles, meant for popular reading, were remarkable for their clarity and penetrating thought; and thus they were highly effective weapons in the battle he was waging on behalf of the Torah's people.

At any rate, not for long was he to enjoy his days of tranquility and peace. His father became stricken with the illness that was destined to be his last. On the advice of physicians, the sick man traveled to Vienna to see if medical doctors there could find a way to save him. The malady only worsened, however, and he asked to send urgently for Yehoshua, the younger of his two sons (since the older one had emigrated by then to America). Yehoshua traveled to Vienna, to be with his father in his unfortunate condition; and he never left his father's bedside, till the end came — when his father was only fifty-one.

The death of the Rabbi of Krushtchenko-Shtchavnitz in a foreign land, far from his own home, struck a strong responsive chord in the Jewish world, as it was reported in the newspapers. When the days of mourning ended, the leaders of his community chose the young man to become their new rabbi, in his father's place. Though still a student, the gifted young scholar yielded to their wishes, believing it incumbent on him: He felt he had to, as a way of honoring his departed father. In truth, however, he felt somewhat aggrieved, since there was still a deep yearning in him to stay on at the yeshiva and go further, toward perfection, in his advanced Torah study.

He was young in years when he was called to put on rabbinic garb, but he fulfilled his duties well, to the complete satisfaction of the community. At the same time he spent hours, by night and by day, to reach further depths in every branch of his precious Torah study. If his learning schedule was disturbed on a given day, he would make up the missing hours of his set, regular program at night. And while he strictly kept his Heavenly account of study time, his relations with his fellow humans remained a model of admirable grace.

Apart from all this, his way of prayer became a heartfelt worship by his entire being, in an uttermost longing to become one with his Maker — like his great teacher and mentor, whose path in life he was striving to follow.

So it was that his reputation spread steadily further, till it reached across the distance to the town of Opotchna, where his father-in-law lived; and the day came when he was called to assume the rabbinic post there.

In Opotchna, considerably larger than Krushtchenko-Shtchavnitz, the Jewish community was correspondingly greater in size and esteem. And as the community was greater, so were the rabbinic duties and problems which made up the burden of responsibility that the young Rav had to carry. Yet he found his bearings in all respects, to the undisputed satisfaction of both his own sizable community and the smaller Jewish settlements in the neighboring little towns and villages.

One result was that the rabbis of the region came to visit the new young rabbi and cultivate his friendship, hoping to improve, through his influence and example, their own management of rabbinic and community matters.

It was told that when this young Rav arrived in the town to take up his position, Chanuka came up on the Jewish calendar. Every evening, after the lighting of the festive candles, the townspeople would get together in the *shul*; and there, in the local synagogue, the new young rabbi would speak every night of Chanuka on a different topic: for example, the timeless permanence of the Torah, the ethics of authentic Judaism, a comparison of chassidic and ethical thought *(mussar)*; and so likewise on current topics that were then of immediate vital interest.

Every talk he gave left a strong, deep impression: for in those evenings, his audience heard, in effect, whole, complete, wide-ranging lectures.

The townspeople, of every social stratum and every political bent or party affiliation, saw in him a source of bountiful blessing and hope for a blossoming growth and new radiant life in their eminent, age-old community.

Yet tragically, the quiet, tranquil days he knew then were not to last long. All too soon the days of doom and destruction arrived. With the invasion of Hitler's armed forces, the great calamity of devastation befell every aspect and fragment of Jewish life in Poland and the surrounding regions. But even in those frightful days, the young Rav did not sit in his own corner, concerned for his safety. He strove and toiled without let-up to rescue and salvage whatever might yet be saved. Till the end he remained at his post, fulfilling his duties as best he could.

On the bitter, unavoidable day in 5703 (1943) when his entire community was sent to the slaughter, the young, beloved Rav marched at the head of them all, giving them words of consolation and courage. Together with them, when he was only about thirty, taking his wife and two young children with him, the great, hallowed Torah scholar went to his death.

****

So was a mighty “cedar of Lebanon” cut down — one of the most esteemed and admired young men of his generation, from whom such great achievements were expected. May the God of vengeance manifest Himself to settle accounts in full for him, his family, his community — among the six million who perished. And may his name have its place of permanence in our annals, until the promised Resurrection brings them all back to life.